THE PARTICIPANTS

THE PARTICIPANTS

The Men of the Wannsee Conference

**Edited by Hans-Christian Jasch and
Christoph Kreutzmüller**

Translated by Charlotte Kreutzmüller-Hughes and Jane Paulick

berghahn
NEW YORK · OXFORD
www.berghahnbooks.com

Published in 2017 by
Berghahn Books
www.berghahnbooks.com

Originally published in German as *Die Teilnehmer:
Die Männer der Wannsee-Konferenz*,
© 2017 Metropol Verlag

English-language edition © 2017 Erinnern für die Zukunft—
Trägerverein des Hauses der Wannsee-Konferenz e.V

Library of Congress Cataloging-in-Publication Data

Names: Jasch, Hans-Christian, 1973- editor. | Kreutzmüller, Christoph,
  editor.
Title: The participants : the men of the Wannsee Conference / edited by
  Hans-Christian Jasch and Christoph Kreutzmüller.
Other titles: Teilnehmer. English
Description: [New York] : Berghahn Books, [2017] | Includes
bibliographical references and index.
Identifiers: LCCN 2017017956 (print) | LCCN 2017018627 (ebook) | ISBN
  9781785336713 (e-book) | ISBN 9781785336331 (hardback : alk. paper)
Subjects: LCSH: Wannsee-Konferenz (1942 : Berlin, Germany) | Holocaust,
  Jewish (1939-1945)--Causes. | War criminals--Germany--Biography. |
  Nazis--Biography. | Germany--Politics and government--1933-1945.
Classification: LCC D804.3 (ebook) | LCC D804.3 .T4313 2017 (print) | DDC
  940.53/11--dc23
LC record available at https://lccn.loc.gov/2017017956

British Library Cataloguing in Publication Data

A catalogue record for this book is available from the British Library

ISBN 978-1-78533-633-1 (hardback)
ISBN 978-1-78533-671-3 (paperback)
ISBN 978-1-78533-634-8 (ebook)

Contents

Illustrations

Foreword

Otto Dov Kulka

> But most of all, they say, a deportation in the near future of all Jews from
> Germany would be warmly welcomed.
> —From the Secret SD-Reports on German Popular Opinion, 2 February 1942

There is a wide range of research in historiography on the significance of the Wannsee Conference for the unfolding of the "Final Solution." The present volume of biographical studies by leading historians on the participants of the conference, which dealt with the planning and implementation of the so-called "Final Solution of the Jewish Question," is unquestionably an important achievement in the field of research on the Nazi perpetrators.

Particularly valuable is the exceptional concept of bringing together these studies in one volume. Furthermore, in addition to examining the participants' individual roles at the conference, the chapters range across their complete biographies. In each case, the reader is led back to the origins of their political activities, generally in the wake of the First World War and during the formative stages of the Nazi movement. One can view the new volume as a continuity and extension of Ulrich Herbert's innovative approach in his acclaimed major biography of Werner Best on *Radicalism, Ideology and Reason*,[1] as well as Hans-Christian Jasch's on *Wilhelm Stuckart, and the Judenpolitik*.[2]

However, unlike the collective biography by Michael Wildt—*An Uncompromising Generation: The Nazi Leadership of the Reich Security Main Office*,[3] on the rather homogeneous body of the RSHA—this volume references a time-specific historical event while also considering a heterogeneous gathering of leading representatives of the Nazi regime from different ministerial offices, security agencies, plenipotentiaries for the occupied territories, and party representatives. Each of the senior representatives invited to the conference, which was convened by Reinhard Heydrich, was indispensable for planning, organizing, and implementing the annihilation of European Jewry.

Thus, the distinction of the present volume derives not only from its ability to take earlier historiographical approaches to a new level, but also from its singular compilation of the biographies of representatives of the leading echelon of the Nazi regime. Hence its innovative value for research about key Nazi figures.

At the same time, the editors and some of the contributors have gone beyond research about the perpetrators. In their introduction, Hans-Christian Jasch and Christoph Kreutzmüller devote considerable space to the unconcealed picture displayed by the German press around the time of the conference, about the impending and indeed already ongoing extermination of European Jews, also referring to Hitler's notorious prophecy from January 1939 and January 1942.

Accordingly, it might be worth posing the question on how the German population reacted to these frank media representations and, beyond that, what their attitude was toward the regime's anti-Jewish policy—and toward the Jews themselves—at this critical stage of the persecution.

Today, we have massive, albeit not yet adequately researched, source material that can shed light on these questions.[4] It turns out that the Nazi regime itself did not accept at face value the monolithic image of state and society that it portrayed in the mass media. The authorities established secret internal reporting systems to provide reliable information about the prevailing popular mood and about activity among the different segments of the population.

The most important as well as the most dependable of these systems was that of the SS Security Service (the SD). The directives to the compilers of the reports emphasized repeatedly that the authorities wanted a true, unembellished picture of the situation and of the population's attitude toward the policy of the regime and of course toward its *Judenpolitik* and toward the Jews themselves.[5] Particular attention was to be paid to critical or even negative attitudes and activities. According to the directive issued by Heydrich in 1937, the purpose of the SD reports—written "for the political leadership of the Reich"—was "to fight the enemy with passion but to be cold as ice and objective in the assessment of the situation and its presentation."[6]

The existence of these reports has been known since the mid 1960s and sporadically quoted in the research literature on various issues, including "the Jews." For the war years, however, the dominant impression was that "the Jewish question" was all but neglected in the reports. Overall, the assessment of the historians on this issue was encapsulated in the phrase: "the silence of documents." Hence, it was concluded, the German population, preoccupied with personal matters of subsistence during the war, was generally indifferent to the fate of the Jews. The result was the ongoing "indifference thesis" in research.

However, the documentation available today allows a re-examination of this thesis.

The comprehensive scholarly edition of the Secret Reports contains nearly 4,000 documents relating to the Jews during the period 1933–1945. Nearly 1,000 of them were written during the war years. Beginning from the invasion of the Soviet Union in June 1941, many of them contain information about the deportations of the Jews to the East and their fate, as well as the reactions of the population in various parts of the Reich.

One such document is the SD report for 10–16 December 1941 of the District Office Bielefeld:

> On Thursday, 11 December 1941, the action began here locally to transport the first Jewish families to Riga. . . . Although this action had been kept secret by the Gestapo, the fact that the Jews were being sent off was the object of discussion in all segments of the population. Accordingly, there were also a number of statements reflecting the prevailing mood. It should be noted that the action was welcomed and approved by the preponderant majority. . . .

It was stated that the Jews were all being deported to Russia. The transport was to be in railway carriages to Warsaw, and then in cattle cars from there on to Russia. In Russia, people were saying, the Jews were being deployed for labor in former Soviet factories, while the elderly and frail Jews were to be shot. It was, some said, inconceivable that the Jews could be treated so brutally. Whether a Jew or an Aryan, we're all the children of God.[7]

Such information obviously came from local personnel, who accompanied the transports to the East. Many more detailed reports on mass executions of Jews in the East were circulated by soldiers on leave. One such report, dated as early as 21 July 1941 is an actual eyewitness testimony:

> According to a report from Major Frantz, 2,600 Jews were recently shot in Bialystok. He drove through a street that had been closed off by the police, and asked a German police officer: "Are Jews being deported here?" "No," he replied, "but they're being shot." The day before, they shot 2,600 Jews, the next day 6,000 were to follow. Supposedly all Jews between the ages of 15 and 60 are being shot. According to the police officer, the operation is being carried out daily, each day by a different unit of men on duty. Several police officers who are no longer able to take part in such operations because of nervous breakdown have reported ill to a German physician on duty there. An execution of Jews in Baranawitschy has as yet not taken place.[8]

The systematic reporting, on all levels, continued until nearly the end of the war. The following section of an SD report of 6 November 1944, from Stuttgart, refers also to the views among the German population regarding the fate of the Jews:

> Didn't we slaughter the Jews by the thousands? Don't soldiers repeatedly tell stories that the Jews in Poland were forced to dig their own graves? And what did we do with the Jews who were in Alsatia in concentration camps? After all, Jews are only human too. In doing this, we gave the enemies an example of what they are allowed to do with us in the event of their victory. (numerous voices from all circles of the population).[9]

One of the most comprehensive, detailed documents compiled close to the time of the Wannsee Conference, and covering the period from September to December 1941, is the nation wide SD report dated 2 February 1942. It summarizes on a national level the reports from all parts of the Reich. The main issue was the population's reactions to the edict of marking the Jews with a yellow patch, though at the end it also relates to people's expectations of further measures regarding the solution of the "Jewish question."

The summarizing section opens as follows:

> According to reports now available from all parts of the Reich . . . the issuance of the ordinance on the marking of the Jews has in general had a favorable impact in the population. It is emphasized everywhere that this ordinance is in keeping with a wish long present among broad circles of the population, especially in localities where there are still a relatively large number of Jews. . ... It is significant that many regard the ordinance on marking not as a final measure of some sort, but rather only as the prelude to further more drastic ordinances, with the goal of a final resolution of the Jewish Question. . ..

And it concludes:

> The population wishes to mark in an appropriate manner also the apartments of the Jews. But most of all, they say, a deportation in the near future of all Jews from Germany would be warmly welcomed. [10]

Like all special reports, this one, about the popular reception of the marking of the Jews, was preceded by a general overview (*Allgemeines*) of the mood of the population in the Reich. This included the first reactions to Hitler's notorious speech of 30 January 1942, in which he reiterated his prophecy of 30 January 1939[11] on the interdependence between a new world war and the extermination of the Jews in Europe, "which is now being realized:"

> We are fully aware that this war can end either in the extermination of the Aryan people or in the disappearance of Jewry from Europe. . . . I wish to avoid making hasty prophesies, but this war will not end as the Jews imagine, namely, in the extermination of the European-Aryan people; instead, the result of this war will be the annihilation of Jewry. For the first time, the old, truly Jewish rule of "an eye for an eye, a tooth for a tooth," will obtain.[12]

The report opens with a description of the tense, impatient expectations of the people for Hitler's speech, owing to the continuing lack of adequate information about the situation on the Eastern Front. In regard to Hitler's prophecy, the report notes:

> The renewed denunciation of the Jews and the emphasis on the phrase from the Old Testament "an eye for an eye and a tooth for a tooth," were interpreted to mean that the Führer's struggle against Jewry will continue on with relentless consistency until it is completed and soon the last Jew will be expelled from European soil.[13]

As we have seen, information about the fate of the Jews deported from Germany was already widespread among the German population. Thus, the question is no longer what the German population knew, but rather which political course for the solution of the "Jewish question" the majority of Germans favored at this stage.

In his historiographical survey of the developments, focusing on the perpetrators, Mark Roseman hints at "the most recent trend of blurring the boundaries between direct perpetration and a wider societal participation."[14] The prolonged, frustrating debate between the so-called Intentionalists and Structuralists, or "Functionalists," gradually changed its focus following Ulrich Herbert's groundbreaking biography of Werner Best and turned its attention more to the early biographies in the Third Reich. As mentioned above, the conceptual framework of the present volume is based on this fruitful approach.

However, the historiographical debate could be resolved by yet another approach. I refer to Ian Kershaw's innovative thesis based on the metaphor of "working towards the Führer" *(dem Führer entgegenarbeiten)*. In his article titled with the same phrase, "Working towards the Führer,"[15] Kershaw developed the theoretical implications of this thesis, based on his earlier empirical research, that he later applied in his monumental biography of Hitler, which is virtually also a social and political history of Nazi Germany:

> The notion of "working towards the Führer" could be interpreted, too, in a more indirect sense where ideological motivation was secondary, or perhaps even absent altogether, but where the objective function of

the actions was nevertheless to further the potential for implementation of the goals which Hitler embodied. . . . The result was the unstoppable radicalisation of the "system" and the gradual emergence of policy objectives closely related to the ideological imperatives represented by Hitler. . . .[16]

Would it be too daring to propose that Kershaw's thesis on the perpetrators is also applicable to the research on the German population as well? That this is indeed the case suggested by the reports about the population's awareness of the radicalization in the regime's "Jewish policy" and its favorable anticipation of even more radical steps against the Jews, such as the already ongoing deportations *(Abschiebung)*.

We have to take into consideration that the reports quoted above on the moods and attitutes of the population reflect the period when Germany under Hitler's uncontestable leadership seemed to be at the peak of its political and military achievements, and anti-Jewish sentiments and policies became widespread not only in Germany but across the continent.

In his above-mentioned chapter, Mark Roseman is well aware of the recently developing trend in the historiography on Nazi Germany, as he takes note of some of the newer studies that "[make] the whole population complicit in genocide."[17] A severe verdict indeed, but one that can be regarded as justified. The present book, as well as my foreword to it, seeks to explore prevailing approaches in historiography that might enable us to understand how this complicity became possible.

Otto Dov Kulka was born 1933 in the Czech Republic, and has lived in Israel since 1949. He is Rosenbloom Professor Emeritus of Jewish History at the Hebrew University of Jerusalem, a historian and a writer. His publications include: *The Jews in the Secret Nazi-Reports* (Yale University Press, 2010) (together with Eberhard Jäckel); and *Landscapes of the Metropolis of Death* (Harvard University Press, 2013).

Notes

Epigraph: *"Am meisten würde jedoch eine baldige Abschiebung aller Juden aus Deutschland begrüßt werden."*

1 Ulrich Herbert, *Best: Biographische Studien über Radikalismus, Weltanschauung und Vernunft 1903–1989* (Bonn, 1996).

2 Hans-Christian Jasch, *Staatssekretär Wilhelm Stuckart und die Judenpolitik: Der Mythos von der sauberen Verwaltung* (Munich, 2012).

3 Michael Wildt, *An Uncompromising Generation: The Nazi Leadership of the Reich Security Main Office* (Madison, 2009).

4 O.D. Kulka and E. Jäckel, ed., *The Jews in the Secret Nazi Reports on Popular Opinion in Germany, 1933–1945* (New Haven, CT and London, 2010). See in particular the Introduction. The book itself presents 752 selected documents of the whole corpus of 3,744 reports that appear in the comprehensive digital edition of the original German documents attached to the book on CD. See also A. E. Steinweis, "An Essential Source Collection on German Popular Opinion and the Jews," *Yad Vashem Studies* 40, no. 2 (2012). The original German edition with the attached CD appeared in 2004. See also the review by Bernward Dörner in: *H-Soz-Kult*, 26 February 2005. Retrieved 12 February 2017 from http://www.hsozkult.de/searching/id/rezbuecher-5053?title=o-kulka-u-a-hgg-juden-in-ns-stimmungsberichten&q=doerner&page=5&sort=&fq=&total=125&recno=87&subType=reb

5 Dörner, review, see in particular the Introduction. This review appeared in the same periodical online as the item in the previous note.

6 Dörner, review, xxviii. See above, note 5.

7 Kulka and Jäckel, *Secret Nazi Reports*, Doc. 605.

8 Kulka and Jäckel, *Secret Nazi Reports*, Doc. 557.

9 Kulka and Jäckel, *Secret Nazi Reports*, Doc. 749.

10 Kulka and Jäckel, *Secret Nazi Reports*, Doc. 618.

11 Hitler invariably dated it wrongly to 1 September 1939, the day of German invasion of Poland.

12 Max Domarus, *Hitler: Reden und Proklamationen 1932–1945.* vol. 4 (Wiesbaden, 1983), 1828–29. English translation retrieved 12 February 2017 https://archive.org/stream/TheEssentialHitlerSpeechesAndCommentary/TheEssentialHitler-SpeechesAndCommentary_djvu.txt. See also Ian Kershaw, "Hitler's Prophecy and the 'Final Solution,'" in *On Germans and Jews: Essays by Three Generations of Historians: A Festschrift in Honor of Otto Dov Kulka,* ed. M. Zimmermann (Jerusalem, 2006), 49–66.

13 Kulka and Jäckel, *Secret Nazi Reports*, Doc. 618.

14 Mark Roseman, "Biographical Approaches and the Wannsee Conference" in this volume.

15 Ian Kershaw, "'Working towards the Führer': Reflections on the Nature of the Hitler Dictatorship," in *Hitler, The Germans and the Final Solution,* ed. I. Kershaw (New Haven, CT and London, 2008), 29–49. The equation "metaphor" for the thesis that appeared in the title of his article was chosen by Kershaw himself.

16 Kershaw, "Reflections on the Nature of the Hitler," 42–43.

17 As in footnote 14 above. It's worth mentioning the works of, for example: Bernward Dörner, *Die Deutschen und der Holocaust: Was niemand wissen wollte, aber jeder wissen konnte* (Berlin, 2007); Peter Longerich, *"Davon haben wir nichts gewusst!" Die Deutschen und die Judenverfolgung 1933–1945* (Munich, 2006); Michael Wildt, *Volksgemeinschaft als Selbstermächtigung: Gewalt gegen Juden in der deutschen Provinz 1919 bis 1939* (Hamburg, 2007);

F. Bajohr, "The 'Folk Community' and the Persecution of the Jews: German Society under the National Socialist Dictatorship, 1933–1945," *Holocaust and Genocide Studies* 20, no. 2 (2006): 183–206; Frank Bajohr and Dieter Pohl, *Der Holocaust als offenes Geheimnis: Die Deutschen: Die NS-Führung und die Alliierten* (Munich, 2006); S. Schrafstetter and A.E. Steinweis, ed., *The Germans and the Holocaust: Popular Responses to the Persecution and Murder of the Jews* (Oxford and New York, 2016).

Bibliography

Bajohr, F. "The 'Folk Community' and the Persecution of the Jews: German Society under the National Socialist Dictatorship, 1933–1945." *Holocaust and Genocide Studies* 20, no. 2 (2006): 183–206.

Bajohr, Frank and Dieter Pohl. *Der Holocaust als offenes Geheimnis: Die Deutschen. Die NS-Führung und die Alliierten.* Munich: C. H. Beck, 2006.

Domarus, Max. *Hitler: Reden und Proklamationen 1932–1945.* Wiesbaden: R. Löwit, 1983.

Dörner, Bernward. *Die Deutschen und der Holocaust: Was niemand wissen wollte, aber jeder wissen konnte.* Berlin: Propyläen, 2007.

Herbert, Ulrich. *Best: Biographische Studien über Radikalismus, Weltanschauung und Vernunft 1903–1989.* Bonn: Dietz, 1996.

Jasch, Hans-Christian. *Staatssekretär Wilhelm Stuckart und die Judenpolitik: Der Mythos von der sauberen Verwaltung.* Munich: Oldenbourg, 2012.

Kershaw, Ian. "Hitler's Prophecy and the 'Final Solution.'" In *On Germans and Jews: Essays by Three Generations of Historians: A Festschrift in Honor of Otto Dov Kulka,* edited by M. Zimmermann, 49–66. Jerusalem: Hebrew University Magnes Press, 2006.

———. "'Working towards the Führer': Reflections on the Nature of the Hitler Dictatorship." In *Hitler, The Germans and the Final Solution,* edited by I. Kershaw, 29–49. New Haven, CT and London: Yale University Press, 2008.

Kulka, O.D. and E. Jäckel, ed. *Die Juden in den geheimen NS-Stimmungsberichten 1933–1945.* Düsseldorf: Droste, 2004. [English: *The Jews in the Secret Nazi Reports on Popular Opinion in Germany, 1933–1945.* New Haven, CT and London: Yale University Press, 2010.]

Longerich, Peter. *"Davon haben wir nichts gewusst!" Die Deutschen und die Judenverfolgung 1933–1945.* Munich: Pantheon, 2006.

Schrafstetter, S. and A.E. Steinweis, ed. *The Germans and the Holocaust: Popular Responses to the Persecution and Murder of the Jews.* Oxford and New York: Berghahn, 2016.

Steinweis, A.E. "An Essential Source Collection on German Popular Opinion and the Jews." *Yad Vashem Studies* 40, no. 2 (2012).

Wildt, Michael. *Die Generation des Unbedingten: Das Führungskorps des Reichssicherheitshauptamtes.* Hamburg: Hamburger Edition, 2002. [English: *An Uncompromising Generation: The Nazi Leadership of the Reich Security Main Office.* Madison, WI: University of Wisconsin Press, 2009.]

———. *Volksgemeinschaft als Selbstermächtigung: Gewalt gegen Juden in der deutschen Provinz 1919 bis 1939*. Hamburg: Hamburger Edition, 2007. [English: *Hitler's Volksgemeinschaft and the Dynamics of Racial Exclusion: Violence Against Jews in Provincial Germany, 1919–1939*. New York and Oxford: Berghahn, 2012.]

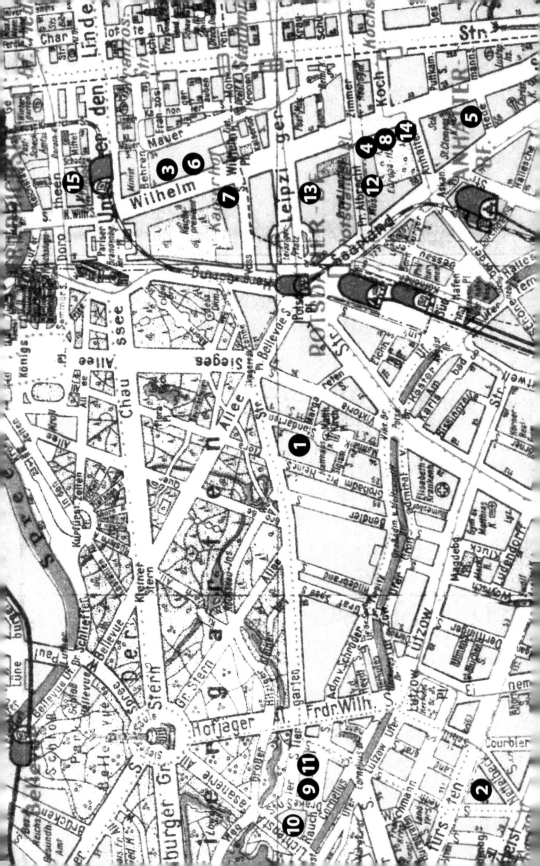

Berlin Offices of the Participants

1 Bühler   Administration of the General Government,
             Standartenstraße 14
2 Eichmann   Reich Main Security Office, Kurfürstenstraße 116
3 Freisler   Reich Ministry of Justice, Wilhelmstraße 65
4 Heydrich   Reich Main Security Office, Wilhelmstraße 101
5 Hofmann   SS Race and Settlement Main Office, Hedemannstraße 24
6 Klopfer   Nazi Party Chancellery, Wilhelmstraße 64
7 Kritzinger Reich Chancellery, Wilhelmstraße 77
8 Lange   Reich Main Security Office, Wilhelmstraße 101
9 Leibbrandt Reich Ministry for the Occupied Eastern Territories,
             Rauchstraße 17/18
10 Luther   Foreign Office, Rauchstraße 11
11 Meyer   Reich Ministry for the Occupied Eastern Territories,
             Rauchstraße 17/18
12 Müller   Reich Main Security Office, Prinz-Albrecht-Straße 8
13 Neumann   Plenipotentiary for the Four Year Plan, Leipziger Straße 3
14 Schöngarth Reich Main Security Office, Wilhelmstraße 101
15 Stuckart   Reich Ministry of the Interior, Unter den Linden 72

Pharus map from 1940. Reproduced with the permission of the publisher.

Introduction

THE PARTICIPANTS

The Men of the Wannsee Conference

Hans-Christian Jasch and Christoph Kreutzmüller

On 20 January 1942 senior German officials came together for a meeting, to be followed by breakfast, in a grand villa overlooking Lake Wannsee to discuss the "Final Solution to the Jewish Question"[1] in Europe. What sort of men were they? This is what most visitors to the House of the Wannsee Conference Memorial and Educational Site ask themselves when they visit the former dining room where the meeting very likely took place.[2]

This volume sets out to provide answers. Inevitably, they will not be exhaustive answers. While the Wannsee Conference has come to be seen as key (and sometimes even as a cipher) to the bureaucratically orchestrated mass murder of European Jews, its participants have not.[3] The fifteen men who attended the Wannsee Conference will be profiled in this volume in readable, concise chapters based on primary sources and intense research. Our goal is to convey a distinct sense of these men with in-depth biographical detail, associations and references. We hope that our volume will contribute to research into Nazi perpetrators,[4] which has been a valuable addition to Holocaust research and is a central element of the Memorial's educational agenda.[5] We also hope the volume provides a glimpse into the private and professional networks of the officials who worked in the offices on Berlin's Wilhelmstraße and whom research has so far neglected.[6]

Who were the conference participants? We must start by stating the obvious: there were no women among them. Given the extreme chauvinism of the Nazis, who tolerated women in leading positions at best in the caring professions, this fact is hardly surprising. Notwithstanding the 2001 TV film *Conspiracy*, and specifically Kenneth Branagh's Heydrich, who seems to have stepped out of a Shakespeare play,[7] these men do not at first glance appear to be evil psychopaths. As shocking as it seems, they were "ordinary men" (Christopher Browning) who knew how to behave, who could appreciate fine architecture (with a view of the lake) and the good things in life, including the refreshments, possibly looted from across Europe, provided after the meeting. The participants at the conference did not make up an established group. The group was convened only for this particular meeting and represented a cross section of the Nazi elite. This illustrates how a "modern division of labor," as Gerald D. Feldman and Wolfgang Seibel observed, was an important premise for the mass murder of European Jews.[8] If nothing else, it allowed the perpetrators to think that they were only one link in a chain of command and therefore not individually responsible for their deeds.

Despite their high ranks, the men profiled in this volume had an average age of little over forty-two, making them relatively young.[9] With the exception of Martin Luther and Wilhelm Stuckart, they came from middle-class families. They were the sons of civil engineers, bakers, farmers and manufacturers. One of them (Friedrich Wilhelm Kritzinger) was the son of a pastor. Eleven of them had Protestant backgrounds. Three were Catholic. Otto Hofmann described himself merely as "a believer" ("gottgläubig") but most probably also came from a Catholic background. The majority of the participants were in SS-terminology Prussians, but Rudolf Lange and Eberhardt Schöngarth came from Saxony, Josef Bühler from Württemberg, Heinrich Müller from Bavaria and Otto Hofmann from Austria, while Georg Leibbrandt was a Russian-German born near Odessa.

Seven of them—Roland Freisler, Hofmann, Kritzinger, Alfred Meyer, Müller, Erich Neumann and Luther—had fought in the First World War and saw themselves as survivors of what Ernst Jünger termed the "Storm of Steel." Only one of them (Müller, who did not graduate from high school) failed to reach the rank of lieutenant. Neumann was badly injured in the White Men's Great War (Arnold Zweig), while quite a few (Freisler, Hofmann, Kritzinger and Meyer) had been prisoners of war. The other eight participants belonged to the so-called "war youth generation"—as described by Ernst Gläser in his excellent novel *Born in 1902*, which was burnt on 10 May 1933 by students on what is now Bebelplatz in Berlin—dubbed the "uncompromising generation" by Michael Wildt.[10] It was shaped by the fervent patriotism and hardship of the war years, as well as by the chaos of the revolution in 1918/19, the brutal Silesian Uprisings, the occupation of the area west of the Rhine and the Ruhr region by French and Belgian troops, and hyperinflation. There is no doubt that these turbulent years had a formative effect. Ultimately, they wanted to win the war their fathers had lost, and to prove their mettle.

Ten of the fifteen participants had been to university. Eight of them had even been awarded doctorates, although it should be pointed out that it was considerably easier to gain a doctorate in law or philosophy in the 1920s than it is today. Eight of them had studied law, which, then as now, was not uncommon in the top positions of public administration. Many first turned to radical politics as members of Freikorps or student fraternities.[11] Three of the participants (Freisler, Klopfer and Lange) had studied in Jena. In the 1920s, the University of Jena was a fertile breeding ground for nationalist thinking. With dedicated Nazi, race researcher and later SS-Hauptsturmbannführer Karl Astel as rector, it developed into a model Nazi university. Race researcher Hans Günther also taught there.[12] Others, such as Reinhard Heydrich, joined the SS because they had failed to launch careers elsewhere, and only became radical once they were members of the self-acclaimed Nazi elite order.

Some participants, chief among them Freisler, Hofmann, Meyer and Stuckart, were *alte Kämpfer*—that is, "old fighters" who had joined the Nazi Party in the 1920s and were therefore permitted to wear the Golden Party Badge. As a Gauleiter (regional head of the Nazi Party), Meyer occupied an especially high position in the Party hierarchy, which is why he appears at the top of the Protocol's list of participants. While Adolf Eichmann, Heydrich and Luther joined the Party in 1931/32, when it performed well in elections, others such as Bühler, Klopfer, Neumann, Leibbrandt and Schöngarth were what was called "the fallen of March" or "Mayflies," one of the hundred thousands who only joined the Party for opportunistic reasons once its power had been consolidated.[13] Lange, Müller and Kritzinger were only admitted to the Party after the ban on membership was lifted in 1937.

The representatives of the Reich Main Security Office and Hofmann, head of the SS Race and Settlement Main Office, were senior figures in the SS. Klopfer, Stuckart and Neumann had long been members of the SS. Ten days after the conference—on the ninth anniversary of the so-called Machtergreifung (seizure of power)—Stuckart was made a SS-Gruppenführer and Klopfer a Brigadenführer. Both thereby attained the rank of general.

The study of these men's biographies provides clear evidence that the participants had met one another well before the conference on 20

January 1942: almost all of them lived in Berlin's affluent south-west or in the fashionable Tiergarten district, and some of them were members of a men's club where many Nazis networked, including many senior officials on Wilhelmstraße.[14] Freisler, Heydrich and Stuckart, as well as Friedrich-Wilhelm Krüger, the Higher SS and Police Leader of the General Government, who had also been invited to the conference, belonged to the German Aero Club, under the patronage of Göring.[15] Freisler, Meyer and Heydrich were members of the Reichstag, where Kritzinger sat on the government bench.[16] Freisler, Kritzinger, Neumann and Stuckart knew one another from the Prussian State Council and the Ministerial Council for Defense of the Reich. Bühler, Freisler and Stuckart would have encountered one another in the Academy for German Law.

Eichmann, Heydrich, Müller, Neumann and Stuckart all attended the high-level meeting held on 12 November 1938 in the Ministry of Aviation, when Göring communicated Hitler's order that "the Jewish Question be now, once and for all, summed up and resolved one way or another."[17] In the course of the four-hour meeting, Heydrich proposed a central office for Jewish emigration, similar to that in Vienna, in order to further expedite the emigration of Jews—which was increasingly becoming more of a desperate flight in the wake of the pogrom still often referred to as Crystal Night.[18] The proposal met with Göring's approval. In January 1939 he established the Reich Central Office for Jewish Emigration within the Interior Ministry and made Heydrich its head.[19] When Heydrich issued his invitations to the Wannsee Conference, he enclosed a certificate of appointment signed on 31 July 1941 by Göring, naming him the coordinator of the "definitive resolution of the Jewish Question in the German sphere of influence in Europe." This explicitly extended the powers granted to Heydrich with the founding of the Reich Central Office for Jewish Emigration and thus made implicit reference to the conference held on 12 November 1938. In this respect, the pogrom of November 1938 and Göring's conference were directly linked to the Wannsee Conference.

By this time, the "Resolution of the Jewish Question" was being debated in various public media with astonishing openness. Anti-Jewish propaganda was stepped up in the wake of the invasion of the Soviet Union in summer 1941 and the first systematic deportations of Jews throughout the Reich in October 1941. The German media by and large adhered to the instruction issued by Reich Press Chief Otto Dietrich[20] in the Daily Watchword *(Tagesparole)* on 26 October 1941 to bear in mind Hitler's "prediction" made on 30 January 1939. "Long before the outbreak of the current war," he wrote, Hitler had

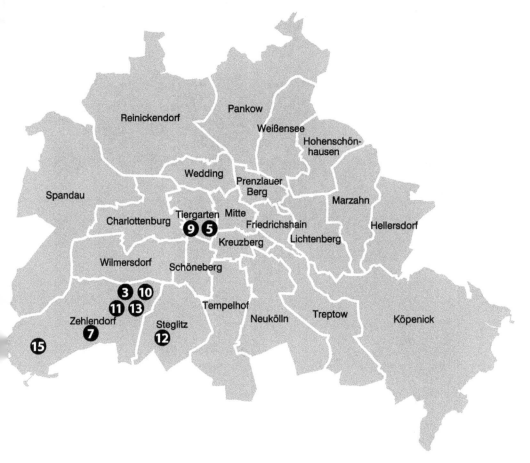

Map 0.1 Map by Felix Hahn via Wikimedia Commons, CC BY-SA 2.5.

Residences of the Participants

1	Bühler	Krakow
2	Eichmann	Prague
3	Freisler	Habelschwerdter Allee 9/Hüttenweg 14 a, Zehlendorf
4	Heydrich	Břežany (near Prague)
5	Hofmann	Woyrschstraße 48, Tiergarten
6	Klopfer	Pullach (near Munich)
7	Kritzinger	Blücherstraße 6, Zehlendorf
8	Lange	Riga
9	Leibbrandt	Keithstraße 22, Tiergarten
10	Luther	Reichensteiner Weg 34–36, Zehlendorf
11	Meyer	Finkenstraße, Zehlendorf
12	Müller	Corneliusstraße 22, Steglitz
13	Neumann	Schwendener Straße 1, Zehlendorf
14	Schöngarth	Münster
15	Stuckart	Am Sandwerder 28, Zehlendorf

Illustration 0.1 Some of the men who attended the Wannsee Conference had previously met at various functions and festivities. At the pictured gathering, organized by the Reich Ministry of the Interior in 1937, Heydrich and Stuckart are seated opposite one another. Seated next to Heydrich is Kurt Daluege the head of the Ordnungspolizei (regular police), and two seats along from Stuckart—with a full beer glass—is Heinrich Himmler. Unknown photographer, 1937, SV-Bilderdienst, 00028000.

"specifically warned international Jewry against starting a war against Nazi Germany." But this, Dietrich continued, is what they did and, just as the Führer predicted, "the Jews are paying for the blood guilt they brought upon themselves by their own crimes. The Jews alone have this war on their conscience. This issue must be addressed in two columns on the front page."[21]

On 16 November 1941 the highest circulation weekly newspaper *Das Reich* carried a lead article headlined "It is the Fault of the Jews!" by Joseph Goebbels, Reich Minister for Propaganda and Gauleiter of Berlin, whose state secretary Leopold Gutterer was also one of the original invitees to the Wannsee Conference:

> We are now seeing the fulfillment of this prophecy, and the Jews are suffering a fate that, albeit hard, they have more than deserved. Compassion or even regret are totally inappropriate. World Jewry has completely underestimated the strength of its own power in its instigation of this war, and is now gradually experiencing a process of destruction which

Illustration 0.2 Some of the later participants in the Wannsee Conference also met through the Academy of German Law. Pictured here, at a meeting in fall 1936 of specialists in administrative and police law, are (from left to right) Chief of the Ordnungspolizei Kurt Daluege (wearing spurs), Wilhelm Stuckart, Reich Minister Hans Frank, Reichsführer-SS and Chief of the German Police Heinrich Himmler, Reinhard Heydrich, his deputy Dr Werner Best, Berlin Chief of Police Graf Wolf-Heinrich von Helldorff, and an unknown person. Photo by Heinrich Hoffmann, 12.10.1936, BpK, 50059276.

> it wanted for us and would have mercilessly imposed on us if it had had enough power. Now the situation we are in is, according to the Jews' own law, an eye for an eye.[22]

The launch of the Soviet counteroffensive, Japan's attack on Pearl Harbor and Germany's declaration of war against the United States turned the war into a world war. Around this time, Goebbels referred in his diary to a meeting on the afternoon of 12 December 1941 between Hitler and the Nazi Reichsleiter and Gauleiter, including Meyer, in his private rooms at the Reich Chancellery:

> With respect of the Jewish Question, the Führer has decided to make a clean sweep. He prophesied to the Jews that if they brought another world war to pass they would experience their own annihilation. That was not just an empty phrase. The world war is here, and the annihilation of the Jews must be the necessary consequence. The question has to

be examined without any sentimentality. We are not here to pity Jews, but to have pity for our own German people. If the German people have sacrificed about 160,000 dead in the battles in the east, the instigators of this bloody conflict will have to pay for it with their lives.[23]

The publication *Deutsches Recht*, which was compulsory reading for many Nazi lawyers, also referred to the solution of the "Jewish Question" "without sentimentality."[24] Jewry was "bound to suffer historical and earthly death . . . as far as the historical phenomenon of Jews in Europe is concerned."[25]

Owing to a lack of historical evidence, we know little of the participants' activities immediately prior to and after the meeting on 20 January 1942—a cold, clear Tuesday in the middle of an unusually long period of frost.[26] Most of them would have read the newspapers' coverage of the fighting in- and outside Europe. That day, a front page article headlined "Japanese Troops on the Southern Tip of Malacca [Malaysia]" in the Berlin edition of the Nazis' official newspaper *Völkischer Beobachter* reported that the town of Feodosia in Crimea had been "recaptured" but that the Red Army—described as "Bolshevists"—was attacking on the Donetsk front with "strong forces." A propaganda unit report on one infantry unit's defensive battle hinted that the Wehrmacht was struggling with inadequate equipment and suffering heavy losses. The article described a speech made by the U.S. president, in which he announced a drastic boost in U.S. war production, as a "bluff." The Berlin Nazi paper *Der Angriff* carried the headline "Germans and Romanians Recapture Feodosia in Bold Attack" and further reported on the successes of the Japanese army in Malaysia. In another article, headlined "Unwavering Defiance," Robert Ley, head of the German Labor Front, maintained that soldiers in the grip of "honest fanaticism" were invincible. But his words—"German men, German women. German workers, citizens and farmers. Only unwavering defiance will ensure victory . . . now more than ever. We will never capitulate!"— indirectly conveyed just how difficult the situation—known as the "winter crisis"—had become.

On the last page of *Der Angriff*, alongside an advertisement for Togal pain relief pills, a newspaper entitled "Global Battle: Quarterly Journal on the Jewish Question" was touted as the "leading publication in the field of the Jewish problem." Published on the day of the conference—"The Jewish Question in politics, law, culture and the economy"—opened with the typical conspiracy theory that the Jews were to blame for the United States entering the war and were ruining the U.S. national budget. In the reviews section of the journal, published by an Institute for Jewish Question Studies, the fourth edition of a paper on "The Jewish Question: Material and How to Treat it in School" was positively received, although the reviewer felt that "the part on method should be extended if a further edition is published." In a special supplement, not intended for general publication, the reader's attention was drawn to an order banning Jews wearing the yellow star from using public telephone booths.

The conference participants presumably knew about this ban already. Having read the newspapers, most of them had probably worked for some hours before driving straight from their offices around Wilhelmstraße to Wannsee. Some of them traveled together, to save on gasoline and discuss the meeting ahead. We know that Klopfer, for instance, drove to Wannsee with Kritzinger. Almost certainly Meyer and his subordinate Leibbrandt would have arrived together, too. It is likely that the staff of the Reich Main Security Office who had traveled from farther afield—Schöngarth and possibly also Lange—stayed in their employers' guest accommodation in the villa, which was fitted with furniture stolen from Jewish homes in Prague,[27] and advertised in a Security Police newsletter as offering "all creature comforts."[28] They would have needed only to descend the stairs from the guest rooms on the first or second floor. It is likely that Eichmann, too, who did not have a permanent residence in Berlin and had arrived from Prague via Theresienstadt the day before, had stayed the night in the villa. This would certainly have made it easier for him to supervise the preparations on site in the morning.

After the "meeting followed by breakfast," which started at noon and was probably officially over by 2 P.M., Heydrich, Müller and Eichmann stayed behind in the guest house—according to Eichmann—to relax over a glass of cognac and review the minutes of the meeting. The unnamed staff of the villa—quite possibly Jewish forced laborers, who looked after the house and gardens until February 1943—will have cleared up the conference room and washed the dishes in the meantime. Eichmann probably got straight to work on writing the Protocol, referring not only to his own notes but, by his own account, also to a transcript written by a—now unknown—shorthand typist.[29] Heydrich flew straight back to Prague to host a reception in Prague Castle for the new government of the Protectorate at 7 P.M. the same day.[30] There is no record of what the other participants did in the afternoon after the conference. The ministry officials probably drove back to Wilhelmstraße to continue working at their desks or to report to their superiors and staff on the outcome of the meeting. After work, perhaps they had a drink in one of the men's clubs—the Nationalklub or the Aero Club—or in a bar on Friedrichstraße or Kurfürstendamm. What did they talk about with other guests or their families at home?

Luther received the Wannsee Protocol some six weeks after the conference. His is the only surviving copy. The covering letter, signed by Heydrich, underlined the consensus achieved at Wannsee: "As now, fortunately, a basic course with respect to the practical implementation of the Final Solution of the Jewish Question has been achieved" and "complete agreement among the offices involved" reached, the "organizational, technical and material preconditions for the practical tackling of the solution" could be sketched out and a draft for the procedure drawn up for Göring. He asked the "offices involved" to appoint specialists to attend the follow-up conference on 6 March 1942.[31] Before Luther consigned the letter to his files, he wrote in the margins that his head of division, Rademacher, should report to Eichmann. A third hand probably highlighted the part of the Protocol that was particularly relevant to the Foreign Ministry: "Instead of emigration, an additional solution has now arisen, following prior authorization by the Führer, of evacuating the Jews to the East."[32] There is no reason to doubt that the other ministries handled their copies of the Protocol in quite a similar manner.

Just nine days after the Wannsee Conference, a meeting was called by the Reich Minister for the occupied Eastern territories. Stuckart's staff member Bernhard Lösener was to report on the points agreed at the Wannsee Conference and a draft law was to be negotiated to regulate the classification of Jews in the occupied Eastern territories. The first follow-up conference, which Heydrich had announced in the letter enclosed with the Protocol, took place on 6 March 1942 in Eichmann's office at Kurfürstenstraße 116. Here, and at the second follow-up meeting on 27 October 1942, the attendees discussed the treatment of "Mischlinge," enforced sterilization, and compulsory divorces of marriages between Jews and Non-Jews. The Propaganda Ministry, now also participating in the discussions, expressed reservations about the latter point in view of the "predictable response of the Vatican."[33] The Protocol and the subsequent correspondence found in Luther's files show that, even after the mass murder had begun, the Nazi authorities still sought to embed it within a political and legal framework. For this reason, the genocide was organized in the manner of a standard administrative procedure, with the cooperation of various offices, even though most of the documents were classified as highly confidential—"Geheime Reichssache"—and only conveyed via special messengers and secret filing departments.[34]

Less than five months after the conference, on 4 June 1942, Heydrich died of injuries caused by an assassination attempt by Czech resistance fighters in Prague. Freisler died during an Allied bombing raid on Berlin in February 1945. Lange and Müller were probably killed fighting at the end of the war, while Meyer, like tens of thousands of others, took his own life as the Allies advanced.[35] Luther fell from grace in 1943, was interned as a special prisoner in Sachsenhausen concentration camp, and died shortly after the camp's liberation by the Red Army in spring 1945. Schöngarth was sentenced to death a short time after the war, but for his involvement in the murder of an Allied pilot, not his participation in the mass murder of Jews—even though news of the talks at Wannsee had been revealed to the public by *The New York Times* in 1945.[36] Bühler was sentenced to death for his role in the administration of the General Government by a Polish court in 1948. Participation in the Wannsee Conference was a central charge in his case. Consequently, Bühler was the first participant to mention the conference, even before the Protocol was discovered in 1947. Meanwhile, Kritzinger and Neumann were questioned as witnesses in Nuremberg and later released on health grounds. Kritzinger died in 1947; Neumann in 1951. Kritzinger was the only one of the Wannsee Conference participants to show any remorse over his involvement.[37]

Hofmann and Stuckart were sentenced by U.S. military courts in Nuremberg (the NMT), but the Wannsee Conference played a central role only in Stuckart's trial.[38] After the war, the surviving conference participants unanimously—and apparently in collusion—claimed that Heydrich had not mentioned the extermination of the Jews at all on 20 January 1942.[39] Thanks to his skillful defense, in which he managed to stylize him as a resistance fighter, and in view of the poor state of his health, Stuckart received only a short term of imprisonment.[40] Hofmann was sentenced to twenty-five years' imprisonment but granted an amnesty in 1954 by U.S. High Commissioner John Jay McCloy.

Despite the first publication of the Wannsee Protocol by the Union of Persecutees of the Nazi Regime, who also filed charges against the participants,[41] Hofmann, Klopfer and Leibbrandt were able to lead quiet lives in Germany, unchallenged and under their real names, right up until the 1980s. Proceedings against Klopfer and Leibbrandt—like many other cases—were abandoned because of statutory limitation periods and supposed problems with evidence. The postwar biographies of the surviving conference participants can, then, be read as proof of the negligence and errors of judgment that occurred in society and the judiciary when dealing with the perpetrators. The fact that the House of the Wannsee Conference Memorial Museum was not opened until 1992 also reflects this state of affairs.

In this volume, Mark Roseman, whose study of the Wannsee Conference remains seminal, considers how the now infamous meeting and those who attended it have been perceived over the years. His analysis is followed by essays on each of the participants, grouped according to their main occupation—either within the SS or Nazi and police ministerial bureaucracy. Within these groups, they have been placed in alphabetical order.

Robert Gerwarth, Professor of Modern History at University College Dublin, analyzes Heydrich on the basis of his own highly acclaimed biography as the social climber, power seeker and mass murderer who was the conference host. Building on many years' research into the Nazis' Germanization and settlement policy, Isabel Heinemann, lecturer in Modern and Contemporary History at Münster University, profiles Otto Hofmann, leader of the SS Race and Settlement Main Office, who was imprisoned after the war and later pardoned. Johannes Tuchel, director of the resistance memorial Gedenkstätte Deutscher Widerstand, considers the sphynx-like figure of "Gestapo Müller," who mutated from an unpolitical policeman to an ideologically motivated perpetrator.

Philosopher and Eichmann-expert Bettina Stangmeth sketches an image of the SS-Obersturmbannführer's character that goes beyond the "banality of evil" that Hannah Arendt observed. The SD commanders who were the practitioners directly involved in mass murder in the East—Lange in Riga and Schöngarth in Lemberg—are profiled by Peter Klein, lecturer in Holocaust Studies at Berlin's Touro College and long-time close associate of the Wannsee Memorial, and Olaf Löschke, who previously portrayed his participant of the Wannsee Conference in a successful documentary-drama project.

Schöngarth's opposite number in the General Government, Bühler, is analyzed by Ingo Loose, a leading expert on German occupation policy in Poland, who studied the Polish case files for this essay. The doyen of perpetrator research, Christopher Browning, describes the rise of shirt-sleeved underdog Martin Luther to the elite Foreign Ministry. Markus Heckmann builds on his extensive research to profile Klopfer, former State Secretary at the Nazi Party Chancellery, who settled in the author's hometown after the war. Leibbrandt, Nazi specialist on Eastern Europe and representative of the Reich Ministry for the occupied Eastern territories, who hailed from the Odessa area and had researched German ethnicity as a Rockefeller scholar in the United States before the Nazis seized power, is sketched by his biographer, Martin Munke. The life and work of his superior and deputy to the Reich Minister for the Occupied Eastern Territories Alfred Rosenberg, Gauleiter of North Westphalia Meyer, is portrayed by Heinz-Jürgen Priamus on the basis of his well received biography.

Freisler, later known as the bloody judge of the People's Court, who was State Secretary in the Reich Ministry of Justice until summer 1942, is portrayed by long-time freelance associate of the Wannsee Memorial Silke Struck. Historian Stefan Paul-Jacobs and our former colleague Lore Kleiber consider Kritzinger, a Prussian official who held the reins of regime communication in the Reich Chancellery, paying special attention to his son's relationship with him — and with the House of the Wannsee Conference Memorial Museum. We, the editors, have turned our attention to two behind-the-scenes perpetrators in the ministries, Wilhelm Stuckart and Erich Neumann.

We owe a large debt of gratitude to the Hamburg foundation "Stiftung zur Förderung von Wissenschaft und Kultur" for its generous and non-bureaucratic support for this volume. We are also deeply grateful to our German publisher Fritz Veitl of Metropol Verlag (Berlin), who advised and assisted the publication from the outset. Back in 1992, Metropol Verlag published the hitherto largest collection of biographical data on the conference participants, collated by Kurt Pätzold and Erika Schwarz, which marked a watershed of research. Without the help of our colleagues from the Memorial's own, excellently stocked library, the Joseph Wulf Mediothek, our many dedicated colleagues and freelance associates, Sandra Keil and Jana Fritsche's editorial work, this book would not have become what it is. Lastly, our thanks are due to the authors, many of whom are seasoned experts on the participants they profile. Our work benefited greatly from their intensive research and compelling reflections.

Hans-Christian Jasch has been the executive director of the Memorial and Educational Site House of the Wannsee Conference since May 2014. He has authored an acclaimed biographical study on the State Secretary in the Reich Interior Ministry Wilhelm Stuckart and the role of the civil service in Jewish policy, which was published in 2012. His other research focuses on the history of state, law and administration in Nazi Germany and the early years of the Federal Republic. He has contributed to the book *The Law in Nazi Germany* (edited by Alan E. Steinweis and Robert D. Rachlin) published by Berghahn in 2013. A lawyer by training, Jasch has also gained practical experience working as a civil servant in the German Federal Ministry of the Interior since 2001. From 2005 to 2011 he was first seconded to work in Rome as a liaison officer and then to the European Commission in Brussels to work on policy development in the field of countering radicalization and terrorism.

Christoph Kreutzmüller has been connected to the House of the Wannsee Conference since 1992. He studied in Berlin and the UK and wrote his Ph.D. thesis on German banks in the Netherlands between 1919 and 1945. Having coordinated two extensive research projects on the fate of Jewish owned businesses in Berlin 1930–1945 and on Jews in Berlin 1918–1938 for the Humboldt-University (Berlin), he joined the Jewish Museum in Berlin as a curator for the new permanent exhibition in 2016. Kreutzmüller's acclaimed study *Final Sale in Berlin: The Destruction of Jewish Commercial Activity 1930–1945* was published in 2015 by Berghahn. Other publications include *Berlin 1933–1945*, Munich (Siedler) 2013 (with Michael Wildt) and *National Economies: Volks-Wirtschaft, Racism and Economy in Europe between the Wars*, Newcastle (Cambridge Scholars Publishing) 2015 (with Michael Wildt and Moshe Zimmermann).

Notes

1   Letter from Reinhard Heydrich to Martin Luther, 8 January 1942, PA AA, R. 100857.
2   On the history of the House, see: Michael Haupt, *Das Haus der Wannsee-Konferenz: Von der Industriellenvilla zur Gedenkstätte* (Berlin, 2009); Johannes Tuchel, *Am Großen Wannsee 56–58: Von der Villa Minoux zum Haus der Wannsee-Konferenz* (Publikationen der Gedenkstätte Haus der Wannsee-Konferenz, vol. 1) (Berlin, 1992). For the history of the Memorial Museum, see: G. Schoenberner, "Der lange Weg nach Wannsee: Von der Gründerzeitvilla zur Gedenkstätte," *Dachauer Hefte* 8 (1992): 150–63; G. Kühling, "Schullandheim oder Forschungsstätte? Die Auseinandersetzung um ein Dokumentationszentrum im Haus der Wannsee-Konferenz (1966/67)," *Zeithistorische Forschungen/Studies in Contemporary History* 5, no. 2 (2008): 211–35.
3   The Wannsee Conference itself is presented in the Wannsee House permanent exhibition and has been analyzed in numerous publications. Suffice it to mention here only: Peter Klein, *Die Wannsee-Konferenz vom 20. Januar 1942: Analyse und Dokumentation* (Berlin, 1995); Peter Longerich, *Die Wannsee-Konferenz: Der Weg zur "Endlösung"* (Munich, 2016); N. Kampe and P. Klein, ed., *Die Wannsee-Konferenz am 20. Januar 1942: Dokumente, Forschungsstand, Kontroversen* (Cologne, Weimar and Vienna, 2013); Mark Roseman, *Die Wannsee-Konferenz: Wie die NS-Bürokratie den Holocaust organisierte* (Berlin, 2002).
4   For more recent biographical approaches, see: Mark Roseman, "Lebensfälle: Biografische Annäherungen an NS-Täter," in *Der Holocaust: Ergebnisse und neue Fragen der Forschung*, ed. F. Bajohr and A. Löw (Frankfurt am Main, 2015), 186–209. An overview can also be found in: Harald Welzer, *Täter: Wie aus ganz normalen Menschen Massenmörder werden* (Frankfurt am Main,

2005); G. Paul, ed., *Die Täter der Shoah: Fanatische Nationalsozialisten oder ganz normale Deutsche?* (Göttingen, 2002); Michael Wildt, *Die Generation des Unbedingten: Das Führungskorps des Reichssicherheitshauptamtes* (Hamburg, 2002); Ulrich Herbert, *Best: Biographische Studien über Radikalismus, Weltanschauung und Vernunft 1903–1989* (Bonn, 1996).

5 Wolf Kaiser, "Die Wannsee-Konferenz: SS-Führer und Ministerialbeamte im Einvernehmen über die Ermordung der europäischen Juden," in *Täter, Opfer, Folgen: Der Holocaust in Geschichte und Gegenwart*, ed. H. Lichtenstein and O.R. Romberg (Bonn, 1997), 24–37.

6 C. Kreutzmüller and M. Wildt, ed., *Berlin 1933–1945* (Munich, 2013), 16.

7 *Conspiracy*, directed by Frank Pierson (United States and Great Britain, 2001).

8 Gerald D. Feldman and Wolfgang Seibel, "The Holocaust as Division-of-Labor-Based Crime: Evidence and Analytical Challenges," in *Networks of Nazi Persecution: Bureaucracy, Business, and the Organization of the Holocaust*, ed. G.D. Feldman and W. Seibel (New York and Oxford, 2005), 1.

9 Götz Aly has pointed out that, on the basis of a statistical survey during the war, Goebbels established that the average age of leading personalities in the middle layer of the Party was thirty-four and inside the machinery of the State forty-four. It could in truth be said that "Germany is today being led by its youth." See Götz Aly, *Hitlers Volksstaat: Raub, Rassenkrieg und nationaler Sozialismus* (Frankfurt am Main, 2006), 12; also Welzer, *Täter*, 53.

10 Wildt, *Generation*.

11 Norbert Kampe, *Studenten und "Judenfrage" im deutschen Kaiserreich: Die Entstehung einer akademischen Trägerschicht des Antisemitismus* (Göttingen, 1988); Dietrich Heither et al., *Blut und Paukboden: Eine Geschichte der Burschenschaften* (Frankfurt am Main, 1997).

12 See U. Hoßfeld et al., ed., *"Im Dienst an Volk und Vaterland": Die Jenaer Universität in der NS-Zeit* (Cologne, Weimar and Vienna, 2005).

13 See Björn Weigel, "'Märzgefallene' und Aufnahmestopp im Frühjahr 1933: Eine Studie über den Opportunismus," in *Wie wurde man Parteigenosse? Die NSDAP und ihre Mitglieder*, ed. W. Benz (Frankfurt am Main, 2009), 91–109.

14 Rüdiger Hachtmann, *Wissenschaftsmanagement im "Dritten Reich": Geschichte der Generalverwaltung der Kaiser-Wilhelm-Gesellschaft* (Göttingen, 2007), 153.

15 Membership list of the Aero Club of Germany, January 1939, see: Archiv zur Geschichte der Max-Planck-Gesellschaft, I Abt., Rep. 0001A. We are grateful to Rüdiger Hachtmann, Berlin, for this information.

16 This is presumably one of the grounds on which the conference was postponed at short notice, after the Japanese attack on Pearl Harbor, from 9 December 1941 to 20 January 1942, since Hitler wished to announce to the Großdeutsche Reichstag on 11 December 1941 that Germany and Italy were issuing a declaration of war against the United States of America.

17 Stenographical report of the discussion of the Jewish Question with Göring, 12 November 1938, in: International Military Tribunal [IMT], *Der Prozeß gegen die Hauptkriegsverbrecher vor dem Internationalen Militärgerichtshof (IMT): Nürnberg 14. November 1945 – 1. Oktober 1946, gemäß den Weisungen des Internationalen Militärgerichtshofes vom Sekretariat des Gerichtshofes unter*

der Autorität des Obersten Kontrollrats für Deutschland veröffentlicht, 42 vols., ed. L.D. Egbert and P.A. Joosten (Nuremberg, 1947–49), vol. 28, 499–540, doc. 1816 PS. See minutes of interrogation of Erich Neumann, 18 November 1947, Institut für Zeitgeschichte (IfZ), ZS 1259.

18 See previous note. On the emigration of Jews from the "Third Reich," see Juliane Wetzel, "Auswanderung aus Deutschland," in *Die Juden in Deutschland 1933–1945: Leben unter nationalsozialistischer Herrschaft*, ed. W. Benz (Munich, 1988), 413–98. After the prohibition of emigration ordered by Himmler in autumn 1941, only an estimated 8,500 persons managed to flee. See M. Richarz, ed., *Jüdisches Leben in Deutschland: Selbstzeugnisse zur Sozialgeschichte 1780–1945*, 3 vols. (Stuttgart, 1976–82), 53.

19 Göring's letter, 24 January 1939, PAAA R 100857, sheet 4 et seq.

20 See Stefan Krings, *Hitlers Pressechef: Otto Dietrich (1897–1952): Eine Biografie* (Göttingen, 2010).

21 Cited from Bernward Dörner, *Die Deutschen und der Holocaust: Was niemand wissen wollte, aber jeder wissen konnte* (Berlin, 2007), 160 et seq.

22 "Die Juden sind schuld," *Das Reich*, 16 November 1941. See Dörner, *Die Deutschen und der Holocaust*, 162 et seq.

23 *Die Tagebücher von Joseph Goebbels* [The Diaries of Joseph Goebbels], commissioned by the IfZ and with the support of the State Archive Service of Russia, ed. E. Fröhlich, Part II: Diktate 1941–1945, vol. 2: October to December 1941 (Munich, 1996), 487 et seq.

24 W. Gross, "Die rassenpolitischen Voraussetzungen zur Lösung der Judenfrage," *Deutsches Recht: Zentralorgan des NS-Rechtswahrerbundes* 12, no. A 1/2 (1942): 8. The article was published in early 1941 in *Weltkampf* 18, no. 1/2 (1941): 52–63.

25 Gross, "Die rassenpolitischen Voraussetzungen," 2.

26 P. Schlaak, "Das Wetter in Berlin von 1933 bis 1945," *Berlinische Monatsschrift* 9, no. 9 (2000): 182.

27 This is documented in a letter of 20 August 1943 from the Prague Gestapo concerning the whereabouts of confiscated furniture, which was dispatched to Berlin and had been used "in Wannsee to furnish a guest house of the Reich Security Main Office," in: Prague state archive, UPR-ST-AMV 109, box 160, sign. 109-12-140.

28 Cit. from "Befehlsblatt der Sicherheitspolizei und des SD," in: Staatsarchiv Nürnberg, PS-709.

29 See the minutes of interrogation of Adolf Eichmann, 5 July 1960, reprinted in: Kampe and Klein, *Wannsee-Konferenz*, 88.

30 "Regierungsneubildung in Protektorat Böhmen und Mähren," *Völkischer Beobachter*, 21 January 1942.

31 Letter from Heydrich to Luther, 26 February 1942, PAAA, R. 100857, 165.

32 Protocol of the Conference on the Final Solution of the Jewish Question, PAAA, R. 100857, 166–80.

33 See the letter of invitation and transcript of the meeting with accompanying letter from Eichmann, 3 November 1942, PAAA R 100 857, sheet 127 et seq. On this meeting, see Hans-Christian Jasch, *Staatssekretär Wilhelm Stuckart und die Judenpolitik: Der Mythos von der sauberen Verwaltung*

(Munich, 2012), 330 et seq.; also Cornelia Essner, *Die "Nürnberger Gesetze" oder die Verwaltung des Rassenwahns 1933–1945* (Paderborn, 2002), 434–42.

34 The sociologist Baumann places the genocide of the European Jews in the context of the modern age, conceived in the midst of a modern, rational society and carried out by the purest form of bureaucracy ("Bürokratie in Reinkultur"). See Zygmunt Bauman, *Dialektik der Ordnung: Die Moderne und der Holocaust* (Hamburg, 1992), 10 and 31.

35 See Christian Goeschel, *Suicide in Nazi Germany* (Oxford, 2009).

36 "Nazi Jewish Files Found: Papers Confirm Aim to Exterminate People in Europe," *The New York Times*, 21 August 1945. Reprinted in Kampe and Klein, *Wannsee-Konferenz*, 61.

37 Minutes of interrogation of Friedrich Wilhelm Kritzingers, 5 March 1947, IfZ, ZS 988-2.

38 In a "Statement on the Extension of the 'Ministries Case' to Include some Additional High Nazis Responsible for the Extirpation of Jews," 20 November 1947, the World Jewish Congress (WJC) had tried unsuccessfully to extend the charges to other participants of the Wannsee Conference— Neumann, Leibbrandt, Hofmann (here named Hoffmann) and Kritzinger— as well as two of Eichmann's members of staff—Krumey and Girzick (here named Girzik). In this statement, the WJC noted that Stuckart was the only participant in the conference to stand trial in Nuremberg although other participants were in U.S. custody (and Krumey in British custody). As the U.S. authorities had decided to conclude the prosecution of war criminals with the Wilhelmstraße trial, the case no. 11 offered the only opportunity to create a "major case of action by the U.S. authorities against the German initiators (and main culprits) of anti-Jewish action in all of Europe." To follow the case "and to assist in the Jewish aspect of this extremely important case," the WJC sent its own representative to Nuremberg. See Records of the Jacob Rader Marcus Center of the American Jewish Archives; also http://www.trumanlibrary.org/whistlestop/study_collections/nuremberg/documents/index.php?pagenumber=1&documentdate=1947-11-20&documentid=C194-3-6&studycollectionid=nuremberg (accessed 15 October 2015).

39 See the statements under oath by Gerhard Klopfer, 16 December 1947 and 12 June 1948, BA Berlin (BAL) 99 US 7, Fall XI, 871, 44–54.; also interrogation of Otto Hofmann on 7 January 1948 before the Military Tribunal no. 1 in case VIII, BArch 99 US 7, Fall XI, 871, 62–68; the statements under oath by Georg Leibbrandt of 4 June 1948, BAL 99 US 7, Fall XI, 871, 55–58 and by Erich Neumann of 29 June 1948, BAL 99 US 7, Fall XI, 874, 34–37; testimonies by Stuckart in the Wilhelmstraße trial, Bundesarchiv Koblenz (BAK) NL Stuckart, N 1292/125. See also Essner, *Nürnberger Gesetze*, 414 et seq.

40 "Nuremberg Terms Run 4 to 25 Years," *The New York Times*, 15 April 1949.

41 Copy of a letter from the public prosecutor to the Director of Public Prosecutions at the Supreme Court, 23 January 1957, LAB, B Rep. 058, 4481.

Bibliography

Aly, Götz. *Hitlers Volksstaat: Raub, Rassenkrieg und nationaler Sozialismus*. 2nd ed. Frankfurt am Main: S. Fischer, 2006. [English: *Hitler's Beneficiaries: Plunder, Racial War, and the Nazi Welfare State*. New York: Henry Holt and Company, 2005.]

Bauman, Zygmunt. *Dialektik der Ordnung: Die Moderne und der Holocaust*. Hamburg: Europäische Verlagsanstalt, 1992. [English: *Modernity and the Holocaust*, Ithaca, NY: Cornell University Press, 1989.]

Dörner, Bernward. *Die Deutschen und der Holocaust: Was niemand wissen wollte, aber jeder wissen konnte*. Berlin: Propyläen, 2007.

Essner, Cornelia. *Die "Nürnberger Gesetze" oder die Verwaltung des Rassenwahns 1933–1945*. Paderborn: Schöningh, 2002.

Feldman, Gerald D. and Wolfgang Seibel. "The Holocaust as Division-of-Labor-Based Crime: Evidence and Analytical Challenges." In *Networks of Nazi Persecution: Bureaucracy, Business, and the Organization of the Holocaust*, edited by G.D. Feldman and W. Seibel, 1–10. New York and Oxford: Berghahn, 2005.

Fröhlich, E. ed. *Die Tagebücher von Joseph Goebbels: Aufzeichnungen 1923–1941*, 14 vols. Munich: Saur, 1998–2006.

Gillott, Nick. *Conspiracy [Die Wannsee-Konferenz]*. DVD. Directed by Frank Pierson. U.S. and GB: Home Box Office and BBC, 2001.

Goeschel, Christian. *Suicide in Nazi Germany*. Oxford: Oxford University Press, 2009.

Gross, W. "Die rassenpolitischen Voraussetzungen zur Lösung der Judenfrage." *Deutsches Recht: Zentralorgan des NS-Rechtswahrerbundes* 12, no. A 1/2 (1942): 2–9 [first in: *Weltkampf* 18, no. 1/2 (1941): 52–63].

Hachtmann, Rüdiger. *Wissenschaftsmanagement im "Dritten Reich": Geschichte der Generalverwaltung der Kaiser-Wilhelm-Gesellschaft*. Göttingen: Wallstein, 2007.

Haupt, Michael. *Das Haus der Wannsee-Konferenz: Von der Industriellenvilla zur Gedenkstätte*. Berlin: Gedenk- und Bildungsstätte Haus der Wannsee-Konferenz, 2009.

Heither, Dietrich, Michael Gehler, Alexandra Kurth and Gerhard Schäfer. *Blut und Paukboden: Eine Geschichte der Burschenschaften*. Frankfurt am Main: Fischer-Taschenbuch-Verlag, 1997.

Herbert, Ulrich. *Best: Biographische Studien über Radikalismus, Weltanschauung und Vernunft 1903–1989*. Bonn: Dietz, 1996.

Hoßfeld, U., J. John, O. Lehmuth and R. Stutz, ed. *"Im Dienst an Volk und Vaterland": Die Jenaer Universität in der NS-Zeit*. Cologne, Weimar and Vienna: Böhlau, 2005.

International Military Tribunal [IMT]. *Der Prozeß gegen die Hauptkriegsverbrecher vor dem Internationalen Militärgerichtshof (IMT): Nürnberg 14. November 1945— 1. Oktober 1946, gemäß den Weisungen des Internationalen Militärgerichtshofes vom Sekretariat des Gerichtshofes unter der Autorität des Obersten Kontrollrats für Deutschland veröffentlicht*, edited by L.D. Egbert and P.A. Joosten. Nuremberg, 1947–1949.

Jasch, Hans-Christian. *Staatssekretär Wilhelm Stuckart und die Judenpolitik: Der Mythos von der sauberen Verwaltung*. Munich: Oldenbourg, 2012.

Kaiser, Wolf. "Die Wannsee-Konferenz: SS-Führer und Ministerialbeamte im Einvernehmen über die Ermordung der europäischen Juden." In *Täter, Opfer, Folgen: Der Holocaust in Geschichte und Gegenwart*, edited by H. Lichtenstein and O.R. Romberg, 24–37. Bonn: Bundeszentrale für Politische Bildung, 1997.

Kampe, Norbert. *Studenten und "Judenfrage" im deutschen Kaiserreich: Die Entstehung einer akademischen Trägerschicht des Antisemitismus*. Göttingen: Vandenhoeck & Ruprecht, 1988.

Kampe, N. and P. Klein, ed. *Die Wannsee-Konferenz am 20. Januar 1942: Dokumente, Forschungsstand, Kontroversen*. Cologne, Weimar and Vienna: Böhlau, 2013.

Klein, Peter. *Die Wannsee-Konferenz vom 20. Januar 1942: Analyse und Dokumentation*. Berlin: Edition Hentrich, 1995.

Kreutzmüller, Christoph and Michael Wildt. "Berlin 1933–1945: Stadt und Gesellschaft im Nationalsozialismus." In *Berlin 1933–1945*, edited by C. Kreutzmüller and M. Wildt, 7–16. Munich: Siedler, 2013.

Krings, Stefan. *Hitlers Pressechef: Otto Dietrich (1897–1952): Eine Biografie*. Göttingen: Wallstein, 2010.

Kühling, G. "Schullandheim oder Forschungsstätte? Die Auseinandersetzung um ein Dokumentationszentrum im Haus der Wannsee-Konferenz (1966/67)." *Zeithistorische Forschungen/Studies in Contemporary History* 5, no. 2 (2008): 211–35. Retrieved 6 October 2016 from http://www.zeithistorische-forschungen.de/2-2008/id%3D4570.

Longerich, Peter. *Die Wannsee-Konferenz: Der Weg zur "Endlösung."* Munich: Pantheon, 2016.

Paul, G., ed. *Die Täter der Shoah: Fanatische Nationalsozialisten oder ganz normale Deutsche?* Göttingen: Wallstein, 2002.

Roseman, Mark. *Die Wannsee-Konferenz: Wie die NS-Bürokratie den Holocaust organisierte*. Berlin: Propyläen, 2002. [English: *The Villa, the Lake, the Meeting: Wannsee and the Final Solution*. London: Penguin Press, 2002.]

———. "Lebensfälle: Biografische Annäherungen an NS-Täter." In *Der Holocaust: Ergebnisse und neue Fragen der Forschung*, edited by F. Bajohr and A. Löw, 186–209. Frankfurt am Main: Fischer-Taschenbuch-Verlag, 2015.

Richarz, M., ed. *Jüdisches Leben in Deutschland: Selbstzeugnisse zur Sozialgeschichte 1780–1945*. Stuttgart: Deutsche Verlags-Anstalt, 1976–82.

Schlaak, P. "Das Wetter in Berlin von 1933 bis 1945." *Berlinische Monatsschrift* 9, no. 9 (2000): 177–84.

Schoenberner, G. "Der lange Weg nach Wannsee: Von der Gründerzeitvilla zur Gedenkstätte." *Dachauer Hefte* 8 (1992): 150–63.

Tuchel, Johannes. *Am Großen Wannsee 56–58: Von der Villa Minoux zum Haus der Wannsee-Konferenz*. Berlin: Edition Hentrich, 1992.

Weigel, Björn. "'Märzgefallene' und Aufnahmestopp im Frühjahr 1933: Eine Studie über den Opportunismus." In *Wie wurde man Parteigenosse? Die NSDAP und ihre Mitglieder*, edited by W. Benz, 91–109. Frankfurt am Main: Fischer-Taschenbuch-Verlag, 2009.

Welzer, Harald. *Täter: Wie aus ganz normalen Menschen Massenmörder werden*. Frankfurt am Main: S. Fischer, 2005.

Wetzel, Juliane. "Auswanderung aus Deutschland." In *Die Juden in Deutschland 1933–1945: Leben unter nationalsozialistischer Herrschaft*, edited by W. Benz, 413–98. Munich: C.H. Beck, 1988.

Wildt, Michael. *Die Generation des Unbedingten: Das Führungskorps des Reichssicherheitshauptamtes*. Hamburg: Hamburger Edition, 2002. [English: *An Uncompromising Generation: The Nazi Leadership of the Reich Security Main Office*. Madison, WI: University of Wisconsin Press, 2009.]

1

BIOGRAPHICAL APPROACHES AND THE WANNSEE CONFERENCE

Mark Roseman

Ever since the summary minutes ("Protokoll") of the meeting were discovered in 1947, the Wannsee Conference has been seen by the general public as the place where the decision to murder European Jewry was made. Specialists have long agreed that both the timing of the meeting and the invited personnel preclude it having quite this fundamental character. But the minutes continue to offer one of the most telling windows on a key phase of Nazi policymaking, when a Europe-wide murder program was taking concrete shape (and a global murder program being imagined).[1] The conference represented also a further gain for the SS, as part of an extended internal turf war for control of Jewish matters, underway since the 1930s. What remains most striking about the event is the juxtaposition of its genocidal agenda with elegant surroundings, diplomatic protocol and (so far as we can tell)[2] collegial niceties. In the two full-length docudramas produced about the Wannsee Conference, the most arresting feature is indeed the array of serious men, some prim and refined, others more vulgar and aggressive, batting their genocidal project back and forth around a conference table. It is quite surprising on one level, therefore, that the present collection represents the first consolidated biographical approach to the men at the table.[3] On another level, however, it is the natural expression of a sea change in the wider historiography of Nazi Germany and the Holocaust that has occurred over the last decade or two. Much of this chapter navigates those historiographical waters, tracing historians' evolving approach to the men who made the conference possible.

It concludes with some reflections on the challenges of perpetrator biography.

Agents or Structures

It might seem odd that perpetrator biography has only fairly recently become a staple element of serious Holocaust historiography. After all, almost since the end of the war, German and international reading and viewing publics have been more fascinated by leading Nazis than by the protagonists of any other dictatorship. Biographies of evil henchmen, dashing but flawed generals, mad scientists, and of course, Hitler, Hitler, Hitler, have found a secure place on bookshop shelves for decades in a way that, say, the lives of the Dzerzhinksys and Berias of Stalin's rule never have. Indeed, in the Soviet case almost no one below Stalin himself is a household name. Despite this public interest, professional historians of Nazi Germany have been slow to embrace the genre of biography. Apart from a few seminal scholarly biographies of Hitler himself, the lives of Nazis that caught the public imagination were until recently mostly written by outsiders to the field. Even many of the salient works that left their mark on scholarship and continue to be worth reading, despite their flaws—Arendt's account of Eichmann, Haffner's short but still telling biography of Hitler, or Sereny's encounter with Franz Stangl, to name but a few examples—were penned by non-historians, or by historians who never gained access to the academy.[4]

Of course the historical profession was slow to engage with the Holocaust in general. In Germany scholarship of the Nazi era as a whole took a while to take off. But beyond that, for biography to make sense, two things were required. Historians had to believe, first, that particular individuals made a difference. It goes without saying that most agreed that Hitler himself had left his disastrous stamp on Germany, Europe, and the world. But what of the men below him? Secondly, it was worth engaging in biography only if scholars believed that the protagonists were more than the offices they held; for example, that they brought essential and distinctive things to the table from their previous lives. Neither of these assumptions carried much weight in historical analysis of Nazi Germany and the Holocaust until recently.

In the postwar decades, the growing influence of social science methods in the postwar period led historians to reject the traditional emphasis on "great men of history" and to foreground social structures. Biography went out of fashion in the academy. As far as the history of the "Third Reich" is concerned, it is true that social forces alone never seemed likely to be the full explanation for the irrationality and destructiveness of the Nazi regime. Moreover, as noted, however suspicious of "great men" theories, few historians challenged Hitler's central function in shaping Germany's fate. But when they looked below Hitler, there was little inclination to believe that the ideas or biographies of his subordinates had much to offer. Nazi policies seemed, after all, so horrifically irrational that to most historians, accustomed to think in terms of recognizable societal interests, it did not make sense to assume that a large body of intelligent men had actively embraced them.

Historians explained involvement in Nazism's murderous and ultimately suicidal project by reference to warped political structures and processes. For the so-called intentionalists, it was all about Hitler, whose megalomaniac ideas were disseminated to functionaries held in thrall by the elixir of totalitarianism—three parts adulation, two parts terror, and one part routine. The so-called structuralists accorded greater significance to energy and competition among the second and third tier of Nazi leaders, jostling and conniving their way upward by radicalizing Hitler's agenda.[5] To that extent, it was no longer just about Hitler. Yet as both labels for this latter school of interpretation ("structuralists" or "functionalists") make clear, what was at stake was less the distinctive contribution or individual ideas of particular figures than the fateful dynamics of an unbalanced system. It was a system kept in place to the bitter end by the centripetal force of Hitler's unassailable status. At the same time, the centrifugal energy of his subordinates' untrammeled competition caused it to spin in ever wilder and more destructive circles. In historical debates in the late 1960s and 1970s, historians narrowed in on increasingly fine-grained accounts of the decision-making process for genocide, and disagreed over whether Hitler sent metaphorical telegrams of murder, or just waved metaphorical flags. Ulrich Herbert has pointed out that this focus on the decision-making process actually represented a loss of an earlier recognition of the importance of the intellectual and mental world of the elites who made Nazism possible.[6] It left the protagonists as pale ciphers, or rooks, knights and pawns in a lethal chess game.

The Wannsee Participants in German Historiography until the 1990s

Within the evolution of the historiography up to 1990 or so, the challenge of making sense of the Wannsee Conference—as it came to be called—was that of relating it to the sequence of decisions that historians were piecing together to explain the origins of the "Final Solution."[7] The problem was that the Protocol suggested that the meeting was being called because some fundamental decisions needed to be taken for a developing program of genocide, but historians found this declaration hard to align with the other evidence they had about the decision-making process. Hitler was, after all, not at the meeting (nor were Himmler or Göring) and the participants' rank did not seem to be that of the decision-making level. The more historians became convinced that some kind of Hitler decision was made in the summer of 1941, the less the claim in the Protocol made sense that a meeting of permanent secretaries taking place on 20 January 1942 had the task of laying the provisional foundations for a fundamental program still in the making. Accordingly, until the 1990s historians saw the meeting as a particular puzzle within the wider mystery of the Holocaust. That is why, as late as 1995, Eberhard Jäckel could write that "the most remarkable thing about the Wannsee Conference is that we do not know why it took place."[8]

Looking at the way historians wrote about the conference in the 1970s and 1980s reminds us that historians' focus on structures and processes did not preclude their examining the role of particular individuals. When historians argued about the balance between Hitler orders on the one hand, and a competitive dynamic among his subordinates on the other, the evidence they adduced often involved the actions of particular figures. In the case of the conference the more historians found it difficult to understand the meeting's function, the more they turned to individual initiative to explain it. The obvious candidate to provide the key was Heydrich, who called and hosted the meeting in a building that belonged to his organization, and whose staff drafted and disseminated the minutes.

In the early postwar period, Heydrich was seen as the evil genius who carried his weak-willed boss, Himmler, on his shoulders. As Robert Gerwarth has recently pointed out, this overestimation of Heydrich's significance (because of an underestimation of Himmler) was already apparent during the war when the British Special Operations Executive (SOE) invested considerable energy and hopes in Heydrich's assassination. In reality, as we know, Heydrich's assassination in May 1942 led merely to a series of Himmler decisions that horribly accelerated the pace of murder.[9] Later historians may have been less likely to underestimate his boss, Himmler, but they still sought to explain the conference in terms of Heydrich's own objectives. In the description of the conference that appears in Helmut Krausnick's influential account of the origins of the "Final Solution," appearing in 1965, no other protagonists really figured, indeed the others were barely mentioned.[10] The less the meeting came to be seen as part of the core decision-making process, the more it was viewed as a move in Heydrich's power-game. Thus the historian Wolfgang Scheffler believed Heydrich's position was under threat at the end of 1941. Himmler was rapidly expanding the role of SS figures not under RSHA (Reich Main Security Office) control, notably the regional Higher SS and Police Leaders and the Concentration Camp empire under Oswald Pohl's management. [11] For Scheffler, Wannsee was a way for Heydrich to demonstrate his relevance by pushing around the civilian representatives. By contrast, Eberhard Jäckel saw Heydrich in the ascendant. Given Heydrich's new-found role as acting protector of Bohemia and Moravia, in addition to his responsibilities in the Himmler empire, he could at last come out from under Himmler's shadow and demonstrate his standing.[12] Both these interpretations discounted what the Protocol said was the meeting's mission, and foregrounded the ambitions of this power-hungry subaltern.

It is understandable that no one else was seen as key to explaining the conference, since whatever brief from above Heydrich may or may not have received, it is clear that this was his event. In the popular mind, it is true; the conference came to be indelibly associated also with Adolf Eichmann. It was, after all, Eichmann's Jerusalem testimony in 1961 that helped to bring the conference to the forefront of popular consciousness. The exaggeration of Eichmann's significance at the conference was an ironic outcome of his trial. Eichmann had highlighted the meeting to downplay his own role. He wanted to demonstrate that senior civilian officials, well above Eichmann's pay grade, had endorsed the murder program at Wannsee in a way that had surprised and delighted Heydrich. Eichmann's aim here was to present himself as merely the dogsbody in a program enjoying high-level consensus. But in 1961 the global notoriety Eichmann had earned through the trial, coupled with misleading accounts like Robert Kempner's *Eichmann und Komplizen*, which made him the lynchpin of the event, meant that Eichmann's testimony produced the opposite of what he had hoped.[13] For most historians, however, it remained clear that Eichmann was by far the most junior person present, bringing organizational support but no institutional or personal firepower.

It was not easy to parse the role of other participants, not least because of the limited sources. After all, we do not have the original stenographic minutes of the meeting. All we can say of the summary account produced by Eichmann for Heydrich is that while it may have been tendentious and selective, it was not sufficiently inaccurate to engender protest strong enough to have been recorded in the files (some later bureaucratic interventions from other participants notwithstanding). The minutes themselves take the form of lengthy lecture notes from Heydrich, with a few interventions from other participants. Beyond the fact that their attendance is recorded, many of those present leave no trace in the minutes at all. To complement this scant resource, there is a paper trail from other meetings on related matters before and after the conference, and there are some surviving ministerial records from the participating ministries, giving us a sense of their objectives. In addition, there is testimony from the immediate postwar period, particularly from interrogations in the context of the so-called Ministries Trial conducted by the Americans in the wake of the International Military Tribunal at Nuremberg, there is also at least one important later memoir, and there is Eichmann's testimony in Jerusalem.[14]

On this basis, three other figures have received some attention in the historiography of the conference up to the 1990s. Historians agree that whatever else may have been at stake at Wannsee, Heydrich was indeed seeking to expand the SS authority at the cost of other government departments. His prime targets were the civilian ministries that retained an interest in Jewish matters, particularly in the issue of mixed-race Jews and Jews in mixed marriages. Most affected were the Interior Ministry, the Ministry of Justice, and the Reich Chancellery. In this context, a number of historians have seen Wilhelm Stuckart from the Interior Ministry and Wilhelm Kritzinger from the Reichskanzlei as seeking to counter Heydrich's efforts.[15] The evidence for the conflict between the departments can be found in the surviving records of the various meetings between representatives of the ministries and the RSHA over the 1941 to 1942 period, and from postwar testimony. We know that the Interior Ministry and the Reich Chancellery sought to resist the assault on Jews of mixed race, while the Justice Ministry was wary of agreeing to the forced dissolution of mixed marriages. The only intervention that the Wannsee minutes themselves record from any of these men, however, came in the form of significant concessions from Stuckart; namely, the proposal that all mixed-race Jews of the first degree (i.e., with two Jewish grandparents) be sterilized, and that mixed marriages be forcibly dissolved.

So how did historians interpret the Ministerial representatives' role at Wannsee? For Uwe-Dietrich Adam, Hans Mommsen and Dieter Rebentisch, it was above all the Reich Chancellery that was seeking to deflect radical initiatives towards the remaining protected Jewish groups.[16] Hans Heinrich Lammers, the minister, seems in 1942 to have maneuvered to prevent new policies from being decided upon. (Ultimately, though, what prevented the "mixed" categories from being systematically murdered was Hitler's own reluctance to grasp thorny issues that might affect German wartime morale and further alienate the churches.) Kritzinger, Lammers' right hand man and the Reich Chancellery's representative at Wannsee, appeared a prime advocate of this effort to kick radical measures into the long grass. His honesty about the conference after the war, which so contrasted with all other participants interrogated by the Allies, has encouraged historians to see him as a dutiful and upright servant of the state, whose major culpability lay simply in having failed to speak out openly against the many measures with which the Reich Chancellery was complicit.[17]

The evaluation of the Interior Ministry's Stuckart was more ambivalent, with Dieter Rebentisch particularly doubtful about Stuckart's claim to have been an opponent of Nazi measures.[18] Most historians, like Adam, were more well-disposed. Adam and others were influenced by the retrospective account of the meeting offered by Bernhard Lösener, head of the "Jewish section" in Stuckart's department, and published by the State Secretary of the (postwar) Federal Ministry of Justice Walther Strauss in 1961 in the *Vierteljahrshefte für Zeitgeschichte*. Strauss, in turn, was seeking to help another former colleague of Stuckart and Lösener, Hans Globke, now head of Adenauer's Chancellery and tried in absentia in East Germany for his involvement in "Jewish matters" during the Nazi era. But whatever it may or may not have done for Globke, the Lösener report certainly helped the posthumous reputation of Stuckart, who was depicted as someone seeking to fend off the radicals, and whose sterilization proposal at Wannsee was presented as a tactical retreat, made in the belief that it would in fact turn out not to be a feasible proposition.[19]

Looking back now at historical research from the 1960s and 1970s it is striking how much even courageous and path-breaking German historians were inclined to take rather dubious postwar testimony on trust. This is true of Rebentisch's account of Lammers' statements at Nuremberg, Mommsen on Kritzinger's postwar testimony, and Adam on Lösener's published account. True, all these historians were well aware—and even Lösener himself had said as much—that for the ministries there was, alongside any moral considerations, considerable institutional amour propre involved in resisting SS advances. For the Interior Ministry and the Justice Ministry, concessions on their remaining prerogatives with regard to mixed race or mixed marriages would mean a significant erosion of power and prestige in relation to the ambitious men in Heydrich's empire. Even so, what emerged from the best German historical scholarship was a clear sense that the last vestiges of decency had not disappeared from the ministries. The picture that emerged was of a battle between a traditional civil service ethos, still present in some departments, particularly in the Reich Chancellery, on the one hand, and the mood and spirit of the SS and party radicals, on the other. That portrayal also influenced the two films about the event, both of which show a dismayed or hesitant Kritzinger, unhappy with the ambitions of an aggressive Heydrich, and a stand-off between Stuckart and Heydrich over the mixed-race question.

Non-German historians who engaged with the men at the conference, as well as the Polish-Jewish outsider to the profession Joseph Wulf, were far less inclined to give the ministerial representatives the benefit of the doubt.[20] In his path-breaking history of the destruction of European Jewry, Raul Hilberg approached the Wannsee Conference as a telling example of the diligence and care which all the relevant institutions brought to removing obstacles to the Holocaust.[21] In his eyes, the meeting was a problem-solving exercise, with a body of intelligent and conscientious men ironing out the kinks in the extermination plan. Hilberg thus pretty well discounted the differences between the various offices, as Dieter Rebentisch for one registered with dismay.[22] Christopher Browning's account of Martin Luther, the Foreign Office representative at Wannsee, reprised in this volume, was similarly damning, though in Browning's case less in making a blanket statement about all the civilian participants, than in identifying the way ambitious figures in different offices sought to bolster their credentials by flying the flag of murderous anti-Semitism. According to Browning, Luther, a business man before he entered the German department of the Foreign Office, earned his place at the Wannsee table among other things by the radical stance he took vis-à-vis the Jews of Serbia in fall 1941. Foreign Office contacts in Serbia had asked the Foreign Office to intercede to protect Jewish men from the Wehrmacht killings then underway, if possible by having the Jews deported. Luther rebutted this suggestion and was an outspoken advocate of murder.[23] Browning did emphasize however, that after Luther's fall from grace, his boss, Ribbentrop, found himself under exactly the same pressure to radicalize in Jewish matters to ensure the Foreign Office stayed "relevant." In foregrounding institutional pressures over ingrained anti-Semitism, Browning was in that sense operating on similar terrain to the German functionalists.

From Functionaries to Perpetrators

The way historians thought about participation in Nazi racial policy and genocide began to change in the 1980s. Scholarship began to take the discourse and objectives of racial policy seriously, and to assume that the protagonists were driven not merely by irrational orders, or by a lust for power, but rather saw meaning in what they were doing. This new turn in scholarly accounts began with the discovery of significant numbers of experts and professional elites who anticipated, legitimated or staffed Nazi killing polices, be it as racial scientists, demographers, geographers, medical experts, and so on. By looking outside the Nazi Party and police apparatus at such a wide array of professional elites, Götz Aly and others showed that science and professional training provided no safeguard against the Nazis' murderous projects, indeed proved surprisingly compatible with them.[24] With the opening of former Soviet and East European archives in the 1990s, other scholars began to take a new interest in the core actors of the Nazi police and policy apparatus. Not least thanks to the impact of Christopher Browning's *Ordinary Men*, the huge treasure trove of German judicial records, so long neglected by scholars, now began to find extensive use.[25] With these new sources on hand, some scholars focused on particular institutions, branches of the SS, regional Gestapo offices, order police and so forth, while others looked at evolution and enactment of racial policy in particular regions, notably in the Eastern European and Soviet killing fields, where mass murder crystallized into genocide. Other historians focused on individual trials, still others on distinct kinds of evidence; for example, photographs of violence or victim testimony. Following the lead of Browning, Bartov, and Goldhagen a growing number of authors sought to examine violence at the grass-roots level.[26]

As part of this exploding interest in participation, there have been a series of excellent biographies of upper and mid-level perpetrators, and a few of lower level perpetrators too.[27] In recent years, there has been a burgeoning set of studies of female perpetrators, and of non-German collaborators in murder. Finally, a point to which I return below, the most recent trend has been to blur the boundary between direct perpetration and wider societal participation, with some studies making the whole population complicit in genocide.[28] If these works have something in common, it has been first to widen the circle of those who are seen as somehow implicated in murder. In addition to the professional groups mentioned above, and large swathes of the ordinary police, the Wehrmacht was now closely implicated in atrocities and mass civilian deaths in a large variety of venues. Secondly, much of this new work operated with the assumption that the functionaries of Nazi racial policy and genocide in some sense "owned" the crimes to which they contributed. The clear marker of this shift was that the vocabulary of the "functionary" itself, so characteristic of scholarship up to the 1980s, began to be replaced by "perpetrator"' or "*Täter*," implying that a much larger group of individuals than previously acknowledged shared not only responsibility for the crimes they committed but also intent.[29] Indeed, as work on perpetrators evolved into a separate sub-discipline, the dominant note became the unsettling scope for individual decisions, initiative and energy, evident all the way down the hierarchy.[30] Postwar jurisprudence on Nazi crimes had established surprisingly early that German servants of the Nazi state could not claim to have acted under duress. Now the historiography decisively shifted the balance from orders to initiative. Neil Gregor has dubbed this the "voluntarist turn."[31]

Clearly, what ownership and intent meant varied significantly depending on the institution or level in the hierarchy under consideration. At the very highest level of the SS, for example, individual players could make a significant difference to the shape and pace of Nazi policy. At lower levels, individuals' ability to shape history on their own was limited, but the willingness of whole groups of men to participate enthusiastically could be a distinctive source of energy in the Nazi killing machine.

For some historians, the willingness of elites to conceive, endorse, or execute murderous policies ultimately revealed the murderous potential of the modern state.[32] This was certainly true of the first wave of work in the late 1980s and early 1990s, which looked at the professional elites involved in euthanasia policy or engaged in murderous demographic planning. Aly, Heim and others were at pains to emphasize the professional rationality and disciplinary logic of these "architects of annihilation" and thus to reject an older view that Nazi racial policy was the irrational fantasy of a tiny circle of völkisch cranks.[33] From the mid 1990s onwards, however, no doubt influenced by the recent experience of renewed violent ethnic-nationalism in the Balkans, the cold and generic rationality of the modern was increasingly displaced as explanation by a distinctive set of racist-nationalist ideas seen as having gained hold in sections of German society in the interwar period. In other words, contrary to the older view of the protagonists as merely dutiful, subordinate or ambitious careerists, the energy behind Nazi racial policies was now traced back to a large body of intelligent young men whose worldview coincided with that of Nazism well before 1933. This trend was profoundly influenced by Ulrich Herbert's 1996 biography of Heydrich's right-hand man, Werner Best.[34] Herbert drew attention to Best's radical ethnic nationalism, already apparent in the early 1920s, but also to Best's habitus and political style that couched this philosophy as hard-headed realism (or "heroic realism" in Best's rhetoric).

Herbert, whose model was subsequently developed by Michael Wildt in the latter's study of Heydrich's SD and Reich Security and Main Office (*An uncompromising generation*),[35] has shaped the approach of a number of other recent studies, including works of direct relevance to the Wannsee Conference.[36]

When I wrote my book offering a critical synthesis of the Wannsee Conference to coincide with its 60th anniversary in 2002, the fruits of this new wave of more perpetrator-focused research were already visible, even though some of the most relevant biographies for understanding the conference—Hans-Christian Jasch's biography of Stuckart and Robert Gerwarth's life of Heydrich—had not yet appeared. It was already clear that our understanding of the conference had evolved in three major ways. First, the timing of the conference began to make more sense, now that we could see that Berlin was being slowly nudged towards genocide through the fall of 1941. Rather than some clear Hitler decision back in the summer shaping political developments (though we cannot rule out there having been such a decision), it was clear that the initiatives undertaken and the problems experienced by Himmler's regional elites in occupied Eastern territories were helping crystallize mass murder in the occupied Soviet Union into something much broader. This not only made the conference's timing easier to understand but also located the demarcation disputes Heydrich was seeking to resolve within a key phase of policy gestation—whether one subscribed to Christian Gerlach's view that Hitler made some decision on the matter early in December 1941 or not.[37] What reinforced our understanding that the period around the time of the conference was a crucial phase of policy coordination was that, thanks to the recovery of Himmler's appointment calendar, Heydrich's actions could now be placed in the context of a series of Himmler meetings around the same time.[38]

Secondly, and equally significantly, the older impression of a cultural divide between civilian and Party and SS agencies was replaced by a much more differentiated and fluid sense of networks of ideas that crossed institutional lines. The impression of timorous educated civil servants ranged against SS thugs no longer held. Most of the best-educated men round the table were long-standing Nazis and in some cases honorary SS-members such as Stuckart and Klopfer. Of the eight people who had doctorates, six were either "old fighters" of the Nazi Party[39] or had at least enjoyed close contacts with the party well before 1933.[40] The other two had long years of right-wing Völkisch-national politics behind them: Rudolf Lange had belonged to the *Burschenschaft Germania*, while Gerhard Klopfer had been a member of the *Deutscher*

Hochschulring.[41] Here was powerful evidence of the degree to which radical nationalist ideas had made substantial inroads into Germany's educated youth even before 1933. In some cases bonds of friendship and shared ideas bridged the different institutions—the most striking being that between the SD's chief architect, Werner Best (not present himself at Wannsee), the party man Gerhard Klopfer, and the civil servant Wilhelm Stuckart. In autumn 1941 these men founded a new journal *Reich—Volksordnung—Lebensraum* (Reich—ethnic order—living space) for "ethnically based (völkisch) constitution and administration."[42] It was clear that men like Stuckart or Freisler were as deeply persuaded by Nazi ethnic-racial power politics as the Party officials or the men in the RSHA. To help understand why this was later lost from view, Jasch's recent Stuckart biography has shown just how much was fabricated in Stuckart's and Lösener's apologetic postwar narratives.[43]

Finally, along with this meshing of civilian and SS representatives, recent work has also offered another set of close connections; namely, that between the desk and field murderers—particularly, but not only, in the SS Reich Security Main Office. The men who arrived at Wannsee with their hands dripping with blood, Lange and Schöngarth, shared the same university background and legal training as most of their civil servant colleagues.

Agency, Culpability and Ambiguity

Is there a danger that by foregrounding the individuals around the table we may end up exaggerating their role, and lose sight of the forces to which they were subject?[44] One way of approaching this question is to ask whether the outcome could have been different if these men had acted differently. On one level this is obvious; any political system depends on the participation of many. If all the locomotive drivers had refused to take their trains to the camps, no one would have been killed there. But a more historically significant question is whether the individuals behaved differently to the way others would have in the same circumstances. In other words, whether there was anything distinctive about their contribution. To take the example just mentioned, Raul Hilberg has expressed skepticism as to whether it makes sense to talk about "Nazi train drivers." The drivers may have been party members, or they may not, but it made little difference to the performance of their duty. It would, in fact, have required an extraordinary person to have stepped out of the cab—and historically more significant, it would have taken extraordinary circumstances to see all or most of the train drivers step out of their cabs.

Of course, the men at Wannsee were very far from being just train drivers. But could they really shape policy? In most historical contexts, we tend not to write the biographies of civil servants or permanent secretaries, because we see them as the executors not the makers of policy. If at all, they tend to be written about in the context of collective accounts—the climate at the Quai D'Orsay, or the rise of the mandarins. True, the Nazi system allowed ambitious, talented party men to rise up fast through the ranks and become in some cases more influential than their bosses. Stuckart and Freisler in the Justice Ministry certainly belonged to this group. Yet, it would be hard to claim that individually either was decisive in determining the trajectory of Jewish policy. Even Heydrich, by far the most powerful man at the event, was operating within Himmler's framework. Heydrich's assassination a few months later had no measurable impact other than prompting Himmler to accelerate extermination in Poland. These men were for the most part individually not setting the goals, even if collectively their work was essential for the development of policy.

That does not rule out the idea that the Stuckarts and Heydrichs brought a distinctive talent and commitment to turning goals into policy. The older historiography recognized very well that Nazism allowed ambitious and ruthless men to make their mark. In that sense historians knew that the regime's servants were not "Everyman"—but then talented civil servants at the top rarely are. The new historiography added the insight that the shared ideas of territorial cleansing, ruthless ethnic nationalism, and so on, provided personal guiding principles for the regime's energetic servants. The problem though, in thinking about what the power of ideas might mean in such cases is that the participants of the Wannsee Conference had moved very far in a very short time. Even just a few years earlier, mass murder does not seem to have been remotely on their horizon or in their vocabulary. For many of our protagonists we are hard put even to find strong evidence of their anti-Semitism before 1933. Some, such as Heydrich or Müller, seem not to have been very political animals at all.

In exploring the relationship between the individuals, the offices they occupied, and the positions they advocated, we face significant hurdles. The sources are in most cases very fragmentary. The refractions of 1933 and 1945 make the serial expressions of our protagonists, where they exist at all, hard to fathom. We are not sure how to read either the rhetoric of the Nazi era, or the postwar apologias. After 1945, many of the civil servants were inscrutable, none more so than Neumann, as

Kreutzmüller's chapter in this volume shows. In that sense, the individual biographies rarely provide us with a vivid micro-historical vantage point. Partly for these reasons the challenge of distinguishing between conviction and opportunism, between agency and structure, limits the degree to which we can draw a clear line between what the protagonists brought to the table, and what circumstance and structure had contrived to make happen with these talented and willing collaborators.

But perhaps that is the point. In the end what is so powerful about these juxtaposed biographies is precisely the tension that emerges between two opposing insights: on the one hand, shared ideas, energy and habitus made the Wannsee Conference possible; on the other, the protagonists had had to make remarkable intellectual and moral journeys from selves for whom, just a few years earlier, a conference about genocide would have been inconceivable.

Mark Roseman is Pat M. Glazer Chair of Jewish Studies and Professor in History at Indiana University, Bloomington. He is the author of numerous books and articles on the Holocaust and modern German history, including a history of the Wannsee Conference (*The Villa, the Lake, the Meeting: Wannsee and the Final Solution* (Penguin, 2002) and multiple international editions).

Notes

1 The Chelmno camp, in effect a fixed site where mobile gas vans were in operation, had been a site of killings since December 1941. In the interest of space, the notes to this chapter have been kept to a minimum.

2 Christian Gerlach points out that we take a lot of Eichmann on trust. Stangneth shows in her contribution that Eichmann has systematically manipulated the "truth" he wanted to convey about his role in Wannsee.

3 Kurt Pätzold and Erika Schwarz, *Tagesordnung: Judenmord: Die Wannsee-Konferenz am 20. Januar 1942. Eine Dokumentation zur Organisation der 'Endlösung'* (Berlin, 1992) contained short biographies of the participants.

4 Hannah Arendt, *Eichmann in Jerusalem: Ein Bericht von der Banalität des Bösen,* (Munich, 1964); Gitta Sereny, *Into that Darkness: From Mercy Killing to Mass Murder* (New York, 1974); Sebastian Haffner, *The Meaning of Hitler* (London, 1979).

5 For discussion of the historiography, see Ian Kershaw, *The Nazi Dictatorship: Problems and Perspectives of Interpretation* (London, 2000).

6 Ulrich Herbert, "Vernichtungspolitik: Neue Antworten und Fragen zur Geschichte des 'Holocaust,'" in *Nationalsozialistische Vernichtungspolitik, 1939 bis 1945: Neue Forschungen und Kontroversen,* ed. U. Herbert (Frankfurt am Main, 1998), 9–66.

7   Mark Roseman, "'Wannsee' als Herausforderung: Die Historiker und die Konferenz," in *Wannsee-Konferenz*, ed. N. Kampe and P. Klein (Cologne, 2013), 401–14.

8   Eberhard Jäckel, "On the Purpose of the Wannsee Conference," in *Perspectives on the Holocaust: Essays in Honor of Raul Hilberg*, ed. James S. Pacy and Alan P. Wertheimer (Boulder, CO, San Francisco, CA and Oxford, 1995), here 39.

9   Robert Gerwarth, *Hitler's Hangman: The Life of Heydrich* (New Haven, CT, 2011).

10 In Martin Broszat, Hans-Adolf Jacobson and Helmut Krausnick, *Konzentrationslager, Kommissarbefehl, Judenverfolgung, vol. 2: Anatomie des SS-Staates* (Olten, 1965).

11 Wolfgang Scheffler, "Die Wannsee-Konferenz und ihre historische Bedeutung," in *Erinnern für die Zukunft: Ansprachen und Vorträge zur Eröffnung der Gedenkstätte*, ed. Gedenk- und Bildungsstätte Haus der Wannsee-Konferenz (Berlin, 1992), 18; Gerald Reitlinger, *The Final Solution: The Attempt to Exterminate the Jews of Europa, 1939–1945* (London, 1953), 102.

12 Jäckel, "Purpose of the Wannsee Conference," 39–50.

13 Robert M. W. Kempner, *Eichmann und Komplizen* (Zurich, Stuttgart and Vienna, 1961).

14 The memoir is from Stuckart's deputy, Bernhard Lösener, "Als Rassereferent im Reichsministerium des Inneren: Dokumentation. Das Reichsministerium des Inneren und die Judengesetzgebung," *Vierteljahrshefte für Zeitgeschichte* 9, no. 3 (1961): 264–313.

15 Among others, see Hans Mommsen, "Aufgabenkreise und Verantwortlichkeit des Staatssekretärs der Reichskanzlei Dr Wilhelm Kritzinger," in *Gutachten des Institutes für Zeitgeschichte, vol. 2: Gutachten*, ed. Institut für Zeitgeschichte (Munich, 1966), 369–98; Uwe Dietrich Adam, *Judenpolitik im Dritten Reich* (Düsseldorf, 1972); Dieter Rebentisch, *Führerstaat und Verwaltung im Zweiten Weltkrieg: Verfassungsentwicklung und Verwaltungspolitik 1939–1945* (Stuttgart, 1989).

16 See note 57.

17 Mommsen, "Aufgabenkreise und Verantwortlichkeit."

18 Rebentisch, *Führerstaat*, 110.

19 Lösener, "Als Rassereferent im Reichsministerium des Inneren."

20 Léon Poliakov and Joseph Wulf, *Das Dritte Reich und seine Diener: Dokumente* (Berlin, 1956).

21 Raul Hilberg, *The Destruction of the European Jews*, 4th ed. (New York, 1985), 166 et seq.

22 Rebentisch, *Führerstaat*, 437 and footnote 207.

23 Christopher R. Browning, *The Final Solution and the German Foreign Office: A Study of Referat D III of Abteilung Deutschland 1940–1943* (New York, 1978), 56 et seq.

24 Götz Aly and Susanne Heim, *Vordenker der Vernichtung: Auschwitz und die deutschen Pläne für eine neue europäische Ordnung* (Hamburg, 1991).

25 Christopher R. Browning, *Ordinary Men: Reserve Police Battalion 101 and the Final Solution in Poland* (New York, 1992).

26 Omer Bartov, *The Eastern Front 1941–45: German Troops and the Barbarisation of Warfare* (London, 1985); Daniel Jonah Goldhagen, *Hitler's Willing Executioners: Ordinary Germans and the Holocaust* (New York, 1996). There is no space here to do justice to the scope of research on perpetrators over the last two decades. For overviews of the evolving historiography of perpetrators, see G. Paul ed., *Täter der Shoah Fanatische Nationalsozialisten oder ganz normale Deutsche?* (Göttingen, 2002) Jürgen Matthäus, "Historiography and the Perpetrators of the Holocaust," in *The Historiography of the Holocaust*, ed. D. Stone (New York, 2004), 197–215; Mark Roseman, "Beyond Conviction? Perpetrators, Ideas, and Action in the Holocaust in Historiographical Perspective," in *Conflict, Catastrophe and Continuity: Essays on Modern German History*, ed. F. Biess, M. Roseman and H. Schissler (New York, 2007), 83–103.

27 Again, space precludes surveying the field, but two of the most influential biographies have been Ulrich Herbert, *Best: Biographische Studien über Radikalismus, Weltanschauung und Vernunft 1903–1989* (Bonn, 1996); and Peter Longerich, *Heinrich Himmler: Biographie* (Munich, 2008).

28 Michael Wildt, *Volksgemeinschaft als Selbstermächtigung: Gewalt gegen Juden in der deutschen Provinz 1919 bis 1939* (Hamburg, 2007); Thomas Kühne, *Belonging and Genocide: Hitler's Community, 1918–1945* (New Haven, CT, 2010).

29 There is of course a more narrowly functional use of the term perpetrator, meaning only those in some way involved in Nazi policies. This is how Raul Hilberg uses the term, but it has not been the dominant note. Raul Hilberg, *Perpetrators, Victims, Bystanders: The Jewish Catastrophe, 1933–1945* (New York, 1992). On the explosion of the work on perpetrators, see Paul, *Täter der Shoah*, and Matthäus, "Historiography and the Perpetrators of the Holocaust."

30 A. Lüdtke, "Fehlgreifen in der Wahl der Mittel: Optionen im Alltag militärischen Handelns," *Mittelweg 36* 12, no. 1 (2003): 75.

31 Neil Gregor, "Nazism—a Political Religion? Rethinking the Voluntarist Turn," in *Nazism, War and Genocide: Essays in Honour of Jeremy Noakes*, ed. N. Gregor (Exeter, 2005), 1–21.

32 Zygmunt Bauman, *Modernity and the Holocaust* (Ithaca, NY, 1989). For a review and critique of the modernity paradigm, see M. Roseman, "National Socialism and the End of Modernity," *American Historical Review* 116, no. 3 (2011): 688–701.

33 Aly and Heim, *Vordenker der Vernichtung*.

34 Herbert, *Best*.

35 Michael. Wildt, *Die Generation des Unbedingten: Das Führungskorps des Reichssicherheitshauptamtes* (Hamburg, 2002).

36 For a critique, see Hans Mommsen, "Probleme der Täterforschung," in *NS-Täter aus interdisziplinärer Perspektive*, ed. H. Kramer (Munich, 2006), 425–33.

37 C. Gerlach, "Die Wannsee-Konferenz, das Schicksal der deutschen Juden und Hitlers politische Grundsatzentscheidung, alle Juden Europas zu ermorden," *WerkstattGeschichte* 18 (1997): 7–44.

38 P. Witte et al., ed., *Der Dienstkalender Heinrich Himmlers 1941/42* (Hamburg, 1999).
39 Freisler, Meyer and Stuckart.
40 Bühler, Schöngarth, Leibbrandt. This information, and that in the preceding note, from Pätzold and Schwarz, *Tagesordnung: Judenmord*, 201 et seq.
41 Herbert, *Best*, 285.
42 Herbert, *Best*, 284.
43 Jasch, *Staatssekretär Wilhelm Stuckart*.
44 On this fear, see Mommsen, "Probleme der Täterforschung."

Bibliography

Adam, Uwe Dietrich. *Judenpolitik im Dritten Reich.* Düsseldorf: Droste, 1972 [reprint Düsseldorf: Droste, 2003].

Aly, Götz and Susanne Heim. *Vordenker der Vernichtung: Auschwitz und die deutschen Pläne für eine neue europäische Ordnung.* Hamburg: Fischer-Taschenbuch-Verlag, 2004 [first published 1991]. [English: *Architects of Annihilation: Auschwitz and the Logic of Destruction.* Princeton, NJ: Princeton University Press, 2002.]

Arendt, Hannah. *Eichmann in Jerusalem: Ein Bericht von der Banalität des Bösen.* Munich: Piper, 2011 [first published 1964]. [English: *Eichmann in Jerusalem: A Report on the Banality of Evil.* New York: Viking, 1963.]

Bartov, Omer. *The Eastern Front 1941–45: German Troops and the Barbarisation of Warfare.* London: Macmillan, 1985.

Bauman, Zygmunt. *Dialektik der Ordnung: Die Moderne und der Holocaust.* Hamburg: Europäische Verlagsanstalt, 1992. [English: *Modernity and the Holocaust,* Ithaca, NY: Cornell University Press, 1989.]

Broszat, Martin, Hans-Adolf Jacobson and Helmut Krausnick. *Konzentrationslager, Kommissarbefehl, Judenverfolgung, vol. 2: Anatomie des SS-Staates.* Olten: Walter, 1965.

Browning, Christopher R. *Ordinary Men: Reserve Police Battalion 101 and the Final Solution in Poland.* New York: HarperCollins, 1992.

———. *Die "Endlösung" und das Auswärtige Amt: Das Referat D III der Abteilung Deutschland 1940–1943.* Darmstadt: WBG, 2010. [English: *The Final Solution and the German Foreign Office: A Study of Referat D III of Abteilung Deutschland 1940–1943.* New York: Holmes & Meier, 1978.]

Gerlach, C. "Die Wannsee-Konferenz, das Schicksal der deutschen Juden und Hitlers politische Grundsatzentscheidung, alle Juden Europas zu ermorden." In *Krieg, Ernährung, Völkermord: Forschungen zur deutschen Vernichtungspolitik im Zweiten Weltkrieg,* edited by C. Gerlach, 79–153. Hamburg: Hamburger Edition, 1998 [first in: *WerkstattGeschichte* 18 (1997): 7–44]. [English: "The Wannsee Conferenz: The Fate of German Jews, and Hitler's Decision in Principle to Exterminate all European Jews." *Journal of Modern History* 70, no. 4 (1998): 759–812.]

Gerwarth, Robert. *Reinhard Heydrich: Biographie*. Munich: Siedler, 2011. [English: *Hitler's Hangman: The Life of Heydrich*. New Haven, CT: Yale University Press, 2011.]

Goldhagen, Daniel Jonah. *Hitler's Willing Executioners: Ordinary Germans and the Holocaust*. New York: Knopf, 1996.

Gregor, Neil. "Nazism — A Political Religion? Rethinking the Voluntarist Turn." In *Nazism, War and Genocide: Essays in Honour of Jeremy Noakes*, edited by N. Gregor, 1–21. Exeter: University of Exeter Press, 2005.

Haffner, Sebastian. *The Meaning of Hitler*. London: Weidenfeld and Nicolson, 1979.

Herbert, Ulrich. *Best: Biographische Studien über Radikalismus, Weltanschauung und Vernunft 1903–1989*. Bonn: Dietz, 1996.

———. "Vernichtungspolitik: Neue Antworten und Fragen zur Geschichte des 'Holocaust.'" In *Nationalsozialistische Vernichtungspolitik, 1939 bis 1945: Neue Forschungen und Kontroversen*, edited by U. Herbert, 9–66. Frankfurt am Main: Fischer-Taschenbuch-Verlag, 1998.

Hilberg, Raul. *Die Vernichtung der europäischen Juden*. Frankfurt am Main: Fischer-Taschenbuch-Verlag, 1990–1992. [English: *The Destruction of the European Jews*. 4th ed. New York: Holmes & Meier, 1985.]

———. *Perpetrators, Victims, Bystanders: The Jewish Catastrophe, 1933–1945*. New York: Aaron Asher, 1992.

Jäckel, Eberhard. "On the Purpose of the Wannsee Conference." In *Perspectives on the Holocaust: Essays in Honor of Raul Hilberg*, edited by J.S. Pacy and A.P. Wertheimer, 39–50. Boulder, CO, San Francisco, CA and Oxford: Westview Press, 1995.

Jasch, Hans-Christian. *Staatssekretär Wilhelm Stuckart und die Judenpolitik: Der Mythos von der sauberen Verwaltung*. Munich: Oldenbourg, 2012.

Kempner, Robert M. W. *Eichmann und Komplizen*. Zurich, Stuttgart, and Vienna: Europaverlag, 1961.

Kershaw, Ian. *The Nazi Dictatorship: Problems and Perspectives of Interpretation*. London: Arnold, 2000.

Kühne, Thomas. *Belonging and Genocide: Hitler's Community, 1918–1945*. New Haven, CT: Yale University Press, 2010.

Longerich, Peter. *Heinrich Himmler: Biographie*. Munich: Siedler, 2008. [English: *Heinrich Himmler: A Life*. Oxford and New York: Oxford University Press, 2012.]

Lösener, B. "Als Rassereferent im Reichsministerium des Inneren: Dokumentation. Das Reichsministerium des Inneren und die Judengesetzgebung." *Vierteljahrshefte für Zeitgeschichte* 9, no. 3 (1961): 264–313. Retrieved 6 October 2016 from http://www.ifz-muenchen.de/heftarchiv/1961_3_4_strauß.pdf.

Lüdtke, A. "Fehlgreifen in der Wahl der Mittel: Optionen im Alltag militärischen Handelns." *Mittelweg 36* 12, no. 1 (2003): 61–75.

Matthäus, Jürgen. "Historiography and the Perpetrators of the Holocaust." In *The Historiography of the Holocaust*, edited by D. Stone, 197–215. New York: Palgrave Macmillan, 2004.

Mommsen, Hans. "Aufgabenkreise und Verantwortlichkeit des Staatssekretärs der Reichskanzlei Dr Wilhelm Kritzinger." In *Gutachten des Institutes für*

Zeitgeschichte edited by Institut für Zeitgeschichte, 369–98. Munich: Institut für Zeitgeschichte, 1966.

———. "Probleme der Täterforschung." In *NS-Täter aus interdisziplinärer Perspektive*, edited by H. Kramer, 425–33. Munich: Martin Meidenbauer, 2006.

Pätzold, Kurt and Erika Schwarz. *Tagesordnung: Judenmord: Die Wannsee-Konferenz am 20. Januar 1942. Eine Dokumentation zur Organisation der `Endlösung.'* Berlin: Metropol, 1992.

Paul, G., ed. *Die Täter der Shoah: Fanatische Nationalsozialisten oder ganz normale Deutsche?* Göttingen: Wallstein, 2002.

Poliakov, Léon and Joseph Wulf. *Das Dritte Reich und seine Diener: Dokumente.* Berlin: Arani, 1956.

Rebentisch, Dieter. *Führerstaat und Verwaltung im Zweiten Weltkrieg: Verfassungsentwicklung und Verwaltungspolitik 1939–1945.* Stuttgart: Steiner, 1989.

Reitlinger, Gerald. *Die Endlösung: Hitlers Versuch der Ausrottung der Juden Europas 1939–1945.* Berlin: Colloquium, 1956. [English: *The Final Solution: The Attempt to Exterminate the Jews of Europa, 1939–1945.* London: Vallentine Mitchell, 1953.]

Roseman, Mark. "Beyond Conviction? Perpetrators, Ideas, and Action in the Holocaust in Historiographical Perspective." In *Conflict, Catastrophe and Continuity: Essays on Modern German History*, edited by F. Biess, M. Roseman and H. Schissler, 83–103. New York: Berghahn, 2007.

———. "National Socialism and the End of Modernity." *American Historical Review* 116, no. 3 (2011): 688–701.

———. "'Wannsee' als Herausforderung: Die Historiker und die Konferenz." In *Die Wannsee-Konferenz am 20. Januar 1942: Dokumente, Forschungsstand, Kontroversen*, edited by N. Kampe and P. Klein, 401–14. Cologne: Böhlau, 2013.

Scheffler, Wolfgang. "Die Wannsee-Konferenz und ihre historische Bedeutung." In *Erinnern für die Zukunft: Ansprachen und Vorträge zur Eröffnung der Gedenkstätte*, edited by Gedenk- und Bildungsstätte Haus der Wannsee-Konferenz, 17–34. Berlin: Gedenk- und Bildungsstätte Haus der Wannsee-Konferenz, 1992.

Sereny, Gitta. *Into that Darkness: From Mercy Killing to Mass Murder.* New York: McGraw-Hill, 1974.

Wildt, Michael. *Die Generation des Unbedingten: Das Führungskorps des Reichssicherheitshauptamtes.* Hamburg: Hamburger Edition, 2002. [English: *An Uncompromising Generation: The Nazi Leadership of the Reich Security Main Office.* Madison, WI: University of Wisconsin Press, 2009.]

———. *Volksgemeinschaft als Selbstermächtigung: Gewalt gegen Juden in der deutschen Provinz 1919 bis 1939.* Hamburg: Hamburger Edition, 2007. [English: *Hitler's Volksgemeinschaft and the Dynamics of Racial Exclusion: Violence against Jews in Provincial Germany, 1919–1939.* New York and Oxford: Berghahn, 2012.]

Witte, P., M. Wildt, M. Vogt, D. Pohl, P. Klein, C. Gerlach, C. Dieckmann and A. Angrick, ed. *Der Dienstkalender Heinrich Himmlers 1941/42.* Hamburg: Christians, 1999.

2

OTTO ADOLF EICHMANN

Reich Main Security Office

The RSHA's "Jewish Expert"

Bettina Stangneth

Illustration 2.1 Unknown photographer, undated (1941), AKG Images, 4217270.

The Wannsee Conference marked the most glorious day of Eichmann's career. In the end, however, he would maintain he had merely been sharpening pencils at a side table and taking the minutes. On 20 January 1942, Reinhard Heydrich ceremoniously made Adolf Eichmann his point man for institutional matters relating to implementation of the "Final Solution of the Jewish Question" in Europe. But barely twenty years later, Eichmann purported not to have known that the entire planning of the conference held at Lake Wannsee, from drawing up an authorization letter for Heydrich, signed by Göring on 31 July 1941, to taking the minutes, had crossed his desk.

By then, though, he was no longer the dynamic, 35-year-old head of the Office of Jewish Affairs at the Reich Main Security Office (RSHA) with a new uniform tailor-made for the conference and a recent promotion to SS-Obersturmbannführer under his belt. He was on trial in Criminal Case 40/61, The State of Israel v Otto Adolf Eichmann, son of Karl Adolf Eichmann.[1]

Childhood and Family

As usual, Eichmann had spent the weekend before the conference visiting his family in their handsome rented house with a garden in the Prague 18 district, near the seat of government and where Heydrich now also resided. The location had been explicitly chosen by his wife (who wanted to live there with her sister and her family and did not want to return to Berlin) after Eichmann's work had required that his family moved repeatedly in a short space of time. At first the couple had lived in the Berlin suburb of Britz, then Vera Eichmann followed her husband to Vienna's second district and from there to Prague in 1939, where he was setting up another headquarters for the organized persecution of Jews as well as installing Theresienstadt as a "model ghetto." After a few months he was summoned back to the Reich capital. When the former headquarters of the Jewish Brotherhood on Kurfürstenstraße 116 were repurposed as the RSHA's Office of Jewish Affairs, it was decided that the family would not move again. This suited Eichmann well, providing his wife and sons with stability and pleasant company while he traveled frequently for work. After the assassination of Heydrich in late May 1942, Eichmann organized a security detail for his family. Molischova 22 (present-day U Laboratoře in Prague 6) was not an exclusive address, but the house was big enough for two families to share. By January 1942 Vera Eichmann was heavily pregnant with her third child. Eichmann kept his official residence in Prague, but when in Berlin used the opportunity to stay in rented rooms, in his office's guest residence, or, as everyone knew, with various lady friends. He had an official car and a driver and he also had his own room in Theresienstadt. On 19 January 1942 he interrupted the five-hour drive from his family in Prague to Berlin to make a stopover there and take part in an inspection, before he was driven on to the conference in Wannsee.[2]

Even though it was no secret that Eichmann had relationships with other women, his family remained his point of reference. He was born in 1906 in Solingen, the first child of Karl Adolf Eichmann and Maria Schefferling, who was seven years older. The couple had married in haste, with their son christened, in a German Evangelical church, Otto Adolf Eichmann after his grandfather just three months later. Four siblings followed. The children had a sheltered upbringing, with the family thriving financially after moving from the Rheinland to Linz, Austria. There, the Eichmanns lived on Bischofstraße, a prime location on an elegant shopping street in the middle of town. Eichmann senior was an active member of the Protestant community and one of Vienna's most respected figures. The children were given every opportunity. The young Adolf took lessons in riding, fencing, dancing, self-defense and violin. When he was ten years old he lost his mother but when his father remarried four years later, his eldest son considered it a sensible move. A father of four could not remain unmarried. He accepted the new woman in the house, affectionately calling her his "second mother" and becoming close to his two stepbrothers, born shortly thereafter.

Decades later, one of them would help Eichmann's wife and organize his defense in court.

Stories of how Adolf Eichmann was bullied as a schoolboy and supposedly had a Jewish appearance were made up at a time when tabloid journalists needed headlines and former colleagues offered their services as witnesses. The fact that Eichmann did not enjoy school, disappointed his father with his lack of interest in books and gave up a trainee position before he was finished is less significant than the fact that none of it did him any harm. His family supported him, facilitating his first work experience until he eventually found a job he enjoyed: he became a petrol salesman, working in one of the sunrise industries of his era and helping build up a network of petrol stations across Upper Austria. His income was good and his company motorbike afforded him both status and freedom. Eichmann was well brought up and seen as sociable and helpful. Although he traveled frequently for work he continued to live with his parents and his decision to join the Nazi Party in 1932 and recruitment by the SS did not adversely affect the family cohesion. On the contrary: his father followed him into the Party, in which many of the family's acquaintances were already active. When Eichmann got married in 1935 his wife was naturally welcomed into the family even though she was Catholic. After 1945 his father told everybody that his eldest son had been the black sheep of the family and that he had burnt all the family's photographs of him out of disappointment. He was unwilling to explain how he himself had come into possession of "Aryanized commodities." In fact, father and son stood steadfastly by one another right up until the death of Karl Adolf Eichmann, shortly before Adolf's capture in 1960. His siblings all signed a plea for clemency when he was sentenced to death as a war criminal.[3]

Career

When Eichmann decided in 1933 to return to Germany he was enough of a party faithful to be entrusted with a suitcase of secret papers that he reliably smuggled over the border. Since his parents had never applied for his nationality to be changed from German to Austrian, crossing the border posed no problem, since he was traveling with German papers. During his military basic training at SS training camp, Eichmann had stood out mainly for two reasons: firstly, because of his ambition to keep up with others, and secondly because of his inclination to overstep his competences. He faced disciplinary action for trying, without any authorization, to stop a guest at a coffee house from listening to

"Jewish music" and demanding to see the guest's papers as a precautionary measure. Only after a scuffle did it transpire that the Richard Tauber enthusiast he had attacked was unfortunately an SS officer with a much higher rank, while Eichmann himself was unable to identify himself because he could not find his own papers.

Overstepping his competences was something that marked Eichmann's career in years to come. However, he increasingly got away with it, with the method even applauded by his superiors. From his requisitioning of a lover's property in the name of the Central Office for Jewish Emigration in Vienna in order to establish the first camp for Jews in Austria, to his duping of the Reich bank in Vienna in 1938 with exchange rates for Jews, which he had arbitrarily set himself— Heinrich Himmler and Reinhardt Heydrich, as Eichmann liked to say later, laughed off such "tricks." Thanks to his arrogance, Eichmann soon gained a reputation specifically because of this presumptuousness as a man for difficult cases. On 12 November 1938, just a few days after the November pogrom and nearly three years before the Wannsee Conference, he was flown to Berlin at short notice to discuss the "Jewish Question" at a meeting chaired by Field Marshal Hermann Göring. This was the Interministerial Meeting at the Reich Aviation Ministry, so that Göring, Goebbels and various other ministers and state secretaries could hear how systematic avoidance of official channels was helping advance the persecution of Jews. At the meeting on 20 March 1941 at the Propaganda Ministry, Goebbels was so impressed by Eichmann's talk that he personally requested he make Berlin *judenrein* (free of Jews) too. When Eichmann said in Jerusalem that he met the state's "men at the top" for the first time at the Wannsee Conference, it was an outright lie. In fact he had met many ministers who knew him by name and saw him as a specialist on "Jewish matters" before. Ever since his successes in Vienna he had been hailed as a skillful architect of methods for putting Jews under pressure and driving them out of the country.[4]

After 1939 and his energetic involvement in the resettlement of the population once Germany had invaded Poland, promotions rained down on Eichmann rather than the disciplinary action demanded from all sides. Eichmann even went unpunished when he challenged an SS General to a duel, even though the general in question was Karl Wolff, Himmler's SS Liaison Officer to Hitler, and he also shrugged off a complaint made by SS-Brigadeführer Friedrich Übelhoer that in the Foreign Ministry he had purported to have intimate knowledge of the Litzmannstadt Ghetto, where he had never actually been, in order to boost the number of people being deported there. Even this lie led to a further promotion. In 1943 his announcement that he intended personally to hunt down Jews in Monaco sparked a diplomatic incident. Officials at the Foreign Ministry were driven to distraction trying to work out what had really happened. In his self-promotion, Eichmann had mastered the trick of making himself look even more successful than he already was.[5]

What made Eichmann so convincing in this was his age. We have become very used to seeing the "Jewish expert" as something of a young upstart. In fact Eichmann was one of the older men in the Nazi movement. Most of his colleagues in the RSHA, such as Rudolf Lange and many of his own staff, were younger than him. Moreover he was allowed to wear the Honor Chevron for the Old Guard, which only those who had joined the Nazi Party prior to 1933 were entitled to wear. Unlike many others, he also had substantial professional experience, which imbued him with a confidence his younger colleagues fresh out of university education lacked. This confidence was combined with a certain talent as a performer and an ability to make the most of scraps of information.

Eichmann garnered the respect of his colleagues at the Sicherheitsdienst (SD) intelligence agency as early as 1935, because he knew Hebrew was read from right to left. On the basis of a cursory story, he even skillfully cultivated the rumor in his own ranks that he had been born in Palestine. That Eichmann had in fact discovered the world of books in the early days of his appointment to the SD's department for Jewish affairs and cursorily absorbed everything he could find about Judaism was enough to make him look like an undisputed specialist. The one-eyed man is king in the land of the blind. Two or three scraps of Yiddish were enough for him to gain recognition as a language expert.

Eichmann's ability to spin a convincing yarn out of nothing when it was of use to him might be reminiscent of a con man—were one to forget the crimes driven on with the help of his trickery. He did not subvert hierarchies and overstep his competences merely for the sake of it. It became a method of manipulating all those who still had faith in bureaucratic rules, chains of command and paperwork. Many years later, Eichmann said that the murder of millions of Jews had only been possible because, in his office, bureaucracy has been a deliberately constructed means to manipulate others.

Himmler, Heydrich and Eichmann's immediate superior, Heinrich Müller, specifically appreciated their protégé's skill in keeping other ministries in check merely with paperwork. So there were many reasons why Eichmann was also tasked with preparing and organizing the conference on the Großer Wannsee.[6] In fact, Eichmann was the only head of a division in the RSHA who never switched positions, even though his division was constantly given new titles and tasks, and was called not only IV B 4 but also IV R, IV D 4 and IV A 4b. At an early stage, it was enough to refer simply to the "Eichmann department" and everyone knew this meant the offices on Kurfürstenstraße 116 and their head. He also successfully held on to the staff in his field. The department's secrecy policy alone does not explain this consistency, as the constant reshuffling of men running the concentration camps goes to show.

As head of the Office of Jewish Affairs he succeeded in building a team whose murderous efficiency was largely due to the fact that its members, from secretaries to *Judenberater* (Jewish advisors) scattered across Europe, all enjoyed working for their boss. Anyone unable to attend one of the department's regular meetings would excuse themselves with regret. One secretary later reported that the department had been a very sociable one; that Eichmann had always treated everyone fairly and had been keen to boost camaraderie. Musical evenings were held, with the boss playing violin—although he apparently felt one of his underlings played better than he did so was happy to play second violin. When the Nazi regime collapsed, few were willing to remember that Eichmann had been a well-respected figure. He had not needed to introduce himself at the Wannsee Conference on 20 January 1942. Everyone present had long known who he was.[7]

The Inductee

When Heydrich recruited Eichmann to prepare the Wannsee Conference and put him in charge of coordinating the "Final Solution," he was not merely delegating a tedious job. The highly tricky plan to resolve, at a single stroke, the tussle over competences between institutions in favor of the RSHA had to be carried out by someone who not only believed wholeheartedly in the necessity of systematically murdering millions of people, but who also had diplomatic skill and the audacity to be economical with the truth and gain support at any price. That someone was Eichmann, a man who had repeatedly shown he was capable of making up any statistics and creating facts whenever these were required by his superiors. Above all, with his reputation as an undisputed expert on Jewish matters, Eichmann was the Joker in the ministries' game over control of a project of such importance to Hitler. Along with significant questions relating to offices and their respective jurisdictions, the day-to-day organization of the lunatic scheme called for someone who would coordinate it down to every last detail. From the outset, it was clear that there was only one man with the experience, the talent, the seniority and the "expertise" for the job—namely, the "Judenreferent," the head of the Office of Jewish Affairs at the RSHA. No other ministry or office had anyone comparable to present to the conference on 20 January 1942.[8]

Alois Schintlholzer, the SS man who, in 1950, drove Eichmann from his hideout on the Lüneburg Heath across Germany to the Austrian border, later stated that there had been just one topic of conversation during the entire trip: the genocide of Jews and the number of Jews murdered. Whoever encountered Eichmann in Argentina in the 1950s would also often ask him about the balance of destruction of Jewry. Their assumption that he was one of the few who even had an overview was entirely correct, because from the early 1930s, Eichmann had been tasked at the SS Sicherheitsdienst with observing the Jewish population and compiling the *Judenkartei* (Jewish File). This work was by no means secret. Eichmann also authored educational material on Judaism and Zionism when others were still exploring methods to eliminate Jews from German cultural and economic life.

Every time the persecution of Jews entered a new phase, he was in the vanguard. When Austria joined Hitler's Reich, Eichmann went to Vienna not only to run the notorious Central Agency for Jewish Emigration but also to set up the first two camps for Jews, where his colleagues from the "Central Agency" were already torturing people. He supervised the first attempt—made in full view of the public—to deport hundreds of people in trains from Vienna to the East, namely to Nisko on the River San, an inhospitable region consisting mainly of swamps. The point was mainly to give the SS Sicherheitsdienst an idea of how the general public would react to such an unheard-of plan. These were pilot schemes, co-drawn up by Eichmann.

After the invasion of Poland and the resettlement and mass executions that began in its wake, Eichmann went there in order to get a first-hand look at the methods being used, and before invitations to the Wannsee Conference had been sent out, Eichmann knew what gas vans were because he had asked to see them at the Kulmhof/Chełmno extermination camp. Not even Rudolf Lange, who came straight to the conference from Latvia, where his mobile killing unit Einsatzgruppe A was mass-murdering Jews, could maintain that Eichmann's involvement in the "Jewish Question" was academic and limited to his desk. The two men who met there knew of the heavy toll that shooting women and children took on soldiers' psyches. All the figures on the Nazis' victims coalesced at the Office of Jewish Affairs at the RSHA, even when the killing operations in question had nothing to do with the department.

The figures given by Eichmann in various stages of the mass murder are accurate, according to current research. Even though Heinrich Himmler now and then did not scrimp on criticism when he was not satisfied with the statistics compiled by Eichmann's office, everyone was well aware that there was no way of collecting data on the murder of Jews without visiting the offices at Kurfürstenstraße 116. At the meeting on 20 January 1942, Heydrich backed up his points with an impressive list of statistics, courtesy of Eichmann or at least the authority of his office—which also allegedly supplied notes for Heydrich's opening speech. The fact that these figures were badly researched did nothing to damage the reputations of either Heydrich or Eichmann. They had already bandied about statistics cobbled together mainly for effect at the Interministerial Meeting at the Reich Aviation Ministry in 1939. [9]

Eichmann was obviously not merely a "minor expert" merely "sharpening pencils at the side table," as he claimed after judgment was pronounced in 1961 in all pathos when facing the gallows.[10] He had a front row seat when the plan devised by Himmler and Heydrich worked and the conference served as what he later termed a *Machtvollkommenheitserweiterung* (expansion of absolute power) for the RSHA and himself. The minutes do not reveal whether he was called upon to speak at the Wannsee Conference. Heydrich opened the conference with a speech based on Eichmann's drafts, while statistics compiled by his department served as a basis for the discussion. Eichmann gave differing accounts of how long the meeting lasted. On one occasion he said it lasted ninety minutes, on another he said it lasted several hours. By the end of it, Heydrich had enthroned him as senior "Jewish expert" at the RSHA's newly revamped section IV B 4—which had been known for the previous month simply as "Jews." This was undoubtedly one of the greatest moments in Eichmann's career, with his key position visible evidence of the new interministerial complicity. No wonder Heydrich toasted him with cognac when they sat down with Heinrich Müller. Even if Adolf Eichmann said nothing himself at the conference, as he later claimed, many of the words spoken there originated from him. The fact that it was Eichmann who later turned the protocol into what we know today as the Minutes of the Wannsee Conference gives his voice a significance that cannot be overestimated. With those Minutes, the RSHA not only consolidated the results of the conference but also influenced the way the meeting on 20 January 1942 was seen by others who were not there. According to Eichmann, the minutes were sent out to many people.[11]

In a sense, Adolf Eichmann staged the Wannsee Conference in three ways. Firstly, with his meticulous planning in close consultation with his superiors, from summer 1941 to the day of the conference. Secondly, by taking the minutes, with which he and his superiors not only consolidated the conclusion of the meeting but which also had far-reaching political repercussions, because they were read not just by the conference participants but also by Goebbels, who was not represented at the meeting. Thirdly, after the war was over, the SS-Obersturmbannführer did everything in his power to draw attention to the Wannsee Conference.

After the Conference

The death of Heydrich in Prague profoundly affected Eichmann but also gave him an opportunity to further boost his own standing. No one contested his most recent appointment. For a few months he was third in the hierarchy after Heinrich Himmler and Heinrich Müller. His "Jewish experts" across the Reich attempted to step up the persecution of Jews and accelerate the deportations. In 1944 Eichmann went with over 100 members of his staff to Budapest to realize the deportation of nearly half a million people to Auschwitz over the course of just six weeks. He emerged from conflicts with other ministries unscathed. Disagreement over the treatment of "Mischlinge" — which had also led to debate at the Wannsee Conference — was the only area that proved difficult, especially with the Interior Ministry and Reich Chancellery. To this day we do not know exactly how many follow-up meetings on the issue were held. But some of them were most certainly hosted by Eichmann's office. Until the very end, Eichmann did his utmost to bring about the destruction of all European Jews There is evidence linking him to the construction of the last gas chambers used and the continued use of gas vans even in the last few weeks of the war.[12]

In the last months of the war, while the Nazi functionary elite took precautionary measures to prepare for the period after the failed "final victory," shredding documents and making joint arrangements, Adolf Eichmann kept his distance from goings-on, even though he would have had every opportunity to involve himself. Mayhem broke out in the offices at Kurfürstenstraße 116 in 1945 — which previously many would have preferred to avoid. But by then they became a meeting place not only for colleagues from the Gestapo and the RSHA but also for high-ranking Nazis. In the last years of the war, Paul Blobel, the head of the "Sonderaktion 1005," along with his men were quartered in Eichmann's offices. The men in charge of what they called "Enterdung"—exhuming mass graves and burning the bodies—were usually drunk and from time to time forgot to clean up their vehicles before driving back to Berlin again. One reason for the new popularity of Eichmann's offices at this point was the simple fact that they boasted a canteen and a well-stocked larder, both of which had become a rarity. Most of the other Nazi offices in and around Wilhelmstraße had long been bombed out. Eichmann suddenly found himself playing host to the very men who would insist just months later that they had never heard of him.

But they were not merely hungry. Kurfürstenstaße 116 had something very different to offer them: genuine documents of genuine German civil servants that could furnish them with fake identities. In 1945, everybody of rank and name had an urgent need to shed both or at least to slightly rewrite their careers. In a matter of weeks, new lives were officially drawn up en masse. Eichmann demonstratively disapproved of what was happening under the roof of his offices. When his oh-so revered superior Heinrich Müller asked him which identity he would like to adopt, Eichmann responded by gesturing to his handgun and declaring steadfast in loyalty and full of pride that there would be no life for him without the Führer. His colleagues remembered this scene very well: "He said he would leap laughing into the pit, because the feeling that he had six million people on his conscience would be a source of extraordinary satisfaction for him."

But despite his avowals of loyalty to the Führer and SS honor, Otto Adolf Eichmann had in fact been pursuing very different objectives in the previous months. We do not know when exactly he began planning his life without the "Führer." There is evidence to suggest it was as early as 1941, because he believed Hitler's invasion of the Soviet Union was a mistake and the beginning of the end. There is no doubt that, by mid 1944, Eichmann was making provision for himself and his family. Whenever he could, he drove from Budapest to visit his father in Linz. He regaled his colleagues with tales of his amazing encounters with the "Grand Mufti" of Jerusalem, Amin Al-Husseini, who was residing in style in a hotel in Linz after his hotel in Berlin had been bombed. Their supposed friendship proved to be advantageous in more ways than one, allowing Eichmann to see his father regularly. The fake papers that he had long ago procured needed to be safeguarded. They chose a place in the Rheinland, where an uncle lived. A family hunting lodge was put at the disposal of Eichmann's wife and three sons and their upkeep secured. Potential hideouts, strategies, meeting points and escape routes needed to be agreed. How would contact be maintained? More importantly, what to do with the family photographs that investigators would no doubt one day look for? How to stop the children giving anything away? As "Adolf Eichmann" he would never be able to return home or even stay in touch with his family. Help would be needed; networks would have to be organized. His colleagues and superiors, Eichmann realized, were not the ones to look to. They would send him to his doom at the first opportunity and even deny their evident responsibilities if it meant saving themselves. Later, at the Nuremberg Trials, even his old friend, Heydrich's successor Ernst Kaltenbrunner, would deny their acquaintance and any direct professional cooperation. Dieter Wisliceny, one of his closest colleagues and friends, would with all knowledge actively help hunt down the man who had named one of his sons after him. Eichmann had moreover long been too high on the Allies' most-wanted men list. "They knew me wherever I went," he said years later, after his successful escape. His former colleagues would become the first willing helpers in the hunt for him. When they congratulated him on his upcoming promotion to SS-Standartenführer in early 1945 and wanted to celebrate, he turned down their invitation. He did not welcome the promotion for two reasons: firstly, because he was attached to his reputation as the RSHA's most redoubtable SS-Obersturmbannführer, and secondly, because he had already distanced himself from his superiors and was no longer interested in being decorated by them. But he also knew them all well enough to be able to hide his true intentions from them, even though they had known him for years and had seen how he behaved under pressure.[13]

Escape and Trial

At the end of the war, the officers of the RSHA who were still alive convened in Austria. After Germany's capitulation Eichmann had left the group and went underground, assuming a number of new identities in American POW camps. In late 1946, when his name was mentioned in the coverage of the Nuremberg Trials in newspapers and on the radio, Eichmann escaped and hid out on the Lüneburg Heath with his false documents from the Rheinland. With the help of the Argentine Immigration Office and various helpers in SS circles and the Catholic Church, he managed to flee and reach Argentina in 1950. Old comrades helped him bring his family over in 1952. He led a quite tolerable life, variously working for a state enterprise and as a manager for a former SS man before joining Mercedes Benz in Buenos Aires. During this period, he contributed to a political book project and spoke openly about what he had done. Eichmann's true identity was no secret within the community of other escaped Nazis and their families. His contact with old comrades prompted him to write a book about his "life's achievements." Interestingly, the manuscript contains no mention of the Wannsee Conference. It seems that he had not considered it a significant event until he learned of its impact—and especially that of the minutes—on others. It was only in 1955, when Léon Poliakov and Josef Wulf published the minutes in a collection of documents that Eichmann realized that a copy of this incriminating document existed and that someone had ignored the order to destroy all copies. From then on, the man who, in 1942, drew up the minutes of the Wannsee Conference as we know them did his best to explain and depict the meeting so as to cast himself, in particular, in a good light.

Even though German intelligence had known the whereabouts of the Nazis' former "Jewish expert" since 1952, it was only in 1960 that the Israeli secret service tracked him down, captured him, took him to Jerusalem and put him on trial. Before, during and after the trial, Eichmann zealously put forward different accounts of the meeting on 20 January 1942 that varied wildly according to whom he was speaking and his own agenda, but which were primarily aimed at incriminating the other participants, as well as various others who had not attended, from Adolf Hitler to Hans Globke. Nevertheless, he resisted all efforts to put him in the witness box in other trials. The tales of Eichmann should be read by anyone who takes an interest in how historiography can be manipulated by eyewitness testimonies. In the end, his trickery got him nowhere. He died by hanging in 1962 in Israel. But it is worth heeding his warning that influencing future generations had always been one of his priorities.[14]

Motivation

Before he was captured and put on trial in Israel, Adolf Eichmann made no secret of the fact that he had acted out of conviction and was proud of the considerable part he played in what we can only call the worst atrocity in the history of mankind. His deeds and exhaustive explanations of his reasons in various recordings and conversations also show that Eichmann never merely parroted rabble-rousing slogans but had a complex worldview that he adapted to changing circumstances, especially after 1945. In broad terms, Eichmann believed that "the Jews" and "the Germans" were rivals in a struggle for world dominion and that only one side could win. Since Eichmann, like Hitler, saw Jews as the cleverer "race", because they wielded the dangerous weapon of intellectualism, the German "race" was justified in resorting to whatever means were necessary to fight against this danger. In his view, anyone who was restrained in this fight by ethical or human considerations was behaving negligently. Eichmann never tired of saying that ethics and reason were obsolete and, moreover, dangerous concepts, because they only served Jewish efforts to undermine the strength of every other human being. It was the Germans' duty to follow "the voice of blood." Eichmann's sole self-reproach was a lack of consistency, insufficient hardness and occasional human weakness. He was not alone in thinking that it was the duty of the German government to murder European Jews in order to protect its public. Eichmann saw himself as a member of the functionary elite, who had to fulfill this duty conscientiously.[15]

He evidently enjoyed the fact that his participation in a "task" of such global historical significance afforded him reputation and power over other human beings. He was hell-bent on winning the supposed fight with Germans' supposedly dangerous enemy, and drew pleasure from manipulating and tricking the very people he accused of trying to get the world to dance to their tune. On trial in Israel, the delusion that he was cleverer, quicker and better than others led to serious mistakes in his defense. Eichmann was convinced that he was fighting a war against Jews, a war that had not ended with the downfall of the Nazi regime. He tried to prolong this war by making recordings, taking part in conversations and consciously manipulating lawyers, historians and all the others who sought to understand him. This included his tireless warning to future generations of the invisible threat, and his encouragement of the Muslim world to continue the Nazis' murderous mission. What sounds like lunacy was ultimately nothing but the logical extension of the widespread assumption that reason is the wrong path, and the idea that men are rational beings and equal is an illusion. Eichmann's deeds were rooted in a strict implementation of pseudoscientific racial theory and concomitant denial of any ethical boundaries when it came to preserving his own "race." Even though Eichmann did everything during his trial to make it seem that he had merely been a cog in the wheel—a clerk following orders—he never regretted his deeds. Repentance, he said during the trial, is for little children.

Bettina Stangneth is an independent philosopher who has written about Immanuel Kant and his concept of "radical evil." She has written extensively about the history of anti-Judaism in the eighteenth-century, as well as National Socialistic philosophy, Adolf Eichmann and Hannah

Arendt. Her main subject of research is a theory of the lie as part of a "Critique of Dialogical Thinking". Stangneth lives in Hamburg.

Notes

1   To date the only attempt at a comprehensive Eichmann biography has been David Cesarani, *Adolf Eichmann: Bürokrat und Massenmörder* (Berlin, 2004). Since, however, a large number of accessible sources were not utilized and several dating errors slipped into that work, this presentation has reverted to the original sources. Since the citation of all sources originates from the said context, see also, in case of doubt, Bettina Stangneth, *Eichmann vor Jerusalem: Das unbehelligte Leben eines* Massenmörders (Zurich, 2011).

2   Information on Eichmann's various places of residence can be found in the documents kept in his SS and RuSHA files (BDC, BArch Berlin). For corroboration as to Eichmann's family relationships and private life, see the statements of his colleague and friend Dieter Wisliceny of 27 October 1946, Bratislava, the "Cell 133-Dokument: A 36-page handwritten report on the former SS-Obersturmbannführer Adolf Eichmann." Prosecution document no. T/84 in the Eichmann Trial. Like all the trial documents it can be found in: State of Israel, Ministry of Justice, The Trial of Adolf Eichmann. Microfiche Copies of the Exhibits submitted by the Prosecution and Defense, vol. IX. (Jerusalem, 1995); Eichmann's own testimony in the police interrogation and trial, ibid. vol. I–VIII. On the visit to Theresienstadt "Tagesbefehl des Ältestenrats Nr. 29," prosecution document T/846.

3   See, for Eichmann's origins, his RuSHA files; Eichmann's statements right at the beginning of the police interrogation; Vera Eichmann 1962 in an interview with Paris Match, typescript from the estate of Robert Servatius, BArch, AllProz 6/252; on his wife's Catholicism, see in particular: Sassen-Transcript, Audiotape no. 3, BArch Coblenz, NL 1497. Myths about Eichmann's impoverished childhood and supposedly Jewish appearance originated from early statements and interviews given by Eichmann's colleague, Wilhelm Höttl, who was known for effectively misleading public opinion with his lies, most recently in: "Der Vernichter," directed by Guido Knopp, from the series *Hitlers Helfer II* (Germany, 1998). Regarding family contact after 1945, comments by Eichmann's brother, Robert and various reports by Simon Wiesenthal, Clemency Appeal, BArch, AllProz 6/182.

4   On the disciplinary proceedings against Eichmann and Fritz Schaub, see the report of the SS-Sturmführer of 23 April 1934, Yad Vashem Archiv (YVA), 0-51/61; message from Eichmann of 30 April 1943, SS file Adolf Eichmann, BDC, BArch Berlin. On the acquisition of the property, see Eichmann's recommendation to Gestapo Head Office in Vienna that Amalia Tallafuss's property be requisitioned, 5 April 1939, facs. in: Tuviah Friedman, *Loewenherz in Wien* (Haifa, 1995); see Stangneth, *Eichmann*, 223; and G. Anderl, "Die 'Umschulungslager' Doppl und Sandhof der Wiener Zentralstelle für jüdische Auswanderung," *David: Jüdische Kulturzeitschrift* 58 (2003) and 60 (2004). For the Reichsbank

affair, see prosecution documents in the Eichmann Trial T/135 and T/149: Eichmann's report and comments on the visit of Reichsbank Board Member Wolf to the Reich Economics Ministry, Vienna, 16 June 1938, and Otto von Bolschwing, "Bericht über die Reise des Bankrats Dr Wolf und Assessor Siegert nach Wien," 20 June 1938; Hagen's note on the file, 25 May 1938, "Besprechung Reichsbankrat Wolf und Six," BArch Berlin Hoppegarten, Doc./K.99, vol. 3; see Theodor Venus and Alexandra Eileen Wenck, *Die Entziehung jüdischen Vermögens im Rahmen der Aktion Gildemeester* (Vienna and Munich, 2004), 65 et seq. On the meeting in the Aviation Ministry, see the telegram from Heydrich to Stahlecker of 11 November 1938, requiring Eichmann's presence the next day at the meeting (BArch Coblenz R58/486,28). Eichmann produced favorable figures for Heydrich that were only partly true, and systematically exaggerated the proportion that could really be traced back to the Central Office. For the minutes of the meeting, see prosecution document T/114 (also IMT 1816-PS). Minutes of the hearing of 20 March 1941, drawn up on 21 March 1942, Reichspropagandaleitung Hauptamt Reichsring, printed in: Hans Günther Adler, *Der verwaltete Mensch: Studien zur Deportation der Juden aus Deutschland* (Tübingen, 1974), 152 et seq.

5 The story of the challenge to a duel rapidly did the rounds and was often mentioned: see, for the most complete version, Sassen-Transcript, Audiotape 14.8 et seq., BArch, NL1497. For the Friedrich Übelhoer affair, see inter alia the telegram from Übelhoer, president of the Lodz district, to Himmler, prosecution document T/220; IVB4a, signed by Heydrich to Himmler, 19 October 1941, prosecution document T/222; Exchange of letters between General Thomas, Wehrwirtschafts- und Rüstungshauptamt / Himmler, 11 October 1941, prosecution document T/248. Eichmann received notice of his promotion on 11 October 1941 with effect from 9 November 1941 (SS-Files). On the supposed hunt for Jews in Monaco, see prosecution documents T/492 et seq., Thadden, Record of a discussion on 21 September 1943 and further correspondence, ibid.

6 For a comprehensive account of Eichmann's methods of manipulation by deliberate instrumentalization of bureaucracy, see Bettina Stangneth, "'Offenes Visier war bei mir ein geflügeltes Wort:' Bekenntnisse des Täuschers Adolf Eichmann," in *Interessen um Eichmann: Israelische Justiz, deutsche Strafverfolgung und alte Kameradschaft*, ed. W. Renz (Frankfurt am Main, 2012), 181–99.

7 For reasons unknown, names of divisions and their remits are often confused in studies of the subject. Eichmann's responsibilities variously included "Evacuation," "Occupied Territories," "Seizure of Anti-German Assets and Withdrawal of German Citizenship," "Ideological Enemies, Confessions, Jews," "Political Churches and Sects," and "Emigrees." See the organigrams of the RSHA and the SSO files. Eyewitness testimonies pertaining to Eichmann feature in the documentary *Erscheinungsform Mensch: Adolf Eichmann*, directed by Rolf Defrank (Hamburg, 1978/79) and *Adolf Eichmann—Begegnugen mit einem Mörder*, directed by Clara Glynn (Germany, U.K., and U.S., 2003).

8   Tellingly, to date no proposal from another ministry opposing Eichmann's being given the job has come to light, although Heydrich died soon afterwards.

9   It is hard to imagine that Eichmann's superiors had nothing to do with the unreliable and often manipulated figures on which they based their policies. The fact that figures are especially easy to employ to give the impression of hard facts is not news.

10 Adolf Eichmann, "Auch hier angesichts des Galgens," handwritten note, New Year A 1961/62. Copy in Servatius estate, BArch, AllProz 6/165.

11 All comments by Eichmann on the Wannsee Conference are reproduced in N. Kampe and P. Klein, ed., *Wannsee-Konferenz am 20. Januar 1942: Dokumente, Forschungsstand, Kontroversen* (Cologne, Weimar and Vienna: Böhlau, 2013).

12 See the interrogations, to date neglected in research, of Eichmann in March 1945, by women who had been sent from Ravensbrueck to Theresienstadt. Testimony of Charlotte Salzburger, Trial hearing 42. Eichmann did not contradict her account that this was an attempt to suppress information concerning the last mass killings and was visibly unpleasantly disturbed by seeing her again. With no knowledge of that source, Stefan Hördler has shown that the last mass killing with gas was probably committed between 15 and 24 April 1945 by the Moll mobile killing unit. S. Hördler, "Die Schlussphase des Konzentrationslagers Ravensbrück: Personalpolitik und Vernichtung," *Zeitschrift für Geschichtswissenschaft* 56, no. 3 (2008): 244.

13 See in this connection the comprehensive "Nachkriegskarriere eines Namens," in: Stangneth, *Eichmann*, 91–107. Eichmann's distrust of both his superiors and subordinates was justified and his skillfulness astonishing in the way that, for a while, he was able to seize the advantage because he correctly calculated in time how they would behave. With all promotions awarded in memory of the Machtergreifung in January, thus taking effect from April, Eichmann's appointment did not become effective, as the end of the War supervened.

14 Bettina Stangneth, "Eichmanns Erzählungen," in *Die Wannsee-Konferenz am 20. Januar 1942: Dokumente, Forschungsstand, Kontroversen*, ed. N. Kampe and P. Klein (Cologne, 2013), 139–50.

15 See, for a comprehensive account, Stangneth, *Eichmann*, 266–300. See, for the National Socialist mindset in all its systematic scope Bettina Stangneth, *Böses Denken* (Hamburg, 2016), 130–42.

Bibliography

Adler, Hans Günther. *Der verwaltete Mensch: Studien zur Deportation der Juden aus Deutschland*. Tübingen: Mohr, 1974.

Anderl, G. "Die 'Umschulungslager' Doppl und Sandhof der Wiener Zentralstelle für jüdische Auswanderung." *David: Jüdische Kulturzeitschrift* 58 (2003) and 60 (2004). Retrieved 2 October 2016 from http://www.doew.at/cms/download/7qvab/anderl_umschulungslager_doppl_sandhof.pdf

Cesarani, David. *Adolf Eichmann: Bürokrat und Massenmörder*. Berlin: Propyläen, 2004. [English: *Becoming Eichmann: Rethinking the Life, Crimes, and Trial of a "Desk Murderer."* Boston, MA: Da Capo Press, 2007.]

Friedman, Tuviah. *Loewenherz in Wien*. Haifa, 1995.

Glynn, Clara. *Adolf Eichmann: Begegnungen mit einem Mörder* [I Met Adolf Eichmann], DVD. Directed by Clara Glynn. Germany, U.K., and U.S: BBC Films, Norddeutscher Rundfunk, and Discovery Channel Pictures, 2003.

Hördler, S. "Die Schlussphase des Konzentrationslagers Ravensbrück: Personalpolitik und Vernichtung." *Zeitschrift für Geschichtswissenschaft* 56, no. 3 (2008): 222–48.

International Military Tribunal [IMT]. *Der Prozeß gegen die Hauptkriegsverbrecher vor dem Internationalen Militärgerichtshof (IMT): Nürnberg 14. November 1945 – 1. Oktober 1946, gemäß den Weisungen des Internationalen Militärgerichtshofes vom Sekretariat des Gerichtshofes unter der Autorität des Obersten Kontrollrats für Deutschland veröffentlicht*, edited by L.D. Egbert and P.A. Joosten. Nuremberg, 1947–1949.

Kampe, N. and P. Klein, ed. *Die Wannsee-Konferenz am 20. Januar 1942: Dokumente, Forschungsstand, Kontroversen*. Cologne, Weimar and Vienna: Böhlau, 2013.

Runze, Ottokar. *Erscheinungsform Mensch: Adolf Eichmann*. DVD. Directed by Rolf Defrank. Hamburg: Aurora Television Productions, 1978/79.

Stangneth, Bettina. *Eichmann vor Jerusalem: Das unbehelligte Leben eines Massenmörders*. Zurich: Arche, 2011. [English: *Eichmann before Jerusalem: The Unexamined Life of a Mass Murderer*, New York: Knopf, 2014.]

———. "'Offenes Visier war bei mir ein geflügeltes Wort': Bekenntnisse des Täuschers Adolf Eichmann." In *Interessen um Eichmann: Israelische Justiz, deutsche Strafverfolgung und alte Kameradschaft*, edited by W. Renz, 181–99. Frankfurt am Main: Campus, 2012.

———. "Eichmanns Erzählungen." In *Die Wannsee-Konferenz am 20. Januar 1942: Dokumente, Forschungsstand, Kontroversen*, edited by N. Kampe and P. Klein, 139–50. Cologne: Böhlau, 2013.

———. *Böses Denken*, Hamburg: Rowohlt, 2016.

———. *Lügen lesen*, Hamburg: Rowohlt, 2017.

Venus, Theodor and Alexandra Eileen Wenck. *Die Entziehung jüdischen Vermögens im Rahmen der Aktion Gildemeester: Eine empirische Studie über Organisation, Form und Wandel von "Arisierung" und jüdischer Auswanderung in Österreich 1938–1941*. Munich: Oldenbourg, 2004.

3

REINHARD HEYDRICH
Reich Main Security Office
The Nazi Terror Enforcer
Robert Gerwarth

Illustration 3.1 Unknown photographer, undated (1940), ullstein bild, 1011103339.

> Jewry as such, the Jewish race and Jewish people, is isolated by the Nuremberg Laws. This keeps Jewish blood directly away from the German people's body. But the indirect influence of the Jewish mind is far from contained. Many people, especially intellectuals and scientists, unwittingly bear traces of Jewish, liberal and freemasonic infection. On the other hand, our own German history has taught us that the Jewish purpose remains unwavering: world domination by a more or less visible Jewish upper class . . . In terms of foreign policy, the Jew uses the apparatus which he already controls completely, Bolshevism and the freemason lodges that exist overseas.
>
> —Reinhard Heydrich, "Bekämpfung der Staatsfeinde"

Since the end of the Second World War, few other leading Nazis have attracted more attention from journalists, filmmakers and writers than Reinhard Heydrich, variously known as the "God of Death" and "Hitler's Hangman." His stellar career in Hitler's dictatorship and the assassination operation in Prague that claimed his life in 1942 inspired several dozen feature films and documentaries, including Fritz Lang's 1943 Hollywood production *Hangmen also Die!* Heinrich Mann's novel *Lidice* (1942) paid literary tribute to the village north-west of Prague destroyed by the Nazis in reprisal for the assassination of Heydrich, while more recent novels including Laurent Binet's bestseller *HHhH* take a postmodern look at the figure of Heydrich.

He was just thirty-eight when he chaired the Wannsee Conference and, until his death in 1942, he held the reins of the Nazis' Jewish policy, along with Hitler and Himmler. Who was this man? Reinhard Heydrich occupied three significant positions in the complex hierarchy of the Third Reich: he was head of the Reich Main Security Office (RSHA), the most important body in the Nazi system of repression and terror; chief officer in charge of the "Final Solution to the Jewish Question," and acting Reich Protector of Bohemia and Moravia. Despite his relative youth, he wielded almost unparalleled power in the Third Reich.[1]

The Radical SS Leader from a Privileged Background

Reinhard Heydrich was born in Halle in 1904 into an affluent and musical Catholic family. Unlike the straight trajectory followed by his superior Heinrich Himmler or his long-term deputy Werner Best, the route of his transformation from an insecure and apolitical loner into the confident and dogmatic chief of the RSHA and main architect of Jewish persecution was a circuitous one. He enjoyed an educated, middle-class upbringing in Wilhelmin Germany. Nothing about his younger years explains the ferocity and evil he would later demonstrate. His father was a successful opera singer, composer and director of the Halle Conservatory, while his mother came from a distinguished family from Dresden. Her father was Eugen Krantz, head of the internationally renowned Royal Conservatory of Dresden. In every respect, Heydrich grew up with privilege. He attended a progressive, non-confessional grammar school specialized in modern languages and the natural sciences, and was allowed to graduate—an opportunity reserved only for a few at the time. Music was part of his life from an early age and he served as an altar boy in the small Catholic community of Halle, a protestant town.[2]

Like many Nazis and participants at the Wannsee Conference, Heydrich belonged to the so-called "war youth generation." As a teenager he witnessed a series of national crises, from Germany's defeat in the First World War to revolution and hyperinflation in the early 1920s, which destroyed his family's once considerable fortune. These experiences had a lasting and formative effect on him, even though, initially, they neither turned him into a fervent anti-Semite nor prompted him to join the fledgling Nazi Party—the responses of many others his age, who went on to become high-ranking officials in the Third Reich. Heydrich kept his distance from any kind of political activity in the 1920s. By his own account, he joined a Freikorps volunteer unit in Halle after 1918, but his involvement in paramilitary organizations in the wake of the First World War was at most marginal and more likely evidence of a youthful spirit of adventure rather than any incipient political belief in radical nationalism. Nor is there evidence dating from this period of any burgeoning racial anti-Semitism in Heydrich.[3]

The loss of the family fortune denied Reinhard Heydrich the opportunity to follow in his father's footsteps and take over as director of the Conservatory in Halle. Instead, in 1922 he joined the Reich navy, a shadow of its former self since 1918 but which promised a steady income and social standing in an uncertain period.[4] However, his career as a lieutenant came to an unexpected and abrupt end when he was thrown out of the navy at the height of the Great Depression after refusing to marry a young lady who believed they were engaged, and behaving in an arrogant fashion when he appeared before a military honor court convened to look into the matter. His dishonorable discharge in 1931 marked a new direction in Heydrich's life. With no job, no prospects and no family support to turn to, he took the advice of his fiancée Lina von Osten, an ardent Nazi, and applied for an administrative position in Munich with the SS, which was at the time little more than a politically insignificant, small paramilitary unit.[5] Lina von Osten played a key role in Heydrich's life. At this point, she took a much greater interest in politics than he did, and he joined the SS not least to prove to his fiancée and her equally nationalistic family that he would make a good husband.

Up until this point, Heydrich's life could have gone in a very different direction. Other than his dogged determination never again to fail, the future head of the Gestapo and the SD and organizer of the genocide showed little obvious ability. With no prior experience of the work done by the SiPo and secret police, and with no Nazi pedigree, Heydrich had no choice but to reinvent himself in order to survive in this politically radical professional world of which he knew nothing. He compensated for the persistent, albeit incorrect, rumors of "flaws" in his background (that is, his alleged Jewish ancestry) which, in 1932, prompted a humiliating party investigation that threatened to terminate his career, and his lack of political engagement prior to 1931 with permanent activism. He thereby displayed the radicalism of the late convert, permanently trying to outperform others, be it in the field of sport, work or political extremism.[6]

Heydrich's political radicalization, his steep learning curve in matters of Nazi ideology and his reinvention as the archetypal SS officer took place between 1931 and 1936. Key to his future development were his experiences and the people he met once he had joined the SS, a very specific political milieu of mainly young, ideologically radical and

Illustration 3.2 Heydrich at his workplace as head of the Bavarian police. Friedrich Franz Bauer, 11.4.1934, BArch Koblenz, 152-50-10.

ambitious men acting out violent fantasies of cleansing Germany of the "enemy inside" and at the same time rejecting the previous generation's bourgeois ethics as obsolete and unsuited to bringing about Germany's "national rebirth."[7] When it came to the ideology propagated by Heinrich Himmler, he soon proved to be a receptive pupil. As of 1931, Himmler rather than Hitler had become a central figure in Heydrich's professional life. Contrary to all the rumors that circulated after the Second World War, the two men had taken an instant liking to one another. Their respective talents were well-matched: Himmler, with his wild-eyed racism, obvious aptitude for developing the inner-party networks that were essential to the Third Reich and undeniable leadership skills, gave Heydrich a second chance and could therefore count on his unconditional devotion forevermore. Heydrich also had outstanding organizational skills, ruthless determination and burning ambition. These complementary "talents" allowed Heydrich and Himmler to successively expand the remit of the SS from a small, insignificant unit into the central organ of the Nazis' terror in their fight against a range of enemies, defined according to an ever-broader and increasingly racial definition.[8] The heady experience of his rapid rise to power, which put a steadily growing pool of resources at the disposal of the disgraced former navy lieutenant, vindicated Heydrich's decision to join the Nazi movement's most radical organization, and held a promise of further opportunities.

But while he originally joined the SS for opportunistic reasons, it took just a few years for him to become a committed Nazi. He was increasingly convinced that in order to bring about the utopian society envisioned by Hitler it was necessary to violently and ruthlessly eliminate all "elements" that he and Himmler considered a danger. This was a task that could only be accomplished by the SS, trained in fighting enemies and ideologically unequivocal. The belief was that a new *Volksgemeinschaft* (community of people) could only arise once German society was "cleansed" of elements categorized as "foreign, sick and hostile," and only then could an inevitable war be won against the Reich's main ideological enemy, the Soviet Union.[9] The means of the "cleansing" foreseen by Heydrich changed dramatically between 1933 and 1942, partly as a reaction to altered circumstances and events beyond his control (from the outbreak of the Second World War to the failure of various deportation plans), and partly as a result of the growing sense of hubris that gripped many high-ranking SS leaders, army officers and resettlement architects after the German invasion of Poland. They were convinced that a unique opportunity in history had arrived when they could wipe out Germany's domestic and foreign enemies. While the systematic murder of Jews was unimaginable even to Heydrich when the war began in 1939, his views on the matter became increasingly radical in the following two and a half years. A combination of the brutalizing effect of war, disappointment over failed expulsion plans, pressure from local authorities in occupied territories and an ideological determination to solve the "Jewish Problem" once and for all unleashed what Hans Mommsen has termed a "cumulative radicalization" that was vented in ever more massacres of Jewish and Slavic people.[10]

Before the war began, the task of solving the "Jewish Question" in the German Reich was dealt with first and foremost by the Central Office for Jewish Emigration, set up by Heydrich, which forced Jews to emigrate. In September 1939 this task was handed over to a new institution, also headed by Heydrich, which coordinated the operational persecution of Jews: the Reich Main Security Office (RSHA) in Berlin. After months of preparation, the RSHA officially opened its doors on 27 September 1939. It represented a new type of organizational body, merging the SiPo (itself a merger of the criminal police and the secret state police) and the SD, the Nazi Party's intelligence agency. In contrast to the conventional party apparatus, its purpose was not only to prosecute criminals but also to cleanse state and society of its political and racial enemies as a preventative measure, as Heydrich had proposed in the mid 1930s and as his apparatus had been doing for years. In the course of the war, Heydrich ensured that the RSHA became a central instrument in the creation of the Nazis' utopian new order.

The "success" of the RSHA in the following years furthered Heydrich's steep career rise, which culminated in the autumn of 1941 in his appointment as SS-Obergruppenführer, General der Polizei, and acting Reich Protector of Bohemia-Moravia.

Mass Murderer

The Second World War afforded Heydrich and Himmler a twofold opportunity to further consolidate their power. Firstly, they were able to extend Reich police jurisdiction to the German-occupied territories, and secondly, Himmler was appointed Reich Commissioner for the Consolidation of German Nationhood in a *Führererlass* (Führer's Decree) on 7 October 1939 and made Heydrich the chief organizer of the "Final Solution to the Jewish Problem." As the man who coordinated the taskforces (made up mainly of members of his apparatus), Heydrich was more directly involved than Himmler in the mass murders of the Jewish population up until 1942. This did not lead to any personal or professional rivalry.

In late November 1941 Reinhard Heydrich issued invitations to the Wannsee Conference, stating that the official purpose of the meeting in the SS guest house on the lake was "to make all the necessary organizational, practical and material preparations for the Final Solution to the Jewish Question with the participation of all the central organs involved." A further topic he wished to discuss was that "since 15.10.1941 Jews from the Reich territory including the Protectorate of Bohemia-Moravia are being evacuated to the eastern territories in ongoing transports."[11] First and foremost, the deportation of Jews from the Reich raised questions about "Mischlinge" (persons with Christian and Jewish parents or grandparents) and "mixed-race" marriages, and how they were to be dealt with in the "Final Solution."[12] The invitation failed to mention what was in fact the most important reason for the meeting, from Heydrich's point of view (although the invitees would have been aware of it nonetheless), namely, to confirm the controversial SS dominance in the planning and implementation of the "Final Solution."

The guests were senior officials as high-ranking in the hierarchy of the "Third Reich" as Heydrich, albeit not quite as powerful. According

to Heydrich's typically dichotomic thinking, the guests broadly consisted of various groups of allies and supposed opponents. The largest group at the table was made up of representatives of the Reich
ministries dedicated to the regime's persecution of Jews. This made
them rivals or potential challengers to the ambitious SS leadership:
Wilhelm Stuckart (Reich Interior Ministry), Roland Freisler (Reich
Justice Ministry), Erich Neumann (Office of the Four Year Plan),
Friedrich-Wilhelm Kritzinger (Reich Chancellery) and Martin Luther
(Foreign Ministry). The two representatives of the Reich Ministry for
the Occupied Eastern Territories, Alfred Meyer and Georg Leibbrandt,
also fell into this category but further represented—along with the
state secretary in Hans Frank's General Government, Josef Bühler—the
civil administration in the occupied Eastern territories, with whom
Heydrich did not get along.[13]

Moreover, Heydrich invited two officials whose special area of
expertise was "race questions": Gerhard Klopfer, Martin Bormann's
deputy at the Reich Chancellery, and Otto Hofmann, head of the SS
Race and Settlement Main Office (RuSHA), as well as two officials
from his own organization in charge of operative persecution of Jews,
namely Gestapo head Heinrich Müller and his expert on Jewish issues,
Adolf Eichmann. The SS and police in the occupied Eastern territories
were represented by Karl Eberhard Schöngarth, head of the SiPo and
SD in the General Government, invited on behalf of Friedrich-Wilhelm
Krüger, Higher SS and Police Leader (HSSPF), and Rudolf Lange, the
head of the SiPo and SD as well as the Einsatzgruppe—a mobile killing unit in the Reichskommissariat Ostland (RKO)—and deputy to
Franz Walter Stahlecker. Atrocities committed by Lange include the
mass executions of over 30,000 Jews in Riga in late November 1941.[14]
Heydrich's relations with his colleagues were cordial but hierarchical.
The notoriously hard-hearted head of the RSHA had few friends. His
main ally was Herbert Backe, who served as state secretary in the
Reich Ministry of Food and was appointed minister in 1942. In 1941
he played a key role in the development and implementation of the
Hunger Plan, which envisioned death by starvation of millions of
civilians in the Soviet Union in order to guarantee food supplies for
German troops.

Heydrich opened the conference with a reminder to the attendees
that Göring had put him in charge of all "preparations for the Final
Solution to the Jewish Question" and that the meeting had been called
to clarify a number of fundamental questions. He told the gathered officials that the Reich Marshal was expecting him to deliver a draft concerning organizational, factual and material interests in relation to the

Illustration 3.3 Heydrich congratulating Hermann Göring on his 49th birthday on 12 January 1942. Eight days before the Wannsee Conference, Heydrich assured Reichsmarschall Göring of his loyalty by personally attending the celebration. Unknown photographer, 12.1.1942, BpK, 30008532.

"Final Solution of the Jewish Question in Europe, (making) necessary an initial common action of all central offices immediately concerned with these questions in order to bring their general activities into line." Heydrich made it clear which body would dictate how exactly this would happen—it would not be the German civil administration in the General Government, nor the Reich Ministry for the Occupied Eastern Territories. According to the minutes of the meeting: "The overall control for organizing the Final Solution to the Jewish Question, irrespective of geographical boundaries, is in the hands of the SS-Reichsführer and the head of the SiPo and SD,"—that is, Heydrich.

Heydrich used the words "irrespective of geographical boundaries" deliberately, so as to emphasize that neither Alfred Rosenberg, as Reich Minister for the Occupied Eastern Territories, nor General Governor Hans Frank, had the authority to make decisions on Jewish policy. Further underscoring his own authority on the "Jewish Question," Heydrich reiterated the success of his organization in the war on Jews but observed that the situation was very different now that German troops had invaded the Soviet Union. Emigration from Germany was no longer possible, he said, and had been outlawed by Himmler in autumn 1941. Heydrich therefore proposed a temporary solution that had recently been approved by Hitler: "the evacuation of Jews to the East." The deportations from the Reich and the protectorate to Łodź, Minsk and Riga, which had begun in October 1941, had taught important "practical lessons" of "great significance for the imminent Final Solution of the Jewish Question." Heydrich's cynical reference to "practical lessons" related to the deportations from Germany, Austria and the Protectorate, which had been underway since October 1941. Conditions on the transports varied considerably. The approximately 20,000 Jews from Luxemburg, Frankfurt, Cologne, Berlin, Prague and Vienna transported to Łodź between 15 October and 3 November 1941 were housed in terrible conditions in the ghetto. Even worse fates awaited other deportees. In November 1941, nearly 12,000 Jews from the Minsk Ghetto were executed by SiPo and Orpo forces to make room for deportees from Hamburg. In late November German deportees had also been executed on arrival in Kaunas and Riga, including nearly 5,000 men, women and children from Berlin, Munich, Frankfurt, Breslau (present-day Wrocław) and Vienna. Between 29 November and 1 December 13,000 Latvian Jews from the Riga Ghetto and 1,000 Jews newly arrived deportees from Berlin were also executed. The German civil administration objected to these massacres, as did Himmler, who had explicitly told Heydrich by telephone there was to be "no liquidation" of people on the Berlin transports. The differing ways the transports were dealt with at their various destinations showed that Berlin had never issued specific instructions as to how Jews deported from Germany should be dealt with. These were the "problems" Heydrich alluded to in his invitation dated 29 November 1941 to the Wannsee Conference.

Heydrich began the meeting with a general introduction and went on to explain exactly what would happen to deported Jews:

> Under proper guidance, in the course of the Final Solution the Jews are to be allocated for appropriate labor in the East. Able-bodied Jews, separated according to sex, will be taken in large work columns to these areas for work on roads, in the course of which action doubtless a large portion will be eliminated by natural causes. The possible final remnant will, since it will undoubtedly consist of the most resistant portion, have to be treated accordingly, because it is the product of natural selection and would, if released, act as a seed of a new Jewish revival (see the experience of history.)

Heydrich made no explicit mention of the fate of women and children who were unfit for work, but it can be assumed that he believed they too would "have to be treated accordingly," because they might otherwise "act as a seed of a new Jewish revival." Heydrich's exposition of the "Jewish Question" contained little that was new. Even at the Wannsee Conference, he held to the belief expressed in early 1941 that a complete solution to the "Jewish Question" would only be possible after the war, and would entail deportations to the East, forced labor and mass murder. Until then, his plan was to step up the systematic mass executions of Jews that had begun in the Soviet Union the previous summer.

A further focus of his lengthy monologue at the Wannsee Conference were such questions as to how persons "of mixed blood" and "full Jews" married to "persons of German blood" were to be dealt with in the course of the "Final Solution." Definitions of Jewishness mattered greatly to Heydrich. According to the Nuremberg Laws, people with three to four Jewish grandparents were defined as Jewish. People with one or two Jewish grandparents were defined as "Mischlinge." In the course of 1941, radical anti-Semites had stepped up their efforts to have the special status of "Mischlinge" abolished—that is, to have "Mischlinge" put on the same legal footing as Jews. Heydrich took a lively interest in the matter, especially when it became necessary to establish which groups were to be deported from the Reich. Heydrich proposed a radical solution to the question of the approximately 20,000 German Jews married to Germans: "evacuation." The meeting was closed with the request of the host to the participants that they afford him appropriate support during the carrying out of the tasks involved in the solution. The meeting lasted roughly ninety minutes, with the minutes of the meeting showing that Heydrich's monologue took up most of that time. As far as the host was concerned, the conference had gone well. As his subordinate Adolf Eichmann recalled during his postwar trial in Jerusalem, when it was over, Heydrich invited him and Heinrich Müller, chief of the Gestapo, to join him "for a glass of cognac and a cigarette." Since Heydrich neither drank nor smoked, he must have been in an exceptionally festive mood.[15]

It was at least partly justified. Heydrich had convened the meeting to achieve three goals. Firstly, he had sought the official approval of the central Nazi instances and the authorities in the occupied eastern territories for the deportations already underway as part of the sweeping solution to the "Jewish Question." Secondly, he had sought confirmation of the SS's controversial dominance of the planning and execution of the "Final Solution," and lastly, he had sought agreement on the question as to which persons should be deported from the Reich. He achieved at least two of these three goals. The participants of the conference accepted Heydrich's leading role in the "Final Solution to the Jewish Question." The representatives of the Reich Interior Ministry, the General Government and the Reich Ministry for the Occupied Eastern Territories had indicated they agreed to his plans and even presented radical new proposals for the occupied Polish territories, such as executing Jews on site in the occupied zones. This appeared to mark the end of the dispute with the civil administration in the General Government that had long been brewing. Heydrich had reached broad agreement with Frank's deputy that the number of Jews in the General Government was to be reduced by mass murder before further Jews could be deported there.

Disagreements over divisions of responsibilities continued even after January 1942, but the "basic fundamentals for the execution of the Final Solution to the Jewish Question" had "fortunately been settled," as Heydrich wrote shortly after the conference in a letter to Martin Luther, Under Secretary at the Foreign Office.[16] However, Heydrich had not succeeded in making headway on the "Mischling" and "mixed–marriage" questions. Both the Reich Propaganda Ministry and the Reich Justice Ministry feared the repercussions of forced divorces. In October 1942, Reich Justice Minister Otto Georg Thierack and Himmler agreed not to deport "Mischlinge" for as long as the war lasted.[17]

The day after the Wannsee Conference, Heydrich telephoned the SS-Reichsführer to tell him what had been agreed. By this point, Heydrich was already back in Prague. As acting Reich Protector of the Protectorate of Bohemia and Moravia, he was preparing for a further ambitious campaign of expulsion and murder, which he planned to put into practice once the "Final Solution to the Jewish Question" was complete: the "Germanization" of the occupied East.[18] The Wannsee Conference was one of many milestones on the path to a pan-European "Final Solution of the Jewish Question" by means of a continuation of the systematic pan-European genocide that had been underway since spring 1942, at the latest. By now, Heydrich had also been entrusted with another key task. Hitler had appointed Heydrich acting Reich Protector of the Protectorate of Bohemia and Moravia in September 1941, just two months after the launch of Operation Barbarossa and at a crucial moment at the start of the systematic mass murder of Soviet Jews and the deportation of Jews from the Reich territory and Protectorate. On the one hand this was linked to the growing resistance in the Protectorate, which was threatening the productivity of the Czech arms industry, which was needed for the war effort. But even more importantly, Heydrich had been sent to Prague to oversee the introduction of the next stage of the Nazis' racist policy—that is, the deportations of Jews from Germany and the Protectorate, which had just been approved by Hitler. On the other hand, it was also a step towards the preparation for the complete Germanization of the Protectorate—that is, the full racist, political and cultural integration of Bohemia and Moravia into the German Reich.[19] "The Solution of the Jewish Question," which Heydrich had been in charge of since the late 1930s, was merely a first step on the path to a bloody unweaving of Europe's complex ethnic composition by means of a zealous campaign of persecuting, resettling and murdering millions of East Europeans.

As acting Reich Protector of the Protectorate of Bohemia and Moravia—an office he held until his death in June 1942—Heydrich ushered in the Germanization of the Protectorate with a highly ambitious program of racist classification and cultural imperialism. However, Heydrich was well aware that that the full Germanization of Eastern Europe would have to wait until the Wehrmacht had defeated the Red Army. In logistical terms, he knew it would be impossible to expel, resettle or murder an estimated 30 million Slavs once the East was occupied, while simultaneously winning the war against an alliance of enemies whose forces outnumbered the Wehrmacht. The murder of European Jews, a far smaller minority and easily identified, posed fewer logistical challenges. For Heydrich and Himmler, a speedy implementation of the "Final Solution" promised to give them a major strategic advantage over rival authorities in the occupied territories: they hoped their efficiency in implementing Hitler's genocidal vision would demonstrate to the Führer that the SS was the organization best suited to leading the Nazis' even more ambitious postwar project—the complete racial reorganization of Europe.[20]

Heydrich did not live to see the failure of these megalomaniac and genocidal fantasies. He died in June 1942, after two Czech and Slovak paratroopers made an assassination attempt on his life as he drove to work in Prague. The British Special Operations Executive and Edvard Beneš's Czechoslovak Government-in-Exile in London were behind it. Secret service documents show the plan to kill Heydrich had been hatched several months earlier and was born out of desperation. Ever since France had been defeated in summer 1940 and Allied soldiers evacuated from the beaches and harbor of Dunkirk, the British government had been under intense pressure to regain the initiative. The Battle of Britain in 1940 and Operation Barbarossa in summer 1941 buoyed Britain somewhat, but the war was far from being won.[21]

The British and Czechoslovaks knew that an assassination of a high-ranking Nazi would have great symbolic value—it would show that the spirit of Czechoslovak resistance remained undiminished and that the Germans could be attacked behind the frontline at any time. As the head of the RSHA and the occupation regime in Prague, Heydrich was an obvious target, especially since he was known to eschew security precautions. On the day of the assassination attempt, Heydrich was driving in a car with an open roof, which cost him his life.

He died from septicemia caused by his injuries several days later. The Nazi leadership paid their respects with a grandiose funeral at the New Reich Chancellery. It was the biggest state funeral in the history of the "Third Reich." Hitler went on to order a wave of reprisals by German SS troops, including the destruction of villages such as Lidice and the killing of some 10,000 Nazi opponents in Bohemia and Moravia, their supporters and families. Himmler himself paid appropriate tribute to Heydrich by giving the systematic murder of some two million Polish Jews between June 1942 and summer 1943 the code name "Operation Reinhard"—a fitting homage to the man who since the November pogrom in 1938 had been the leading planner of Nazi Germany's Jewish policy.[22]

Lina Heydrich was thirty-one years old and pregnant when her husband was buried in Berlin. She spent the next two years living with her children in Panenské Břežany outside Prague. In 1943 her eldest son Klaus was killed in a car accident. As the Red Army approached in April 1945 Himmler ordered the evacuation of the family to Bavaria. When the Third Reich collapsed and Germany announced its unconditional surrender, Heydrich's widow and her children went to live with her parents on the island of Fehmarn. In 1947 the military government in the British occupation zone refused a request submitted by the Beneš government to extradite Lina Heydrich to Prague.

It was not the only example of the authorities turning a blind eye to her history. She was officially cleared during the denazification proceedings, despite accusations that she had mistreated forced laborers in Panenské Břežany. Her house on Fehmarn, confiscated by the British in 1945, was returned to her. She turned it into a small inn called "Imbria Parva," where her late husband's former SS colleagues traded memories of "better days" at regular reunions. In 1956 and again in 1959 Lina Heydrich won cases against the West German state, which had denied her the right to a widow's pension. Even though the prosecution had ample evidence of the leading role played by her late husband in the murder of Jews, the court decided to award her the right to a pension because he had been killed in action. As if to mock the prosecution and the media—which had angrily criticized the court ruling—she called her memoirs, published in the 1970s, *Life with a War Criminal.*

Lina Heydrich died in August 1985, still consumed by disgust at a society that refused to honor the "sacrifices" her family made during the war. By then, few shared her warped view of history. An overwhelming majority of Germans understood that even by the standards of his time, Reinhard Heydrich had been a war criminal. Until his assassination in 1942 he had been the chief enforcer of Nazi terror, complicit every step of the way in establishing the SS police state and the escalation of the mass murder of Jews. The role he played in implementing the extermination policy developed by Hitler and Himmler make him a key figure of the Third Reich and its murderous agenda.

Robert Gerwarth is Professor of Modern History at University College Dublin where he is also Director of the Centre for War Studies. After studying history and political science in Berlin, he completed his DPhil and a British Academy Postdoctoral Fellowship at Oxford University. He is an elected Member of the Royal Irish Academy and the Academia Europaea, and the author of three monographs, including a critically acclaimed biography of Reinhard Heydrich (Yale University Press, 2011) and, most recently, *The Vanquished: Why the First World War Failed to End* (Allen Lane, 2016). His work has been translated into more than twenty languages.

Notes

1   On Heydrich's life and role in the "Third Reich," see: Robert Gerwarth, *Heydrich: Biographie* (Munich, 2011).
2   On his childhood, see Gerwarth, *Heydrich*, chapter II; Shlomo Aronson, *Reinhard Heydrich und die Frühgeschichte von Gestapo und SD* (Stuttgart, 1971), 16.
3   On the general climate: Andrew Donson, *Youth in the Fatherless Land: War Pedagogy, Nationalism and Authority in Germany, 1914–1918* (Cambridge, MA, 2010), 239; Ulrich Herbert, "'Generation der Sachlichkeit': Die völkische Studentenbewegung der frühen zwanziger Jahre in Deutschland," in *Zivilisation und Barbarei: Die widersprüchlichen Potentiale der Moderne: Detlev Peukert zum Gedenken*, ed. F. Bajohr, W. Johe and U. Lohalm (Hamburg, 1991), 115–44.
4   Günther Deschner, *Reinhard Heydrich: Statthalter der totalen Macht* (Esslingen, 1977), 26 et seq.
5   Lina Heydrich, *Leben mit einem Kriegsverbrecher: mit Kommentaren von Werner Maser* (Pfaffenhofen, 1976), 7 et seq.; Gerwarth, *Heydrich*, 59–64.
6   Aronson, *Heydrich*, 63; K. Flachowsky, "Neue Quellen zur Abstammung Reinhard Heydrichs," *Vierteljahrshefte für Zeitgeschichte* 48, no. 2 (2000): 319 et seq.

7   Eckhart Conze, "Adel unter dem Totenkopf: Die Idee eines Neuadels in den Gesellschaftsvorstellungen der SS," in *Adel und Moderne: Deutschland im internationalen Vergleich im 19. und 20. Jahrhundert*, ed. E. Conze and Monika Wienfort (Cologne, 2004), 151–76.

8   On Himmler: Peter Longerich, *Heinrich Himmler: Biographie* (Munich, 2008); on the relationship between the two: Gerwarth, *Heydrich*, 71 et seq.

9   Gerwarth, *Heydrich*, 111 et seq. An important insight into Heydrich's views on the "enemy" in the mid 1930s is provided by his work: Reinhard Heydrich, *Wandlungen unseres Kampfes* (Berlin, 1935).

10 Hans Mommsen, "'The Realization of the Unthinkable': The 'Final Solution of the Jewish Question' in the Third Reich," in *The Policies of Genocide: Jews and Soviet Prisoners of War in Nazi Germany*, ed. G. Hirschfeld (London, 1986), 93–144; and Hans Mommsen, "Der Nationalsozialismus: Kumulative Radikalisierung und Selbstzerstörung des Regimes," in *Meyers Enzyklopädisches Lexikon* (Munich, 1976), vol. 16, 785–90.

11 Heydrich to Luther, 29 November 1941, PAAA, R 100857, Inland II g 177, sheet. 188.

12 On NS policy to "Judenmischlingen" see Cornelia Essner, *Die "Nürnberger Gesetze" oder die Verwaltung des Rassenwahns 1933–1945* (Paderborn, 2002), 410 et seq.; J. Noakes, "The Development of Nazi Policy towards the German-Jewish 'Mischlinge', 1933–1945," *Leo Baeck Institute Yearbook* 34 (1989): 291–354. For a detailed examination of the fate of Hamburg "Judenmischlinge" see Beate Meyer, *"Jüdische Mischlinge": Rassenpolitik und Verfolgungserfahrung 1933–1945* (Hamburg, 1999); and Claudia Koonz, *The Nazi Conscience* (Cambridge, MA and London, 2003), 163–89.

13 On the participants, see Mark Roseman, *Wannsee-Konferenz: Wie die NS-Bürokratie den Holocaust organisierte* (Berlin, 2002), 95 et seq.; Wolf Kaiser, "Die Wannsee-Konferenz: SS-Führer und Ministerialbeamte im Einvernehmen über die Ermordung der europäischen Juden," in *Täter, Opfer, Folgen: Der Holocaust in Geschichte und Gegenwart*, ed. H. Lichtenstein and O.R. Romberg (Bonn: Bundeszentrale für Politische Bildung), 1997, 24–37. CVs of the participants can be found in: Kurt Pätzold and Erika Schwarz, *Tagesordnung: Judenmord: Die Wannsee-Konferenz am 20. Januar 1942: Eine Dokumentation zur Organisation der 'Endlösung'* (Berlin, 1992), 201–45.

14 Roseman, *Wannsee-Konferenz*, 95–97.

15 David Cesarani, *Adolf Eichmann: Bürokrat und Massenmörder* (Berlin, 2004),161.

16 Heydrich to Luther, 26 February 1942, PAAA, R100857, 156.

17 On the two related conferences on the treatment of "Mischlingen" and "Mischehen" in 1942, see Raul Hilberg, *Die Vernichtung der europäischen Juden*, 3 vols. (Frankfurt am Main, 1990–92), vol. 2, 436 et seq; Saul Friedländer, *Das Dritte Reich und die Juden: Verfolgung und Vernichtung*, 2 vols. (Munich, 2006), vol. 2, 327. See also the minutes of the meeting in the RSHA, 6 March 1942, IfZ, Eich 119.

18 P. Witte et al., ed., *Der Dienstkalender Heinrich Himmlers 1941/42* (21 January 1942) (Hamburg, 1999), 331.

19 Ian Kershaw, *Hitler: 1936–1945* (Stuttgart, 2000), 641; Witte et al., *Dienstkalender*, 217. On the Protectorate generally: Chad Bryant, *Prague in Black: Nazi Rule and Czech Nationalism* (Cambridge, MA, 2007).
20 Longerich, *Himmler.*
21 On the assassination: Hellmut G. Haasis, *Tod in Prag: Das Attentat auf Reinhard Heydrich* (Reinbek, 2002); Callum MacDonald, *The Killing of SS Obergruppenfuehrer Reinhard Heydrich, 27 May 1942* (London, 1992); Michal Burian et al., *Assassination: Operation Anthropoid 1941–1945* (Prague, 2002).
22 Detlef Brandes, *Die Tschechen unter deutschem Protektorat*, 2 vols. (Munich, 1969 and 1976), vol. 1, 263 et seq.; Vojtech Mastny, *Czechs under Nazi Rule: The Failure of National Resistance, 1939–1942* (New York, NY, 1971), 215 et seq.; Peter Steinkamp, "Lidice 1942," in *Orte des Grauens: Verbrechen im Zweiten Weltkrieg*, ed. G.R. Ueberschär (Darmstadt, 2003), 126–35.

Bibliography

Aronson, Shlomo. *Reinhard Heydrich und die Frühgeschichte von Gestapo und SD.* Stuttgart: Deutsche Verlags-Anstalt, 1971.

Brandes, Detlef. *Die Tschechen unter deutschem Protektorat.* Munich: Oldenbourg, 1969 and 1976.

Bryant, Chad. *Prague in Black: Nazi Rule and Czech Nationalism.* Cambridge, MA: Harvard University Press, 2007.

Burian, Michal, Aleš Knížek, Jiří Rajlich and Eduard Stehlík. *Assassination: Operation Anthropoid 1941–1945.* Prague: Ministry of Defence of the Czech Republic — AVIS, 2002. Retrieved 7 October 2016 from http://www.army.cz/ images/id_7001_8000/7419/assassination-en.pdf

Cesarani, David. *Adolf Eichmann: Bürokrat und Massenmörder.* Berlin: Propyläen, 2004. [English: *Becoming Eichmann: Rethinking the Life, Crimes, and Trial of a "Desk Murderer."* Boston, MA: Da Capo Press, 2007.]

Conze, Eckhart. "Adel unter dem Totenkopf: Die Idee eines Neuadels in den Gesellschaftsvorstellungen der SS." In *Adel und Moderne: Deutschland im internationalen Vergleich im 19. und 20. Jahrhundert*, edited by E. Conze and M. Wienfort, 151–76. Cologne: Böhlau, 2004.

Deschner, Günther. *Reinhard Heydrich: Statthalter der totalen Macht.* Esslingen: Bechtle, 1977. [English: *Reinhard Heydrich: A Biography.* New York: Stein and Day, 1981.]

Donson, Andrew. *Youth in the Fatherless Land: War Pedagogy, Nationalism and Authority in Germany, 1914–1918.* Cambridge, MA: Harvard University Press, 2010.

Essner, Cornelia. *Die "Nürnberger Gesetze" oder die Verwaltung des Rassenwahns 1933–1945.* Paderborn: Schöningh, 2002.

Flachowsky, K. "Neue Quellen zur Abstammung Reinhard Heydrichs." *Vierteljahrshefte für Zeitgeschichte* 48, no. 2 (2000): 319–27.

Friedländer, Saul. *Das Dritte Reich und die Juden: Verfolgung und Vernichtung.* Munich: C.H. Beck, 2006. [English: *Nazi Germany and the Jews.* New York: HarperCollins, 1997.]

Gerwarth, Robert. *Reinhard Heydrich: Biographie*. Munich: Siedler, 2011. [English: *Hitler's Hangman: The Life of Heydrich*. New Haven, CT: Yale University Press, 2011.]

Haasis, Hellmut G. *Tod in Prag: Das Attentat auf Reinhard Heydrich*. Reinbek: Rowohlt, 2002.

Herbert, Ulrich. "'Generation der Sachlichkeit': Die völkische Studenten-bewegung der frühen zwanziger Jahre in Deutschland." In *Zivilisation und Barbarei: Die widersprüchlichen Potentiale der Moderne: Detlev Peukert zum Gedenken*, edited by F. Bajohr, W. Johe and U. Lohalm, 115–44. Hamburg: Christians, 1991.

Heydrich, Lina. *Leben mit einem Kriegsverbrecher: mit Kommentaren von Werner Maser*. Pfaffenhofen: Ludwig, 1976.

Heydrich, Reinhard. *Wandlungen unseres Kampfes*. Berlin: Eher, 1935.

Heydrich, R. "Bekämpfung der Staatsfeinde." *Deutsches Recht* 6 (1936): 121–23.

Hilberg, Raul. *Die Vernichtung der europäischen Juden*. Frankfurt am Main: Fischer-Taschenbuch-Verlag, 1990–1992. [English: *The Destruction of the European Jews*. 4th ed. New York: Holmes & Meier, 1985.]

Kaiser, Wolf. "Die Wannsee-Konferenz: SS-Führer und Ministerialbeamte im Einvernehmen über die Ermordung der europäischen Juden." In *Täter, Opfer, Folgen: Der Holocaust in Geschichte und Gegenwart*, edited by H. Lichtenstein and O.R. Romberg, 24–37. Bonn: Bundeszentrale für Politische Bildung, 1997.

Kershaw, Ian. *Hitler: 1936–1945*. Stuttgart: Deutsche Verlags-Anstalt, 2000. [English: *Hitler, 1936–1945: Nemesis*. London: Penguin Press, 2000.]

Koonz, Claudia. *The Nazi Conscience*. Cambridge, MA and London: Belknap Press of Harvard University Press, 2003.

Longerich, Peter. *Heinrich Himmler: Biographie*. Munich: Siedler, 2008. [English: *Heinrich Himmler: A Life*, Oxford and New York: Oxford University Press, 2012.]

MacDonald, Callum. *The Killing of SS Obergruppenfuehrer Reinhard Heydrich, 27 May 1942*. London: Papermac, 1992.

Mastny, Vojtech. *Czechs under Nazi Rule: The Failure of National Resistance, 1939–1942*. New York: Columbia University Press, 1971.

Meyer, Beate. *"Jüdische Mischlinge": Rassenpolitik und Verfolgungserfahrung 1933–1945*. Hamburg: Dölling und Galitz, 1999.

Mommsen, Hans. "Der Nationalsozialismus: Kumulative Radikalisierung und Selbstzerstörung des Regimes." In *Meyers Enzyklopädisches Lexikon*, 785–90. Munich: Bibliographisches Institut, 1976.

———. "'The Realization of the Unthinkable': The 'Final Solution of the Jewish Question' in the Third Reich." In *The Policies of Genocide: Jews and Soviet Prisoners of War in Nazi Germany*, edited by G. Hirschfeld, 93–144. London: HarperCollins, 1986.

Noakes, J. "The Development of Nazi Policy towards the German-Jewish 'Mischlinge', 1933–1945." *Leo Baeck Institute Yearbook* 34 (1989): 291–354.

Pätzold, Kurt, and Erika Schwarz. *Tagesordnung: Judenmord: Die Wannsee-Konferenz am 20. Januar 1942: Eine Dokumentation zur Organisation der 'Endlösung.'* Berlin: Metropol, 1992.

Roseman, Mark. *Die Wannsee-Konferenz: Wie die NS-Bürokratie den Holocaust organisierte*, Berlin: Propyläen, 2002. [English: *The Villa, the Lake, the Meeting: Wannsee and the Final Solution*. London: Penguin Press, 2002.]

Steinkamp, Peter. "Lidice 1942." In *Orte des Grauens: Verbrechen im Zweiten Weltkrieg*, edited by G.R. Ueberschär, 126–35. Darmstadt: WBG, 2003.

Witte, P., M. Wildt, M. Vogt, D. Pohl, P. Klein, C. Gerlach, C. Dieckmann and A. Angrick, ed. *Der Dienstkalender Heinrich Himmlers 1941/42*. Hamburg: Christians, 1999.

4

Otto Hofmann

SS Race and Settlement Main
Office

A Pragmatic Enforcer of Racial
Policy?

Isabel Heinemann

Illustration 4.1 Unknown photographer,
BArch, R 9361-I/17613 (Slg. BDC).

"The R.u.S.H. [Race and Settlement Main Office], as far as I recall, did
not deal with the Jewish Question in the sense of propagandist handling
or carrying out a directive,"[1] Otto Hofmann, former SS-Gruppenführer,
police and Waffen-SS general, and long-time head of the SS Race and
Settlement Main Office, said to Larry Wolf, the U.S. investigator questioning him in May 1947. Hofmann was in the dock at the U.S. Military
Court in Nuremberg, charged with crimes against humanity.[2] If the
institution that he represented had had nothing to do with the "propagandist handling" of the "Jewish Question" or "carrying out" genocide,
as he claimed, why was he among the high-ranking Nazis present at the
Wannsee Conference? This chapter sets out to profile Otto Hofmann,
the man, and outline the role of the organization he represented at the
Wannsee Conference, before considering the punishment of his crimes
and his postwar biography.

A Radical Ethnonationalist in the SS

Otto Ludwig Karl Adam Hofmann was born on 16 March 1896, the son
of Adam Hofmann, a merchant, and his wife Hermine Rosmanith.[3] He
attended elementary and high school in Munich. From the age of eight,
he lived with his step-grandfather, a retired major. A few days after
the outbreak of the First World War, he volunteered for the army and
was deployed in a field artillery regiment. In March 1917 he was made

liaison officer for an Austrian fighter pilot unit. He was shot down by a Russian fighter jet in June 1917 and held as a prisoner of war for five weeks before managing to escape. He subsequently trained as a pilot, and reached the rank of reserve lieutenant. Among the many honors he received were the first-class and second-class Iron Crosses.[4]

In March 1919 Hofmann was released from military service. Having not learned any other profession, he decided to join a Freikorps, the "Batterie von Axthelm," in which he fought until fall 1919 at the border between Bavaria and Czechoslovakia. He eventually made the transition into civilian life in 1920, when he started working for his father-in-law's wine wholesale business in Nuremberg. Five years later, he and his wife (with whom he had a daughter) were divorced and he set up his own business representing a large wine company. In 1927 Hofmann married his second wife, Gertrud Maria Strerath from Rheydt (now part of Mönchengladbach).[5] They had two sons, born in 1935 and 1936.

Hofmann was one of the old guard—an early member of the Nazi Party, first joining in 1923. The Party was banned in November that year, but re-founded on 1 August 1929, and Hofmann became a member again with the membership number 145,729.[6] On 1 April 1931, he joined the SS with the membership number 7,646. This marked the start of Hofmann's career within the Nazi regime: after earning initial merits for motorizing various SS sections, he was entrusted with the job of chief-of-staff of the greater north-west section of the SS (Braunschweig) under SS-Gruppenführer Jeckeln, a personal friend of his.[7] He subsequently led various SS formations (SS-Standarte) and the SS section XV (Hamburg), before becoming a full-time staff member of the SS in September 1935. Assigned a post as SS leader in the RuSHA in early 1937, this former sales representative started working as SS Leader for Race and Settlement (RuS-Führer) in the greater west section of the SS (Düsseldorf). His field of responsibility included indoctrination of SS members, selection, welfare and ethnonational policy. In February 1939 he assumed directorship of the "kinship office" (Sippenamt) set up to issue proof of descent for SS members.[8] On account of his success building up the kinship office, he was promoted to SS-Brigadeführer and deputy head of the race office in the RuSHA.[9] In the latter function, he organized physical examinations of ethnic Germans and those "suitable for re-Germanization" in occupied Poland in 1939 to 1940, garnering the emphatic praise of then chief of the RuSHA Gunther Pancke. Hofmann then acted as head of the race and settlement main office for the duration of the war.[10]

When the Second World War broke out, Himmler gave orders for the head of the RuSHA to also assume the task of Reich Commissioner for the Consolidation of German Nationhood (Reichskommissar für die Festigung deutschen Volkstums, RKF), in which capacity Hofmann shaped the racial policy aspects of the Nazis' Germanization and resettlement program in occupied Europe, especially in the countries of Eastern Europe.[11] This program was based on the notion that people had a "racial value," true to Himmler's concept of creating a "Germanic Europe" under German supremacy, populated only by the "racially valuable." Some 500 so-called race experts from the RuSHA were charged with registering the details of several million people (SS members and their wives, ethnic Germans, and non-Germans).[12] They recorded their impressions—arranged according to twenty-one categories of anthropological characteristics—on a "race card" from which they ultimately deduced a "racial formula" to predetermine the treatment of people in each category. In the annexed Polish territories, staff of the RuSHA ruled on whether to expel undesirable Poles, whose businesses were to be transferred to ethnic Germans, and supervised their "resettlement." At the same time, SS suitability inspectors selected "racially valuable" individuals from the mass of expellees for "re-Germanization." The RuSHA also ran field offices in the other occupied regions of Europe.

As head of the RuSHA, Hofmann constantly extended its remit. Under his leadership, it assumed the following tasks: selecting candidates for the general SS and the Waffen-SS, their brides, and civilians considered suitable for Germanization; training new "suitability inspectors" (Eignungsprüfer) to carry out selections; cooperating on the expulsion of "racially undesirable" Poles and the settling of ethnic Germans; issuing attestations of Jewish identity and "crossbreed Jewish" identity; setting up SS farms in the East; providing welfare and accommodation for SS families, invalids and surviving dependents; and genealogical research.[13] In March 1943, his tendency to broaden the RuSHA's domain led to a serious dispute with Himmler, who was highly critical of Hofmann's solo efforts and eventually discharged him from his duties as head of the RuSHA.[14] The SS-Reichsführer subsequently appointed him senior SS and police leader for southwest Germany (HSSPF Südwest), and simultaneously RuS leader, as of 20 April 1943, to give him the chance of "practical probation."[15] But Hofmann displeased Himmler again, this time by ordering the hasty withdrawal of SS and police units from the Alsace in November 1944.[16]

Despite his tense relationship with the SS chief, Hofmann was soon promoted—in June 1943—to the rank of SS-Obergruppenführer and police general,[17] and in June 1944 he was appointed a general of the Waffen-SS and the police.[18] He was also awarded a large number of

SS honors *(Totenkopfring, Ehrendegen, Ehrendolch, Julleuchter)* and in December 1944 received the 500 Reichmarks "Christmas donation from the Reich Führer of the SS."[19] In addition, he was awarded the Golden Party Badge, the first-class and second-class War Merit Cross, and the Nazi Party service medal in bronze.[20]

Yet even in the 1930s, Hofmann was a somewhat controversial figure in the SS. As early as March 1935, when he still ran the twenty-first SS formation in Magdeburg, his immediate superior noted that he liked to push himself to the fore and was "very full of his own importance," though he also found him "honest, open and reliable." His friend Jeckeln, in contrast, wrote the following about him: "Hofmann is an SS leader who runs his formation with great zeal and skill. On duty, forceful, off duty, a good comrade, he completely fulfils his responsibilities."[21] But Hofmann repeatedly garnered negative attention. In 1933, he was accused of using his cover as an SS member to spy for the police authority in Nuremberg; an internal SS inquiry was launched but came to nothing.[22] In August 1934, Himmler reprimanded him following another inquiry: Hofmann and a friend had broken up a dance in Leipzig, torn down the swastika flag and insulted the participants for playing jazz.[23] Hofmann lived with his family in the old West side of central Berlin, at Woyrchstraße 48 (now Genthiner Straße), not far from Eichmann's office.[24] It was only a one and a half mile walk to his own office at Hedemannstraße 24, opposite the RSHA. He used his position to draw advantages for his family, securing a job for his daughter in the "Hegewald" German settlement area near Himmler's headquarters in Shitomir in 1943, and in the marriage office of the RuSHA in 1944.[25] At home, his wife gained the assistance of a young Polish girl found "suitable for re-Germanization." She had been deemed "racially valuable" by RuSHA suitability inspectors working on the re-Germanization program, and had been sent to the German homeland (the "Altreich") to be re-educated as a German. Girls such as these were often de facto treated as forced laborers, and this was apparently also the case in the Hofmanns' household.[26] In a letter to a friend and SS leader, the RuSHA chief explained: "I myself employ a young Polish girl, a re-Germanization candidate, who we can only keep under control by treating her strictly."[27] Hofmann also arranged such forced household-helps for several friends, acquaintances and Party comrades. As a long-serving SS leader, Hofmann had many connections within the SS and was a personal friend of several of the protagonists of the Holocaust, including Friedrich Jeckeln and Ludolf-Hermann van Alvensleben (later Himmler's chief adjutant, leader of the ethnic German "self-defense" organization Volksdeutscher Selbstschutz in West Prussia and SSPF

(SS und Polizeiführer) in Ukraine) and Richard Hildebrandt, long-time higher SS and police leader (HSSPF) in Danzig/West Prussia, later to be his successor in the RuSHA.[28]

Self-will and Self-initiative: Hofmann at the Wannsee Conference

When the Western world was informed of the talks that had taken place at Lake Wannsee in south-west Berlin by a report in *The New York Times* of 21 August 1945, Otto Hofmann was particularly implicated. U.S. investigators had found the invitations addressed to him of 29 November 1941 and 8 January 1942, sent by Reinhard Heydrich, in the files of the RuSHA.[29] What role, then, did the man play whom *The Times* described as "chief of the infamous SS Race and Settlement Office" and among whose documents they found "conclusive proof that the extermination of Europe's Jewry was plotted by the Nazi inner circle" at the Wannsee Conference?[30] Hofmann was no passive attendee of the talks at Wannsee; he was quite familiar with the progress of efforts toward the solution to the "Jewish Question." In 1941 he had been in frequent contact with Heydrich to discuss the Nazis' Germanization policy in Eastern Europe.[31] Along with Stuckart and Klopfer, they had been made permanent members of the newly created authority on questions of ethnicity in the annexed Eastern territories, charged with ruling on contentious cases of Germanization.[32] Moreover, the kinship office within the RuSHA kept an "index of crossbreed Jews," intended to help track down individuals with partially Jewish origins in the various regions of Europe as well as in the Reich. The RuSHA played a key role in the SS resettlement project, and Hofmann represented the SS at the conference.

Hofmann put forward his own suggestions on several occasions at the conference. He first commented on the issue of launching the "Final Solution" in Hungary; Heydrich and Eichmann estimated there were some 742,000 people to be murdered here.[33] Hungarian Jews were, then, the third largest national group affected, after the Jews from the Soviet Union (5 million) and those from the General Government (2.28 million). Hofmann declared his intention to "send an administrator from the Race and Settlement Main Office to assist with general orientation when the matter is tackled there by the Chief of the Security Police and the SD."[34] By getting the RuSHA involved, which considered itself the main authority on questions of Jewish identity due to its experience and its index of Jews in Europe, he presumably aimed to ensure that the extermination program was conducted as thoroughly as possible. It is not clear from the Protocol if the other participants approved of his intentions, but they agreed to deploy a RuSHA staff member, "to remain initially inactive, as a temporary assistant to the police-attaché."

Hofmann's suggestions for dealing with people with partially Jewish origins were more concrete and more controversial. As is known, the fate of "crossbreed Jews" ("Mischlinge") and people with Jewish spouses was one of the central points discussed at the conference. Indeed, the effectiveness of "maintaining the purity of the German national body" by mass murder was seen to depend on how the "Mischling Question" was solved—and here Hofmann and the RuSHA had the relevant expertise of the SS at its disposal.

In May 1939 a national census had counted 112,500 Jewish "Mischlinge" resident in the Reich. By 1942, with the occupied and annexed territories included, a far larger number were at the mercy of the Germans.[35] According to the Wannsee Protocol, "first-degree crossbreeds" were to be "treated the same [as full Jews] with regard to the Final Solution of the Jewish Question." In other words, they were to be included in the Nazis' deportation and murder plans,[36] based on the Nuremberg laws. Hofmann, however, suggested for this group of people—that is, individuals with two Jewish grandparents—that "extensive use must be made of sterilization; especially as the crossbreed, given the choice of whether to be evacuated or sterilized, would rather undergo sterilization."[37] In this way, Hofmann revealed his awareness of the fact that "evacuation" was equal to "murder."[38] At the same time, he disagreed with Heydrich's suggestion to only allow "first-degree crossbreeds" to stay in the Reich following their "voluntary steriliza- tion" in exceptional cases, as in his view, sterilization was sufficient to render the "crossbreed biologically harmless."[39] Heydrich, meanwhile, proposed classifying "second-degree crossbreeds" as German, albeit also with a few exceptions (if both parents were "Mischlinge," or the individual had a distinctly unfavorable appearance, a police record or was a known political agitator).

Taking up Hofmann's proposal to introduce "voluntary sterilization," Wilhelm Stuckart from the Reich Ministry of the Interior immediately demanded "compulsory sterilization" for all "first-degree crossbreeds." This was, he claimed, the only way to minimize the administrative workload and still "accommodate the biological facts."[40] Apparently there was, then, far less agreement on the concrete handling of the "Final Solution of the Mischling Question" than on the overall "Final Solution" as such. Further meetings were required to clarify them, two of which were on 6 March 1942 and 24 October 1942 in Eichmann's

Illustration 4.2 Hofmann at a lecture in the Netherlands in July 1942. SS propaganda photographer, July 1942, BArch Koblenz, 183-B26445.

office at Kurfürstenstraße 116, each also attended by representatives of the RuSHA.[41] Although Stuckart's idea of mass-scale compulsory sterilization was discussed at the meeting in March 1942, Hofmann's proposal of "voluntary sterilization of the remaining crossbreeds as a return service for mercifully allowing them to stay in the Reich" found more favor.[42] This plan was deemed easier to implement than Stuckart's hardline proposal, as statements by the ministries involved show.[43]

With regard to "second-degree crossbreeds," Hofmann developed more radical plans for "maintaining the purity of German blood." One of his last official acts as head of the RuSHA in March 1943 was to ask whether it would perhaps be better to "not integrate them without exception into those of German blood but to subject them to a racial inspection by the SS Race and Settlement Main Office." A measure such as this would serve to "place those second-class crossbreeds with prominent racial characteristics on the same footing in terms of treatment as first-class crossbreeds."[44] Hofmann based his arguments on the findings of an expertise by the head of his Race Office, the racial anthropologist Professor Dr Bruno Kurt Schultz, which he enclosed in his letter to the SS-Reichsführer. Himmler endorsed the expertise and sent it on to Reichsleiter Martin Bormann, who used it to formulate a directive for the heads of the district authorities on "evaluating the hereditary disposition of Jewish second-degree crossbreeds for their political assessment by the Party."[45]

Himmler and Bormann were the two highest-ranking policymakers in the Nazi regime at the time, after Hitler, to back Hofmann's initiative "for the Final Solution of the Jewish Mischling Question." In Germany, the people affected were not immediately subjected to mass murder or compulsory sterilization, but they were exposed to more intense discrimination.[46] In the "Altreich" — unlike in the Protectorate, for instance, where "Jewish crossbreeds" were subjected to "racial inspections" from 1941, and barred from "membership of the German nation" if they were found "racially unfit" from 1942 — tackling the "Final Solution of the Jewish Mischling Question" was postponed until after the war.

An "Idealist Betrayed"?

"The major error of the prosecution is that it makes Hofmann responsible for the persecution of the Jews." With this statement, Oswald Schwarz, Hofmann's defense attorney in the eighth Nuremberg follow-up trial against the SS institutions that dealt with nationhood policy (also known as the "RuSHA case"), brought his argument to a climax. The U.S. prosecutors aimed to have the Nazis' resettlement and Germanization policy in occupied Europe condemned as "part of a systematic program of genocide."[47] As well as representatives of the RuSHA, such as Hofmann and his successor Richard Hildebrandt, SS leaders from the main office of the Reich Commissioner for the Consolidation of German Nationhood (including office chief Ulrich Greifelt and head of the SS planning office Konrad Meyer), and staff members of the welfare office for ethnic Germans (Volksdeutsche Mittelstelle) and the SS association for Aryan procreation "Lebensborn e.V." stood in the dock. In total, the defendants comprised thirteen SS leaders and one woman.[48] The three main charges under the Allies' Control Council Law no. 10 were: 1) crimes against humanity; 2) war crimes; and 3) membership in a criminal organization. The prosecutors supported the charge of genocide

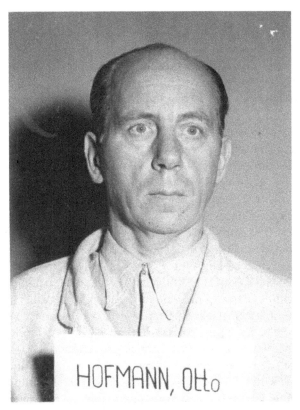

Illustration 4.3 Hofmann following his arrest in Nuremberg. Public Relations Photo Section, Office Chief Counsel for War Crimes, APO 696-A.

with nine sub-counts: a) abducting children for Germanization; b) enforcing compulsory sterilization of forced laborers; c) murdering the children of forced laborers; d) punishing sexual intercourse between forced laborers and German women; e) obstructing the reproduction of enemy nationals; f) enforcing compulsory expulsion and resettlement; g) enforcing compulsory Germanization, slave labor and forced recruitment; h) plundering foreign property; i) participating in the persecution and extermination of Jews.[49] All these counts, with which Hofmann was also individually charged, were supported by the prosecutors with a profuse amount of documentary evidence and witness statements. In retrospect, the prosecuting authorities seem to have had sound reasons for holding Hofmann responsible for the Nazis' criminal resettlement and Germanization policy in occupied Europe (which was in turn a prerequisite for the genocide of the Jews). Why, then, was Hofmann not more severely punished?

The explanation lies partly in the strategy of the defense, who very effectively portrayed Hofmann as an "idealist betrayed," who "believed in the National Socialist idea and saw only the good in it. He lived according to Himmler's SS laws of loyalty, honor and self-sacrifice, was incorruptible, and tried to be an understanding and just superior and flawless role model. He led a good family life. He helped his fellow men wherever he could."[50] Second, Hofmann managed to present himself as good-willed and honorable (as did his co-defendants), and the institution he represented as insignificant and powerless—a view that indeed predominated in historical research right up until the mid 1990s.[51] When questioned, Hofmann shifted the entire responsibility on to Himmler, the Reich Security Main Office and SS members who were already dead or missing.[52] And he and his co-defendants from the RuSHA actively ensured that the defense pursue a cover-up strategy by co-writing guidelines for portraying the history and duties of the Race and Settlement Main Office of the SS.[53] These recommendations played down the role of the RuSHA as having been primarily to "care for maintaining the health of SS members' families as the main foundation of the nation and the state."[54] In view of the evidence that RuSHA staff members had not only carried out racial examinations as the basis on which the Nazis' resettlement policy was enforced in the occupied territories of Europe, but had also had children abducted and pregnancies compulsorily terminated as well as forced laborers singled out for "special treatment", this was a knowing misrepresentation of the facts.

The defense pursued the same strategy with respect to Hofmann's participation in the Wannsee Conference:

> Hofmann was invited to the meeting about the Final Solution of the Jewish Question without his cooperation and without any objective connection, obviously on a personal whim of Heydrich's. He had no choice but to accept this invitation from the most powerful man after Himmler. At the meeting, Hofmann, in contrast to Heydrich, supported a position that was more favorable for first-degree Jewish Mischlinge. Had he been a Jew-hater he would have agreed with Heydrich. Due to his objection, the issue was put on the back burner. The meeting ended without result. The sterilization of Mischlinge was not enforced after all.[55]

During his many interrogations by Larry Wolf, the U.S. investigator, Hofmann tried to adhere to this account. He denied having known anything about the existence of a "Jewish Mischling index" at the RuSHA, compiled in order to track down people of partly Jewish descent, not only within the Reich but also in the various regions of Europe. He also claimed he was mistakenly present at the Wannsee Conference.[56] Both statements are implausible. For one, Hofmann himself was head of the kinship office (Sippenamt) from 1939 onward and later, as head of the RuSHA, personally gave the order to confiscate "Jew indices" and "registers" in France, the Netherlands and Norway.[57] Second, the Wannsee Protocol showed that he had played an active part in the state secretaries' meeting, often speaking and contributing his own ideas.

Furthermore, if one is to believe the statement by former HSSPF for central Russia, Erich von dem Bach-Zelewski, it was common knowledge among SS circles that the RuSHA held a "Jewish Mischling index" at the kinship office. As witness for the prosecution, Bach-Zelewski had said that "in Berlin, in the Race and Settlement Main Office, a Jew index existed that could provide information on every family right back to the early centuries." It had been very useful for identifying Jews in occupied Europe, as "on the basis of this index, this Jew index, the Security Police did preparatory work before the invasion of foreign territories ... making sudden strikes possible." Despite the fact that there was no doubt about the existence of the "Jewish Mischling index" or the RuSHA's initiatives toward the "Final Solution of the Jewish Mischling Question," the relativizing arguments of the defense ultimately prevailed.[58] Although Hofmann was found guilty on all three main counts, he received a comparatively lenient sentence of twenty-five years' imprisonment. Maintaining the charges relating to enforced Germanization and resettlement (count one: genocide / "crimes against humanity"), the judges acquitted Hofmann only of plundering foreign property.[59] But they dropped the charge of "participation of the RuSHA in the persecution and extermination of the Jews" due to lack of evidence, and argued that the Nazis' criminal resettlement policy had targeted Poles and Jews equally.[60] Though objectively correct, this blurred the fact that the resettlement and murder of Jews were intermeshed processes, each pushing the other to more radical extremes. As a consequence, Hofmann, a participant in the Wannsee Conference, was cleared of all charges of involvement in the genocide of the Jews.[61] Like many other Nazis, Hofmann only served a fraction of his sentence, benefiting from an amnesty declared by U.S. High Commissioner McCloy in 1954.[62] Thereafter he led a quiet life as a clerk with his family in the south German town of Künzelsau, Baden-Württemberg.

After his release, between 1959 and 1982, Hofmann was questioned again during preliminary investigations conducted by the Central Office of the State Justice Administrations in Ludwigsburg (ZSt.) into cases of participation in National Socialist crimes.[63] The Eichmann trial in Jerusalem in 1961, in particular, aroused renewed interest in the Wannsee Conference. Hofmann was questioned several times in the years 1962, 1965 and 1966 in connection with these investigations.[64] In two cases, the preliminary investigations even led to criminal proceedings against Hofmann. In the first action (1959–61), brought by the Heilbronn public prosecutors, he was charged with participation in criminal killings in Natzweiler concentration camp in his capacity as HSSPF Südwest.[65] In a second action (in 1982), the Stuttgart public prosecution conducted investigations specifically into the participants of the Wannsee Conference.[66] Both cases were eventually dismissed. The public prosecutors faced the major obstacle of Hofmann's previous conviction in Nuremberg for his activities as head of the RuSHA and his participation in crimes against humanity. Under German law, he could not be prosecuted for the same crimes again, only questioned as a witness.[67]

For his part, Hofmann purposefully made light of his involvement in identifying Jews and Jewish "Mischlinge," in racial inspections in the context of "re-Germanization procedures," and especially in the order to kill Eastern European forced laborers classified as "racially inferior." Although there was evidence to prove that he had ordered the murder of forced laborers who had violated the ban on sexual intercourse with German women while HSSPF in Stuttgart, and had instructed his suitability inspectors on how to proceed in such "special treatment cases" as head of the RuSHA, when questioned in 1966 by the Baden-Württemberg state criminal investigation department, he brazenly declared: "Nobody at the RuS Main Office had a precise idea about the concept of 'special treatment.' It might be interpreted as a term in a concentration camp, imprisonment or the death penalty."[68] The investigators realized that Hofmann was aiming to play down and cover up the facts but could do nothing about it:

> Although the witness Hofmann readily followed the questioning, he nevertheless created the impression that he was withholding essential knowledge. He stated several times, but did not want it put in the protocol, that this particular case had already been heard before the American Military Court in Nuremberg. It was from these files that the specific circumstances of the special treatment procedure became apparent.[69]

Unlike the forced laborers he had condemned to "special treatment" and the victims of the Holocaust, Otto Hofmann was able to live to an advanced age. He died on 31 December 1982 in Bad Mergentheim, aged eighty-six.[70]

Summary

Hofmann's biography includes the typical stations of a radical ethnonationalist of the SS pioneer generation: military service in the First

World War, Freikorps service, early membership of the Nazi Party and the SS, professional advancement within the SS to the position of head of an SS main office, and highest rank in the general SS and the Waffen-SS. Hofmann was a convinced racist and anti-Semite who, as head of the RuSHA, had a key influence on the Nazis' nationhood and racial policy in occupied Europe. As such, he was instrumental in the murder of the European Jews.[71] He was certainly not an "idealist betrayed" by Himmler, as his defense attorney in Nuremberg claimed. At the Wannsee Conference, Hofmann had demonstrated self-will and self-initiative, especially with regard to the "Final Solution of the Jewish Mischling Question," which was so important to him, a pragmatic enforcer of racial policy. Even after the conference, he worked on a strategy for permanently "maintaining the purity of German blood" by rendering "first- and second-degree Mischlinge" biologically harmless, based on an expertise by the head of his Race Office. He did not even shy away from confrontation with Himmler when it came to pursuing racial and settlement policy in occupied Europe.

Hofmann was convicted for his part in the Nazis' policy of resettlement and extermination by the U.S. military court in Nuremberg in 1948, but of the twenty-five years he received, he served only nine before being released in 1954. His life as a clerk was not significantly disturbed by the many investigations conducted by Germany's Federal prosecutors. Due to the broad sweep of the prosecution at Nuremberg (where he was accused of being "part of a genocidal program"), Hofmann could not be convicted again without new charges being brought. Hence he was merely questioned as a witness in several cases. Ironically, then, it was the thoroughness of the Nuremberg prosecution that ultimately allowed Hofmann to live out his life to a peaceful old age.

Isabel Heinemann is Assistant Professor of Contemporary History at Münster University, Germany. Her research interests include the history of National Socialism and NS racism, the cultural history of the United States in the twentieth century, gender history and the history of science. She is the author of *'Rasse, Siedlung, deutsches Blut': Das Rasse- und Siedlungshauptamt der SS und die rassenpolitische Neuordnung Europas* (Wallstein Verlag, second edition 2003), and *Familienwerte im gesellschaftlichen Wandel: Debatten um Ehescheidung, Frauenarbeit und Reproduktion in den USA des 20. Jahrhunderts* (to appear with DeGruyter-Oldenbourg, 2017).

Notes

1 "Zeugenvernehmung Otto Hofmann durch Larry Wolf," 20 May 1947, IfZ, 75-797-31.
2 This was the eighth Nuremberg follow-up trial, the so-called RuSHA case. On the Nuremberg follow-up trials, see K.C. Priemel and A. Stiller, ed., *NMT: Die Nürnberger Militärtribunale zwischen Geschichte, Gerechtigkeit und Rechtschöpfung* (Hamburg, 2013); also my article on case VIII in: Isabel Heinemann, *"Rasse, Siedlung, deutsches Blut": Das Rasse- und Siedlungshauptamt der SS und die rassenpolitische Neuordnung Europas*, 2nd ed. (Göttingen, 2003), 100–26. On Hofmann, see also Isabel Heinemann, *Rasse* and Isabel Heinemann, "Otto Hofmann und das Rasse- und Siedlungshauptamt: Die 'Lösung der Judenfrage' als Element der rassenpolitischen Neuordnung Europas," in *Die Wannsee-Konferenz am 20. Januar 1942: Dokumente, Forschungsstand, Kontroversen*, ed. N. Kampe and P. Klein (Cologne, 2013), 323–40.
3 For details of Hofmann's biography, employment and military status, decorations, etc., see his SS personal file in Bundesarchiv Berlin, BDC, SSO. See also the statutory declaration by Hofmann before the military court in Nuremberg, 19 June 1947, IfZ ZS-797-65.
4 "Wehrdienstnachweis Otto Hofmann,", BArch BDC, SSO Otto Hofmann, p. 44.
5 On Hofmann's marriage, see his RuS file, BArch R 9361-III-79662.
6 See the information in Hofmann's undated CV (1936) in his SS personal file, BArch BDC, SSO Otto Hofmann.
7 "Stellenbesetzungsvorschlag des Führers des SS-OA Nord-West, SS-Gruf. Friedrich Jeckeln," 15 January 1934. Hofmann was officially appointed on 15 January 1934, BArch BDC, SSO, Otto Hofmann.
8 "Anschreiben Chef RuSHA an RFSS," 12 January 1939, "Bestätigung durch RFSS," 20 January 1939, BArch BDC, SSO Otto Hofmann.
9 BArch BDC, SSO Otto Hofmann.
10 "Ernennungsschreiben des RFSS," 12 July 1940, BArch BDC, SSO Otto Hofmann.
11 On Hitler's Reichstag address of 6 October 1939, see M. Wildt, "'Eine neue Ordnung der ethnographischen Verhältnisse': Hitlers Reichstagsrede vom 6. Oktober 1939," *Zeithistorische Forschungen/Studies in Contemporary History* 3, no. 1 (2006): 129–37. On the RKF, see Robert L. Koehl, *RKFDV: German Resettlement and Population Policy 1939–1945: A History of the Reich Commission for the Strengthening of Germandom* (Cambridge, 1957); Alexa Stiller, *Germanisierung und Gewalt: Nationalsozialistische Politik in den annektierten Gebieten 1939–1945* (Basel, 2015); Alexa Stiller, "Gewalt und Alltag der Volkstumspolitik: Der Apparat des Reichskommissars für die Festigung deutschen Volkstums und andere gesellschaftliche Akteure der veralltäglichten Gewalt," in *Gewalt und Alltag im besetzten Polen 1939–1945*, ed. J. Böhler and S. Lehnstaedt (Osnabrück, 2012), 45–66; Peter Longerich, *Heinrich Himmler: Biographie* (Munich, 2008); Gerhard Wolf, *Ideologie und Herrschaftsrationalität: Nationalsozialistische*

Germanisierungspolitik in Polen (Hamburg, 2012); Isabel Heinemann, "Wissenschaft und Homogenisierungsplanungen für Osteuropa: Konrad Meyer, der 'Generalplan Ost' und die DFG," in *Wissenschaft, Planung, Vertreibung: Neuordnungskonzepte und Umsiedlungspolitik im 20. Jahrhundert* (Beiträge zur Geschichte der Deutschen Forschungsgemeinschaft, vol. 1), ed. P. Wagner and I. Heinemann (Stuttgart, 2006), 45–72.

12   For more on this procedure, see Heinemann, *Rasse*.

13   Hofmann was named head of the RuSHA as of 9 July 1940 "for the duration of the war": "Schreiben des RFSS an Otto Hofmann," 17 July 1940, BArch BDC, SSO Otto Hofmann.

14   "Briefentwurf Himmlers an Otto Hofmann," 12 March 1943; "Niederschrift Himmlers über eine Besprechung mit Otto Hofmann," 13 March 1943, BArch BDC, SSO Otto Hofmann.

15   "Briefentwurf Himmlers an Otto Hofmann," 12 March 1943; "Niederschrift Himmlers über eine Besprechung mit Otto Hofmann," 13 March 1943; Führers decree, 20 April 1943. "Telegramm Hofmanns an den RFSS über Dienstantritt zum 21 April 1943," 22 April 1943; "Schreiben des RFSS an Hofmann," 29 September 1943, BArch BDC SSO Otto Hofmann.

16   Himmler to the HSSPF Südwest, 29 November 1944, BArch BDC SSO Otto Hofmann.

17   "Beförderung durch Adolf Hitler," 21 June 1943, BArch BDC SSO Otto Hofmann.

18   "Ernennung durch Adolf Hitler," 20 June 1944, BArch BDC SSO Otto Hofmann.

19   "Dankesschreiben Hofmanns an Himmler," 31 December 1944, BArch BDC SSO Otto Hofmann.

20   "Eidesstattliche Erklärung Hofmanns," 19 June 1947, IfZ ZS-797-65.

21   "Stellungnahme des Führers des SS-Abschnittes XVI, SS-Oberf. Harnys," 19 March 1935; "Stellungnahme des Führers des SS-OA Nordwest, SS-Gruf. Jeckeln," 23 March 1935, BArch BDC SSO Otto Hofmann.

22   "Meldung Hofmanns an den Führer der SS-Gruppe Süd, SS-Gruf. Jeckeln," 12 June 1933, BArch BDC SSO Otto Hofmann.

23   "Verweis des RFSS vom 22. August 1934: Vernehmung Hofmanns," 9 May 1934; "Gnadengesuch Hofmanns vom 17. Oktober 1934"; "Ablehnung durch den RFSS mit Schreiben vom 10. Dezember 1934." See also the entire record of the investigation proceedings in Hofmann's personal file, BArch BDC SSO Otto Hofmann.

24   Letter from Otto Hofmann to the Wehrbezirkskommando Berlin VI, Abteilung Luftwaffe, 11 August 1939, BArch BDC SSO Otto Hofmann.

25   "Briefentwurf Himmlers an Otto Hofmann," 12 March 1943; letter from Otto Hofmann to the RFSS, 20 March 1943; letter from Hofmann to the Chief of RuSHA, 14 December 1943; letter from Hofmann to the RFSS, 18 January 1945, BArch BDC Otto Hofmann.

26   See Heinemann, *Rasse*.

27   "Der Chef des RuSHA, gez. Otto Hofmann, an den SS-Ogruf. Heißmeyer," 25 September 1942, BArch NS 2/82.

28 See for instance the correspondence in Hofmann's and the other SS leaders' personal SS files, BArch BDC, SSO Otto Hofmann; SSO Richard Hildebrandt.

29 Staatsarchiv Nürnberg, PS-709.

30 Although *The New York Times* mistakenly wrote "Philipp Hoffmann," there is no doubt that Otto Hofmann was implied. "Nazi Jewish Files Found," *The New York Times*, 21 August 1945. Reprinted in Kampe and Klein, *Wannsee-Konferenz*, 61.

31 "Heydrich an Hofmann über Maßnahmen zur Senkung der Geburtenrate der Polen," 3 May 1941, BArch NS 2/68. "Heydrich an Hofmann über rassische Musterungen von Angehörigen der DVL," 26 May 1941, AGK 167/41. Entry in Himmler's diary of 20 March 1941: "Himmler, Heydrich, Hofmann und andere hohe Funktionäre aus Partei und SS besuchen gemeinsam die Umsiedlungs-Ausstellung 'Planung und Aufbau im Osten' in Berlin." *Der Dienstkalender Heinrich Himmlers 1941/42*, (Hamburg, 1999), 135.

32 "Brief RFSS/RKF an die Mitglieder des Obersten Prüfungshofes für Volkszugehörigkeitsfragen," 14 April 1942, BArch NS 2/80.

33 "Protokoll der Besprechung über die Endlösung der Judenfrage," 20 January 1942. Reprinted in Peter Klein, *Die Wannsee-Konferenz vom 20. Januar 1942: Analyse und Dokumentation* (Berlin, 1995), 47.

34 "Protokoll," 51. In a letter to Himmler of 24 April 1942, Hofmann explained that he had arranged with Heydrich to "send e.g. a staff member of the Race Office to Hungary when the time comes, to study the Jewish question there especially." Hofmann to RFSS, 24 April 1941, BArch NS 2/58.

35 According to the census of 17 May 1939, 71,126 "first-degree Mischlinge" and 41,456 "second-degree Mischlinge" lived in Germany. Statistik des Deutschen Reiches, vol. 552, Die Bevölkerung des Deutschen Reiches nach den Ergebnissen der Volkszählung von 1939, no. 4: Die Juden und jüdischen Mischlinge im Deutschen Reich, Berlin 1944. Cit. from Beate Meyer, *"Jüdische Mischlinge": Rassenpolitik und Verfolgungserfahrung 1933–1945* (Hamburg, 1999), 162.

36 "Protokoll," 51.

37 "Protokoll," 52, 54–55.

38 The judges hearing the case against the staff of the Foreign Ministry, the so-called Wilhelmstraße Trial, also recognized this. "Urteil in Fall XI der Nürnberger Nachfolgeprozesse," BArch All. Proz. 1, LVI Z/2, 515.

39 "Protokoll," 52.

40 "Protokoll," 55. On Stuckart, see the chapter in this volume by Hans-Christian Jasch.

41 On 6 March 1942, the representatives were two SS leaders from the Race Office of the RuSHA, SS Hauptsturmführer Preusch and SS Obersturmführer Dr Hans Georg Grohmann; on 24 October 1942, Preusch again, accompanied by head of the Race Office, SS Obersturmführer Georg Harders. "Besprechungsniederschrift über die am 6. März 1942 im RSHA, Referat IV B 4 stattgefundene Besprechung über die Endlösung der Judenfrage." Robert M. W. Kempner, *Eichmann und Komplizen* (Zurich, Stuttgart and Vienna, 1961), unpag. Letter from Stuckart to Freisler, Klopfer,

Neumann, Luther, Meyer, Heydrich, and Hofmann, 16 March 1942; doc. no. NG-2586-I. "Zusammenfassung der Konferenz vom 27 October 1942," doc. no. NG-2586-M. "Sitzungsprotokoll mit einem Schreiben des Referats IV B 4, geh. Rs., an den Gesandschaftsrat Dr Klingenfuß im AA," 3 November 1942, reprinted in: Kempner, *Eichmann und Komplizen,* unpag.

42 "Besprechungsniederschrift über die am 6. März 1942 im RSHA, Referat IV B 4 stattgefundene Besprechung über die Endlösung der Judenfrage," reprinted in Kempner, *Eichmann und Komplizen,* unpag.

43 See Klein, *Wannsee-Konferenz,* 58–61.

44 Letter from the RuSHA-Chiefs, signed SS-Gruf. Otto Hofmann, to the RFSS on 17. März 1943 about the "Final Solution on the Mischling Question," BArch NS 19/1049.

45 "Gutachten Schultz'," 18 January 1943 "zur rassebiologischen Beurteilung der 'jüdischen Mischlinge II. Grades,'" BArch NS 19/1047; letter from the RFSS to the Reichsleiter Martin Bormann, 22 May 1943; "Rundschreiben des Leiters der Partei-Kanzlei, 22. August 1943 über die Bewertung der Erbanlagen von jüdischen Mischlingen 2. Grades bei ihrer politischen Beurteilung durch die Partei," BArch NS 19/1047. The same letter was sent on 3 September 1943 to the RuSHA and the RSHA.

46 For example, through admission restrictions to schools, forced labor etc. See J. Noakes, "The Development of Nazi policy towards the German-Jewish 'Mischlinge', 1933–1945," *Leo Baeck Institute Yearbook* 34 (1989): 348–52. See also Raul Hilberg, *Die Vernichtung der europäischen Juden,* 3 vols. (Frankfurt am Main, 1990–1992), vol. 2, 444–45.

47 Indictment: Count One—Crimes Against Humanity, TWC, vol. IV, 2, 669–70.

48 The woman was Inge Viermetz of the Lebensborn e.V. association. The case files along with the documents of the prosecutors and defense are held in Staatsarchiv Nürnberg, with a copy in BArch, All. Proz. 1, Rep. 501; an excerpt from the case files is reproduced in TWC, vol. 4.2 and 5.1. On the Nuremberg follow-up trials, see Priemel and Stiller, *NMT;* on case VIII, see also my article, 100–26.

49 Prosecution Otto Hofmann, Opening Statement of the Prosecution, BArch All. Proz. 1, XXXXIV, Rep. 501, Be 3, 69–81. Indictment: Count One—Crimes Against Humanity, TWC, vol. IVm 2, 669–70.

50 "Eröffnungsrede für den Angeklagten Otto Hofmann vor dem Militärtribunal I in Nürnberg im Fall 8 gegen Greifelt und andere. Gehalten von Dr Otfried Schwarz, Verteidger," BArch All. Proz. 1, XXXXIV, Rep. 501, J 1, 29.

51 Koehl, *RKFDV;* Hans Buchheim, "Rechtsstellung und Organisation des Reichskommissars für die Festigung deutschen Volkstums," in *Gutachten des Instituts für Zeitgeschichte,* ed. Institut für Zeitgeschichte (Munich, 1958), vol. 1, 239–79; Michael H. Kater, *Das "Ahnenerbe" der SS 1935–1945: Ein Beitrag zur Kulturpolitik des Dritten Reiches,* 4th ed. (Munich, 2001); Georg Lilienthal, *Der Lebensborn e.V. Ein Instrument nationalsozialistischer Rassenpolitik* (Forschungen zur neueren Medizin- und Biologiegeschichte, vol. 1) (Stuttgart and New York , 1985).

52 See his witness statements during trial in: BArch All. Proz. I, XXXXIV, Rep. 501. R-3271, R-3274.

53 "Geschichte und Aufgaben des Rasse- und Siedlungshauptamtes SS. Ein Leitfaden für unsere Verteidiger," BArch, All. Proz. 1, XXXXIV, Rep. 501, C 5.

54 "Geschichte und Aufgaben des Rasse- und Siedlungshauptamtes SS. Ein Leitfaden für unsere Verteidiger," BArch, All. Proz. 1, XXXXIV, Rep. 501, C 5, 22.

55 "Eröffnungsstatement für Otto Hofmann," BArch, All. Proz. 1, XXXXIV, Rep. 501, J1. 23–24.

56 "Vernehmung Otto Hofmann durch Larry Wolf," 20 May 1947, IfZ ZS-797-30, 31–32.

57 See Heinemann, "Otto Hofmann."

58 See Closing Brief of the Prosecution on the Organization of the Race- and Settlement Main Office, BArch All Proz. 1, Rep. 501, XXXIV, Be 47, 124–28.

59. "Urteil gegen den Angeklagten Otto Hofmann," BArch All Proz. 1, XXXXIV, Rep. 501, S 1, 141.

60 "Urteil gegen den Angeklagten Otto Hofmann," 130. Opinion and Judgement, TWC, vol. V, 152.

61 On the connection between the murder and resettlement of the Jews and the Nazis' Germanization policy, see Götz Aly, *"Endlösung": Völkerverschiebung und der Mord an den europäischen Juden* (Frankfurt am Main, 1995).

62 See Heinemann, *Rasse*.

63 Among other counts, these preliminary investigations concerned Otto Hofmann's activity as head of the RuSHA and as HSSPF Südwest. "Vorermittlungsverfahren gegen Angehörige der SS wegen Mordes im Konzentrationslager Natzweiler," AR-Z 33/61; "Vorermittlungsverfahren gegen die Angehörigen des Rasse- und Siedlungshauptmat der SS," AR 122/65; "Vorermittlungsverfahren gegen die ehemaligen Höheren SS- und Polizeiführer der SS," AR 1501/65; "Ermittlungen der Staatsanwaltschaft Berlin gegen Teilnehmer der Wannsee-Konferenz," AR 72/82.

64 See the records of Hofmann's interrogations of 17 April 1962, ZSt. AR-Z 33/61; of 27 April 1965, ZSt. AR 1501/65; of 10 November 1966, ZSt. AR 1501/65 and AR 122/65.

65 ZSt. 419 AR-Z 33/61, Staatsanwaltschaft Hechingen 1 Js 4288/59 and 1 Js 6069/60. Staatsanwaltschaft Heilbronn 1 Js 6 247/1959, "wegen Beihilfe zum Mord. Einstellungsverfügung," 27 September 1961.

66 ZSt. 415 AR 269/82. Staatsanwaltschaft Stuttgart 7 Js 497/82, "Strafanzeige gegen die Teilnehmer der Wannsee-Konferenz wegen Völkermordes. Einstellungsverfügung vom 30. September 1982."

67 See, for example, the statement of reasons for the order to stop proceedings by Staatsanwaltschaft beim Landgericht Heilbronn of 27 September 1961, signed Dr Lorenz, 1 JS 6 247/59.

68 "Vernehmung Hofmanns durch das LKA Ludwigsburg," 10 November 1966, ZSt. AR 122/65.

69 "Bericht des LKA Ludwigsburg an die ZSt.," 11 November 1966. ZSt. AR 122/65.

70 Notice from the Künzelsau (Hofmann's last place of residence) registry office to the Central Office of the State Justice Administrations in
Ludwigsbrug of 6 August 1984. Entry in the Bad Mergentheim register of
deaths Reg. Nr. 623/1982. ZSt. Personenkartei Otto Hofmann.

71 On this specific type of perpetrator (younger and more established than
the "uncompromising generation"), see Ulrich Herbert, *Best: Biographische
Studien über Radikalismus, Weltanschauung und Vernunft 1903–1989* (Bonn,
1996), 42–50; also Michael Wildt, *Die Generation des Unbedingten: Das
Führungskorps des Reichssicherheitshauptamtes* (Hamburg, 2002), 847–71.

Bibliography

Aly, Götz. *"Endlösung": Völkerverschiebung und der Mord an den europäischen
Juden.* Frankfurt am Main: S. Fischer, 1995. [English: *"Final Solution": Nazi
Population Policy and the Murder of the European Jews.* New York: Oxford
University Press, 1999.]

Buchheim, Hans. "Rechtsstellung und Organisation des Reichskommissars
für die Festigung deutschen Volkstums." In *Gutachten des Instituts für
Zeitgeschichte*, edited by Institut für Zeitgeschichte, 239–79. Munich: Institut
für Zeitgeschichte, 1958.

Der Dienstkalender Heinrich Himmlers 1941/42. Edited by Peter Witte et al.
Hamburg: Christians, 1999.

Heinemann, Isabel. *"Rasse, Siedlung, deutsches Blut": Das Rasse- und Siedlungshauptamt der SS und die rassenpolitische Neuordnung Europas.* Göttingen:
Wallstein, 2003.

———. "Wissenschaft und Homogenisierungsplanungen für Osteuropa: Konrad
Meyer, der 'Generalplan Ost' und die DFG." In *Wissenschaft, Planung,
Vertreibung: Neuordnungskonzepte und Umsiedlungspolitik im 20. Jahrhundert*,
edited by P. Wagner and I. Heinemann, 45–72. Stuttgart: Steiner, 2006.

———. "Otto Hofmann und das Rasse- und Siedlungshauptamt: Die 'Lösung
der Judenfrage' als Element der rassenpolitischen Neuordnung Europas."
In *Die Wannsee-Konferenz am 20. Januar 1942: Dokumente, Forschungsstand,
Kontroversen*, edited by N. Kampe and P. Klein, 323–40. Cologne: Böhlau,
2013.

Herbert, Ulrich. *Best: Biographische Studien über Radikalismus, Weltanschauung
und Vernunft 1903–1989.* Bonn: Dietz, 1996.

Hilberg, Raul. *Die Vernichtung der europäischen Juden.* Frankfurt am Main:
Fischer-Taschenbuch-Verlag, 1990–1992. [English: *The Destruction of the
European Jews.* 4th ed. New York: Holmes & Meier, 1985.]

Kampe, N. and P. Klein, ed. *Die Wannsee-Konferenz am 20. Januar 1942: Dokumente,
Forschungsstand, Kontroversen.* Cologne, Weimar and Vienna: Böhlau, 2013.

Kater, Michael H. *Das "Ahnenerbe" der SS 1935–1945: Ein Beitrag zur Kulturpolitik
des Dritten Reiches.* Munich: Oldenbourg, 2001.

Kempner, Robert M. W. *Eichmann und Komplizen.* Zurich, Stuttgart and Vienna:
Europaverlag, 1961.

Klein, Peter. *Die Wannsee-Konferenz vom 20. Januar 1942: Analyse und Dokumentation.* Berlin: Edition Hentrich, 1995.

Koehl, Robert L. *RKFDV: German Resettlement and Population Policy 1939–1945: A History of the Reich Commission for the Strengthening of Germandom.* Cambridge, MA: Oxford University Press, 1957.

Lilienthal, Georg. *Der Lebensborn e.V. Ein Instrument nationalsozialistischer Rassenpolitik.* Stuttgart and New York: Fischer-Taschenbuch-Verlag, 1985.

Longerich, Peter. *Heinrich Himmler: Biographie.* Munich: Siedler, 2008. [English: *Heinrich Himmler: A Life,.* Oxford and New York: Oxford University Press, 2012.]

Meyer, Beate. *"Jüdische Mischlinge": Rassenpolitik und Verfolgungserfahrung 1933–1945.* Hamburg: Dölling und Galitz, 1999.

Noakes, J. "The Development of Nazi Policy towards the German-Jewish 'Mischlinge', 1933–1945." *Leo Baeck Institute Yearbook* 34 (1989): 291–354.

Priemel, K.C. and A. Stiller, ed. *NMT: Die Nürnberger Militärtribunale zwischen Geschichte, Gerechtigkeit und Rechtschöpfung.* Hamburg: Hamburger Edition, 2013.

Stiller, Alexa. "Gewalt und Alltag der Volkstumspolitik: Der Apparat des Reichskommissars für die Festigung deutschen Volkstums und andere gesellschaftliche Akteure der veralltäglichten Gewalt." In *Gewalt und Alltag im besetzten Polen 1939–1945,* edited by J. Böhler and S. Lehnstaedt, 45–66. Osnabrück: Fibre, 2012.

———. *Germanisierung und Gewalt: Nationalsozialistische Politik in den annektierten Gebieten 1939–1945.* Basel, 2015.

Wildt, Michael. *Die Generation des Unbedingten: Das Führungskorps des Reichssicherheitshauptamtes.* Hamburg: Hamburger Edition, 2002. [English: *An Uncompromising Generation: The Nazi Leadership of the Reich Security Main Office.* Madison, WI: University of Wisconsin Press, 2009.]

———. "'Eine neue Ordnung der ethnographischen Verhältnisse': Hitlers Reichstagsrede vom 6. Oktober 1939," *Zeithistorische Forschungen/Studies in Contemporary History* 3, no. 1 (2006): 129–37. Retrieved 6 October 2016 from http://www.zeithistorische-forschungen.de/1-2006/id=4759

Wolf, Gerhard. *Ideologie und Herrschaftsrationalität: Nationalsozialistische Germanisierungspolitik in Polen.* Hamburg: Hamburger Edition, 2012.

5

RUDOLF LANGE

Reich Main Security Office

Academic, Ideological Warrior
and Mass Murderer

Peter Klein

Illustration 5.1 Unknown photographer,
undated (1942), BArch Berlin, R 9361-
III/113921 (formerly BDC).

The youngest participant at the meeting of State Secretaries was 31-year-old Rudolf Erwin Lange, who held a doctorate in law. He would not live to see his 36th birthday. On 23 February 1945 the SS-Standartenführer, who was decorated with a German Cross in gold as well as two Iron Crosses, died defending the Posen/Poznań Fortress against the advancing Red Army. In early February 1945, Heinrich Himmler and Ernst Kaltenbrunner had agreed that this spirited SS leader who wholeheartedly embraced Nazism deserved to be decorated. "It is first and foremost thanks to his courage and fortitude that the SiPo-SD garrison in Posen, which had fallen into enemy hands, could be reclaimed. In the course of combat seven enemy tanks at the fortress were destroyed."[1] Such bravery had been accompanied by other deeds required of Nazi leaders, from arresting numerous "saboteurs and deserters" to locating and returning dispersed soldiers in order to boost the strength of Germany's defending forces. Lange suffered serious injuries in the Battle of Posen/Poznań, which was militarily hopeless, and either died during the Red Army's assault on the fortified position or committed suicide.[2] He is buried in the military cemetery in Poznań-Miłostowo.

Studies and Professional Ambitions

Clearly Rudolf Lange was to all intents and purposes an ideal Gestapo officer of the so-called "war youth generation." Born on 18 April 1910 to a railway construction supervisor in the village of Weisswasser in Saxony, he spent his early childhood in Treptow in Western Pomerania. When he was ten, he and his Protestant parents moved to Stassfurt in the Prussian administrative district of Magdeburg. During the Weimar Republic's years of crisis and the short period of deceptive recovery in the mid 1920s he attended the local grammar school, graduating in spring 1928. He went on to study law at the universities of Jena, Munich and Halle. In summer 1942, by which time his social standing had risen considerably, he had little to say about his years as a student, although he felt compelled to mention that before Hitler seized power he had not belonged to any political party or association.[3] Barely twenty, he had joined Germania, the anti-democratic and anti-Semitic traditional Jena fencing fraternity. His social life as a student revolved around the club, leaving Lange's face covered with dueling scars and a case of gonorrhea that was treated in 1930. His loyalty to Germania survived its conver- sion into a National Socialist German Students' League fraternity in 1936, when he joined its old boys' network.

In July 1932 Lange passed his first state law exams and began his doctorate on "the instruction right of the employer." He was working as a trainee lawyer with judicial authorities in Stassfurt, Magdeburg, Torgau and Naumburg when the Nazis seized power in clear breach of the rule of law and basic democratic principles. In summer 1933 he spent five weeks doing voluntary labor service in Gartz on the River Oder, joining the SA in November. The fact that Lange, a fledgling lawyer aged just twenty-four, volunteered for these duties indicates strong support for the new regime. Lange never joined the Association of National Socialist German Legal Professionals (which later became the National Socialist Association of German Legal Professionals), apparently preferring to play his part with voluntary labor service and membership of the youthful, activist Storm Troopers. Youthful enthusi- asm counted for more than a professional Nazi association, which may have struck working-class Lange as exclusive, academic and elitist. He completed the last stage of his traineeship with the state police in Halle in late 1935, gaining experience in administrative matters before sitting his final exams. By August 1936, having been awarded his Ph.D. and passed his second state exams, he was employed on a trial basis by the Berlin Gestapo. By September 1936, Rudolf Lange appeared to have found his vocation. The following months saw him switch his focus to the career with the SS and police that was beckoning. He left the SA, either when he joined the Gestapo or in September 1937— records are contradictory[4]—and at the same time joined the SS; he left the church and applied to become a member of the Nazi Party. On 24

August 1937 Lange learned, during his two-month military service as a gunner with the II Flak Regiment 12 in Berlin-Lankwitz, that he had been made a government assistant lawyer and therefore a civil servant. This God-fearing civil servant, party member and experienced potential Wehrmacht leader was made an SS officer with the Security Service of the SS-Reichsführer (SD) on 30 September 1937, aged just twenty-seven. Now all he had to do was prove himself.[5]

Gestapo Adviser in Vienna

He got his chance in May 1938, when he was appointed head of Division II B at Gestapo headquarters in Vienna, which had been set up two months earlier and was not yet fully operational. It soon became the largest Gestapo headquarters in the Greater German Reich in terms of staff.[6] Lange's executive responsibilities included "fighting the enemy," specifically Jews and the church. Until June 1939 he therefore occupied a key position in the persecution of Viennese and Austrian Jews. Given the exceptionally brutal arrests of political enemies and Jews taking place at this time, as well as the atrocities committed against Jews during the November pogrom and ongoing state-organized looting of Jewish assets, it is easy enough to form a picture of Rudolf Lange's activities, even in the absence of complete records.[7]

The head of the Vienna Israelite Community soon made his acquaintance. On 19 July 1938, before the Central Agency for Jewish Emigration had been founded, Joseph Löwenherz was summoned to Lange's office for a meeting with senior senate councilor Otto Schaufler and other city officials. "Herr Dr Lange began the meeting by announcing a plan to treat Jewish patients in fund and city hospitals separately because Aryan nurses cannot be expected to care for Jewish patients." Lange forced Löwenherz to prepare for this separation to take place immediately.[8] Around the same time, Lange was involved in the organization of an illegal transport of some 400 Viennese Jews to Palestine. He and Adolf Eichmann were reportedly both present at the station when a train departed.[9] However, their plan to smuggle Jews into Palestine via Greece, Rhodes and Cyprus failed. Such plans met with the disapproval of Walther Stahlecker, SD leader of the Danube Higher Section and inspector with the security police (SiPo) and the Vienna SD and, as such, of higher-rank than Eichmann and Lange. On 12 August 1938 he informed the Reich Main Security Office that "on 9.7.1938 a steamship set sail to Palestine with some 400 . . . Jewish émigrés on board. This emigration to Palestine was illegal."[10] Shortly after the founding of the

Central Agency for Jewish Emigration, when it emerged that the journey had been aborted and the Jewish passengers were bound for Vienna, Lange was instructed to house them in a police jail in Karajangasse and to secure legal papers for their emigration to Palestine.[11] On 20 January 1942, when Reinhard Heydrich gave a retrospective account of the "legal" efforts to speed up Jewish emigration, Eichmann and Lange believed they could recall their association in Vienna a few years earlier.[12]

The only personal information available on Lange during his years in Vienna was provided by his successor, Dr Karl Ebner. When faced with a potential death sentence at the People's Court in Vienna in 1948, Ebner sought to prove he had shown humanity as a Gestapo officer.[13] He described Lange as a deeply ideological and ambitious division head who had radicalized his colleagues and turned them into committed Nazis, saying "it cost me at least six months to counterbalance the radical ideas that had been pumped into people and which had partly fallen on fertile ground."[14] It did not help Lange's reputation that the former deputy director of the Vienna Gestapo was obviously trying to cover his own tracks. In fact his statement attested to a Nazi conception of duty shared by both men.

A Senior Official

Lange was next appointed deputy head of the Gestapo regional headquarters in Stuttgart and then a senior civil servant. But his spell in Swabia was short-lived. Less than a year later he moved on to the Gestapo offices in Weimar and Erfurt, and was promoted to the rank of SS-Hauptsturmführer and deputy head of the office of the inspector of the SiPo and the SD in military district IX in Kassel. His next career leap came on 17 September 1940. Just thirty years old, the SS-Hauptsturmführer was appointed deputy to Walter Blume, the 34-year-old head of the Gestapo regional headquarters in Berlin.[15] Lange, who was a bachelor, rented a room at Waitzstraße 10, Charlottenburg, from the Sieg family. After six months in the Reich capital he was promoted to the rank of SS-Sturmbannführer and was sent to Pretzsch on the River Elbe as part of plans to strategically deploy SiPo and SD taskforces. Here he joined Taskforce A, led by his former boss Walther Stahlecker, and was among the 1,000 SiPo troops deployed in the assault on the Soviet Union. His job was to develop Gestapo and criminal police procedures (Division IV/V). Later, Lange maintained he also led a so-called subdetachment, a highly mobile, small squadron assembled as required, which would visit villages off the routes taken by the taskforces and special units and follow orders to murder ideological enemies and potential opponents of the Nazis—that is, Jews, communists, deserters, unidentified persons and anyone else deemed suspicious.[16]

Riga

The Latvian city of Riga was the largest and most important city along the route taken by Taskforce A in the three Baltic countries. On 1 July 1941 the squadron arrived in Latvia on the heels of the Wehrmacht and began security policing. The city initially served as a base for Stahlecker's taskforce. The routes and tasks of the various units and mobile detachments were coordinated from there and from the base in Kaunas. As the taskforce's point man for combating enemies, Lange was responsible for carrying out the persecution of official enemies of the Nazis. In cooperation with the Latvian auxiliary police led by Viktors Arājs, the squadron was quick to set up a local detachment that followed anti-Semitic and anti-communist commands to the letter but also pursued the Nazis' goals by frequently seizing the initiative.[17] The terror that reigned in Riga in late summer 1941 had less to do with pogroms than with an auxiliary police body that willingly followed German orders. Arājs' police and the SiPo set up their own prisons. Random arrests, kidnaps and murders became commonplace.[18] This did not change in the wake of the introduction of German civil administration on 17 July 1941, when a further occupation organization also gained influence. Riga now served as the headquarters of the Reich Commissioner for the Occupied Eastern Territories, the General Commissioner in Latvia and the German mayor. Himmler, meanwhile, installed his own regional representative, the Higher SS and Police Leader (HSSPF).[19]

The fact that Lange managed to insinuate himself into Berlin's favor despite this considerably higher-ranking company attests to his efficiency in knowing when and when not to follow orders. For example, he sided with his superior Reinhard Heydrich when the civil administration was reluctant to make Riga the point of arrival for deported German Jews. No sooner had Heydrich, as head of the Reich Main Security Office (RSHA), selected Riga, Minsk and Kaunas as potential points of arrival for German, Austrian and Czech Jews and Stahlecker had informed Otto-Heinrich Drechsler, the General Commissioner of Latvia on 11 October 1941, than Rudolf Lange began implementing the decision against the wishes of the civil administration. He chose a site for what would become the Salaspils camp, but when the construction of the camp for deported and Latvian Jews took longer than he expected, Lange had deportees on board the first four trains interred in an improvised camp on the former estate of Jungfernhof. These dilapidated buildings leased by the SS and police were located close to the Šķirotava railway station and the Salaspils concentration camp, which was still under construction. It served as provisional housing for some 4,000 people from Nuremberg, Stuttgart, Vienna and Hamburg.[20]

In Berlin's eyes, Rudolf Lange was an SS-Sturmbannführer who did not shy away from conflict and was capable of thinking on his feet. But the young lawyer from Weißwasser also instinctively knew exactly how far he could go. When Friedrich Jeckeln, newly appointed HSSPF, made an autonomous decision to execute Jews deported to Kaunas and deployed the regional commander of the SiPo-SD (KdS) and his men to carry out the executions, the KdS men in Riga refused to cooperate. Jeckeln also planned to execute Jews from Berlin who arrived in Riga-Šķirotava on 31 November 1941. Jeckeln implemented this autonomous decision to murder 1,053 Jews from Berlin, but Lange's men only arrived on the scene after the mass murder had taken place and Latvian Jews from the ghetto were being executed to make room for Jews arriving from Germany.[21] The local SiPo were also present on 8 December 1941 when the second massacre of the remaining Latvian Jews in the ghetto took place. Two days later, the regional commissioner protested when the first German transports reached the ghetto. But Lange was undeterred.

. A copy of a letter to Lange from Streckenbach, dated 3 December 1941, is proof of his promotion to KdS in the Latvia General Region.[22] The RSHA praised his vigorous commitment. In a résumé he penned shortly thereafter, Lange maintained he had been appointed KdS in February 1942. This discrepancy cannot be explained.[23] The minutes of the Wannsee Conference list and describe the participants, and state that on 20 January 1942 Lange was appointed KdS in the Latvia General Region. It is easy to understand why he was invited to the meeting rather than Stahlecker, whose position meant he had little to do with the deportations. Not only could Lange refer to the mass murders of Jews carried out by his taskforce, he also effectively stood for the practical enforcement of Heydrich's unilateral control of the "Final Solution to the Jewish Question" when necessary and against all previous resistance on the part of the Occupation's civilian administration, as represented by Meyer and Georg Leibbrandt. Moreover, the KdS for Latvia had only just returned from the trenches of Biķernieki outside Riga. There, with the help of Arājs' men, almost all the Jews who had been

Illustration 5.2 This snapshot of Lange was also found in the files of the SS race and settlement main office. It shows him on a cold, sunny day standing at the edge of a forest, in front of a car with the driver's door open. Unknown photographer, (1942), BArch Berlin R 9361-III/113921 (formerly BDC).

transported four days earlier from the Theresienstadt ghetto were murdered on 19 January 1942. Given that Lange was aware of the trouble encountered by HSSPF Jeckeln after the murder of the Berlin Jews on 30 November, and the fact that the Bohemian Jews from Theresienstadt fell under Heydrich's protectorate, it can be assumed with hindsight that the massacre of deported Jews would never have taken place without the approval of the Wannsee Conference host. Lange's presence at the meeting reflected a new departure in the Nazis' policy of annihilation. While the mass murder of deportees, whether they could be used as labor or not, was not officially sanctioned on 30 November 1941, by the eve of the Wannsee Conference it was.[24]

Rudolf Lange and the Holocaust

If Lange is to be viewed not merely as Heydrich's henchman in the execution of deportees to Riga and light shed on his role as a perpetrator of mass murder as a step towards the "Final Solution," it is necessary to take into account the actions of the KdS in the immediate aftermath of the Wannsee Conference. Lange now knew that his superiors' strategy extended beyond Latvia; he had been privy to discussions that are deeply shocking in hindsight, and he was aware of what was expected of regional decision-makers such as himself. By the time he returned to Riga after the conference, two transports carrying Jews from Berlin and Saxony were on their way to the city, while two transports from Vienna, one from Berlin and one from Dortmund were expected. On 30 or 31 January Lange ordered the mass execution of Jews brought to Riga whether from Berlin or Vienna. On Saturday 31 January, page two of the *Deutsche Zeitung im Ostland*, available in kiosks in Riga, ran a column with the headline "This War Will Destroy Jewry." Rudolf Lange saw the printed affirmation of his actions in another newspaper article quoting a speech given by Hitler the previous day.[25] On 5 February the Nazis sifted out people they considered fit for work from the ghetto where Jews from Vienna and Berlin lived.[26]

In the same week, a progress report was drawn up in Lange's office that illustrates how the KdS obfuscated the mass murders taking place under his supervision:

> Transports of Jews from the Reich have been arriving at frequent intervals since December 1941. A total of 19,000 Jews from the Reich and the Protectorate have been deported to Riga. Some of them are housed in a ghetto, others in a provisional reception camp and others in a newly-built barracks near Riga. A minority of these Jews from the German Reich are fit for work. 70–80% of them are women and children, or old men who are unfit for work. Mortality rates among evacuated Jews are climbing steadily. In particular old and frail Jews lack the strength to survive the exceptionally harsh winter. In order to fight the risk of epidemic in the ghetto and the two camps, a number of Jews afflicted with contagious diseases (dysentery and diphtheria) were singled out and executed. Their removal was disguised as a transferal to a Jewish home for the sick and elderly, to prevent word of the executions reaching local Jews and Jews in the Reich. A number of mentally ill Jews were dealt with in the same way. All Jews housed in barracks that have already been built continue to work on the construction of new barracks for Jews from the Reich. By spring, the camp will be ready to house all the evacuated Jews who survive the winter.[27]

Lange alluded in his report to the subject of the Wannsee Conference, referring to those Jews who were fit to work and those who were not, even though he masked the murder of the latter as deaths induced by frailty. In spring 1942 the execution of Jews unfit for work spiraled into further organized local massacres of deportees in the Jungfernhof concentration camp and the ghetto. The so-called "Dünamünde Aktion" resulted in the murder of 4,800 people. On Lange's orders, they were trucked to the Biķernieki woods, shot, and buried in previously dug mass graves. The KdS in Riga was following the strategy described in the Wannsee Conference Minutes to the letter.[28]

After the war, many survivors of the deportations gave statements in criminal proceedings or wrote their memoirs. They all remembered the notorious SS-Sturmbannführer Rudolf Lange. He made frequent, unannounced appearances in the Jungfernhof concentration camp, the ghetto and at the Salaspils construction site, where he would inevitably claim more Jewish victims. From the SiPo's point of view, Lange was a highly capable regional leader who dealt efficiently with the arrival of transports at the Riga-Sķirotava station and supervised the Salaspils camp. When he immediately and ruthlessly punished the slightest mis-demeanor with death he was merely acting in accordance with his superiors' barbaric expectations. Whenever he visited Jews laboring outside the ghettos, their lives were in danger.

In general, Jews put to work were a nuisance to the KdS. But the shortage of labor in the Latvian capital meant Lange could not afford to murder Jews fit for work, who moreover spoke German. The KdS was repeatedly obliged to make tactical concessions to the civilian admin-istration. Every day, several thousand Jews left the ghetto to work in forced labor projects. Some of them were even "in barracks" at their place of work, a development approved by Lange. Many Jews even worked in the KdS headquarters.[29] When another 5,000 people from Berlin and Theresienstadt were deported to Riga between 15 August and 26 October 1942, Lange did not even find living quarters for them. Whether they were fit for work or not, they were removed from the authority of the civil administration and taken by bus or truck to the Biķernieki woods and shot. Only a few survived because they were deployed, without the involvement of the civil administration, as labor for the SiPo in Riga or the Todt Organization.[30]

During this period, when transports were arriving in Riga, Bohemian Jews were being murdered and countless individuals executed, Lange fell in love with a shorthand and foreign-languages secretary who worked in Division III of Stahlecker's office. In autumn 1941 Lange began encountering her in the office on a regular basis. Else Schmitt had previously worked at the migration office in Litzmannstadt (present-day Łódź), celebrating her twenty-first birthday shortly after arriving in Riga. She gave notice in May 1942 and the couple married shortly thereafter at the registry office in Mannheim, her hometown.[31] The new-lyweds moved into a new home on Kronwaldring 7, opposite an idyllic park in Riga. When Schmitt gave birth to a daughter in July 1943, Lange was locked in a serious dispute with the civil labor administration over Jewish forced labor. By this point, Himmler had decided to redefine the inhabitants of the Riga Ghetto as concentration camp inmates, thereby securing control of their fate. The KdS therefore sabotaged the well-established routine that saw Jews sent to work every day by the labor administration. Lange put a stop to these convoys and had the forced laborers brought back to the ghetto, maintaining that he needed to review whether their labor made a vital contribution to the war. In the meantime, a small concentration camp was set up in Kaiserwald near Riga, to where Jews from the Riga Ghetto were briefly sent, so that they could then be registered as concentration camp inmates.[32] Once again, Lange prevailed over the civil administration. Although a new father himself, Lange had all the children and elderly people remaining in the ghetto deported to Auschwitz on 2 November 1943, while their families continued to be sent to the last sites still supplied with forced labor from the ghetto.[33]

The exact date on which Rudolf Lange, now promoted to the rank of SS-Obersturmbannführer, left Riga cannot be established. His final task was to shut down "Aktion 1005." The operation used prisoners to exhume mass graves and burn the bodies of victims of German atrocities before the Soviet army arrived. Together with the SS economic officer, Lange also removed the many subordinate commands of the Kaiserwald concentration camp.[34] He began serving as KdS in Posen/Poznań on 1 January 1945 and was promoted to the rank of SS-Standartenführer later that month. In January and February 1945, violent fighting raged in Posen/Poznań, which had been declared a stronghold and was the chief city of the Reichsgau Wartheland. Rudolf Lange died during the final assault on the citadel in the heart of Posen/Poznań. He fulfilled his duties until his last breath, the blood of thousands on his hands.

Summary

There are no surviving personal documents pertaining to this member of the Heydrich elite.[35] It is not clear if he was born into an anti-Semitic family or whether his views were formed by his social life at university. His entry into the SA and voluntary labor service reflect the beginnings of identification with National Socialism, but little more. Alone, these decisions do not mark him out as a perpetrator. However, his subsequent career rise was meteoric, unimpeded by even the slightest disciplinary problem. He was twice sent to offices—in Vienna in 1938 and in Riga in 1941—that were still in their infancy and where he took the initiative when it came to furthering the Nazi agenda. In retrospect, the pressure he exerted on Jews in Vienna to emigrate at any cost and his massacre of Latvian Jews and Jews deported from the Reich seem like a test of the limits of his power. What means ultimately served the end? Was even illegal emigration acceptable? Was a dispute with the civil administration a risk worth taking in order to secure the arrival of transports, come what may? What did his refusal to participate in the execution of Berlin Jews on 30 November 1941 mean for his career, given that it had been approved by Himmler's SS and police commands. Despite his limited experience, Rudolf Lange was faced with such questions when he was in his late twenties and early thirties. He rose to every challenge, as was expected by the Reich Security Main Office of a man in his office. In this respect, Rudolf Lange was a typical example of the proactive, well-educated young men that the SiPo sought to recruit, trusting in the motivating effect of their identification with the organization. When he was appointed KdS Riga, Rudolf Lange believed he was making decisions that would be seen as correct and welcome, which was why he later found himself attending a high-level meeting where he was able to slot his own regional activities into the context of a Europe-wide strategy. The Wannsee Conference was the most significant recorded meeting of Lange's career.

Peter Klein is a historian and Professor of Holocaust Studies at Touro College Berlin. His research focuses on the history of Nazi persecution of the Jews and the Holocaust in Eastern Europe and on biographical research on German politicians between 1900 and 1950. His recent publications include: "Die Wannsee-Konferenz als Echo auf die gefallene Entscheidung zur Ermordung der europäischen Juden." In *Die Wannsee-Konferenz am 20. Januar 1942: Dokumente, Forschungsstand, Kontroversen*, edited by N. Kampe and P. Klein. Weimar, Cologne, Vienna, 2013; "Behördenbeamte oder Gefolgschaftsmitglieder? Arthur Greisers Personalpolitik in Posen." In *Gewalt und Alltag im besetzten Polen 1939–1945*, edited by J. Böhler and S. Lehnstaedt. Osnabrück, 2012; and "Massentötung durch Giftgas im Vernichtungslager Chełmno." In *Neue Studien zu nationalsozialistischen Massentötungen durch Giftgas: Historische Bedeutung, technische Entwicklung, revisionistische Leugnung* (= Schriftenreihe der Stiftung Brandenburgische Gedenkstätten Bd. 29), edited by G. Morsch and B. Perz. Berlin, 2011.

Notes

1   All biographical background data on Dr Rudolf Lange and his career are based on his personal file in the Bundesarchiv Berlin BAB, SSO-Rudolf Lange and on the Rasse and Siedlungshauptamt (R.u.S.) questionnaire relating to his marriage application. Evidence from those files is adduced only in quotes. Proposal to award the German Cross in gold, 5 February

1945, signed by Kaltenbrunner with the note "RFSS einverstanden" of 6 February1945, BAB, SSO-Rudolf Lange, unpag.

2 Sworn declarations of the Ic of the Fortress Commander, Hans-Kurt Moser dated 21 April 1948 and 15 March 1951, 1 Js 9/65 LG Berlin, Dossier Lange.

3 Handwritten CV 1942, Rudolf Lange, BAB, SSO-Rudolf Lange, unpag.

4 Andrej Angrick and Peter Klein, *Die "Endlösung" in Riga: Ausbeutung und Vernichtung 1941–1944* (Darmstadt, 2006), 54, footnote 27.

5 Handwritten CV for the R.u.S. questionnaire, undated, BAB SSO-Rudolf Lange.

6 Franz Weisz, "Personell vor allem ein 'ständestaatlicher' Polizeikörper: Die Gestapo in Österreich," in *Die Gestapo: Mythos und Realität,* ed. G. Paul and K-M. Mallmann (Darmstadt, 1995), 439–62; Thomas Mang, *"Gestapo-Leitstelle Wien—Mein Name ist Huber"* (Münster, 2003). Comprehensive: Franz Weisz, "Die Geheime Staatspolizei, Staatspolizeileitstelle Wien 1938–1945: Arbeitsweise und personale Belange" (Ph.D. dissertation, University of Vienna, 1991).

7 The eyewitness reports are impressive, in: B. Barkow, R. Gross and M. Lenarz, ed., *Novemberpogrom 1938: Die Augenzeugenberichte der Wiener Library, London* (Frankfurt am Main, 2008), 711–876. Perpetrator perspectives: Brigitte Bailer and Wolfgang Form, ed., "Deutsche Geschichte im 20. Jahrhundert online: Tagesrapporte der Gestapoleitstelle Wien 1938–1945," *Deutsche Geschichte im 20. Jahrhundert Online.* This Data bank has about 750 daily reports of the approximately 820 sent that can be fully downloaded.

8 Note on the file, Vienna, 29 July 1938, in: Leo Baeck Institute Archive, Joseph Loewenherz Collection (AR 250559), folder 1, sheets 30–32.

9 Doron Rabinovici, *Instanzen der Ohnmacht: Wien 1938–1945: Der Weg zum Judenrat* (Frankfurt am Main, 2000), 118–19.

10 Communication from the SD-Führer of the SS-Oberabschnitts Donau, II 112, to the Sicherheitshauptamt, Abt. II 112, Berlin, concerning Emigrants' organization in Wien, dated 12 August 1938, RGVA 500-1-675, sheets 4–5.

11 From the SD-Hauptamt to the SD-Führer of the OA Donau, II 112, concerning the illegal transport of Jews to Palestine, signed by Hagen, dated 12 September 1938, RGVA 500-1-675, sheet 36.

12 Minutes of the Conference, 3.

13 Vienna District Court, see 12i Vr. 1223/47./. Dr Karl Ebner. On Ebner see Thomas Mang, *Die Unperson: Karl Ebner, Judenreferent der Gestapo Wien: Eine Täterbiographie* (Bozen, 2013).

14 Quote from Werner L. Schubert, *Der Judenmörder von Riga: eine Dokumentation zum Leben des Dr Rudolf Erwin Lange, geboren am 18. April 1910 in Weißwasser O.L. Kreis Rothenburg, Teilnehmer der Wannseekonferenz am 20. Januar 1042, Stabschef der Einsatzgruppe A und Kommandeur der Sicherheitspolizei und des SD in Lettland 1941–1944* (Beiträge zur Stadtgeschichte des Fördervereins Glasmuseum e.V.) (Weißwasser, 2001), 12.

15 On Blume as a representaive of the Führungskorps of the Reichssicherheitshauptamtes see Michael Wildt, *Die Generation des Unbedingten: Das Führungskorps des Reichssicherheitshauptamtes* (Hamburg, 2002), 180–84.

16 Helmut Krausnick and Hans-Heinrich Wilhelm, *Die Truppe des Weltanschauungskrieges: Die Einsatzgruppen der Sicherheitspolizei und des SD 1938–1942* (Stuttgart, 1981), 281–637. Handwritten CV for the R.u.S. questionnaire, undated, BAB SSO-Rudolf Lange.

17 Margers Vestermanis, "Der lettische Anteil an der 'Endlösung': Versuch einer Antwort," in *Die Schatten der Vergangenheit: Impulse zur Historisierung des Nationalsozialismus*, ed. U. Backes, E. Jesse and R. Zitelmann (Berlin, 1990), 426–49; Andrew Ezergailis, *The Holocaust in Latvia 1941–1944: The Missing Center* (Riga, 1996), 173–202; Björn Michael Felder, *Lettland im Zweiten Weltkrieg: Zwischen sowjetischen und deutschen Besatzern 1940–1946* (Paderborn, 2009), 203–28. More recently in: R. Plavnieks, "The Pursuit, Prosecution, and Punishment of the Latvian War Criminal Viktors Arājs," *Yad Vashem Studies* 40, no. 2 (2012): 81–106.

18 Angrick and Klein, *"Endlösung" in Riga*, 63–137.

19 On the setting up of and friction between the individual occupation organizations, see Sven Jüngerkes, *Deutsche Besatzungsverwaltung in Lettland 1941–1945: Eine Kommunikations- und Kulturgeschichte nationalsozialistischer Organisationen* (Constance, 2010).

20 On the numbers and names of those deported to that camp, see Wolfgang Scheffler and Diana Schulle, *Buch der Erinnerung: Die ins Baltikum deportierten deutschen, österreichischen und tschechoslowakischen Juden*, 2 vols. (Munich, 2003). For the departure and arrival dates of those transports, see Alfred Gottwaldt and Diana Schulle, *Die "Judendeportationen" aus dem Deutschen Reich von 1941–1945: Eine kommentierte Chronologie* (Wiesbaden, 2005), 110–36, 248–59. On Jungfernhof, see Wolfgang Scheffler, "Das Schicksal der in die baltischen Staaten deportierten deutschen österreichischen und tschechoslowakischen Juden 1941–1945: Ein historischer Überblick," in Scheffler and Schulle, *Buch der Erinnerung*, vol. 1, 9–13.

21 Peter Klein, "Die Erlaubnis zum grenzenlosen Massenmord: Das Schicksal der Berliner Juden und die Rolle der Einsatzgruppen bei dem Versuch, Juden als Partisanen 'auszurotten,'" in *Die Wehrmacht: Mythos und Realität*, ed. Rolf-Dieter Müller and Hans-Erich Volkmann (Munich, 1999), 923–47; Christoph Dieckmann, *Deutsche Besatzungspolitik in Litauen 1941–1944* (Göttingen, 2011), vol. 2, 960–67.

22 RFSSuChdDtPol, I A 1 d Nr. 12103/41 g.VO, to SS-Sturmbannführer, Regierungsrat Dr Lange, Riga, 3 December 1941, BAB, SSO-Rudolf Lange.

23 Between 6 and 14 January 1942 there were announcements in Latvian newspapers of the destruction of the village of Audrini by SS-Obersturmbannführer Eduard Strauch. KdS Lettland, see *Rēzeknes Ziņas*, no. 4 (14 January 1942): 1; *Daugavas Vestnesis*, no. 4 (6 January 1942): 1. handwritten CV annexed to R.u.S. questionnaire, undated, BAB SSO-Rudolf Lange.

24 Peter Klein, "Die Wannsee-Konferenz als Echo auf die gefallene Entscheidung zur Ermordung der europäischen Juden," in *Wannsee-Konferenz am 20. Januar 1942: Dokumente, Forschungsstand, Kontroversen*, ed. N. Kampe and P. Klein (Cologne, 2013), 197–198

25 *Deutsche Zeitung im Ostland* 2, no. 31 (31 January 1942): 2. Very similarly, in the high-circulation *Feldzeitung*, which was printed in Riga, on page two the headline above all the columns was: "Dieses Krieg wird die Vernichtung des Judentums sein," *Feldzeitung* 368 (Saturday 3 January 1942): 2.

26 Angrick and Klein, *"Endlösung" in Riga*, 237–45.

27 Undated Camp Report "Judentum", LVVA Riga, P 1026-1-3, sheets 262–64, printed in: A. Angrick et al., ed., *Deutsche Besatzungsherrschaft in der UdSSR 1941–1945: Dokumente der Einsatzgruppen in der Sowjetunion*, vol. 2 (Veröffentlichungen der Forschungsstelle Ludwigsburg der Universität Stuttgart, vol. 23) (Darmstadt, 2013), doc. 98, 257–58.

28 Angrick and Klein, *"Endlösung" in Riga*, 338–45.

29 Angrick and Klein, *"Endlösung" in Riga*, 276–97, 323–37.

30 Angrick and Klein, *"Endlösung" in Riga*, 378–90.

31 R.u.S questionnaire and handwritten CV of Else Schmitt, BAB, SSO-Rudolf Lange, unpag.

32 Franziska Jahn, "Riga-Kaiserwald: Stammlager," in *Der Ort des Terrors: Geschichte der nationalsozialistischen Konzentrationslager, vol. 8: Riga. Warschau. Kaunas. Vaivara. Plaszów. Klooga. Chelmo. Belzec. Treblinka. Sobibor*, ed. W. Benz and B. Distel (Munich, 2008), 17–63.

33 Gertrude Schneider, *Reise in den Tod: Deutsche Juden in Riga 1941–1944* (Berlin, 2006), 154–55.

34 Angrick and Klein, *"Endlösung" in Riga*, 391–405, 416–46.

35 Jens Banach, *Heydrichs Elite: Das Führerkorps der Sicherheitspolizei und des SD 1936–1945* (Paderborn, 1998).

Bibliography

Angrick, Andrej and Peter Klein. *Die "Endlösung" in Riga: Ausbeutung und Vernichtung 1941–1944*. Darmstadt: WBG, 2006. [English: *The "Final Solution" in Riga: Exploitation and Annihilation, 1941–1944*. New York: Berghahn Books, 2009.]

Angrick, A., K-M. Mallmann, J. Matthäus and M. Cüppers, ed. *Deutsche Besatzungsherrschaft in der UdSSR 1941–1945: Dokumente der Einsatzgruppen in der Sowjetunion*. Darmstadt: WBG, 2013.

Bailer, B. and W. Form (ed.). n.d. "Deutsche Geschichte im 20. Jahrhundert online: Tagesrapporte der Gestapoleitstelle Wien 1938–1945," *Deutsche Geschichte im 20. Jahrhundert Online*. Retrieved 13 March 2017 from https://www.degruyter.com/staticfiles/pdfs/produktpraesentationen/Tagesrapporte%20der%20Gestapoleitstelle%20Wien%201938-1945.pdf

Banach, Jens. *Heydrichs Elite: Das Führerkorps der Sicherheitspolizei und des SD 1936–1945*. Paderborn: Schöningh, 2002 [first published 1998].

Barkow, B., R. Gross and M. Lenarz, ed. *Novemberpogrom 1938: Die Augenzeugenberichte der Wiener Library, London*. Frankfurt am Main: Jüdischer Verlag im Suhrkamp Verlag, 2008.

Dieckmann, Christoph. *Deutsche Besatzungspolitik in Litauen 1941–1944*. Göttingen: Wallstein, 2011.

Ezergailis, Andrew. *The Holocaust in Latvia 1941–1944: The Missing Center*. Riga: Historical Institut of Latvia, 1996.

Felder, Björn Michael. *Lettland im Zweiten Weltkrieg: Zwischen sowjetischen und deutschen Besatzern 1940–1946*. Paderborn: Schöningh, 2009.

Gottwaldt, Alfred and Diana Schulle. *Die "Judendeportationen" aus dem Deutschen Reich von 1941–1945: Eine kommentierte Chronologie*. Wiesbaden: Marixverlag, 2005.

Jahn, Franziska. "Riga-Kaiserwald: Stammlager." In *Der Ort des Terrors: Geschichte der nationalsozialistischen Konzentrationslager*, edited by W. Benz and B. Distel, 65–87. Munich: C.H. Beck, 2008.

Jüngerkes, Sven. *Deutsche Besatzungsverwaltung in Lettland 1941–1945: Eine Kommunikations- und Kulturgeschichte nationalsozialistischer Organisationen*. Constance: UVK Verlagsgesellschaft, 2010.

Klein, Peter. "Die Erlaubnis zum grenzenlosen Massenmord: Das Schicksal der Berliner Juden und die Rolle der Einsatzgruppen bei dem Versuch, Juden als Partisanen 'auszurotten.'" In *Die Wehrmacht: Mythos und Realität*, edited by R-D. Müller and H-E. Volkmann, 923–47. Munich: Oldenbourg, 1999.

———. "Die Wannsee-Konferenz als Echo auf die gefallene Entscheidung zur Ermordung der europäischen Juden." In *Die Wannsee-Konferenz am 20. Januar 1942: Dokumente, Forschungsstand, Kontroversen*, edited by N. Kampe and P. Klein, 182–201. Cologne: Böhlau, 2013.

Krausnick, Helmut and Hans-Heinrich Wilhelm. *Die Truppe des Weltanschauungskrieges: Die Einsatzgruppen der Sicherheitspolizei und des SD 1938–1942*. Stuttgart: Deutsche Verlags-Anstalt, 1981.

Mang, Thomas. *"Gestapo-Leitstelle Wien—Mein Name ist Huber"*. Münster: Lit, 2003.

———. *Die Unperson: Karl Ebner, Judenreferent der Gestapo Wien: Eine Täterbiographie*. Bozen: Edition Raetia, 2013.

Plavnieks, R. "The Pursuit, Prosecution, and Punishment of the Latvian War Criminal Viktors Arājs." *Yad Vashem Studies* 40, no. 2 (2012): 81–106.

Rabinovici, Doron. *Instanzen der Ohnmacht: Wien 1938–1945: Der Weg zum Judenrat*, Frankfurt am Main: Jüdischer Verlag im Suhrkamp-Verlag, 2000. [English: *Eichmann's Jews: The Jewish Administration of Holocaust Vienna, 1938–1945*. Cambridge and Malden, MA: Polity, 2011.]

Scheffler, Wolfgang. "Das Schicksal der in die baltischen Staaten deportierten deutschen österreichischen und tschechoslowakischen Juden 1941–1945: Ein historischer Überblick." In *Buch der Erinnerung: Die ins Baltikum deportierten deutschen, österreichischen und tschechoslowakischen Juden*, edited by W. Scheffler and D. Schulle, 9–13. Munich: Saur, 2003.

Scheffler, Wolfgang and Diana Schulle. *Buch der Erinnerung: Die ins Baltikum deportierten deutschen, österreichischen und tschechoslowakischen Juden*. Munich: Saur, 2003. [English: *The German, Austrian and Czechoslovakian Jews Deported to the Baltic States*. Berlin and Boston, MA: De Gruyter Saur, 2011.]

Schneider, Gertrude. *Reise in den Tod: Deutsche Juden in Riga 1941–1944*. Berlin: Edition Hentrich, 2006. [English: *Journey into Terror: Story of the Riga Ghetto*. Westport, CT and London: Praeger, 2001.]

Schubert, Werner. *Der Judenmörder von Riga: eine Dokumentation zum Leben des Dr Rudolf Erwin Lange, geboren am 18. April 1910 in Weißwasser O.L. Kreis Rothenburg, Teilnehmer der Wannseekonferenz am 20. Januar 1042, Stabschef der Einsatzgruppe A und Kommandeur der Sicherheitspolizei und des SD in Lettland 1941–1944.* Weißwasser: Förderverein Glasmuseum e.V., 2001.

Vestermanis, Margers. "Der lettische Anteil an der 'Endlösung': Versuch einer Antwort." In *Die Schatten der Vergangenheit: Impulse zur Historisierung des Nationalsozialismus,* edited by U. Backes, E. Jesse, and R. Zitelmann, 426–49. Berlin: Propyläen, 1990.

Weisz, Franz. "Die Geheime Staatspolizei, Staatspolizeileitstelle Wien 1938–1945: Arbeitsweise und personale Belange." Ph.D. dissertation. University of Vienna, 1991.

———. "Personell vor allem ein 'ständestaatlicher' Polizeikörper: Die Gestapo in Österreich." In *Die Gestapo: Mythos und Realität,* edited by G. Paul and K-M. Mallmann, 439–62. Darmstadt: WBG, 1995.

Wildt, Michael. *Die Generation des Unbedingten: Das Führungskorps des Reichssicherheitshauptamtes.* Hamburg: Hamburger Edition, 2002. [English: *An Uncompromising Generation: The Nazi Leadership of the Reich Security Main Office.* Madison, WI: University of Wisconsin Press, 2009.]

6

HEINRICH MÜLLER

Reich Main Security Office

The Archetypal Desktop
Perpetrator

Johannes Tuchel

Illustration 6.1 Unknown photographer,
undated (after November 1941), BArch
Berlin, SSO 286 6400030508 (formerly
BDC).

> It's inevitable that where wood is chopped, splinters will fall, and it's
> obvious that the enemy will always try to exaggerate the measures taken
> against him with the aim of rousing sympathy and averting them. The Jew,
> in particular, has consistently tried to evade his deserved fate, ever since
> I assailed the task of ousting this enemy, by sending anonymous letters to
> almost all the authorities on Reich territory.
> —Letter written by Müller, 28 February 1942

This distinctly anti-Semitic letter was Heinrich Müller's response
to Foreign Ministry Undersecretary Martin Luther's mention of an
anonymous complaint about the "Solution of the Jewish Question in
Warthegau" shortly after the Wannsee Conference. Müller, chief of the
Gestapo, was the closest associate of Reinhard Heydrich and his successor, Ernst Kaltenbrunner, and the superior of Adolf Eichmann. His
nickname "Gestapo Müller" was practically synonymous with the institution he ran. He played a leading or coordinating role in many Nazi
atrocities.[1] They ranged from the murder campaigns conducted by the
Einsatzgruppen special units in the occupied territories of the Soviet
Union and the killing of Soviet prisoners of war[2] to the mass murder
of the European Jews. On the day of the Wannsee Conference, he lin-
gered after the talks, smoking, drinking cognac and relaxing around the
fire with Heydrich and Eichmann. The overview below aims to trace
Müller's participation in the persecution of Jews in Germany and the
mass murder of Jews in Europe before and after the Wannsee Conference.

Childhood and Youth

Müller was born on 28 April 1900 in Munich, the son of Alois Müller, a Catholic administrator and trained gardener who worked as a medical corps sergeant and police officer, and his wife Anna, née Schreindl.[3] Although he changed schools several times, he was regarded as a good pupil.[4] In 1914 he became an apprentice airplane mechanic at Bayerische Flugzeugwerke. On completion of his apprenticeship in June 1917 he volunteered for the Imperial German Army Air Service.[5] In April 1918 Müller was transferred to the Western Front and in 1919 he was demobilized, a highly decorated sergeant with a war injury.

In late 1919 Müller successfully applied for a job with the Munich police authority. In the next four years, he worked his way up the administration, becoming junior assistant *(Kanzleigehilfe)* on 1 May 1921, administrative assistant *(Kanzleiassistent)* on 1 August 1922, and promoted to police assistant *(Polizeiassistent)* on 1 April 1923.[6] He was ambitious: in March 1923 he belatedly took his high-school diploma at Munich's König Ludwig county middle school as an external student, the best in his year.[7] At this point, he worked for the political police in Department VI a, in charge of investigating political crimes such as high treason and breaches of The Law for the Defense of the Republic *(Republikschutzgesetz)* throughout Bavaria.[8] Müller's main tasks were observing and combating the communist movement.[9] In April 1929 he passed the test to enter the middle grade civil service with one of the best results in his year and was promoted to police secretary *(Polizeisekretär)*.

Heading the Gestapo

Along with over ninety percent of the staff of the Munich police authority's political department, Müller was transferred to the Bavarian Political Police (BPP) when it was founded.[10] On 1 May 1933, he was appointed senior police secretary *(Polizeiobersekretär)*, and on 16 November 1933, police inspector *(Kriminalinspektor)*, by Bavarian police chief Reinhard Heydrich.[11] In April 1934, shortly after joining the SS as Sturmführer, Müller, along with his colleagues Anton Dunkern, Reinhard Flesch, Franz Josef Huber and Josef Meisinger, followed Heydrich to Berlin, where he had been made head of the Prussian Gestapo authority. Flesch and Müller were placed in charge of Subsection II 1 (ideological opponents). Müller was responsible for the bureaus II 1 A (communist and Marxist movement, director: Müller), II 1 C (reaction, opposition, Austrian affairs, director: Huber), II 1 D (preventive detention, director: Tesmer) and II 1 H (Nazi Party affairs and organization, director: Meisinger).[12] Thus the contours of Müller's future field of activity began to emerge.

From the new Gestapo headquarters in Berlin, Müller helped coordinate the Nazis' murder campaign of 30 June 1934,[13] targeting SA leaders and political opponents, and was subsequently made SS-Obersturmführer as of 4 July 1934. On 1 November 1934, he was promoted to senior police inspector *(Kriminaloberinspektor)*.[14] In fall 1935, Flesch was made head of Subsection II 1 and Müller—now SS-Hauptsturmführer, like Flesch—became his deputy while retaining responsibility for bureau II 1 A (communist and Marxist movement and subsidiary movements).[15] In late 1935, Flesch was transferred back to Bavaria and Müller took over his job in Berlin. In summer 1936, by which time Müller had risen to SS-Sturmbannführer, he was appointed head of Gestapo Department II in the course of the reorganization of the German police system.[16]

His career was not even significantly impeded by a positively venomous assessment made by the Munich-Upper Bavarian Gau leadership in early 1937:[17]

> In terms of political sympathies, he belongs to the national camp, shifting between the German National People's Party and the Bavarian People's Party. But he was in no way a National Socialist. As far as Müller's character traits go, we regard them in an even more negative light than his political ones. He is ruthless, blatantly uses his elbows, and while always seeking to highlight his own efficiency, he also unashamedly takes the credit for others' achievements.[18]

In June 1937 Müller was promoted to the rank of senior councilor and specialist in criminal investigation *(Oberregierungs- und Kriminalrat)*. This, too, was just a stepping stone: on 20 April 1939 he became SS-Oberführer; on 1 July 1939 he was appointed Reichskriminaldirektor; in December 1940, police major general and SS-Brigadeführer and on 29 November 1941, SS-Gruppenführer. This rapid advancement is evidence of Müller's key position in the Nazi machinery of persecution.

In June 1924 Müller married Sophie Dischner from Pasing in Munich, who was two months older than he. Her father, Otto Dischner, publisher of the local newspaper *Der Würmtalbote*, was considered by the Nazi Party to be a supporter of the Bavarian People's Party.[19] For some years after their marriage, Müller lived in Pasing. After moving to Berlin in 1934, he initially lived in a guest house, "Pension am Knie," at Hardenberg Straße 37, Charlottenburg. He finally took an apartment, at

Illustration 6.2 In November 1939 Heinrich Himmler met with close associates to discuss the progress of investigations against Georg Elser, who had attempted to assassinate Hitler in a Munich beer hall on 8 November 1939. This photo of the meeting was published in the Nazi Party newspaper *Illustrierter Beobachter*. Pictured (from left) are: SS-Obersturmbannführer Franz Josef Huber, Chief of the German Criminal Police SS-Oberführer Arthur Nebe, Reichsführer-SS and Chief of the German Police Heinrich Himmler, SS-Gruppenführer and Chief of the Security Police Reinhard Heydrich, and Gestapo Chief SS-Oberführer Heinrich Müller. Photo by Heinrich Hoffmann, 1939, BArch Koblenz, 183-R98680.

Kühlebornweg 11 in Berlin-Steglitz, in 1938, and his wife and two children—their son, Reinhard, born in 1927, and daughter Elisabeth, born in 1936—left Munich to join him in Berlin. In 1941 the family moved to a house at Cornelius Straße 22 in a respectable middle-class neighborhood in Steglitz. According to Müller's biographer, Seeger, the marriage was fraught with tension.[20] Müller had a long-time affair with a close colleague, *Polizeiobersekretärin* Barbara Helmuth, who had joined the staff of the Munich police headquarters in 1919.[21] This relationship ended in 1939 but in 1940 Müller became romantically involved with Anna Schmid, a secretary for the Reich railways, born in 1913. Sophie Müller, whom Schmid described as a "humble and simple woman, who didn't quite keep pace with her husband's advancement,"[22] knew about both relationships. As the end approached in late 1944, Müller made sure that his family was safe in south Germany; he said a final goodbye to his lover in Berlin in April 1945. Questioned after the war, both women said that Müller had been very attached to his children, especially his son, and had been "down-to-earth" and a "nature-lover." The pictures drawn by former colleagues, who were naturally concerned to cover up their own part in Nazi crimes, were quite different. Franz Josef Huber stated after the war:

> His most prominent characteristic was his thirst for power. He did not allow any insight into his office. He was not capable of true friendship as he was too egocentric . . . Müller was above averagely intelligent, diligent, sober and very reserved. One of his characteristic features was his constantly pursed mouth. He hardly ever came out of his office. He did not have any real pleasures. Even after a little enjoyment, he carried on working in his office. His marriage was troubled. He did not start drinking cognac until the end of the war. He chain-smoked *Brasil* cigars . . . He was not afraid of anyone, not even Heydrich.[23]

Müller's relationship to Nazism was not unambiguous. He did not join the Nazi Party until 1937, and consequently held a very high membership number, 4,583,199.[24] He was, however, known to be fiercely anti-communist. Schmid remembered:

> I didn't have the impression that Müller was a convinced Nazi. I only knew that he completely opposed the communists. I talked to him about that on many occasions. Müller didn't have a very good relationship with Himmler. They didn't like each other. His relationship with Heydrich, on the other hand, was excellent.[25]

Müller's sphere of influence grew steadily. The Gestapo authority, which became Department IV of the newly founded Reich Main Security Office (RSHA) in autumn 1939, coordinated the persecution of political opponents and the racially undesirable throughout Germany.[26] All committals of political prisoners to concentration camps were approved by Müller; all the basic regulations governing political persecution were drafted or issued by his department.[27] In 1936 Müller gained authorization to order the implementation of "intensified interrogations" — in other words, torture[28] — and in autumn 1939, executions without trial.[29] Müller had worked on the third floor of the Gestapo headquarters at Prinz Albrecht Straße 8 in Berlin since 1934.[30] But on 3 February 1945 the building was severely damaged during one of the heaviest air raids Berlin had seen. A temporary workplace was found for Müller in a cabin at Wannsee. He is said to have met delegates from the International Red Cross as late as 20 April 1945 in what is now the

House of the Wannsee Conference memorial site. Müller's subordinate, Eichmann, in contrast, was still centrally based at Kurfürstenstraße 115–116. During his interrogation by the Israeli police in 1961, Eichmann stated that the RSHA chief Kaltenbrunner and the RSHA department heads, including Müller, started holding their lunchtime briefings here in February 1945. In March 1945 Müller moved his entire office there. In spring 1945, this building, later described by Eichmann as a fox's den ("Fuchsbau"), stood amidst the ruins of Berlin, surrounded by makeshift bunkers and tunnels.

A Lynchpin in the Murder of the Jews

As Heydrich's closet associate, Müller was involved in all measures toward disenfranchising and persecuting Jews by 1938 at the latest. To his confidante Anna Schmid he even claimed to have initiated certain anti-Jewish measures. According to her, it had been his idea "that Jews had to wear the yellow star."[31] Records show that the idea of labeling Jews, or at least those in Berlin, was discussed at a large meeting in the Reich Propaganda Ministry on 15 August 1941. The specialist on Jewish affairs of the Reich Ministry of the Interior, Bernhard Lösener, noted:

> On the question of labelling, the speaker for the Reich Main Security Office, Sturmbannführer Eichmann, stated that an application in this respect had been recently sent to the Reichsmarschall. He had sent it back with the comment that the Führer had to decide on the matter. For this reason, the Reich Main Security Office amended the application; it will be directed to Reichsleiter Bormann so that he can inform the Führer.[32]

Four days later, on 19 August 1941, Goebbels enforced the labeling of Jews. Eichmann's account suggests that the initiative did indeed come from the RSHA and the head of the relevant department, Müller.

While the SD (Sicherheitsdienst des Reichsführers-SS) was in charge of preparing the persecution of German Jews until 1938,[33] Eichmann, the leading specialist in the field, assumed a managing role as early as spring 1938 while head of the Central Office for Jewish Emigration in Vienna.[34] There had been indications even earlier that Jewish policy would increasingly involve executive and repressive measures, implemented by the Gestapo, and later Department IV of the Reich Main Security Office. The November pogrom in 1938 was a key turning point. The Security Police used the pogrom, initiated by Goebbels and carried out across the country by regional branches of the Nazi Party and the SA, for its own aims. Although the SS leadership had not been previously informed, Müller told all branches of the Gestapo about the "campaigns against Jews and especially their synagogues" by 11.55 P.M. on 9 November 1938, giving the order: "Prepare for the arrest of 20–30,000 Jews in the Reich. Select wealthy Jews. Further instructions will be issued in the course of the night."[35] The aim of the action was clear: to intensify the pressure on German Jews to emigrate. On 10 November 1938, Müller reported that the concentration camps Dachau, Buchenwald and Sachsenhausen had each admitted an additional 10,000 prisoners, and requested information on the planned transports.[36] He also let it be known that "the arrest campaign will be continued by the State Police" after the "protest actions" had stopped.[37] Heydrich finally gave the order to end the campaign in the evening of 16 November 1938 and stipulated conditions for releasing the Jewish prisoners.[38]

A few days after the pogrom, on 12 November 1938, talks were held in the Ministry of Aviation, chaired by Göring, concerning plans to strip the Jews of further rights.[39] Müller most probably attended this meeting along with Heydrich, and Eichmann from Vienna. The latter had impressed Heydrich by devising a "Viennese model" for expelling Jews from Germany's sphere of influence while heading the Central Office for Jewish Emigration in Vienna,[40] as he pointed out to Göring at several points during the meeting. Consequently, on 24 January 1939, Göring authorized the installation of a "Reich Central Office for Jewish Emigration" in the Ministry of the Interior, to be directed by the chief of the Security Police. Thus Göring placed Heydrich in charge of the emigration of German Jews, and made him henceforth chief policy-maker on the "Jewish Question."[41] In July 1941, Göring delegated further powers to Heydrich.

On 11 February 1939, Heydrich informed the Reich ministries and regional governments that "SS-Standartenführer Oberregierungsrat Müller" had been appointed executive director of the "Reich Office of Jewish Emigration."[42] This established the Himmler-Heydrich-Müller-Eichmann chain of command within the SS and RSHA apparatus that was to be instrumental in the mass murder of the European Jews. After Germany invaded Poland and the RSHA was set up, it was these men who pushed ahead with radicalizing Nazi policy on Jews.

After July 1939, Müller no longer participated in setting up Einsatzgruppen units for the German invasion of Poland; responsibility was handed to Werner Best.[43] On 21 September 1939, Heydrich informed the department heads at the RSHA, including Müller, and the leaders of the Einsatzgruppen, that Jews were to be driven out of Reich territory to Poland within a year: "RFSS Himmler (Reichsführer-SS) will be deployed as settlement commissioner for the East. The deportation of Jews to the foreign Gau, removal across the demarcation line, has been approved by the Führer."[44] A short time later, the representatives of the RSHA presumed to have received orders from Hitler permitting them to "regroup 300,000 impecunious Jews from Germany *(Altreich)* and occupied Austria *(Ostmark)*."[45] On 6 October 1939, Müller charged Eichmann with preparing the "removal" of 70,000 to 80,000 Jews from Katowice and Ostrava across the Vistula, "in order to gain the experience necessary for evacuating large masses."[46] Consequently, some 3,900 Jews were deported in five transports, starting on 18 October 1939, to the area around Nisko on the San River; many of them were chased over the demarcation line into Soviet-occupied territory under gunfire.[47] Just one day later, in a bid to ensure some "central leadership" to the "resettlement and deportation of Poles and Jews into the territory of the future Polish rump state," Müller decreed that "authorization from the local authority must always be presented."[48] He also informed Eichmann that the Oberkommando der Wehrmacht (OKW) "has not forbidden all transports into the Lublin area up to mid-November. It would be possible to fit in a few deportation transports of Jews from Vienna."[49]

In fact, however, it was not possible to carry out any large-scale deportations because of the amount of troops that needed to be transported in the following weeks, as a consequence of which Müller informed all Gestapo authorities on 21 December 1939 that Himmler had "prohibited the deportation of Jews from the Altreich, the Ostmark and the Protectorate into the occupied Polish territories until further notice."[50] Eichmann's special bureau on Kurfürstenstraße, now directly answerable to Müller, was set up the same day[51] to "centrally process the affairs of the Security Police concerning the implementation of evacuations in the Eastern territories" and to coordinate the further deportations.[52] On 12 February 1940, Müller gave the order to "restrict the Jews' freedom of movement in the Reich and group them together in large collecting points" in order to keep them under surveillance.[53]

But the RSHA had to wait to put its grand plans into practice, as Göring put a stop to all deportations until further notice on 23 March 1940.[54] For this reason, Müller still issued "guidelines for the emigration of Jews" as late as 24 April 1940:

> Jewish emigration from Reich territory must continue to be intensively pursued even during the war. The chief of the Security Police and the SD has informed Herr Minister-President Generalfeldmarschall Göring, with whose explicit approval Jewish emigration is being continued, that Jews fit to fight and work should not emigrate to foreign European countries if possible, and not by any means to enemy European countries.

There would be no "evacuation of Jews, whatever their nationality, to the General Government."[55] Nevertheless, the RSHA did not abandon its deportation plans. A memorandum on the "Madagascar Project," concerning the fate of four million Jews living on German territory, sent on 15 August 1940 by a close associate of Eichmann to the Foreign Office, declared that, "the central management [for the Altreich, Sudeten Gaus and new German Gaus in the East] lies in the hands of the Reich Office for Jewish Emigration in Berlin."[56] On 4 August 1941, Müller laid down regulations for the "treatment of Jews of foreign nationality."[57]

During spring and summer 1941 Müller made several visits to the border police academy in Pretzsch, where the Einsatzgruppe special units were being drilled,[58] and in all probability also attended the concluding discussion on 17 June 1941 in the RSHA in Berlin.[59] On 28 June 1941, he declared Department IV A I to be the "central authority for the Russian campaign."[60] A telex of 29 June 1941 to the leaders of the Einsatzgruppen, bearing the letterhead "Head of Dept. IV" but Heydrich's signature, decreed that no steps should be taken to prevent "the autonomous cleansing efforts of anti-communist or anti-Jewish circles." They were, "on the contrary, to be stimulated, intensified if necessary and steered in the right direction, albeit imperceptibly."[61] Hence it is not surprising that the first report of a massacre of Jews in the Memel area, on 1 July 1941, was addressed to Müller.[62] Indeed, on 3 July 1941, Heydrich ordered the installation of a staff of command, and an RSHA campaign information service, to be directed by the Gestapo chief. Müller was to be handed new reports by 9.30 every morning, which he in turn was to pass on.[63] From the start, then, reports on the Einsatzgruppen movements were compiled, and forwarded as "USSR event notifications" *(Ereignismeldungen UdSSR),* under his supervision. The first seven summarized reports of June 1941 were all signed by Müller; he refrained from signing later ones.[64] He even responded to some reports with specific instructions. On 1 August 1941, for instance, he requested "particularly interesting illustrative material," as the Führer was to be "presented with ongoing reports on the work of the Einsatzgruppen in the East."[65] Later that month, when a number of regional commissioners of the civilian occupation regime Reichskommissariat Ostland petitioned to end the campaigns against communists and Jews, Müller ordered "such requests to be declined and immediately reported here."[66] And on 30 August, he informed the leaders of the Einsatzgruppen that "the Chief of the Security Police and the SD asks you, on account of experience previously gained, to prevent groups of observers congregating at mass executions if possible, even if they are officers of the German army."[67] Much of the reporting concerned statistics on fatalities. On 4 July 1942, Müller issued regulations to the Einsatzgruppen for "the number of persons subjected to special treatment during the Security Police's pacification campaigns" to be reported monthly "in order of: 1. Partisans, 2. Communists and functionaries, 3. Jews, 4. Mentally ill, 5. Other Reich-hostile elements, total number, previous total, final total."[68]

With Heydrich appointed Deputy Protector of Bohemia and Moravia in October 1941, Müller's role as a coordinator became even more prominent, as the surviving files show. Once deportations from Germany had started, Himmler issued instructions for "the emigration of Jews to be prevented with immediate effect," although these did not affect the "evacuation campaigns," as Müller reported on 23 October 1941. One day later, Müller issued general regulations for the "conduct of those of German blood toward Jews." Henceforth, "friendly relations with Jews" could lead to imprisonment in a concentration camp: "The Jewish party is in any case to be taken into preventive detention by committal to a concentration camp."[69]

All the links in the Heydrich-Müller-Eichmann chain of command were participants in the Wannsee Conference. The protocol gives no indication of Müller's conduct at the conference, merely that he attended. Yet he played a key role in implementing the plan that Heydrich presented at this meeting. Eichmann later remembered: "While Heydrich was making his introductory remarks I thoroughly scrutinized the others present . . . My own superior, [Gruppenführer] Müller, sat there like a well-behaved schoolboy. With his hands folded in his lap, he looked a picture of humility."[70] Eichmann also described the famous scene after the conference: "I remember how after this 'Wannsee Conference,' Heydrich, Müller and my humble self, sat cozily around a fire . . ., not to talk shop but to unwind after the long, exhausting hours."[71]

Müller was, in Andrej Angrick's view, the "institutional lynchpin" that Heydrich needed to mediate between the practical man Rudolf Lange and the planner Eichmann.[72] Yet Müller was more than that; he supervised and documented the Einsatzgruppen's killing campaigns and, as Eichmann's superior, had the final word on the execution of deportations. And as Angrick points out, it was Müller who supervised the entire course of "Aktion 1005" — the campaign to cover up the traces of the Nazis' mass murder.[73] In fall 1941, he had sent Eichmann to Minsk to observe the executions of Jews there. In January 1942, Eichmann reported back to him about the extermination campaigns using gas vans in the Chełmo/Kulmhof camp. During his later interrogation by Israeli police, he described Müller's reaction to this report:

Müller tended not to say anything. Ever! Not concerning these things or anything else. He was always very reticent and quiet, said only what was necessary. Said yes or no. And when he didn't say either yes or no he tended to say, "Comrade Eichmann. . .," which wasn't yes or no. He didn't say much.[74]

After the Wannsee Conference, Müller issued instructions to deport Jews from Germany. On 15 May 1942, he endorsed the "guidelines on the technical implementation of the evacuation of Jews to Theresienstadt old people's ghetto" with his signature.[75] Less than a week later, he sent the Gestapo authorities throughout the Reich the following urgent message:

> In the course of the Lublin/Izbica evacuation measures, all the evacuation authorities in the Altreich, with a few isolated exceptions, were able to capture the Jews concerned under the guidelines for evacuation. In order to be able to thoroughly exploit all the available accommodation possibilities in the East for further evacuations, I request information of the number of Jews still remaining in your area of responsibility who could still be evacuated under precise observation of the guidelines.[76]

On 16 June 1942, Müller gave orders to deport the relatives of Jewish concentration camp prisoners to the East when the transports were resumed.[77] On 1 July 1942, Müller ordered the closure of all Jewish schools and the deportation of their staff.[78] On the same day, he passed on a notice from the Reich Ministry of Transport that Jews were henceforth prohibited from "using waiting rooms, restaurants and other facilities provided by the transport services."[79]

In a briefing on 23 June 1942,[80] Himmler informed Müller that "all Jews resident in France were to be deported as soon as possible."[81] Müller told Eichmann, who immediately set off for Paris to prepare the transports. Although he regularly reported back to Müller, he kept some things to himself, such as the fact that on 15 July 1942 a deportation train destined for Auschwitz did not leave France as scheduled, allegedly because not enough "stateless Jews" could be found.[82]

Lastly, on 11 August 1942, Müller and Eichmann discussed the deportation of Jews from Romania, which was due to begin in a short time.[83] But this part of the plan announced at the Wannsee Conference had to be abandoned when Marshall Antonescu withdrew his consent. Müller's involvement in detailed planning is evidenced by his letter of assurance in September 1942 to Himmler's chief of staff Wolff that the Jewish workers at the Beskiden oil company would only be deported when replacements could be provided for them.[84]

Müller cooperated closely with the Foreign Office on preparing the deportations of Jews from German-occupied countries.[85] In January

1943, problems arose with the Italian military administration concerning the deportation of foreign Jews from the newly occupied part of France.[86] Müller asked Senior Commander of the Security Police Helmut Knochen for the details. Subsequently, on 25 February 1943, he complained to the Foreign Office that

> the Italians' attitude toward the total European solution has greatly impeded the measures, and even to some extent blocked them, as the governments of all sorts of European countries use our axis partner's standpoint as grounds to excuse themselves. This general attitude of the Italians toward the question we are tackling quite simply frustrates the demand that the Führer has made in all his speeches and proclamations.[87]

In late March 1943, Müller traveled to Rome to seek a settlement "in Germany's interests."[88] But the Inspector General of the Italian police, Lospinoso, managed to evade him. Eventually, on 22 June, Lospinoso talked to Knochen, who informed Müller of the outcome.[89] On 28 June, Knochen announced to Müller that the deportations from France were due to be resumed, as the French government had declared all Jews naturalized after 10 August 1927 to be stateless. Knochen therefore requested "permission to have 250 leaders and men provided on call in the Reich for the duration of ten days."[90] Müller, however, turned the request down due to the shortage of staff at the RSHA.[91]

A note written by legation councilor Eberhard von Thadden demonstrates how closely Müller and the Foreign Office cooperated. Von Thadden visited Müller "as directed" on 16 October 1943 "on the matter of the technical implementation of the Jewish Question in the newly occupied territories." At this meeting, they discussed the situation in Albania, Croatia, the parts of Greece and France previously occupied by Italy, and in Italy. Taking a realistic view of the military circumstances, Müller "was obviously somewhat concerned about the practical implementation of the Führer's order to arrest 8,000 Jews in Rome."[92] Indeed, when the order was carried out in Rome that same day, only around 1,250 Jews were arrested, some 1,000 of whom were deported to Auschwitz two days later. By March 1944 Müller had relayed the order to deport the Hungarian Jews to Eichmann.[93] Starting in May 1944, over 420,000 Jews were deported from Hungary in less than two months; most were murdered in Auschwitz. This "last chapter" of the "Final Solution," then, also occurred with Müller's participation.

In summer 1944, Müller personally led the special task force set up to investigate the failed plot to assassinate Hitler (*Sonderkommission 20. Juli 1944*) and even participated in the interrogations.[94] Consequently he was proposed for decoration in October 1944 on the following grounds: "Owing its unified political and ideological orientation to Müller, the Gestapo must take further considerable credit for the rapid suppression, capture and eradication of the traitors of 20 July 1944 and their followers."[95]

Müller decided to stay in Berlin in April 1945. He met his lover one last time in Kurfürstenstraße on 24 April. Clad in uniform, replete with medals, he appeared "completely official and very composed." He gave her a phial of cyanide and said he "did not have much time and had to get to the Reich Chancellery; Göring had already been taken prisoner."[96]

The End

Müller was seen in the bunker of the Reich Chancellery on the night of 1 to 2 May 1945 by Hitler's chauffeur, Erich Kempka, Hitler's pilot, Hans Baur, and the chief of the Reich Security Service, Johann Rattenhuber. They suggested he flee with them, but Müller dismissed the idea.[97] He spent some hours on the night of 2 May in the company of Hans Krebs and Wilhelm Burgdorf, who had decided to commit suicide. Hitler's adjutant, Otto Günsche, reported: "He [Müller] said he was going to shoot himself in the Reich Chancellery because he did not want to fall into the Russians' hands for anything in the world."[98] Certainly, on the morning of 2 May 1945, he visited the sick bay under the Reich Chancellery together with SS-Obersturmbannführer Schädle.

Soviet troops who occupied the area a short time later found the bodies of Krebs, Burgdorf and Schädle, who had all committed suicide. Müller's body was not among them. Rumors persisted after the war that the Gestapo chief had survived.[99] They were not true. Müller died on 2 May 1945. In August 1945 a corpse in a general's uniform, containing a duty pass bearing the name Heinrich Müller, was found on the grounds of the former Ministry of Aviation.[100] He was buried in the central section of three mass graves on the old Jewish Cemetery on Große Hamburger Straße.[101] Müller, one of the chief offenders responsible for the Nazis' atrocities, now lies in this cemetery along with over 2,700 war victims and over 3,000 Jews buried here between 1672 and 1827.

Summary

Müller's biographer Andreas Seeger described his subject as follows:

> Heinrich Müller always linked his own advancement to the needs of the regime. For those in power, his career was the surest guarantee of loyalty. He was the mundane kind of functionary who performed his duties as a police official in a monomaniacal way. A police expert from humble beginnings, his character equipped him with the means to rise up from the mass of capable officials. When it came to persecuting the "enemies of the Reich" he had neither sympathy nor scruples. Misanthropic, but not sadistic, cynical without deriving any personal satisfaction from killing, he was a product of authoritarian traditions and became one of the Nazi regime's key henchmen in its state-orchestrated crimes.[102]

Yet Heinrich Müller was not merely a henchman; he was an actor, a perpetrator, a mass murderer. Mass shootings of Jews in the occupied territories of the Soviet Union, deportations from Germany and Europe, the removal of evidence—due to his position, Müller played a leading role in all of these. Nevertheless, beyond his ambition and thirst for power, his motives—especially his ideological convictions—remain largely in the dark still today.

Johannes Tuchel studied political science in Hamburg and Berlin. Between 1988 and 1991 he worked on the staff of the Berlin Senate. Since 1991 he has been Director of the German Resistance Memorial Center and Chief Executive Officer of the German Resistance Memorial Center Foundation (German Resistance Memorial Center, Ploetzensee Memorial, Otto Weidt's Workshop for the Blind, and the Silent Heroes Memorial). Since 1992 he has held a teaching post at the Otto Suhr Political Sciences Institute at the Free University of Berlin, and was promoted to the status of Privatdozent in 2001. Since 2008 he has served as adjunct Professor for Political Sciences at the Free University of Berlin, and since 2011 as visiting professor at the Touro College Berlin.

Notes

1 See the hitherto best biography of Heinrich Müller: Andreas Seeger, *Gestapo-Müller: Die Karriere eines Schreibtischtäters* (Berlin, 1996), 86 et seq. For a summary, see: Andreas Seeger, "Heinrich Müller: Der Gestapo-Chef," in *Die SS: Elite unter dem Totenkopf*, ed. R. Smelser and E. Syring (Paderborn, 2003), 346–63. The work by Joachim Bornschein, *Gestapochef*

Heinrich Müller: Technokrat des Terrors (Leipzig, 2004), does not provide any more insights than Seeger's book. There are few personal documents on Müller in the files on SS leaders. More in-depth information on Müller can be found in the case files of the Zentrale Stelle Ludwigsburg (415 AR 422/60) and the Staatsanwaltschaft Berlin (1 Js 1/68 RSHA). The very small estate of Müller's wife Sophie, held in the IfZ (ED 404), is not accessible until the end of 2026.

2   See Reinhard Otto, *Wehrmacht, Gestapo und sowjetische Kriegsgefangene im deutschen Reichsgebiet 1941/42* (Munich, 1998), 143 et seq.

3   CV Heinrich Müller, 11 August 1937, BArch, former BDC, SSO Heinrich Müller.

4   See Seeger, *Gestapo-Müller*, 12.

5   CV Heinrich Müller, 11 August 1937, BArch, former BDC, SSO Heinrich Müller.

6   This information is taken from "Vorschlag zur Ernennung Müllers zum Generalmajor der Polizei," BArch, R 2/12150, fol. 135 et seq.

7   "Aussage von Heinrich Zanker," 22 February 1954, BArch, B 162/3233, sheet 5.

8   On the remit of Department VI, see Martin Faatz, *Vom Staatsschutz zum Gestapo-Terror: Politische Polizei in Bayern in der Endphase der Weimarer Republik und der Anfangsphase der nationalsozialistischen Diktatur* (Würzburg, 1995), 51.

9   See Seeger, *Gestapo-Müller*, 30 et seq.

10   See Faatz, *Vom Staatsschutz zum Gestapo-Terror*, 398.

11   This information is taken from "Vorschlag zur Ernennung Müllers zum Generalmajor der Polizei," BArch, R 2/12150, fol. 135 et seq. Interestingly, in his own CV (see also note 3), Müller predated this appointment to October 1933.

12   "Geschäftsverteilungsplan des Geheimen Staatspolizeiamtes," 25 October 1934, BArch, R 58/840, fol. 34 et seq.

13   See Ulrich Herbert, *Best: Biographische Studien über Radikalismus, Weltanschauung und Vernunft 1903–1989* (Bonn, 1996), 144.

14   In his CV, Müller also falsely dated this promotion as occurring in 1935.

15   "Geschäftsverteilungsplan des Geheimen Staatspolizeiamtes," 1 October 1935, BArch, R 58/840, fol. 60 et seq.

16   Decree by Heydrich, 30 June 1936, BArch, R 58/239, fol. 136.

17   Shlomo Aronson, *Reinhard Heydrich und die Frühgeschichte von Gestapo und SD*, (Stuttgart, 1971), 96; also Seeger, *Gestapo Müller*, 14 and 40.

18   "Politische Beurteilung der Gauleitung München Oberbayern für Heinrich Müller," 4 January 1937, BArch, former BDC, SSO Heinrich Müller.

19   The information in this paragraph is cited from various documents in: BArch, former BDC, SSO Müller.

20   Seeger, *Gestapo-Müller*, 78 et seq.

21   "Vernehmungsniederschrift Barbara Helmuth," 12 December 1960, BArch, B 162/3233, sheet 40 et seq.

22   "Vernehmungsniederschrift Anna Schmid," 13 February 1961, BArch, B 162/3233, sheet 59 et seq.

23 "Vernehmungsniederschrift von Franz Josef Huber," 3 October 1961, BArch, B 162/3233, sheet 129 et seq. For an another description of Müller, see Seeger, *Gestapo-Müller*, 39 et seq. In Wilhelm Höttl (as "Walter Hagen"), *Die geheime Front: Organisation, Personen und Aktionen des deutschen Geheimdienstes* (Stuttgart, 1952), 75, Müller is described as having a "personality without any hinterland."

24 "SS-Offizierspersonalkarte Heinrich Müller," BArch, former BDC, SSO Müller.

25 "Vernehmungsniederschrift Anna Schmid," 13 February 1961, BArch, B 162/3233, sheet 59 et seq.

26 Decree by RfSSuChDtPol, 27 September 1939, BArch, R 58/245, fol. 215 et seq. See also Gerhard Paul, "'Kämpfende Verwaltung': Das Amt IV des Reichssicherheitshauptamtes als Führungsinstanz der Gestapo," in *Die Gestapo im Zweiten Weltkrieg: "Heimatfront" und besetztes Europa*, ed. G. Paul and K-M. Mallmann (Darmstadt, 2000), 42–81.

27 See Seeger, *Gestapo-Müller*, 78 et seq.

28 "Auszug aus der Abwehrbesprechung im Gestapa Berlin," 19 October 1936, Landesarchiv NRW, RW 43/24, fol. 2.

29 On executions without trial ordered by Himmler, Heydrich and Müller, see Johannes Tuchel and Reinhold Schattenfroh, *Zentrale des Terrors: Prinz Albrecht Straße 8: Hauptquartier der Gestapo* (Berlin, 1987), 103 et seq., and the facsimiles therein of the implementing regulations for executions (*Durchführungsbestimmungen für Exekutionen*), 6 January 1943.

30 See "Geschäftsverteilungsplan des Geheimen Staatspolizeiamtes," 25 October 1934, BArch, R 58/840, fol. 35; also "Standortverzeichnis der Dienststellen des Reichssicherheitshauptamtes," 7 December 1943, BArch, R 58/840, fol. 345.

31 "Vernehmungsniederschrift Anna Schmid," 13 February 1961, BArch, B 162/3233, sheet 59 et seq.

32 Cited from Bernhard Lösener, "Als Rassereferent im Reichsministerium des Inneren: Dokumentation: Das Reichsministerium des Inneren und die Judengesetzgebung," *Vierteljahrshefte für Zeitgeschichte* 9, no. 3 (1961): 303. On the problematic nature of this document, see Bettina Stangneth, "Eichmanns Erzählungen," in *Die Wannsee-Konferenz am 20. Januar 1942: Dokumente, Forschungsstand, Kontroversen*, ed. N. Kampe and P. Klein (Cologne, 2013), 146.

33 See M. Wildt, ed., *Die Judenpolitik des SD 1935–1938: Eine Dokumentation* (Schriftenreihe der Vierteljahrshefte für Zeitgeschichte, vol. 71) (Munich, 1995).

34 Michael Wildt has rightly pointed out that in view of Heydrich's order of 1 July 1937, it was only logical that Eichmann became incorporated into the emerging RSHA apparatus, first as Sonderreferent IV R, then as Referatsleiter IV D 4, and later as Referatsleiter IV B.

35 "Blitz-Fernschreiben," 9 November 1938, BArch, R 58/272, fol. 128.

36 "Blitz-Fernschreiben," 10 November 1938, BArch, R 58/272, fol. 137.

37 "Blitz-Fernschreiben," 10 November 1938, BArch, R 58/272, fol. 138.

38 "Blitz-Fernschreiben," 16 November 1938, BArch, R 58/272, fol. 149.

39 See "Stenographische Niederschrift (Teilübertragung) der Besprechung vom 12. November 1938," in: International Military Tribunal [IMT], *Der Prozeß gegen die Hauptkriegsverbrecher vor dem Internationalen Militärgerichtshof (IMT): Nürnberg 14. November 1945—1. Oktober 1946, gemäß den Weisungen des Internationalen Militärgerichtshofes vom Sekretariat des Gerichtshofes unter der Autorität des Obersten Kontrollrats für Deutschland veröffentlicht.*, ed. L.D. Egbert and P.A. Joosten (Nuremberg, 1947–49), vol. 28, 499 et seq. (IMT-Beweisdokument 1816-PS).

40 See Hans Safrian, *Die Eichmann-Männer* (Vienna and Zurich, 1993), 23 et seq.

41 Letter from Göring to the Reichsminister des Innern, 24 January 1939, LA Berlin, Pr. Br. Rep. 57, no. 375.

42 Letter from Heydrich to the Obersten Reichsbehörden, 11 February 1939, LA Berlin, Pr. Br. Rep. 57, no. 375.

43 See K-M. Mallmann, J. Böhler and J. Matthäus, *Einsatzgruppen in Polen: Darstellung und Dokumentation* (Darmstadt, 2008), 116 et seq.

44 "Besprechungsprotokoll, 21 September 1939," in T. Berenstein and A. Rutkowski, "Dokument o konferencji w Urzędzie Policji Bezpieczeństwa z 21 IX 1939 r," *Biuletyn Żydowskiego Instytutu Historycznego* 49, no. 1 (1964): 68 et seq.

45 See the relevant note by Rolf Günther, 9 October 1939, reprinted in: S. Heim and G. Aly, ed., *Die Verfolgung und Ermordung der europäischen Juden durch das nationalsozialistische Deutschland 1933–1945* [VEJ], 16 vols. (Berlin, 2008–), vol. 3, 118 et seq.

46 Note by Eichmann, 6 October 1939, cit. from: Mallmann et al., *Einsatzgruppen in Polen*, 65.

47 See Alfred Gottwaldt and Diana Schulle, *Die "Judendeportationen" aus dem Deutschen Reich von 1941–1945: Eine kommentierte Chronologie* (Wiesbaden, 2005), 31 et seq.

48 Telex, 19 October 1939, cited from Safrian, *Eichmann-Männer*, 79.

49 Safrian, *Eichmann-Männer*, 79.

50 Decree by Müller, BArch, R 58/276, fol. 245.

51 Decree by Heydrich, 21 December 1939, BArch, R 58/276.

52 At a meeting in Berlin on 30 January 1940, which Müller and all functionaries of the police and government apparatus closely involved in the deportation of Poles and Jews attended, Heydrich stressed the importance of "Department IV D 4 for the purpose of centrally governing the evacuation activities." Minutes of the meeting, 30 January 1939, in: Staatsarchiv Nürnberg, KV-Anklage, NO [Nazi Organisation] 5322; also reproduced in: VEJ, vol. 4, 218 et seq.

53 Decree by the RSHA, signed Müller, 12 February 1940, cit. from VEJ, vol. 3, 165 et seq.

54 See the file note, 1 April 1940, cit. from: Jüdisch Historisches Institut Warsaw, ed., *Faschismus, Getto, Massenmord: Dokumentation über Ausrottung und Widerstand der Juden in Polen während des 2. Weltkrieges*, 2nd ed., (Berlin, 1961), 54.

55 Decree, 24 April 1949, cit. from VEJ, vol. 3, 207 et seq.

56 "Reichssicherheitshauptamt: Madagaskar-Projekt," PA AAA, Inland II g 177, fol. 199 et seq., here: fol. 206 et seq.

57 Decree RSHA IV B 4 b, 4 August 1941, BArch, R 58/459, fol. 209 u. RS.

58 See Ralf Ogorreck, *Die Einsatzgruppen und die "Genesis der Endlösung"* (Berlin, 1996), 59.

59 See Ogorreck, *Einsatzgruppen,* 82 et seq.

60 Circular decree by the RSHA, 28 June 1941, cit. from: A. Angrick et al., ed., *Deutsche Besatzungsherrschaft in der UdSSR 1941–1945: Dokumente der Einsatzgruppen in der Sowjetunion* (Veröffentlichungen der Forschungsstelle Ludwigsburg der Universität Stuttgart, vol. 23) (Darmstadt, 2013), vol. 2, 35.

61. Telex by Heydrich, 29 June 1941, cit. from: Angrick et al., *Besatzungsherrschaft,* 35 et seq.

62 Report by Stapostelle Tilsit, 1 July 1941, reprinted in: Angrick et al., *Besatzungsherrschaft,* 41 et seq.

63 Circular decree by the RSHA, 3 July 1941, reprinted in: Angrick et al., *Besatzungsherrschaft,* 49 seq.

64 See "Ereignismeldungen UdSSR 1–8," in: K-M. Mallmann et al., ed., *Die "Ereignismeldungen UdSSR" 1941: Dokumente der Einsatzgruppen in der Sowjetunion* (Darmstadt, 2011), 40 et seq.

65 Radio message from Müller, 1 August 1941, transcript in: Angrick et al., *Besatzungsherrschaft,* 86.

66 Radio message from Müller, 25 August 1941, transcript in: Angrick et al., *Besatzungsherrschaft,* 109.

67 Radio message from Müller, 30 August 1941, transcript in: Angrick et al., *Besatzungsherrschaft,* 117.

68 Express letter from RSHA IV D 5, 4 July 1942, signed Müller, reprinted in: Angrick et al., *Besatzungsherrschaft,* 366.

69 Decree RSHA IV B 4 b, 24 October 1941, BArch, R 58/276, fol. 312; also "Fernschreiben," 24 December 1941, CDCJ Paris, XXVI–5.

70 Eichmann, "Meine Flucht", in Kampe and Klein, *Wannsee-Konferenz,* 91.

71 Hannah Arendt, *Eichmann in Jerusalem: Ein Bericht von der Banalität des Bösen* (Munich, 1964), 149.

72 Andrej Angrick, "Die inszenierte Selbstermächtigung? Motive und Strategie Heydrichs für die Wannsee-Konferenz," in Kampe and Klein, *Wannsee-Konferenz,* 249.

73 Angrick, "Motive und Strategie," 257.

74 J. von Lang, ed., *Das Eichmann-Protokoll: Tonbandaufzeichnungen der israelischen Verhöre* (Berlin, 1982), 72.

75 Decree RSHA IV B 4, 15 May 1942, in: Zentrale Stelle Ludwigsburg, Ordner Verschiedenes, 133.

76 "Fernschreiben vom 21 Mai 1942," IfZ, Fa 506/8.

77 "Fernschreiben vom 16 Juni 1942," Zentrale Stelle der Landesjustizverwaltungen, Judendeportationen aus dem Reichsgebiet, MS, Ludwigsburg o.J., vol. 2 Anl. 80/1.

78 Decree RSHA IV B 4 b 921/42, 1 July 1942, BArch, R 58/276, fol. 341.

79 Decree Der Reichsminister des Innern, Pol. S IV B 4 b, 1 July 1942, BArch, R 58/276, fol. 342.

80 See P. Witte et al., ed., *Der Dienstkalender Heinrich Himmlers 1941/42* (Hamburg, 1999), 465.

81 Note by Eichmann and Dannecker, 1 July 1942, reprinted in: Serge Klarsfeld, *Vichy–Auschwitz: die "Endlösung der Judenfrage" in Frankreich* (Darmstadt, 2007), 390.

82 "Notiz SS Ostuf: Röthke, IV J Paris," 15 July 1942, CDCJ Paris, RF-1226, cit. from: Klarsfeld, *Vichy–Auschwitz*, 406 et seq.

83 See Witte et al., *Dienstkalender*, 513.

84 Letter from Müller to SS-Obergruppenführer Karl Wolff, 17 September 1942, BArch, NS 19/1757.

85 See Christopher R. Browning, *Die "Endlösung" und das Auswärtige Amt: Das Referat D III der Abteilung Deutschland 1940–1943* (Darmstadt, 2010), 92 et seq.

86 See the relevant documents in: Klarsfeld, *Vichy–Auschwitz*, 495 et seq.

87 Letter, 25 February 1943, cit. from: Klarsfeld, *Vichy–Auschwitz*, 495 et seq.

88 Telex from Müller, 2 April 1943, cit. from: Klarsfeld, *Vichy–Auschwitz*, 519.

89 See the relevant documents in: Klarsfeld, *Vichy–Auschwitz*, 536 et seq.

90 Telex, 28 June 1943, signed Knochen, cit. from Klarsfeld, *Vichy–Auschwitz*, 538.

91 "Fernschreiben Müllers," 2 July 1943, CDCJ Paris, XXVII–23.

92 "Vortragsnotiz Eberhard von Thaddens," 22 October 1943, PA AAA, Inland II A 36.

93 On the difficulty of precisely dating this development and the problematic nature of the general context, see Christian Gerlach and Götz Aly, *Das letzte Kapitel: Der Mord an den ungarischen Juden* (Munich, 2002), 249.

94 See Ulrike Hett and Johannes Tuchel, "Die Reaktionen des NS-Staates auf den Umsturzversuch vom 20. Juli 1944," in *Widerstand gegen den Nationalsozialismus*, ed. P. Steinbach and J. Tuchel (Bonn, 1994), 377 et seq.

95 "Vorschlagsliste Nr. 1 für die Verleihung des Ritterkreuzes zum Kriegsverdienstkreuz mit Schwertern," 7 October 1944, BArch, former BDC, SSO Heinrich Müller. Hitler awarded Müller the proposed honor, with the support of Kaltenbrunner and Himmler, on 10 October 1944.

96 "Aussage von Anna Schmid," 13 February 1961, BArch, B 162/3233, sheet 59 et seq.; also Seeger, *Gestapo-Müller*, 63.

97 On the following, including detailed evidence, see Johannes Tuchel, ". . . und ihrer aller wartete der Strick": Das Zellengefängnis Lehrter Straße 3 nach dem 20. Juli 1944* (Berlin, 2014), 214 et seq.

98 Statement by Günsche, in: H. Eberle and M. Uhl, ed., *Das Buch Hitler: Geheimdossier des NKWD für Josef W. Stalin, zusammengestellt aufgrund der Verhörprotokolle des Persönlichen Adjutanten Hitlers, Otto Günsche, und des Kammerdieners Heinz Linge Moskau 1948/49* (Bergisch Gladbach, 2005), 454.

99 See Seeger, *Gestapo-Müller*, 70 et seq.

100 For a more in-depth account, see: Tuchel, ". . . *und ihrer aller wartete der Strick,*" 217 et seq.

101 Interrogation Walter Lüders, 7 October 1963, BArch, B 162/3234, sheet 426 et seq.; also Seeger, *Gestapo-Müller*, 69.

102 Seeger, *Gestapo-Müller*, 27.

Bibliography

Angrick, Andrej. "Die inszenierte Selbstermächtigung? Motive und Strategie Heydrichs für die Wannsee-Konferenz." In *Die Wannsee-Konferenz am 20. Januar 1942: Dokumente, Forschungsstand, Kontroversen*, edited by N. Kampe and P. Klein, 241–58. Cologne, Weimar and Vienna: Böhlau, 2013.

Angrick, A., K-M. Mallmann, J. Matthäus and M. Cüppers, ed. *Deutsche Besatzungsherrschaft in der UdSSR 1941–1945: Dokumente der Einsatzgruppen in der Sowjetunion*. Darmstadt: WBG, 2013.

Arendt, Hannah. *Eichmann in Jerusalem: Ein Bericht von der Banalität des Bösen.* Munich: Piper, 2011 [first published 1964]. [English: *Eichmann in Jerusalem: A Report on the Banality of Evil*. New York: Viking, 1963.]

Aronson, Shlomo. *Reinhard Heydrich und die Frühgeschichte von Gestapo und SD.* Stuttgart: Deutsche Verlags-Anstalt, 1971.

Berenstein, T. and A. Rutkowski. "Dokument o konferencji w Urzędzie Policji Bezpieczeństwa z 21 IX 1939 r." [Das Dokument der Konferenz im Büro der Sicherheitspolizei vom 21. September 1939.] *Biuletyn Żydowskiego Instytutu Historycznego* [Bulletin of the Jewish Historical Institute] 49, no. 1 (1964): 68–73. Retrieved 6 October 2016 from http://cbj.jhi.pl/documents/754488/69/

Bornschein, Joachim. *Gestapochef Heinrich Müller: Technokrat des Terrors*. Leipzig: Militzke, 2004.

Browning, Christopher R. *Die "Endlösung" und das Auswärtige Amt: Das Referat D III der Abteilung Deutschland 1940–1943*. Darmstadt: WBG, 2010. [English: *The Final Solution and the German Foreign Office: A Study of referat D III of Abteilung Deutschland 1940–1943*. New York: Holmes & Meier, 1978.]

Eberle, H. and M. Uhl, ed. *Das Buch Hitler: Geheimdossier des NKWD für Josef W. Stalin, zusammengestellt aufgrund der Verhörprotokolle des Persönlichen Adjutanten Hitlers, Otto Günsche, und des Kammerdieners Heinz Linge Moskau 1948/49*. Bergisch Gladbach: Lübbe, 2005. [English: *The Hitler Book: The Secret Dossier Prepared for Stalin from the Interrogations of Hitler's Personal Aides.*New York: Public Affairs, 2005.]

Faatz, Martin. *Vom Staatsschutz zum Gestapo-Terror: Politische Polizei in Bayern in der Endphase der Weimarer Republik und der Anfangsphase der nationalsozialist-ischen Diktatur*. Würzburg: Echter, 1995.

Gerlach, Christian and Götz Aly. *Das letzte Kapitel: Der Mord an den ungarischen Juden*. Munich: Deutsche Verlags-Anstalt, 2002.

Gottwaldt, Alfred and Diana Schulle. *Die "Judendeportationen" aus dem Deutschen Reich von 1941–1945: Eine kommentierte Chronologie*. Wiesbaden: Marixverlag, 2005.

Heim, S. and G. Aly, ed. *Die Verfolgung und Ermordung der europäischen Juden durch das nationalsozialistische Deutschland 1933–1945* [VEJ]. Berlin: Oldenbourg, 2008–.

Herbert, Ulrich. *Best: Biographische Studien über Radikalismus, Weltanschauung und Vernunft 1903–1989*. Bonn: Dietz, 1996.

Hett, Ulrike and Johannes Tuchel. "Die Reaktionen des NS-Staates auf den Umsturzversuch vom 20. Juli 1944." In *Widerstand gegen den*

Nationalsozialismus, edited by P. Steinbach and J. Tuchel, 377–90. Bonn: Bundeszentrale für Politische Bildung, 1994.

Höttl, Wilhelm (as "Walter Hagen"). *Die geheime Front: Organisation, Personen und Aktionen des deutschen Geheimdienstes*. Stuttgart: Veritas, 1952. [English: *The Secret Front: The Story of Nazi Political Espionage*. London: Weidenfeld & Nicolson, 1954.]

International Military Tribunal [IMT]. *Der Prozeß gegen die Hauptkriegsverbrecher vor dem Internationalen Militärgerichtshof (IMT): Nürnberg 14. November 1945 – 1. Oktober 1946, gemäß den Weisungen des Internationalen Militärgerichtshofes vom Sekretariat des Gerichtshofes unter der Autorität des Obersten Kontrollrats für Deutschland veröffentlicht*, edited by L.D. Egbert and P.A. Joosten. Nuremberg, 1947–1949.

Jüdisch Historisches Institut Warsaw, ed. *Faschismus, Getto, Massenmord: Dokumentation über Ausrottung und Widerstand der Juden in Polen während des 2. Weltkrieges*. 2nd ed. Berlin (East): Rütten & Loening, 1961.

Klarsfeld, Serge. *Vichy–Auschwitz: die "Endlösung der Judenfrage" in Frankreich*. Darmstadt: WBG, 2007.

Lang, J. von, ed. *Das Eichmann-Protokoll: Tonbandaufzeichnungen der israelischen Verhöre*. Berlin: Severin and Siedler, 1982. [English: *Eichmann Interrogated: Transcripts from the Archives of the Israeli Police*. New York: Vintage Books, 1984.]

Lösener, B. "Als Rassereferent im Reichsministerium des Inneren: Dokumentation. Das Reichsministerium des Inneren und die Judengesetzgebung." *Vierteljahrshefte für Zeitgeschichte* 9, no. 3 (1961): 264–313. Retrieved 6 October 2016 from http://www.ifz-muenchen.de/heftarchiv/1961_3_4_strauß.pdf

Mallmann, K-M., A. Angrick, J. Matthäus and M. Cüppers, ed. *Die "Ereignismeldungen UdSSR" 1941: Dokumente der Einsatzgruppen in der Sowjetunion*. Darmstadt: WBG, 2011.

Mallmann, K-M., J. Böhler and J. Matthäus. *Einsatzgruppen in Polen: Darstellung und Dokumentation*. Darmstadt: WBG, 2008.

Müller, Heinrich. 1942. Letter – 28 February PA AAA, Inland II A 11/3.

Ogorreck, Ralf. *Die Einsatzgruppen und die "Genesis der Endlösung."* Berlin: Metropol, 1996.

Otto, Reinhard. *Wehrmacht, Gestapo und sowjetische Kriegsgefangene im deutschen Reichsgebiet 1941/42*. Munich: Oldenbourg, 1998.

Paul, Gerhard. "'Kämpfende Verwaltung': Das Amt IV des Reichssicherheitshauptamtes als Führungsinstanz der Gestapo." In *Die Gestapo im Zweiten Weltkrieg: "Heimatfront" und besetztes Europa*, edited by G. Paul and K-M. Mallmann, 42–81. Darmstadt: WBG, 2000.

Safrian, Hans. *Die Eichmann-Männer*. Vienna and Zurich: Europaverlag, 1993. [English: *Eichmann's Men*. New York: Cambridge University Press, 2010.]

Seeger, Andreas. *Gestapo-Müller: Die Karriere eines Schreibtischtäters*. Berlin: Metropol, 1996.

———. "Heinrich Müller: Der Gestapo-Chef." In *Die SS: Elite unter dem Totenkopf*, edited by R. Smelser and E. Syring, 346–63. Paderborn: Schöningh, 2003.

Stangneth, Bettina. "Eichmanns Erzählungen." In *Die Wannsee-Konferenz am 20. Januar 1942: Dokumente, Forschungsstand, Kontroversen,* edited by N. Kampe and P. Klein, 139–50. Cologne: Böhlau, 2013.

Tuchel, Johannes. *". . . und ihrer aller wartete der Strick": Das Zellengefängnis Lehrter Straße 3 nach dem 20. Juli 1944.* Berlin: Lukas, 2014.

Tuchel, Johannes and Reinhold Schattenfroh. *Zentrale des Terrors: Prinz Albrecht Straße 8: Hauptquartier der Gestapo.* Berlin: Siedler, 1987.

Wildt, M., ed. *Die Judenpolitik des SD 1935–1938: Eine Dokumentation.* Munich: Oldenbourg, 1995.

Witte, P., M. Wildt, M. Vogt, D. Pohl, P. Klein, C. Gerlach, C. Dieckmann and A. Angrick, ed. *Der Dienstkalender Heinrich Himmlers 1941/42.* Hamburg: Christians, 1999.

7

EBERHARD SCHÖNGARTH
Reich Main Security Office
A Practitioner of Mass Murder
Olaf Löschke

Illustration 7.1 Unknown photographer, undated, Yad Vashem Archives, 5511 Item 80024.

"He was a proper, decent officer but strongly influenced by the fighting in the East. Methods were used in the East that were very unpleasant. He brought these methods back with him from the East."[1] Without going into greater detail, the former higher SS and police leader (Höhere SS- und Polizeiführer, HSSPF) in the Netherlands, Hanns Albin Rauter, thus hinted at the brutality of his successor, Eberhard Schöngarth.

Schöngarth was one of the less prominent participants in the Wannsee Conference. Perhaps this was because his attendance was not surprising, as the extended arm of Reinhard Heydrich in German-occupied Poland. Yet he was not Heydrich's first choice to represent the General Government. Initially, the higher-ranking HSSPF in the General Government Friedrich-Wilhelm Krüger was deemed more suitable to attend.[2] Nevertheless, there were a number of compelling reasons for Schöngarth's participation in the Wannsee Conference.

From Berlin to Krakow—A Gestapo Career

Born on 22 April 1903, the son of a master brewer in Leipzig, he belonged to the "war youth generation," who had experienced the First World War from the home front.[3] He identified with ethnonationalistic tendencies at an early age and joined the Reich army for five months shortly before embarking on his study of law in 1924.[4]

In 1928 he passed his first state examination in Naumburg and in 1929 gained a doctorate in law, graded "cum laude," with a thesis on the subject of "the refusal of notices of termination of employment contracts."[5] Having gained a rarely bestowed "good" for his second state examination, he started working for the Prussian judicial service as a junior judicial officer and assistant judge at various regional courts.[6]

Schöngarth's Gestapo career began on 1 November 1935 in the department of church politics in the Gestapo headquarters in Berlin. It is unclear why he found employment specifically here. A letter from Heydrich to the Reich Ministry of the Interior, recommending Schöngarth for employment in the Secret State Police on account of "his services to the movement," suggests that he was appointed at Heydrich's or Himmler's initiative.[7] In April 1936, even before his trial period was over, he was accepted into the civil service as a government assessor on account of his "good legal knowledge" and "broad administrative experience," placing him "finally" at the service of the Gestapo. Soon afterward, he joined the SD, the intelligence service of the SS. In the ensuing two years he was variously deployed as chief of the local Gestapo office in Dortmund, Arnsberg, Bielefeld and Münster. He received consistently positive assessments. Schöngarth was considered "open and honest"; he had a "strong will" and was "assertive." His attitude to Nazi ideology was "completely affirmative." Not only that, he was a "trusty old fighter who was completely dedicated to the cause of the SS and the SD."[8] In 1935 Schöngarth married Dorothea Gross, three years his senior, with whom he had two sons.

In his personal information form, he declared his faith to be "believer" (gottgläubig), the standard term for members of the SS.[9] Appointed senior councilor (Oberregierungsrat) in August 1939, Schöngarth was transferred to Dresden as Inspector of the Security Police and the SD in December and, a short time later, also assumed the task of Inspector of the Security Police and the SD for the Reich Governor in the Sudetenland in Reichenberg.[10] After taking part in the Battle of France as a reserve lieutenant in the Luftwaffe, he was made police lieutenant-colonel (Oberstleutnant der Polizei) in December 1940. On 20 November 1940, at the age of thirty-seven, Schöngarth became Bruno Streckenbach's[11] successor as Commander of the Gestapo in the General Government of Poland. Just a few weeks later, on 23 January 1941, Reich Minister of the Interior Frick proposed his promotion to police colonel (Oberst der Polizei) to Hitler. A short time later he was duly promoted and declared an SS-Oberführer.[12]

The Gestapo Commander's headquarters at Magdeburger Straße 1 in Krakow was structured to mirror the RSHA in Berlin and was immediately answerable to the latter.[13] The main task of the Gestapo Command in occupied Poland was to monitor and combat potential political opponents, the Polish "leading class" and churches. In addition, the Gestapo Command was responsible for the persecution of the Jewish population in close cooperation with the higher SS and police authorities (HSSPF Ost under Friedrich-Wilhelm Krüger), which in turn were directly subordinate to Himmler, the Reich leader of the SS and chief of the German police.

Together with the commanders of the Security Police and the SD stationed in the districts, the Gestapo Command authorities acted as the extended arm of the RSHA in the occupied territories and played a key role in enforcing its brutal occupation policy. A clear indication of this was the "extraordinary pacification campaign" *(außerordentliche Befriedungsaktion)*, launched on 10 May 1940. This campaign, known as the "AB-Aktion," was engineered to coincide with Germany's invasion of France, and aimed to eliminate the Polish intelligentsia and resistance movement without the knowledge of the international public.[14]

The Gestapo Commander was also involved in actions against the Jewish population. At a police meeting in late May 1940, a conflict arose between the civil administration and the SS over the division of responsibilities with regard to Jewish policy. Then Gestapo Commander Streckenbach, Schöngarth's predecessor, argued that "the Security Police . . . was particularly interested in the Jewish Question for obvious reasons." The Jewish councils of elders, he went on, had proven useful for allowing the supervising Security Police officials to gain insights into "Jewish cultural methods" and to "keep a permanent overview of the situation among the Jewry."[15] Streckenbach hoped to secure the sole right of access to the Jewish councils.[16]

Schöngarth was also directly involved in the genocide of the Jews. Following the invasion of the Soviet Union in late June 1941, he consulted with the Reich chief of the criminal police and chief of Einsatzgruppe B, Arthur Nebe, about deploying extra troops to support the Gestapo Commands from Warsaw and Lublin.[17] Consequently, in early July 1941, Schöngarth arrived in Lemberg with his own special task force *(Einsatzkommando zur besonderen Verfügung, z.b.V.)*, which began murdering the Jewish population shortly after arriving.[18] On 5 July, Schöngarth's men murdered Polish professors in Lemberg and their families.[19] In one incident report, he noted applying to deploy special task forces to "perform tasks of a security police and SD nature in the newly occupied areas adjacent to the General Government."[20] The same report gives indications that Jewish councils were to be formed and compulsory labeling introduced.

Following the murder campaigns in Lemberg, some of the task forces were sent to the neighboring towns and villages.[21] During a "trial shooting," Schöngarth briefed his men on procedure, from digging out ditches and rounding up victims to different kinds of shooting and positioning the corpses. The killings were usually followed by drinking sprees.[22] In his operations report to the RSHA of 3 August 1941, Schöngarth reported the killing of 3,947 persons in the period from 21 to 31 July 1941.[23] In late August 1941, he returned to Krakow. Both Schöngarth and the RSHA regarded mass shootings in East Galicia to be the main task of the Security Police.[24] This came to a tragic climax on the "Stanislau Bloody Sunday" of 12 October 1941, which claimed the lives of some 10,000 to 12,000 people. During this time, Nazi policy on Jews in the General Government focused on isolating the ghettos, as the residents' deportation to the East was becoming imminent. On 21 November 1941, Schöngarth issued orders to shoot any Jews "wandering around" outside the ghettos.[25]

Conflicts in the General Government and the Wannsee Conference

In winter 1941/42, a conflict escalated that had been simmering for some time between the SS leadership and the civil administration over police violence in the General Government. Himmler appointed Krüger HSSPF Ost in October 1939 in a bid to start making inroads into General Governor Frank's far-reaching powers. Although the higher SS and police leader was officially subordinate to the General Governor, in practice Himmler and Krüger tended to operate over Frank's head.[26]

Krüger, born 1894 in Strasbourg, was instrumental in the persecution and murder of the European Jews and Polish leading class.[27] The son of an officer, he served in the First World War as a lieutenant, was injured several times and, by the time of his release, highly decorated. Between 1919 and 1920 he was a Freikorps member and worked later as a representative for a book publishing company. Following a subsequent period as a board member of the Berlin refuse collection service, he worked as a self-employed tradesman. A personal friend of Himmler's, with whom he was on first-name terms, Krüger joined the Nazi Party in 1929 and became a member of the SS in 1931.[28]

Krüger's relationship with Himmler seems to have been very close for some years. Though six years younger, Himmler acted like a benevolent uncle toward Krüger. The surviving correspondence between them shows Himmler repeatedly cautioning "his Krüger" in an avuncular

Illustration 7.2 On this slightly retouched press photograph, Hans Frank is presenting HSSPF Friedrich-Wilhelm Krüger with a certificate of appointment to the office of "State Secretary for Security" in the General Government. Schöngarth (left) is looking on in the background, alongside an unknown man. Photo by Otto Rosner, early May 1942, NAC 2-4470.

way to become more independent and cooperate better with the various offices. However, Krüger's pedantry and scheming were a constant source of conflict,[29] and Himmler became increasingly irritated by Krüger's frequent telephone calls, sometimes refusing to answer.[30] In October 1943 Krüger was headhunted for Himmler's staff and in May 1944 he was transferred to the Waffen-SS. He committed suicide in May 1945. Before he fell from grace, Krüger rose to become HSSPF, the most powerful man in the General Government. He considered himself answerable only to Himmler and took orders from nobody else. He regarded General Governor Frank as a raging fool.[31] Nevertheless, the civil administration and the office of the HSSPF cooperated relatively smoothly right up until 1940, partly because Himmler was preoccupied with problems with the army. The Supreme Commander of the German forces in the East, *Generaloberst* Johannes Blaskowitz, had filed a complaint about SS methods in Poland, requiring Himmler to make a statement to the army leadership.[32] In the event, Himmler owed Frank a debt of gratitude for supporting his opposition to Blaskowitz.[33]

Once the division of responsibilities between the German army and the SS in occupied Poland had been clarified, a power struggle broke out between Frank and Himmler. They not only disagreed on policy concerning the protection of German ethnicity and culture (*Volkstumspolitik*), which Himmler, as Reich Commissioner for the Consolidation of German Nationhood (Reichskommisar zur Festigung des Deutschen Volkstums, RKF), regarded as his field of expertise, but above all on questions of who held authority in which field, especially with respect to the General Governor's control over the police executive. Krüger's appointment as commissioner for the RKF in the General Government went some way to limiting Frank's power.[34] The latter tried to subordinate himself to the HSSPF but was repudiated.[35] Within this complex set-up, Schöngarth, Commander of the Security Police, operated under three immediate superiors: Heydrich in Berlin or Prague; Hans Frank, the General Governor in Krakow; and Krüger, Himmler's representative in the General Government. This was bound to lead to conflicts sooner or later. In winter 1941/42, the power struggle between Frank and Himmler culminated in a scandal concerning Frank's long-term friend Karl Lasch, the governor of Galicia. Lasch, who was having an affair with Frank's wife Brigitte, was arrested on 24 January 1942, officially for contravening customs and foreign exchange regulations. Charges were pressed against him of "parasitical crimes against the people ... on the largest scale."[36] Schöngarth, among others, was assigned to conduct the investigations. He not only accused Lasch of trafficking rugs and art objects but also of undermining military morale (*Wehrkraftzersetzung*) and committing racial defilement (*Rassenschande*). Frank dropped Lasch and he was handed over to the public prosecutors in Breslau on 12 March.[37] In early June 1942 Lasch died of unknown causes in prison.[38]

Disputes over respective areas of authority also arose with regard to the "Final Solution of the Jewish Question" and the fates of over 2.2 million Jews in the General Government, which Heydrich took into account when deciding whom to invite to the Wannsee Conference. In late November 1941, for instance, Krüger complained to Himmler and Heydrich "that the General Governor is seeking to completely take over the handling of the Jewish problem."[39] Consequently, Heydrich asked Eichmann to write two drafts of invitations for 9 December 1941, the date first earmarked for the meeting. As well as Krüger, who had already received one of the earlier invitations of 29 November 1941, State Secretary Bühler was now invited to attend instead of his superior, Hans Frank. Apparently, Heydrich hoped this would settle the rivalry between the institutions while serving his own interests.[40] Hence the second letter of invitation of 8 January 1942 was addressed to the same "circle of gentlemen mentioned in the last letter of invitation."[41]

One week before the conference, Himmler spoke to Schöngarth prior to a briefing with Bühler due to take place the same day.[42] The following day, Schöngarth attended a dinner in the company of Himmler and Heydrich and most heads of the RSHA.[43] It is quite possible that the decision to invite Schöngarth to Wannsee was made in the semi-official mood of this dinner.

In terms of Nazi hierarchy, Krüger, the HSSPF directly subordinate to Himmler, would have been the more logical candidate to attend on 20 January 1942, as he was in charge of both the local Ordnungspolizei (Orpo) and the Commander of the Security Police. There are three plausible reasons for Krüger's absence from the conference. For one, he was nursing a broken arm. Second, he had probably been informed of the planned division of responsibilities during talks with Himmler and Heydrich in late November. But the most convincing reason is that Heydrich wanted the meeting to run smoothly and end in an agreement, not an argument, undisturbed by any personal animosities or controversies surrounding the work of the police in the General Government. Bringing together Krüger and Frank, or Krüger and Bühler, might have jeopardized this aim.[44]

Schöngarth's participation in the Wannsee Conference, alongside his superior, was probably a high point of his career. After all, it placed him among state secretaries, key figures in the Nazi regime. Along with Rudolph Lange, he was concerned with the practical side of committing murder on a mass scale. Having participated in the murder campaign in Lemberg and the surrounding areas, he knew about the methods used by the Einsatzgruppen, and passed this knowledge on to newly recruited SS officers when he became head of the Security Police School in Bad Rabka a short time later. Here, students not only attended lectures by high-ranking SS leaders but also seminars on torture and shooting, practicing on live victims.[45] Although no talks by Schöngarth are documented, the subjects taught at the school tallied with his field of responsibility.

The call to murder, encoded in the order to "take the evacuated Jews . . . step by step to so-called transit ghettos in order to be transported further East from there,"[46] directly involved Schöngarth's office. "Transit ghettos" were to be set up in Izbica and Piaski in the Lublin district, among other places.[47] In view of this, it certainly interested Schöngarth to know who would be in command in future and how the transports were to be coordinated with the authorities. "Evacuation to the East" was nothing less than a euphemism for systematic mass murder in eastern Poland.[48]

After the conference in Wannsee, Schöngarth, as Heydrich's extended arm in the General Government, could rest assured that he would be able to operate freely and rely on the support of the civilian authorities. Bühler's comments (recorded in the Protocol), calling for the "Final Solution" in the "General Government [to be] launched" because the "transport problem [was] not significant," were further indication of this. The fact that Bühler caved in to Heydrich, and accepted him as being "in charge" of the murder of the European Jews, illustrated the increased power the RSHA now wielded.[49]

Stationary killing was not officially Heydrich's domain. The RSHA was not "in charge" of setting up extermination camps; Himmler and his HSSPF were responsible for this.[50] Schöngarth, together with the SS and police leader (SSPF) Odilo Globocnik, was responsible for receiving the deportees; the Reich railways were instructed to inform them of the arrival of transport trains.[51] In this regard, Schöngarth cooperated closely with the directors of the eastern railways and Eichmann's department.[52]

Heydrich's announcement at the Wannsee Conference that the Jews were to be "led" to the East "building roads" not only referred to the plan to fatally exploit their labor but also to the construction of forced labor camps along transit road IV, which had begun in October 1941.[53] Schöngarth was not informed until construction was already underway and so presented with a fait accompli. He had no personal control over the outcome of this vanity project of Himmler's.[54]

In summer 1942 disputes broke out over whether to retain Jewish forced laborers in armaments industries and the German army.[55] They were sparked by a secret letter from Himmler to Krüger of 19 July 1942, which can be regarded as firing the starting shot for the deportation and murder of all Jews working in industry.[56] Krüger soon began seizing Jewish forced laborers from their workplaces, eliciting protests from employers who feared they would lack skilled workers as a result. Schöngarth, too, argued that the Jews in the armaments industry were irreplaceable.[57] Disputes such as these, as well as his agreement with Hans Frank to relax policy on Poland, ultimately led to his dismissal in summer 1943.

Gradual Decline—Trial and Transferal to the Netherlands

In June 1942, proceedings were started against Schöngarth on grounds of embezzlement, corruption, plundering and art racketeering.[58] They centered around his friendly relationship with the Dutchman Pieter van Menten, who had been suspected of dubious business practices even before the war. Shortly after the outbreak of war in 1939, Menten started working as a sworn valuer and financial advisor and was appointed a trustee of Jewish art galleries. Over the years, he acquired considerable wealth liquidating Jewish businesses.[59] Menten was fascinated by the SS and its ideology. Barely able to contain his pride, he wrote to the fourth SS and police court in Krakow that he had been "the first Dutchman . . . to volunteer for the Einsatzkommando z.b.V when war broke out with Russia."[60] In summer 1941 he gained the post of interpreter for Einsatzkommando z.b.V. through his connection with Schöngarth, and was henceforth allowed to wear an SS uniform, which he regarded as an honor. Schöngarth and his closest associates were frequent guests in Menten's house, where they indulged in regular drinking binges.[61] In the course of the investigations into Schöngarth's circles, Menten was accused of stealing art and arrested. On Himmler's orders, he was expelled from the General Government for good, but permitted to take his considerable assets with him.[62]

As the proceedings progressed, the allegations against Schöngarth were corroborated, but the chief of the fourth SS and police court in Krakow, Kurt Sachs, was later obliged to hand over the incriminating evidence to the SS judge at the RFSS.[63] Himmler decided to postpone Schöngarth's dismissal to avoid exacerbating the widespread rumors that corruption was rife within the staff of the General Government, who were known in the vernacular as "Eastern hyenas" (*Osthyänen*).

By late 1942, Schöngarth also faced Krüger's intrigues. Krüger complained to Himmler that Schöngarth had contravened orders by attending a government meeting and subsequent dinner in Krakow castle, and displayed "sympathy for the views and opinions of the civil administration." Not only that, Krüger felt that the "momentary relationship between Oberführer Schöngarth and the General Governor, State Secretary Dr Bühler, and the individual government members . . . conflicts directly with the reasons . . ." for leaving him in office. Indeed, Krüger explicitly called on Himmler to either release himself or Schöngarth from his office, as the two could no longer cooperate.[64]

At a meeting with the two men in early December 1942, Himmler made it clear that although he, too, was under the impression that

Schöngarth had become "weak and lukewarm," he would retain him in office.[65] Schöngarth, meanwhile, continued to show concern about the growing level of resistance in Poland, stating at a government meeting on 20 April 1943 that "the situation [would] inevitably escalate . . . if one did not admit that the [Germans'] treatment of the Polish people had hitherto been wrong on many points. One should summon up the courage to change the German course at last."[66] In view of the repressive policy that Himmler and Krüger continued to pursue in Poland, this almost amounted to an internal putsch.

Despite his shaky standing, Schöngarth was promoted once again in early 1943 to SS-Brigadeführer and police major general. But in early July he was abruptly dismissed from his post as Commander of the Security Police and, in September 1943, transferred (for disciplinary reasons) to the SS antiaircraft artillery replacement-regiment in Munich. His successor in Krakow was Walter Bierkamp. After a short training period, Schöngarth was deployed as commander of an infantry company *(Kompanief ührer)* in the fourth SS police Panzergrenadier division stationed in Lamia, Greece.[67] Some of this division was implicated in the Distomo massacre in June 1944, but it is unlikely that Schöngarth was involved, having been transferred to the Netherlands in May. In June he resumed the function of Commander of the Security Police, based in The Hague. Here, he caught up with his friend Pieter Menten and returned to his former activities.[68] Following the Dutch resistance attack on HSSPF Nord-West Hanns Albin Rauter on the night of 6 to 7 March 1945, Schöngarth ordered the shooting of 250 Dutch men.[69] One hundred and seventeen Dutch citizens were murdered the next day, on 8 March, near Woeste Hoeve, where the attack had taken place. In total, 263 people fell victim to Schöngarth's "reprisal action." On 10 March he was assigned to represent Rauter as HSSPF.[70]

During his postwar trial before a British military court, Schöngarth admitted that an order had been given to shoot 100 people as retribution for the attack on Rauter. Later on in the trial, he also admitted giving orders to shoot 150 to 200 people, all of whom, he insisted, had received "regular" death sentences.[71] The crucial charge against him, however, was that he gave the order to shoot an Allied pilot, who crashed on 21 November 1941 over Enschede. Seen as the killing of a prisoner of war, this act violated international law.[72]

The Allied pilot had crashed close to the villa Hooge Boekel, which had been confiscated in 1944 by a department of the SD, the intelligence service of the SS, and where a conference was held on 20 and 21 November, followed by drinks and informal talks. Asked whether he had seen or heard the airplane, Schöngarth replied that he had not because he had been speaking to one of his subordinates at the time. He also denied having seen the parachutist. Questioned directly about Nazi treatment of prisoners of war, he stated that nobody spoke about it, as there was no reason to. During his cross-examination, he was asked about his own role in dealing with prisoners of war, to which he replied that he had nothing to do with them, as downed pilots were a matter for the Luftwaffe and therefore not his remit. He added, however, that this would not have been the case had the pilot been a secret agent.[73] But whenever asked if he had given the order to shoot, Schöngarth professed his innocence. He did, however, describe in detail the official procedure for executions by a summary court martial of the Security Police or SD. Asked where the men learned to kill by shooting their victims in the back of the neck, Schöngarth maintained that no orders were given for this kind of execution. But he did not deny that they might have occurred, referring to the experience the German forces had gained in the East.

On the basis of witness statements, the court found it fact that Schöngarth was responsible for the pilot's death and had given the order to execute. The former Commander of the Security Police and the SD was executed on 16 March 1946 in Hameln.[74]

Schöngarth's activities as chief of Einsatzkommando z.B.V. in Lemberg and his participation in the Wannsee Conference were not significant counts in his postwar trial.[75] Yet he was one of the men at the Wannsee Conference, along with Rudolf Lange, who virtually had blood dripping from their hands. Former associates described him as being both eloquent and jovial and choleric and hotheaded. To some, he was a drunken, brutal, intimidating boss; to others he was a "proper and decent officer."[76]

Olaf Löschke is a Freelancer in the Memorial House of the Wannsee Conference, and works as a researcher and historical consultant for film and theatre productions. Löschke is first chairman at the association "Historikerlabor e.V." in Berlin, his thematic focuses are: Holocaust research, the history of the military and police as well as the history of media in the twenty-first century.

Notes

1   Cit. from A.E. Cohen, "Een onbekende tijdgenoot: De laatste Befehlshaber der Sicherheitspolizei und des SD in Nederland," ["An Unknown Contemporary: The Last Commander of the Security Police and the SD in

the Netherlands"] in *Studies over Nederland in Oorlogstijd*, ed. A.H. Paape (The Hague, 1972), 173, footnote 20.

2   Notice of invitation of 29 November 1941 to Otto Hofmann and Martin Luther et al., reprinted in Kurt Pätzold and Erika Schwarz, *Tagesordnung: Judenmord: Die Wannsee-Konferenz am 20. Januar 1942: Eine Dokumentation zur Organisation der `Endlösung'* (Berlin, 1992), 88–90.

3   On the concept of the "war youth generation" (Kriegsjugendgeneration), see Ulrich Herbert, *Best: Biographische Studien über Radikalismus, Weltanschauung und Vernunft 1903–1989* (Bonn, 1996), 43; also Michael Wildt, *Die Generation des Unbedingten: Das Führungskorps des Reichssicherheitshauptamtes* (Hamburg, 2002), 46.

4   By his own account, he took part in the Kapp Putsch in 1920. He was active in the Thuringian Freikorps 1919–20, and a member of the Wiking-Bund and the Jungdeutscher Orden 1920–22. Following the ban on the Nazi Party in Prussia, he became active in various local groups in Bavaria. He was arrested during the Hitler Putsch but later amnestied. Between 1922 and 1924 he was a member of the Nazi Party (membership no. 43,870) and the SA. He also completed an apprenticeship at Deutsche Bank. See handwritten CV Schöngarth, 26 September 1936, BArch, BDC, SSO-Akte Schöngarth.

5   Eberhard Schöngarth, *Die Zurückweisung von Kündigungen des Arbeitsvertrages* (Erfurt, 1929).

6   In an attachment to a personnel information form of 30 August 1933, Schöngarth is listed as Dr jur. Utr. (doctor juris utriusque) as of 17 October 1929. Hence he was a doctor of church law as well as secular law. This additional qualification was later dropped. See "Personalfragebogen," 30 August 1933, BArch, R 3001/75144.

7   "Preußische Geheime Staatspolizei, Der Stellvertretende Chef, Schreiben Heydrichs an den Reichsminister des Innern, z. Hd. ORR von Wedelstädt," 21 February 1936, BArch, BDC, SSO-Akte Schöngarth.

8   Cit. from "Personalbericht vom 15 Juli 1938," BArch, BDC, SSO-Akte Schöngarth. He joined the SS on 1 March 1933 (SS no. 67,174); a short time later he re-joined the Nazi Party (membership no. 2,848,857). The authorities had a "particular functional interest" in employing him. See the letter from Heydrich to the RMdI of 21 February 1936. On 1 April 1936 he was made government assessor, having served since 6 June 1932, employed by the Prussian state, and changed from the postal service to the Prussian Gestapo. "Ernennungsurkunde vom 3 April 1936," BArch, BDC, SSO-Akte Schöngarth.

9   "Ernennungsvorschlag Fricks," 23 January 1941, Sonderarchiv Moskau, Fonds 720-2-48-28. Until 1933 he declared himself to be Protestant. See "Personalfragebogen," 30 August 1933, BArch, R 3001/75144.

10 See: BArch, R 601/1820, sheet 074. "Vermerk vom 16 Juni 1943," BArch, BDC, SSO-Akte Schöngarth.

11 On Bruno Streckenbach, see Klaus-Michael Mallmann, Jochen Böhler and Jürgen Matthäus, *Einsatzgruppen in Polen: Darstellung und Dokumentation* (Darmstadt, 2008), 20–21; also Wildt, *Generation*, 55–57. The chief of

Einsatzgruppe I in Poland was made head of Department I in the RSHA in June 1940. Schöngarth was officially appointed in early 1941.

12 "Ernennungsvorchlag Fricks," 23 January 1941, Sonderarchiv Moskau, Fonds 720-2-48-28. Within the SS at that time he held the rank of SS-Standartenführer and was originally to be promoted to SS-Oberführer. He was made SS-Oberführer at Himmler's request. See BArch, BDC, SSO-Akte Eberhard Schöngarth.

13 See Ruth Bettina Birn, *Die Höheren SS- und Polizeiführer: Himmlers Vertreter im Reich und in den besetzten Gebieten* (Düsseldorf, 1986), 87–91. On the role of the Gestapo Commander, see also Alwin Ramme, *Der Sicherheitsdienst der SS: Zu seiner Funktion im faschistischen Machtapparat und im Besatzungsregime des sogenannten Generalgouvernements Polen* (Berlin, 1970), 225. For a critical commentary on Ramme, see Wildt, *Generation*, 31, footnote 44.

14 On the "AB-Aktion," see, for example, Dieter Schenk, *Hans Frank: Hitlers Kronjurist und Generalgouverneur* (Frankfurt am Main, 2006), 188–91; also Gerhard Eisenblätter, "Grundlinien der Politik des Reichs gegenüber dem Generalgouvernement 1939–1945" (Ph.D. dissertation, Goethe University Frankfurt, 1969), 173–78.

15 Cit. from the police meeting of 30 May 1940, transcript in W. Präg and W. Jacobmeyer, ed., *Das Diensttagebuch des deutschen Generalgouverneurs in Polen 1939–1945* (Stuttgart, 1975), 215–16. In late 1939 there were large-scale "actions" against the Polish intelligentsia in Krakow and Kielce. See Eisenblätter, "Grundlinien der Politik des Reichs", 159.

16 See Jacek Andrzej Młynarczyk, *Judenmord in Zentralpolen: Der Distrikt Radom im Generalgouvernement 1939–1945* (Darmstadt, 2007), 105.

17 Operations report from the chief of Einsatzgruppe B for the period 23 June 1941 to 13 July 1941, BstU, ZUV 9, vol. 31, sheet 3–17, reprinted in P. Klein, ed., *Die Einsatzgruppen in der besetzten Sowjetunion 1941/42: Die Tätigkeits- und Lageberichte des Chefs der Sicherheitspolizei und des SD* (Publikationen der Gedenk- und Bildungsstätte Haus der Wannsee-Konferenz, vol. 6) (Berlin, 1997), 378–79. On the support troops from the General Government, see Christian Gerlach, "Die Einsatzgruppe B 1941/42," in Klein, *Einsatzgruppen in der besetzten Sowjetunion*, 52–70.

18 Dieter Schenk, *Der Lemberger Professorenmord und der Holocaust in Ostgalizien* (Bonn, 2007), 93–100; also Dieter Pohl, *Nationalsozialistische Judenverfolgung in Ostgalizien 1941–1944: Organisation und Durchführung eines staatlichen Massenverbrechens* (Studien zur Zeitgeschichte, vol. 50) (Munich, 1996), 59–65.

19 Thomas Sandkühler views this as a continuation of the "AB-Aktion" of 1940. See Thomas Sandkühler, *"Endlösung" in Galizien: Der Judenmord in Ostpolen und die Rettungsinitiativen von Berthold Beitz 1941–1944* (Bonn, 1996), 118; also Schenk, *Lemberger Professorenmord*, 96.

20 Cit. from "Ereignismeldung UdSSR Nr. 25," 17 July 1941, Barch R58/214.

21 "Einsatzorte der Kommandos mit Stand vom 12 Juli 1941 in Kowel, Rowno, Luck und Lemberg, Rawa-Ruska, Przemysl, Drohobycz und Tarnopol. KTB, Bfh. Rückw. H. Geb. 103, 'Betrifft: Maßnahmen auf dem Ic-Gebiet,'" 14 July 1941, Barch, R70 Sowjetunion 18, sheet 1.

22   See Schenk, *Lemberger Professorenmord*, 97–98.

23   "Ereignismeldung Nr. 43," 3 August 1941, BArch, R58/215, sheet 159. Thomas Sandkühler estimates that at least 4,000 Jews were murdered in the Lemberg massacre. See Sandkühler, *"Endlösung" in Galizien*, 119. According to Dieter Schenk, some 9,247 people were murdered by Schöngarth's men in Galicia. See Schenk, *Lemberger Professorenmord*, 98.

24   See Pohl, *Judenverfolgung*, 295.

25   Pohl, *Judenverfolgung*, 142–47, here 147 and 163.

26   Express letter from Himmler on 4 October 1939 to Krüger, "Einsetzung Krügers als HSSPF, sowie die Einsetzung Beckers als Chef der Ordnungspolizei und Bruno Streckenbachs als BdS," BArch, BDC, SSO-Akte Friedrich-Wilhelm Krüger.

27   Krüger and his SS leader and police chief (SSPF) Jürgen Stroop were responsible for suppressing the uprising in the Warsaw ghetto in spring 1943 and for destroying the Jewish ghetto. See W. Scheffler and H. Grabitz, ed., *Der Ghetto-Aufstand Warschau 1943 aus der Sicht der Täter und Opfer in Aussagen vor deutschen Gerichten* (Munich, 1993).

28   Date of joining the Nazi Party: 15 November 1929; party membership no. 171,199; date of joining the SS: 1 February 1931; SS membership no. 6,123.

29   As far back as 1939, he reprimanded his "dear Krüger" for his part in failed negotiations and reminded him that he had already "failed once in [his] life"; see "Persönlicher Brief Himmlers an Krüger," 29 December 1939, BArch, BDC, SSO-Akte Friedrich-Wilhelm Krüger, sheets 1059–60.

30   "Aktennotiz Himmlers," 15 August 1940, BArch, BDC, SSO-Akte Friedrich-Wilhelm Krüger, sheet 838.

31   See Schenk, *Hans Frank*, 184. Himmler forbade his HSPPF from reporting to Bühler in any form. See Birn, *Höheren SS- und Polizeiführer*, 198–99.

32   "Ich tue nichts, was der Führer nicht weiß." Cited from Helmut Krausnick and Hans-Heinrich Wilhelm, *Die Truppe des Weltanschauungskrieges: Die Einsatzgruppen der Sicherheitspolizei und des SD 1938–1942* (Stuttgart, 1981), 105. On Himmler's pleadings, see Klaus-Jürgen Müller, "Dokumentation: Zu Vorgeschichte und Inhalt der Rede Himmlers vor der höheren Generalität am 13. März 1940 in Koblenz," *Vierteljahrshefte für Zeitgeschichte* 18, no. 1 (1970): 95–120.

33   In mid February 1940, Frank petitioned Göring to replace Blaskowitz as Supreme Commander in the East. See Schenk, *Hans Frank*, 188.

34   Eisenblätter, "Grundlinien der Politik des Reichs", 134. Peter Longerich, *Heinrich Himmler: Biographie* (Munich, 2008), 449–51.

35   See Eisenblätter, "Grundlinien der Politik des Reichs", 133. On the emergence of these problems, see Eisenblätter, "Grundlinien der Politik des Reichs", 135–44.

36   "Verfahren wegen Volksschädlingsverbrechen . . . allergrößtem Stils." Cited from a secret letter from Hans Frank to Oberregierungsrat Stademann personally of 16 March 1942, "Strafsache gegen Lasch," BArch, R3001/20040, sheet 02/397.

37   "Verfahren wegen Volksschädlingsverbrechen . . . allergrößtem Stils."

38 Less than one month after Lasch's arrest, proceedings were started to withdraw his doctorate. They dragged on for almost a year and were finally stopped with the terse observation that the "withdrawal [was unnecessary] as Lasch had died." See "Schreiben des Rektors der Universität Köln an das Reichsministerium für Wissenschaft, Erziehung und Bildung," 2 February 1943, BArch, R4901/12860, sheet 104. Eisenblätter, "Grundlinien der Politik des Reichs", 246. Młynarczyk, *Judenmord*, 85.

39 Cit. from file memo by Eichmann of 1 December 1941, reprinted in N. Kampe, "Dokumente zur Wannsee-Konferenz," in Kampe and Klein, *Wannsee-Konferenz*, 25–27. An entry in Heinrich Himmler's diary of 28 November 1941 records a meeting that day between Krüger, Heydrich and Himmler from 4 to 4.30 PM to discuss "the matter of Frank." See P. Witte et al., ed., *Der Dienstkalender Heinrich Himmlers 1941/42* (Hamburg, 1999), 277.

40 See Mark Roseman, *Die Wannsee-Konferenz: Wie die NS-Bürokratie den Holocaust organisierte* (Berlin, 2002), 86.

41 See the letter from Heydrich to Hofmann of 8 January 1942, reproduced in Pätzold and Schwarz, *Tagesordnung: Judenmord*, 100.

42 On Bühler's talk with Himmler on 13 January 1942, see the chapter in the present book by Ingo Loose.

43 Präg and Jacobmeyer, *Diensttagebuch des deutschen Generalgouverneurs*, entries from 13 to 14 January 1942, 315 and 317.

44 HSSPF Ost to the chief of the SS-Personalhauptamt of 3 January 1942: "Infolge eines leichten Sportunfalls, den der SS-Obergruppenführer Krüger am 30.12.1941 erlitten hat," sei "mit einem Dienstantritt vor Ende Januar 1942 nicht zu rechnen," BArch, BDC, SSO-Akte Friedrich-Wilhelm Krüger. Letter from Krüger to Himmler of 17 January 1942: "Mein Gesundheitszustand bessert sich von Tag zu Tag. ... ich [hoffe], dass Anfang der kommenden Woche bereits der Oberarm wieder entschient werden kann, . . .," BArch NS19/2653. See Peter Klein, *Die Wannsee-Konferenz vom 20. Januar 1942: Analyse und Dokumentation* (Berlin, 1995), 13–14.

45 Robin O'Neil, *The Rabka Four: Instruments of Genocide and Ground Larceny: A Warning from History* (London, 2011), 67–84.

46 Cit. from the Protocol of the Wannsee Conference, facsimile in Kampe, "Dokumente zur Wannsee-Konferenz," 47.

47 See Robert Kuwałek, "Die Durchgangsghettos im Distrikt Lublin (u.a. Izbica, Piaski, Rejowiec und Trawniki)," in *"Aktion Reinhardt": Der Völkermord an den Juden im Generalgouvernement 1941–1944* (Einzelveröffentlichungen des Deutschen Historischen Instituts Warschau, vol. 10), ed. B. Musial (Osnabrück, 2004), 199.

48 The Maly Trostinez camp outside Minsk was certainly also inferred by "deportation to the East." See Petra Rentrop, *Tatorte der "Endlösung": Das Ghetto Minsk und die Vernichtungsstätte von Maly Trostinez* (Berlin, 2011).

49 See Kampe, "Dokumente zur Wannsee-Konferenz," 53–54.

50 See Klein, *Wannsee-Konferenz*, 9.

51 Transportrichtlinien Adolf Eichmanns, Hauptstadtarchiv Düsseldorf, Film A28, sheets 15–18 and 20R, reprinted in Alfred Gottwaldt and Diana

Schulle, *Die "Judendeportationen" aus dem Deutschen Reich von 1941–1945: Eine kommentierte Chronologie* (Wiesbaden, 2005), 148–55, 170–77.

52 See letter from Ganzenmüller to Wolff, 28 July 1942: "Seit dem 22.7. fährt täglich ein Zug mit je 5000 Juden von Warschau . . . nach Treblinka, außerdem zweimal wöchentlich ein Zug mit 5000 Juden von Pzemysl nach Belzek [!] . . . Die Züge werden mit dem Befehlshaber der Sicherheitspolizei im Generalgouvernement vereinbart. . .," BArch, NS19/2655; see also "Geheimschreiben Eichmanns an Wolff vom 17 September 1942, Betreff 'Endlösung der Judenfrage'": ". . . ich [habe] den Befehlshaber der Sicherheitspolizei und des SD in Krakau anweisen lassen, die Evakuierung dieser Juden nur in solchem Ausmaß vorzunehmen, als Ersatzkräfte eingesetzt werden können," BArch, NS19/1757.

53 See Kampe, "Dokumente zur Wannsee-Konferenz," 46.

54 SSPF Friedrich Katzmann was in charge of the project. On Durchgangsstraße IV, see Hermann Kaienburg, "Jüdische Arbeitslager an der 'Straße der SS,'" *1999: Zeitschrift für Sozialgeschichte des 20. und 21. Jahrhunderts* 11, no. 1 (1996): 19–21.

55 Pohl, *Judenverfolgung*, 235.

56 "Geheimschreiben RFSS an Krüger," 19 July 1942, BArch NS 19/4064, sheet 1. In September 1942 Wilhelm Keitel called on the Wehrkreisbefehlshaber in the General Government to "replace all Jews employed in industries ancillary to the military or in armaments industries . . . immediately with Poles (non-Jews)." See the letter from Keitel to the Wehrkreisbefehlshaber im Generalgouvernement, 5 September 1942, BArch NS19/2462.

57 See Pohl, *Judenverfolgung*, 235.

58 Christopher Theel, "'Parzifal unter Gangstern'? Die SS- und Polizeigerichtsbarkeit in Polen 1939–1945," in *Die Waffen-SS: Neue Forschungen*, ed. J.E. Schulte, P. Lieb and B. Wegner (Paderborn, 2014), 75.

59 See Schenk, *Lemberger Professorenmord*, 136.

60 Cit. from Schenk, *Lemberger Professorenmord*, 137.

61 See Schenk, *Lemberger Professorenmord*, 138.

62 Schenk, *Lemberger Professorenmord*, 137–39, 165–67. During Menten's first postwar trial, eyewitnesses confirmed that he had been present at shootings in Podhorodce, Galicia, on 7 July 1941.

63 Theel, "SS- und Polizeigerichtsbarkeit in Polen," 75, footnote 72.

64 See "Schreiben Krügers an Himmler, Personalangelegenheit Dr Schöngarth," BArch, NS 19/2028, sheets 2–6.

65 See "Gesprächsniederschrift einer Besprechung Himmlers mit Krüger und Schöngarth," 2 December 1942, BArch, NS19/2028, sheet 7.

66 See "Regierungssitzung," 20 April 1943, in Witte et al., *Dienstkalender*, 652. On the same day, the Polish resistance made an attempt on Krüger's life, which he survived unharmed. Schöngarth led the subsequent investigations, which went on until early June 1943.

67 "Personalverfügung des SS-Führungshauptamtes," 10 November 1943, BArch, BDC, SSO-Akte Eberhard Schöngarth.

68 On 11 September 1944 he gave orders for a massacre to "combat terrorists and saboteurs." See Frank Van Riet, *Handhaven onder de nieuwe orde: De*

politieke geschiedenis van de Rotterdamse politie tijdens de Tweede Wereldoorlog (Zaltbommel, 2008), 255.

69 Gerhard Hirschfeld, *Fremdherrschaft und Kollaboration: Die Niederlande unter Deutscher Besatzung 1940–1945* (Stuttgart, 1984), 38. Cohen, "Een onbekende tijdgenoot," 170.

70 "Fernschreiben Himmlers," 10 March 1945, BArch, BDC, SSO-Akte Eberhard Schöngarth.

71 Military Court for the Trial of War Criminals, Burgsteinfurt, Germany, 7 and 8 February 1946, 43–44, National Archives, Kew, WO 235/102A. On this case, see also the files of the Generalstaatsanwaltschaft in the National Archives, Kew, WO 311/1304.

72 The man whose plane crashed near Enschede was most probably Americo S. Galle, co-pilot of a B-17 bomber jet of the 493rd bomber group of the U.S. Air Force. See O'Neil, *The Rabka Four*, 175–89.

73 Military Court for the Trial of War Criminals, Burgsteinfurt, Germany 7 and 8 February 1946, 39. National Archives Kew, WO 235/102A.

74 Military Court for the Trial of War Criminals, Burgsteinfurt, Germany 7 and 8 February 1946, 42. Military Government—Germany, Military Court—War Criminals, Death Warrant, 16 May 1946, National Archives, Kew, WO 235/102A.

75 See Pohl, *Judenverfolgung*, 392.

76 See Cohen, "Een onbekende tijdgenoot," 172–74.

Bibliography

Birn, Ruth Bettina. *Die Höheren SS- und Polizeiführer: Himmlers Vertreter im Reich und in den besetzten Gebieten*. Düsseldorf: Droste, 1986.

Cohen, A.E. "Een onbekende tijdgenoot: De laatste Befehlshaber der Sicherheitspolizei und des SD in Nederland." ["An Unknown Contemporary: The Last Commander of the Security Police and the SD in the Netherlands"] In *Studies over Nederland in oorlogstijd*, edited by A.H. Paape, 170–91. The Hague: Nijhoff, 1972.

Eisenblätter, Gerhard. "Grundlinien der Politik des Reichs gegenüber dem Generalgouvernement 1939–1945." Ph.D. dissertation, Goethe University Frankfurt, 1969.

Gerlach, Christian. "Die Einsatzgruppe B 1941/42." In *Die Einsatzgruppen in der besetzten Sowjetunion 1941/42: Die Tätigkeits- und Lageberichte des Chefs der Sicherheitspolizei und des SD*, edited by P. Klein, 52–70. Berlin: Edition Hentrich, 1997.

Gottwaldt, Alfred and Diana Schulle.. *Die "Judendeportationen" aus dem Deutschen Reich von 1941–1945: Eine kommentierte Chronologie*. Wiesbaden: Marixverlag, 2005.

Herbert, Ulrich. *Best: Biographische Studien über Radikalismus, Weltanschauung und Vernunft 1903–1989*. Bonn: Dietz, 1996.

Hirschfeld, Gerhard. *Fremdherrschaft und Kollaboration: Die Niederlande unter Deutscher Besatzung 1940–1945*. Stuttgart: Deutsche Verlags-Anstalt, 1984.

[English: *Nazi Rule and Dutch Collaboration: The Netherlands under German Occupation 1940–1945*. Oxford: Berg, 1988.]

Kaienburg, Hermann. "Jüdische Arbeitslager an der 'Straße der SS,'" 1999: *Zeitschrift für Sozialgeschichte des 20. und 21. Jahrhunderts* 11, no. 1 (1996): 13–39.

Kampe, Norbert. "Dokumente zur Wannsee-Konferenz." In *Die Wannsee-Konferenz am 20. Januar 1942: Dokumente, Forschungsstand, Kontroversen*, edited by N. Kampe and P. Klein, 17–115. Cologne: Böhlau, 2013.

Klein, P., ed. *Die Einsatzgruppen in der besetzten Sowjetunion 1941/42: Die Tätigkeits- und Lageberichte des Chefs der Sicherheitspolizei und des SD*. Berlin: Edition Hentrich, 1997.

———. *Die Wannsee-Konferenz vom 20. Januar 1942: Analyse und Dokumentation*. Berlin: Edition Hentrich, 1995.

Krausnick, Helmut and Hans-Heinrich Wilhelm. *Die Truppe des Weltanschauungskrieges: Die Einsatzgruppen der Sicherheitspolizei und des SD 1938–1942*. Stuttgart: Deutsche Verlags-Anstalt, 1981.

Kuwałek, Robert. "Die Durchgangsghettos im Distrikt Lublin (u.a. Izbica, Piaski, Rejowiec und Trawniki)." In *"Aktion Reinhardt": Der Völkermord an den Juden im Generalgouvernement 1941–1944*, edited by B. Musial, 197–232. Osnabrück: Fibre, 2004.

Longerich, Peter. *Heinrich Himmler: Biographie*. Munich: Siedler, 2008. [English: *Heinrich Himmler: A Life*. Oxford and New York: Oxford University Press, 2012.]

Mallmann, Klaus-Michael, Jochen Böhler and Jürgen Matthäus. *Einsatzgruppen in Polen: Darstellung und Dokumentation*. Darmstadt: WBG, 2008.

Młynarczyk, Jacek Andrzej. *Judenmord in Zentralpolen: Der Distrikt Radom im Generalgouvernement 1939–1945*, Darmstadt: WBG, 2007.

Müller, K-J. "Dokumentation: Zu Vorgeschichte und Inhalt der Rede Himmlers vor der höheren Generalität am 13. März 1940 in Koblenz." *Vierteljahrshefte für Zeitgeschichte* 18, no. 1 (1970): 95–120.

O'Neil, Robin. *The Rabka Four: Instruments of Genocide and Ground Larceny: A Warning from History*. London: Spiderwize, 2011. Retrieved 7 October 2016 from http://www.jewishgen.org/Yizkor/Galicia3/galicia3.html

Pätzold, Kurt and Erika Schwarz. *Tagesordnung: Judenmord: Die Wannsee-Konferenz am 20. Januar 1942: Eine Dokumentation zur Organisation der 'Endlösung.'* Berlin: Metropol, 1992.

Pohl, Dieter. *Nationalsozialistische Judenverfolgung in Ostgalizien 1941–1944: Organisation und Durchführung eines staatlichen Massenverbrechens*. Munich: Oldenbourg, 1996.

Präg, W. and W. Jacobmeyer, ed. *Das Diensttagebuch des deutschen Generalgouverneurs in Polen 1939–1945*. Stuttgart: Deutsche Verlags-Anstalt, 1975.

Ramme, Alwin. *Der Sicherheitsdienst der SS: Zu seiner Funktion im faschistischen Machtapparat und im Besatzungsregime des sogenannten Generalgouvernements Polen*. Berlin: Deutscher Militärverlag, 1970.

Rentrop, Petra. *Tatorte der "Endlösung": Das Ghetto Minsk und die Vernichtungsstätte von Maly Trostinez*. Berlin: Metropol, 2011.

Riet, Frank van. *Handhaven onder de nieuwe orde: De politieke geschiedenis van de Rotterdamse politie tijdens de Tweede Wereldoorlog* [Working the New Order: The Political History of the Police of Rotterdam during the Second World War]. Zaltbommel: Aprilis, 2008.

Roseman, Mark. *Die Wannsee-Konferenz: Wie die NS-Bürokratie den Holocaust organisierte*. Berlin: Propyläen, 2002. [English: *The Villa, the Lake, the Meeting: Wannsee and the Final Solution*. London: Penguin Press, 2002.]

Sandkühler, Thomas. *"Endlösung" in Galizien: Der Judenmord in Ostpolen und die Rettungsinitiativen von Berthold Beitz 1941–1944*. Bonn: Dietz, 1996.

Scheffler, W. and H. Grabitz, ed. *Der Ghetto-Aufstand Warschau 1943 aus der Sicht der Täter und Opfer in Aussagen vor deutschen Gerichten*. Munich: Goldmann, 1993.

Schenk, Dieter. *Hans Frank: Hitlers Kronjurist und Generalgouverneur*. Frankfurt am Main: S. Fischer, 2006.

———. *Der Lemberger Professorenmord und der Holocaust in Ostgalizien*. Bonn: Dietz, 2007.

Schöngarth, Eberhard. *Die Zurückweisung von Kündigungen des Arbeitsvertrages*. Erfurt, 1929.

Theel, Christopher. "'Parzifal unter Gangstern'? Die SS- und Polizeigerichtsbarkeit in Polen 1939–1945." In *Die Waffen-SS: Neue Forschungen*, edited by J.E. Schulte, P. Lieb and B. Wegner, 6–79. Paderborn: Schöningh, 2014.

Wildt, Michael. *Die Generation des Unbedingten: Das Führungskorps des Reichssicherheitshauptamtes*. Hamburg: Hamburger Edition, 2002. [English: *An Uncompromising Generation: The Nazi Leadership of the Reich Security Main Office*. Madison, WI: University of Wisconsin Press, 2009.]

Witte, P., M. Wildt, M. Vogt, D. Pohl, P. Klein, C. Gerlach, C. Dieckmann and A. Angrick, ed. *Der Dienstkalender Heinrich Himmlers 1941/42*. Hamburg: Christians, 1999.

8

Josef Bühler

State Secretary for the General Government

A Behind-the-Scenes Perpetrator

Ingo Loose

Illustration 8.1 Portrait found in personal file (approx. 1933) BArch R 3001, 53056.

When Josef Bühler stood in the dock at the Supreme National Tribunal of Poland (Najwyższy Trybunał Narodowy, NTN) in Krakow, the former State Secretary of the General Government seemed to find the case against him quite incomprehensible. Despite the fact that he had given evidence in several previous trials of formerly active Nazis, and his superior, General Governor Hans Frank, had been sentenced to death in Nuremberg in 1946, he did not appear to see why he should be prosecuted for his actions during the German occupation of Poland between 1939 and 1945. He was probably aware that he, too, might face the death penalty, yet still hoped the court would accept that he had merely been an "official acting on orders"[1] and thus be able to escape with his life. He believed, he said, that "with God's help he would manage" to convince the court that he "did not besmirch my hands with the blood of innocent people or use them to terrorize, murder or rob."[2] But one of the central charges brought against him in Poland was his participation in the Wannsee Conference.

Early Career

Josef Bühler was born on 16 February 1904 in Waldsee in Württemberg, the eleventh of twelve children born to Friedrich Bühler, a master baker, and his wife Maria, née Achilles. Raised a Catholic, Bühler later insisted to the Polish investigating judge that he had "always remained a Catholic, never left the Church."[3] After attending boarding school and completing his Abitur school-leaving examinations in 1922, Bühler went to Munich to study law. Apart from his eldest brother, a priest, he was the only one of the family to graduate from university. Continuing his studies in Kiel, Berlin and Erlangen, he gained a doctorate and took his second state examination in 1930. Toward the end of the 1930s, Bühler married a considerably younger woman, Hedwig Almus (born 1920). In 1943 the Bühlers' daughter was born and in 1945, their son.

In 1930 Bühler joined the legal firm of Hans Frank, only four years his senior, who regularly defended Adolf Hitler and the Nazi Party in court. By his own account, it was a chance appointment: "How happy I was to find a steady job in the legal firm of the then attorney, Frank."[4] Bühler worked as a lawyer-candidate and attorney in Frank's law firm for two years, before the chance came for him to join the civil service when Frank was appointed Bavarian Minister of Justice on 10 March 1933. Bühler was among the many who joined the Nazi Party on 1 April 1933, and consequently had the high membership number of 1,663,751.[5] In 1948 he stated that one of his most "compelling motives" for joining the party had been the fact that it was Frank's wish, which he had "made clear to him and repeatedly expressed" for some time.[6] Even after 1933, Bühler's entire professional and political career, indeed his whole life right up to his execution, remained inextricably linked with the career and person of Hans Frank.[7]

On 1 October 1932, Bühler became a probationary judge at Munich district court, moving on in March 1933 to a post as lawyer for the Bavarian Ministry of Justice.[8] At the same time, he also took a senior position in the National Socialist Association of German Legal Professionals (Nationalsozialistischer Rechtswahrerbund, NSRB).[9] He climbed another rung of the career ladder one year later when he took a job at the Reich Ministry of Justice in Berlin in October 1934—again on Frank's initiative—and another in 1935, when he was appointed senior prosecutor at the Munich Higher Regional Court. Finally, in the same year, Bühler joined the staff in Frank's ministerial office. As a Reich minister without portfolio, Frank's remit consisted predominantly of matters concerning the Academy for German Law (Akademie für Deutsches Recht), which he himself had founded in summer 1933. Bühler became a presidium member of the academy and a contributor to the academy journal, though he rarely published articles.[10]

State Secretary in the General Government

As previously, Bühler did not earn his next promotion—to the General Government in Krakow—by his services to the Nazi Party but by his now almost ten-year loyal service to Frank. Conscripted to the German army in late August 1939, Frank had him released just a few days later. He had been appointed head of the administration in occupied Poland, and he wanted Bühler with him. While the German-occupied territories in western Poland were declared annexed by the Reich in October 1939, the status of the "General Government" was deliberately left unclear. From the outset, the Nazi authorities tended to look down on these parts of Poland as a mere labor pool, a "heap of rubble,"[11] and a "racial garbage dump." But they were pleased to control the General Government, as they also regarded it as a place to deport Jews. The first measures toward deporting German and Austrian Jews to the General Government were promptly introduced in fall 1939 by the Reich Main Security Office (Reichssicherheitshauptamt, RSHA) under Adolf Eichmann.[12]

In a draft paper completed in January 1940, the Academy of German Law wrote the following reflections on "legal aspects of German policy on Poland":

> It is not possible to destroy a nation as large and ancient as the Polish nation; such an act has not occurred in European history in all the last centuries . . . However the situation in Eastern Europe develops, the Polish people face a hard and difficult future. They will suffer want in every respect and therefore be compelled to hate.[13]

Initially Bühler was chief of staff of the General Government in Krakow; on 8 December 1939 he was made head of the General Governor's office for the occupied Polish territories.[14] On 8 March 1940 Bühler took over from Arthur Seyß-Inquart as "State Secretary of the administration of the General Government," now holding the rank of a *Ministerialrat.*

Even though Bühler later claimed that his activities had "predominantly involved completing personal errands for the General Governor,"[15] in fact he had had some scope for autonomous action, especially in the fields that did not much interest Frank, a despotic and melodramatic General Governor, mockingly dubbed "Frank-Reich" (which also means "France" in German). These were primarily the legal system, regulations, and the organization of the administration in the General Government.[16]

Illustration 8.2 Slightly retouched press photograph taken to mark a meeting between (from left to right) Friedrich-Wilhelm Krüger, Heinrich Himmler, Hans Frank and Bühler, wearing a State Secretary's uniform complete with riding breeches. Unknown photographer, undated (probably mid March 1942), NAC 2-3142.

In April 1940 Bühler personally laid down the "guidelines for the conduct of Germans in Poland" in a general newsletter. According to these, "enemy territory" demanded "special physical and mental fitness"; furthermore, Germans should avoid "social intercourse with Poles or Jews of either sex," as it would be "undignified and pose a health risk."[17] Bühler, a professing Catholic, also stressed that attending religious services celebrated by Polish clergymen was "incompatible with maintaining a German sense of honor."[18] As the head of the academy of administration in Krakow (since July 1941), Bühler was also responsible for ensuring the party-political education of officials in the General Government and their adherence to the Führer principle.[19]

Bühler soon found himself caught in the crossfire of conflicts over jurisdiction between Frank and Heydrich, or Frank and Himmler. In the early spring 1940, the higher SS and police chief in the East (HSSPF), Friedrich-Wilhelm Krüger, complained at great length to Himmler that Frank had made Bühler the former's deputy in his absence. According to Krüger, this meant "that not only the civil administration sector has gained a lead over the SS and the police but also that the man in question, i.e. Dr Bühler as head of the bureau, is superior to myself, the Höherer SS- und Polizeiführer, should he deputize for the General Governor."[20] The dispute between the civil administration and the SS and police under Krüger was exacerbated by Bühler's participation in the Wannsee Conference. Otherwise, however, the German civil administration and police cooperated on mass crimes in the General Government. In view of this, Bühler's postwar claim to the court that he had been ill-informed of the crimes committed mostly by Krüger and the SS units he commanded was implausible. All the district heads' official statements had to be approved by Bühler.[21] Senior civil servants and district governors wrote monthly situation reports, describing the gradual progress of the campaign to exterminate the Jews in each of the districts, the brutal raids in which over one million Poles were captured for forced labor by summer 1943, the disastrous supply situation and the rapid decline in security as the Polish resistance movement grew from 1942 onward.[22] These reports were all sent directly to Bühler.

In March 1942 Bühler personally informed the district governor of Lublin that transit ghettos had been set up in the Lublin area for thousands of Jews "evacuated" from the German Reich (and Slovakia). Having attended the Wannsee Conference and been informed of the launch of "Aktion Reinhard," the mass murder campaign in the General Government, it must have been clear to Bühler that these ghettos were mere facades behind which the Jewish victims were selected to be forced laborers or murdered.[23] At a meeting of 25 January 1943, Frank said to his staff members (including Bühler): "We should remember that all of us present here now figure in Mr. Roosevelt's list of war criminals. I have the honor of being number one. We have therefore become accomplices, so to speak, in a globally historic sense."[24]

In addition to the special legislation introduced in the annexed Polish territories, known as *Polenstrafrechtsverordnung*, which aimed to deprive the Polish and Jewish populations of virtually all their rights,[25] Frank signed a decree of 20 December 1941 "on the administration of the power of pardoning in the General Government," delegating the prerogative of mercy to the district governors. This mostly concerned cases of Jews who had left the ghetto without permission, an offence made punishable by death in October 1941. On 12 January 1942—one week before the Wannsee Conference—Bühler wrote to inform his colleagues that the decree was designed to "enable the prompt and speedy enforcement of judgements in those cases where no grounds for granting a pardon are offered. That will be the large majority of cases."[26] In

1948, the Polish investigating judge summed up Bühler's activity on the clemency board thus: "The surviving files show that Frank made more frequent use of his prerogative of mercy than you."[27]

In November 1943 Wilhelm Koppe replaced Krüger as HSSPF Ost. Bühler was incomparably better disposed to Koppe than he had been to Krüger. Their relationship even took on a "comradely form," according to Bühler. In February 1944 the two friends amicably agreed that all "movable Jewish assets" should be placed at the disposal of the General Government administration following the murder of the legal owners by the SS.[28]

At the Wannsee Conference in January 1942

As the year 1941 progressed, the idea gained ground on various levels of the Nazi regime to murder the Jewish population in the German sphere of control. A number of resettlement and deportation projects had foundered or failed due to local resistance.[29] After the failure of the Madagascar Plan, Hitler assured General Governor Frank that the Jews "would be removed from the General Government in the foreseeable future."[30] In summer 1941, in the wake of the massacre committed by Einsatzgruppen special units in the occupied Soviet Union, the ministry in charge of the conquered Eastern territories (*Ostministerium*) laid down "guidelines for dealing with the Jewish Question." They conveyed a clear message:

> All measures concerning the Jewish Question in the occupied territories in the East must be implemented in the light of the fact that, after the war, the Jewish Question will be solved across-the-board for all of Europe. They should therefore be applied as preparatory and partial measures ... On the other hand, the experience gained dealing with the Jewish Question in the occupied territories in the East can point to solutions for the entire problem, as the Jews in these territories form the strongest contingent of European Jewry together with the Jews of the General Government.[31]

By this point, the Gauleiter of Wartheland, Arthur Greiser, had already gained authorization from Heydrich and Himmler to murder 100,000 Jews in Warthegau. In the first stationary extermination camp at Kulmhof am Ner (Chełmno nad Nerem), north-west of Litzmannstadt (Łódź), the mass murder of deportees began on 8 December 1941 using exhaust fumes from trucks. Meanwhile, Hans Frank sought a way to rid the General Government of Jews. Apparently Heydrich had not initially planned to invite any representatives of the General Government to the conference at Wannsee, originally scheduled to take place on 9 December 1941. But at a meeting hosted by Himmler in late November 1941, HSSPF Krüger put word out that "the General Governor is striving to take control of the entire handling of the Jewish problem." After consulting with Eichmann in early December 1941, Heydrich concluded that "in the interests of clearing up" the conflict between Krüger and Frank, it would be better to invite both State Secretary Bühler and HSSPF Krüger.[32]

Bühler's invitation from Heydrich came at just the right time for General Governor Frank. Subsequently, at a government meeting on 16 December 1941, he made his intentions absolutely clear:

> I will therefore proceed in the expectation that the Jews disappear. They have to go. To this end, I have organized negotiations on expelling them to the East. A major conference on this question will take place in Berlin in January, to which I will send Herr State Secretary Dr Bühler. This conference is to be held in the Reich Main Security Office under the aegis of SS-Obergruppenführer Heydrich. In any case, a large-scale migration of Jews will be launched. . . . But what will happen to the Jews? Do you believe they will be accommodated in settlement villages in Ostland? In Berlin they said to us: why all this bother; we can't deal with them in Ostland or the Reichskommisariat, liquidate them yourselves.[33] Gentlemen, I must ask you to steel yourselves against all notions of sympathy. We have to exterminate the Jews, wherever we encounter them and wherever humanly possible . . . We can't shoot these 3.5 million Jews, we can't poison them, but we will be able to carry out procedures that somehow lead to their successful extermination, namely those relating to the important measures to be discussed in the Reich. The General Government must become as free of Jews as the Reich.[34]

The Wannsee Protocol contains an enlightening passage on Bühler's participation in the talks:

> State Secretary Dr Bühler observed that the General Government would welcome the launch in the General Government of the Final Solution of this problem, because the transport problem is not a significant issue here and there is nothing to hinder the progress of the campaign in terms of labor resources. Jews must be removed from the territory of the General Government as quickly as possible because here, especially, the Jew poses an extreme danger as a carrier of disease and, second, causes constant disorder in the economy of the land by his continued illicit trade. Furthermore, of the two-and-a-half million Jews concerned, the majority are unfit for work.

State Secretary Dr Bühler also observed that the chief of the Security Police and the SD held responsibility for the "Solution of the Jewish Question" in the General Government, and his work would be supported by the authorities of the General Government. His one request was that the "Jewish Question" in this area should be solved as quickly as possible.

Lastly, the various possibilities for solving the question were discussed, prompting both Gauleiter Dr Meyer and State Secretary Dr Bühler to declare their intentions to immediately carry out certain preparatory works toward the "Final Solution" in the territories in question, while noting that it was imperative to avoid alarming the population.[35]

What Bühler referred to as "certain preparatory works" was nothing less than mass murder, planned and carried out on a regional level. The thrust of Bühler's statement, recorded in the Wannsee Protocol, that "the majority" of Jews in the General Government were "unfit to work" and that the transport problem was not a significant issue, was similarly unambiguous—because transports "further East" were not planned, and the construction of extermination camps for "Aktion Reinhard" was already well underway (Bełżec), at the planning stages (Sobibór), or due to begin a short time later (Treblinka, April 1942).

During Eichmann's interrogation in Israel in 1960, Avner Less asked him what exactly had been meant by the statement that of the 2.5 million Jews in the General Government "the majority . . . are unfit to work." He answered that Bühler had wanted to intimate that "they should be killed."[36] To Eichmann, Bühler, alongside Stuckart, had been the "biggest surprise" at the conference. He alleged that Heydrich had not expected any "cheerful assent" from him, or at least not his full approval of the SS taking key responsibility.[37] However, there is evidence to suggest that the division of responsibilities had already been agreed upon at talks between Himmler and Bühler one week before the conference in Berlin. Bühler is said to have been "delighted" with this meeting on 13 January 1942, which he himself initiated.[38] As the General Government had originally been conceived as a destination for expellees, it seems likely that arrangements had previously been made with Bühler to murder the Jews in the General Government where possible to make room for more Jews to be deported from the Reich. When Himmler visited the General Government in mid March 1942, and convened with Frank, Krüger and Bühler, he emphasized his awareness of "the significance of this land for the current and future tasks of the Reich in the East." Frank, on the other hand, expressed his gratitude toward the "men of the SS and the police" in the General Government for their "excellent work."[39] One can only assume that both men were thinking of the recently launched "Final Solution of the Jewish Question" as they spoke.

A short time previously, in early March 1942, Bühler had announced he had given "his approval for a total of 14,000 Jews to temporarily stay in the district of Lublin in the course of the next month."[40] And in the ensuing months, when mass murder was being conducted at full speed in the "Aktion Reinhard" extermination camps, Bühler was kept informed of the progress of the murders. "We started with three-and-a-half million Jews here," Hans Frank said in early August 1943, "of whom only a few work columns remain; the rest have—let's say—emigrated."[41]

On Trial

Bühler was arrested on 30 May 1945 in Schrobenhausen, north of Munich, Bavaria, and taken to Nuremberg as an important witness in the case against former General Governor Frank, who had been in custody since early May. As Bühler was the key witness for the defense, his consistently apologetic bearing was unsurprising, even if it served to incriminate Frank more than exonerate him.[42] The defense strategy pursued by Frank and Bühler was simple: both tried to systematically shift responsibility for the crimes against humanity committed in the General Government upon Krüger, the higher SS and police leader in the East, and his superiors Heydrich and Himmler. However, there was documentary evidence of several extremely brutal comments they had made that refuted their claim of innocence. Nevertheless, the court failed to question Bühler specifically on his part in Nazi policy on Jews in the General Government, although Soviet senior counselor Lev N. Smirnov did highlight a number of aspects of Bühler's and Frank's direct involvement in crimes.

Questioned in Nuremberg on the uprising in the Warsaw ghetto in April 1943, Bühler gave the cynical response of a German perpetrator: "I heard the same as just about everyone else: that an uprising had broken out in the ghetto, which had been prepared well in advance; that the Jews had used the building material delivered to the ghetto for air raid protection purposes to build fortifications, and that during the uprising there was heavy resistance to the German forces."[43]

In effect, Bühler was the first participant in the Wannsee Conference to mention it after 1945. Having initially avoided mentioning the conference to the U.S. officers questioning him,[44] he finally admitted his participation in February 1946 when cross-examined by the Polish prosecutors Jerzy Sawicki and Stefan Kurowski.[45] On 13 January 1942, he had asked to speak to Heydrich alone, primarily to discuss the disastrous conditions that had arisen "as a consequence of the unauthorized admittance of Jewish people into the General Government." Heydrich had replied that this was precisely the reason for inviting Frank, or himself as Frank's representative, to the conference. Bühler also claimed that Heydrich had informed him the Jews would be resettled "in north-east Europe, in Russia," from which he had drawn the "firm conviction" that "if not for the Jews' sake, for the sake of the reputation and standing of the German people, the resettlement of the Jews would proceed in a humane way."[46] A few days later, Bühler actually admitted that a "plan to exterminate the Jews" had been discussed at the conference.[47] To the military tribunal, however, he admitted only that the meeting had concerned "Jewish Questions." "When the Jewish ghettos were emptied," Bühler had assumed "that they would be resettled in north-east Europe, as the head of the Reich Main Security Office intended, which had been explicitly explained to me [Bühler] at the meeting in February [*sic*] 1942."[48] He was careful not to mention his own contribution to the talks, which later provided a key to interpreting the Protocol, either to the military tribunal or the Polish investigators, and the Protocol itself had not yet been found among the documents of the Ministry of Foreign Affairs.

At the end of the war, the Polish state stood in ruins, having lost a fifth of its population and suffered terrible material and immaterial losses, and faced the difficult question of how to deal with the German war criminals they were able to capture. In the Moscow Declaration on Atrocities of 30 October 1943, the signatories declared that German war criminals would be extradited to the countries where they had committed their crimes. But the question remained whether war criminals should be brought to trial at all or just court-martialed; whether court proceedings should be conducted simply to determine the quantum of the penalties or whether even in these cases the accused should be presumed innocent at first.[49]

Soon after the war ended, the first special criminal courts were set up. A Polish military mission for investigating German crimes was founded in a bid to expedite the Allies' extradition of German war criminals for sentencing in Poland. A few German war criminals were sentenced in Poland before the International Military Tribunal in Nuremberg passed judgement in 1946. Subsequently, Polish courts also took the Nuremberg principles as a guide for dealing with war criminals.[50]

The Supreme National Tribunal of Poland (NTN) started operating on 21 June 1946.[51] By August 1948—Bühler was the last person to be judged by the NTN—it had sentenced forty-nine people, thirty-one of them to death. The Allies extradited over 1,800 Germans to Poland, mostly from the U.S. zone of occupation; the NTN subsequently tried such key figures as Reichsstatthalter Arthur Greiser, the commanders of the Auschwitz and Płaszów concentration camps, Rudolf Höss and Amon Goeth, and staff of the Majdanek and Auschwitz concentration camps as well as Josef Bühler.

On 25 May 1946, U.S. forces committed Bühler to Poland. Then aged forty-two, another two years passed before his trial began. During pre-trial interrogations, Bühler adhered firmly to his tactic of claiming that his mission in the General Government was purely technical, not political. He maintained he had believed that the many forced laborers in Poland were voluntary workers, although he was forced to admit that he knew about the Nazi regulations on compulsory labor and had himself ordered contingents of laborers from some districts. "Of course I, as a German," said Bühler, "sought to satisfy the justified interests of my people, but always aspired to remain within the bounds of fairness and humaneness with respect to the foreign nation, toward whom I never inwardly bore any hate."[52]

For the rest, Bühler frequently uttered the most blatant lies. As a prisoner of war Krüger had killed himself in an American POW camp in Austria; Frank had been executed in 1946. It stood to reason, then, that Bühler should try and shift the responsibility for all charges upon these two. Accused of enforcing discriminatory measures against Poles and Jews through the administration that he headed, Bühler claimed either not to remember, to have had no executive powers, or to have been too convinced a resistor. He professed never to have allowed his activity in the clemency commission "to be used to camouflage mass murders." Jan Sehn, the well-prepared investigating judge, countered: "Until now you have consistently spoken of your protests against the use of violent measures. I can find no evidence of these protests in the documents."[53]

With regard to the Wannsee Conference, Bühler persisted with the story that he had been informed of the "Führer's order" to "assemble all European Jews and resettle them in north-east Russia."[54] He was obviously convinced that the minutes would never be discovered. Later the investigating judge was able to remind him of his own words at the conference by quoting from the Protocol.[55] "My wish," Bühler said, "that the Jews be resettled from the General Government as quickly as possible was dictated not least by consideration of the fact that the Jews would thus be freed from the sorry conditions in the ghettos of the General Government and the hands of the police." Thereupon the investigating judge asked: "So this statement of yours was made for the Jews' sake?" And the accused replied: "I said, in the interests of both sides."[56]

The bill of indictment submitted by the prosecutors in May 1948 was 200 pages long; the evidence consisted of 33,000 pages filling 139 files. Comprising a total of almost 300 case records, it is probably the largest cohesive collection of material on the German occupation in the General Government.[57] Closely following the example of the war crimes trials in Nuremberg, the Supreme National Tribunal found Bühler guilty of crimes against peace, war crimes, and crimes against humanity. The charge of sharing responsibility for "the persecution and extermination in general of Polish citizens of Jewish ethnicity or Jewish origins" was crucially based on Bühler's participation in the Wannsee Conference.[58] The prosecutors took his comment that it was imperative not to "alarm" the local population as evidence that the topic under discussion was not resettlement but mass murder. On account of Bühler's participation in the Wannsee Conference, the prosecutors judged him to be "accountable for involvement in all the crimes that the German authorities committed against the Jews in the G.G."[59]

Bühler's trial lasted from 17 June to 5 August 1948. The presiding judge, Alfred Eimer, was an experienced lawyer who had served as judge and prosecutor at the district court in Poznań even before 1939 and also led the proceedings against Rudolf Höss and Amon Goeth. The prosecutors, Jerzy Sawicki and Tadeusz Cyprian, had previously cooperated on several trials of German war criminals and had first questioned Bühler in Nuremberg in 1946. Bühler's assigned counsels, Stefan Kosiński and Bertold Rappaport—they too had previously worked for the NTN—argued that he had not been directly involved in crimes and that Frank and Krüger bore much of the responsibility, and claimed that Bühler was being turned into a "symbol of all the German occupiers' crimes in the General Government."[60]

During trial, Bühler professed his innocence, insisting that merely the resettlement of Jews to northern Russia had been discussed at Wannsee, even though he knew by this point that the conference Protocol had been found in March 1947. Yet he claimed that there had been no talk of gassing or killing centers at the Wannsee Conference, just of the resettlement of the Jewish population. However, the prosecutors reminded him of Frank's speech of 16 December 1941, in which he had quite openly spoken of exterminating the Jewish population.[61] Moreover, case assessor Nachman Blumenthal, director of the main committee for Jewish history in Poland, convincingly showed what expulsion, resettlement, evacuation and emigration—recurring terms in the Wannsee Protocol—actually signified.[62]

While incarcerated, Bühler was called upon to give evidence in the trial of Ludwig Fischer, the governor of the Warsaw district, in January

1947. Bühler stated that he had gone to Berlin in January 1942 in the hope of improving the terrible conditions in which the Jews lived in the General Government. The prosecutor then asked if he had wanted to defend the Jews, which he affirmed, raising bitter laughter in the courtroom.[63]

The verdict was pronounced on 10 July 1948: Bühler was found guilty and sentenced to death.[64] The court argued that Bühler represented "a certain type of war criminal, namely a behind-the-scenes perpetrator *(przestępca gabinetowy)*, who did not personally commit any crimes but was nevertheless directly involved in their execution," primarily by their efforts toward legitimizing them "within the frame of Nazi law." However, the court granted that Bühler had not demonstrated the same brutality in public and toward the Polish population that Hans Frank characteristically did, and that he had been under Frank's powerful influence since 1930. But the court did not find these to be mitigating circumstances, as it was convinced that Bühler was not only aware of the significance of the Wannsee Conference but had also been informed of the details of exterminating the Jews in the General Government in particular and in Europe in general, and subsequently promoted the procedure within his field of responsibility.[65] Thus Bühler's participation in the Wannsee Conference was a crucial factor in determining his sentence.

Pleas for clemency were made by Bühler's wife, Cardinal Michael von Faulhaber of Munich, Bühler's defense attorneys and Bühler himself, but all were rejected by the Polish president, Bolesław Bierut, in early August 1948.[66] Like all other death sentences imposed by the Supreme National Tribunal, Bühler's sentence was enforced by hanging—on 21 August 1948 at 6 PM in Krakow's Montelupich prison. In an irony of history, the only item of value Bühler had in his possession at the end was one gold dental crown.[67]

Throughout his working life Bühler had remained almost entirely in the background, but his organizational work had been a vital support to Hans Frank, the high-profile representative of the Nazi regime. In view of this, Bühler seems to fit the common, though not uncontroversial, image of the behind-the-scenes perpetrator. Bühler gained a position of considerable power in occupied Poland and, as Frank's deputy, was not only well informed of the German crimes, but also played his part in planning and implementing Nazi Germany's occupation policy and the Holocaust in the General Government.

Ingo Loose taught contemporary history at Humboldt University of Berlin for more than ten years. Since 2010 he has worked as a researcher for the sixteen-volume edition of Holocaust-related documents at the

Institute of Contemporary History Munich—Berlin (IfZ), specializing in Polish and Yiddish sources. To his numerous publications belong books and articles about German, Polish and Jewish modern history, among others about the role of German banks in occupied Poland, the transformation of reborn Poland after 1918, the Ghetto of Litzmannstadt/Lodz 1940–1944, and the Nazi extermination camp at Kulmhof/Chełmno.

Notes

1 See: Archiwum Instytutu Pamięci Narodowej (IPN), GK 196/385, 40: Interrogation transcript of 2 to 5 May 1948.
2 IPN, GK 196/241, 52: Minutes of the proceedings of 17 June 1948.
3 IPN, GK 196/385, 3: Interrogation transcript of 2 to 5 May 1948; for the following ibid., sheet 3 et seq.
4 IPN, GK 196/241, 62: Minutes of the proceedings of 17 June 1948.
5 See: BArch, R 3001/53056, sheets 32–38, here 32: Personalakte Josef Bühler in RJM.
6 IPN, GK 196/385, 16: Interrogation transcript of 2 to 5 May 1948.
7 Christoph Kleßmann, "Hans Frank: Parteijurist und Generalgouverneur in Polen," in *Die braune Elite: 22 biographische Skizzen*, ed. R. Smelser, E. Syring and R. Zitelmann (Darmstadt, 1999), 41–51; Dieter Schenk, *Hans Frank: Hitlers Kronjurist und Generalgouverneur* (Frankfurt am Main, 2006).
8 On the following, see IPN, GK 196/386, 93 et seq.: Polish War Crimes Liaison Detachment and Military Governor, U.S. Zone, Germany, 23 April 1946; BArch, R 3001/53056, here sheet 35 et seq.: Personalakte Josef Bühler in RJM.
9 This was named Bund Nationalsozialistischer Deutscher Juristen (BNSDJ) until 1936.
10 Josef Bühler, "Das Reichsjustizkommissariat," in *Nationalsozialistisches Handbuch für Recht und Gesetzgebung*, ed. H. Frank (Munich, 1935), 1581–84; Josef Bühler. "Nationalsozialistische Strafrechtspolitik," *Zeitschrift der Akademie für Deutsches Recht* 9(1939): 232 et seq.
11 W. Präg and W. Jacobmeyer, ed., *Das Diensttagebuch des deutschen Generalgouverneurs in Polen 1939–1945* (Stuttgart, 1975), 90 et seq.
12 Hans Safrian, *Die Eichmann-Männer* (Vienna and Zurich, 1993), 68–81.
13 IPN, GK 196/252, 1–40, here 3: "Rechtsgestaltung deutscher Polenpolitik nach volkspolitischen Gesichtspunkten."
14 There was also a plenipotentiary of the General Governor based in Berlin, with a residence at Standarten-Straße 14, Tiergarten (today Herbert-von-Karajan-Straße).
15 IPN, GK 196/385, 37: Transcript of the interrogation of 2 to 5 May 1948.
16 See Josef Bühler, "Deutsche Ordnung im Generalgouvernement," in *Das General-Gouvernement*, ed. M. Freiherr du Prel (Würzburg, 1942), 51–55.
17 IPN, GK 196/252, 121: "Grundsätze für das Verhalten der Deutschen in Polen," signed Bühler, 24 April 1940.

18   BArch, R 52 II/252, sheet 22: Regierung des Generalgouvernements, signed
      Bühler, addressed to "Die Herren Chefs der Distrikte in Krakau, Lublin,
      Radom, Warschau," 25 January 1941. See also Adam Ronikier, *Pamiętniki
      1939–1945* (Krakow, 2001), 218.

19   See IPN, GK 196/240, 25: Bill of indictment of 31 May 1948.

20   IPN, GK 196/254, 190–92: HSSPF Ost, signed Krüger, addressed to RFSS
      and Chef der deutschen Polizei Himmler, 3 June 1940; see Mark Roseman,
      Die Wannsee-Konferenz: Wie die NS-Bürokratie den Holocaust organisierte
      (Berlin, 2002), 123.

21   Präg and Jacobmeyer, *Diensttagebuch des deutschen Generalgouverneurs*, 341.

22   See Ingo Loose, "Zygmunt Klukowski und das Generalgouvernement," in
      Zygmunt Klukowski: Tagebuch aus den Jahren der Okkupation 1939–1944, ed.
      C. Glauning (Berlin, 2017).

23   Cit. from Robert Kuwałek, *Das Vernichtungslager Bełżec* (Berlin,
      2013), 130.

24   Präg and Jacobmeyer, *Diensttagebuch des deutschen Generalgouverneurs*,
      612; International Military Tribunal [IMT], *Der Prozeß gegen die
      Hauptkriegsverbrecher vor dem Internationalen Militärgerichtshof (IMT):
      Nürnberg 14. November 1945 – 1. Oktober 1946, gemäß den Weisungen des
      Internationalen Militärgerichtshofes vom Sekretariat des Gerichtshofes unter der
      Autorität des Obersten Kontrollrats für Deutschland veröffentlicht*, 42 vols., ed.
      L.D. Egbert and P.A. Joosten (Nuremberg, 1947–49), vol. 12, 103.

25   "Verordnung über die Strafrechtspflege gegen Polen und Juden in den
      eingegliederten Ostgebieten," 4 December 1941, RGBl., 1941, 759–61.

26   IPN, GK 196/312, 27 et seq., here 27: Regierung der GG, signed Bühler,
      "an die Herren Gouverneure," 12 January 1942, "betr. Ausübung des
      Gnadenrechts" (duplicate).

27   IPN, GK 196/385, sheets 84–91, citation 91: Interrogation transcript of 2 to 5
      May 1948; also Schenk, *Hans Frank*, 186 et seq.

28   IMT, vol. 12, 112, 115.

29   Magnus Brechtken, *"Madagaskar für die Juden": Antisemitische Idee und poli-
      tische Praxis 1885–1945* (Munich, 1997).

30   Cit. from: Susanne Heim and Götz Aly, ed., *Die Verfolgung und Ermordung
      der europäischen Juden durch das nationalsozialistische Deutschland 1933–
      1945* [VEJ], 16 vols. (Berlin, 2008–), vol. 3, 59; also Präg and Jacobmeyer,
      Diensttagebuch des deutschen Generalgouverneurs, 337.

31   GARF, 7021-148-183: Richtlinien des Reichsministeriums für die besetzten
      Ostgebiete für die Zivilverwaltung in den besetzten Ostgebieten (Braune
      Mappe), Teil II: Reichskommissariat Ukraine; reprinted in: VEJ, vol. 8,
      87–89, here 87.

32   Cit. from: VEJ, vol. 9, 144 et seq.

33   In mid October 1941 Alfred Rosenberg, Minister for the Occupied Eastern
      Territories, informed Frank that he would not accept any Jews from the
      General Government. See Raul Hilberg, *Die Vernichtung der europäischen
      Juden*, 3 vols. (Frankfurt am Main, 1990–92), 505.

34   Präg and Jacobmeyer, *Diensttagebuch des deutschen Generalgouverneurs*, 452–
      29, here 457 et seq.; also Hilberg, *Vernichtung*, 505–7.

35 Cit. from the facsimile of the Protocol in: N. Kampe and P. Klein, ed., *Die Wannsee-Konferenz am 20. Januar 1942: Dokumente, Forschungsstand, Kontroversen* (Cologne, Weimar and Vienna, 2013), 53 et seq.

36 Cit. from Kampe and Klein, *Wannsee-Konferenz*, 86.

37 Kampe and Klein, *Wannsee-Konferenz*, 96; see Roseman, *Wannsee-Konferenz*, 86.

38 P. Witte et al., ed., *Der Dienstkalender Heinrich Himmlers 1941/42* (Hamburg, 1999), 316; also Hilberg, *Vernichtung*, 421–25.

39 *Krakauer Zeitung* 63 (15 March 1942), 1: "Reichsführer SS Himmler bei Dr Frank; on Himmler's visit to Krakow on 13 to 14 March 1942," see Schenk, *Hans Frank*, 267.

40 Cit. from Dieter Pohl, *Von der Judenpolitik zum Judenmord: Der Distrikt Lublin des Generalgouvernements 1939–1944* (Münchner Studien zur neueren und neuesten Geschichte, vol. 3) (Frankfurt am Main, 1993), 107.

41 Präg and Jacobmeyer, *Diensttagebuch des deutschen Generalgouverneurs*, 715.

42 See Schenk, *Hans Frank*, 393.

43 Schenk, *Hans Frank*, 86.

44 Jerzy Sawicki, *Przed polskim prokuratorem: Dokumenty i komentarze* (Warszawa, 1961), 196–99.

45 IPN, GK 196/386, 186: Interrogation led by Jerzy Sawicki in Nuremberg on 14 February 1946. Two days later Bühler made a rather awkward attempt (ibid., 208) to deny any involvement by claiming that the conference had not taken place at all.

46 IMT, vol. 12, 79.

47 IPN, GK 196/386, 224: Interrogation led by Jerzy Sawicki in Nuremberg on 14 February 1946.

48 IMT, vol. 12, 114.

49 On the following, see Włodzimierz Borodziej, "Hitleristische Verbrechen: Die Ahndung deutscher Kriegs- und Besatzungsverbrechen in Polen," in *Transnationale Vergangenheitspolitik: Der Umgang mit deutschen Kriegsverbrechen in Europa nach dem Zweiten Weltkrieg*, ed. N. Frei (Göttingen, 2006), 399–437; B. Musial, "NS-Kriegsverbrecher vor polnischen Gerichten," *Vierteljahrshefte für Zeitgeschichte* 47, no. 1 (1999): 25–56; J. Lubecka, "Karanie niemieckich zbrodniarzy wojennych w Polsce," *Zeszyty Historyczne WiN-u* 20, no. 34 (2011): 11–44.

50 J. Sawicki, "Prawo norymberskie a polskie prawo karne," *Państwo i Prawo* 3, no. 3 (1948): 54–63; Elżbieta Kobierska-Motas, *Ekstradycja przestępców wojennych do Polski z czterech stref okupacyjnych Niemiec 1946–1950*, cz. 1–2 (Warszawa, 1991–1992), 5–27.

51 A. V. Prusin, "Poland's Nuremberg: The Seven Court Cases of the Supreme National Tribunal, 1946–1948," *Holocaust and Genocide Studies* 24, no. 1 (2010): 1–25.

52 IPN, GK 196/385, 21: Transcript of interrogation of 2 to 5 May 1948.

53 IPN, GK 196/385, 65, 83: Transcript of interrogation of 2 to 5 May 1948.

54 IPN, GK 196/385, 93–96.

55 IPN, GK 196/385, 107 et seq., 124.

56 IPN, GK 196/385, 110. See also Andrej Angrick, "Die inszenierte Selbstermächtigung? Motive und Strategie Heydrichs für die Wannsee-Konferenz," in Kampe and Klein, *Wannsee-Konferenz*, 242.
57 IPN, GK 196/240, 1–198: Bill of indictment against Josef Bühler and statement of reasons of 31 May 1948.
58 IPN, GK 196/240, 27.
59 IPN, GK 196/240, 181 et seq., 189.
60 IPN, GK 196/244, 116: Protocol of proceedings of 5 July 1948.
61 IPN, GK 196/241, 87–89, 95 et seq., 173–75: Protocol of proceedings of 17 and 18 June 1948.
62 IPN, GK 196/243, 40–86, esp. 81 et seq.: Expert opinion by Nachman Blumenthal of 25 June 1948.
63 IPN, GK 162/348, 106, 131: Transcript of interrogation of Josef Bühler in the case against Ludwig Fischer of 10 February 1947.
64 IPN; GK 196/245, 1–98 (transcript in: IPN, Kr 425/63, 23–122): Judgement against Josef Bühler of 10 July 1948.
65 IPN; GK 196/245, 33, 98, 52 et seq., 82–84.
66 IPN; GK 196/245, 99 [envelope]/1 et seq.
67 IPN, Kr 425/63, 7: Protocol of the enforcement of the death sentence of 21 August 1948; IPN, Kr 425/63, 197: List of the deceased's personal estate of 25 October 1948.

Bibliography

Angrick, Andrej. "Die inszenierte Selbstermächtigung? Motive und Strategie Heydrichs für die Wannsee-Konferenz." In *Die Wannsee-Konferenz am 20. Januar 1942: Dokumente, Forschungsstand, Kontroversen*, edited by N. Kampe and P. Klein, 241–58. Cologne, Weimar and Vienna: Böhlau, 2013.
Borodziej, Włodzimierz. "Hitleristische Verbrechen: Die Ahndung deutscher Kriegs- und Besatzungsverbrechen in Polen." In *Transnationale Vergangenheitspolitik: Der Umgang mit deutschen Kriegsverbrechen in Europa nach dem Zweiten Weltkrieg*, edited by N. Frei, 399–437. Göttingen: Wallstein, 2006.
Brechtken, Magnus. *"Madagaskar für die Juden": Antisemitische Idee und politische Praxis 1885–1945*. Munich: Oldenbourg, 1997.
Bühler, Josef. "Das Reichsjustizkommissariat." In *Nationalsozialistisches Handbuch für Recht und Gesetzgebung*, edited by H. Frank, 1581–84. Munich: Eher, 1935.
———. "Deutsche Ordnung im Generalgouvernement." In *Das General-Gouvernement*, edited by M. Freiherr du Prel, 51–55. Würzburg: Triltsch, 1942.
Bühler, J. "Nationalsozialistische Strafrechtspolitik." *Zeitschrift der Akademie für Deutsches Recht* 9 (1939): 232ff.
Heim, S. and G. Aly, ed. *Die Verfolgung und Ermordung der europäischen Juden durch das nationalsozialistische Deutschland 1933–1945 [VEJ]*. Berlin: Oldenbourg, 2008–.

Hilberg, Raul. *Die Vernichtung der europäischen Juden*, Frankfurt am Main: Fischer-Taschenbuch-Verlag, 1990–1992. [English: *The Destruction of the European Jews*. 4th ed. New York: Holmes & Meier, 1985.]

International Military Tribunal [IMT]. *Der Prozeß gegen die Hauptkriegsverbrecher vor dem Internationalen Militärgerichtshof (IMT): Nürnberg 14. November 1945— 1. Oktober 1946, gemäß den Weisungen des Internationalen Militärgerichtshofes vom Sekretariat des Gerichtshofes unter der Autorität des Obersten Kontrollrats für Deutschland veröffentlicht*, edited by L.D. Egbert and P.A. Joosten. Nuremberg, 1947–1949.

Kampe, N. and P. Klein, ed. *Die Wannsee-Konferenz am 20. Januar 1942: Dokumente, Forschungsstand, Kontroversen*. Cologne, Weimar and Vienna: Böhlau, 2013.

Kleßmann, Christoph. "Hans Frank: Parteijurist und Generalgouverneur in Polen." In *Die braune Elite: 22 biographische Skizzen*, edited by R. Smelser, E. Syring and R. Zitelmann, 41–51. Darmstadt: WBG, 1999.

Kobierska-Motas, Elżbieta. *Ekstradycja przestępców wojennych do Polski z czterech stref okupacyjnych Niemiec 1946–1950*, 2 vols. Warszawa: Główna Komisja Badania Zbrodni Przeciwko Narodowi Polskiemu, 1991–1992.

Kuwałek, Robert. *Das Vernichtungslager Bełżec*. Berlin: Metropol, 2013.

Loose, Ingo. "Zygmunt Klukowski und das Generalgouvernement." In *Zygmunt Klukowski: Tagebuch aus den Jahren der Okkupation 1939–1944*, edited by C. Glauning. Berlin: Metropol, 2017.

Lubecka, J. "Karanie niemieckich zbrodniarzy wojennych w Polsce." *Zeszyty Historyczne WiN-u* [Historical Booklets of the Association "Freedom and Independence"] 20, no. 34 (2011): 11–44.

Musial, B. "NS-Kriegsverbrecher vor polnischen Gerichten." *Vierteljahrshefte für Zeitgeschichte* 47, no. 1 (1999): 25–56.

Pohl, Dieter. *Von der Judenpolitik zum Judenmord: Der Distrikt Lublin des Generalgouvernements 1939–1944*. Frankfurt am Main: Lang, 1993.

Präg, W. and W. Jacobmeyer, ed. *Das Diensttagebuch des deutschen Generalgouverneurs in Polen 1939–1945*. Stuttgart: Deutsche Verlags-Anstalt, 1975.

Prusin, A. V. "Poland's Nuremberg: The Seven Court Cases of the Supreme National Tribunal, 1946–1948." *Holocaust and Genocide Studies* 24, no. 1 (2010): 1–25.

Ronikier, Adam. *Pamiętniki 1939–1945* [Memoirs 1939–1945]. Krakow: Wydawnictwo Literackie, 2001.

Roseman, Mark. *Die Wannsee-Konferenz: Wie die NS-Bürokratie den Holocaust organisierte*. Berlin: Propyläen, 2002. [English: *The Villa, the Lake, the Meeting: Wannsee and the Final Solution*. London: Penguin Press, 2002.]

Safrian, Hans. *Die Eichmann-Männer*. Vienna and Zurich: Europaverlag, 1993. [English: *Eichmann's Men*. New York: Cambridge University Press, 2010.]

Sawicki, J. "Prawo norymberskie a polskie prawo karne." ["The Nuremberg Laws and the Polish Criminal Law"] *Państwo i Prawo* [State and Law] 3, no. 3 (1948): 54–63.

——. *Przed polskim prokuratorem: Dokumenty i komentarze*. Warszawa: Iskry, 1961. [German: *Vor dem polnischen Staatsanwalt*. Berlin: Deutscher Militärverlag, 1962].

Schenk, Dieter. *Hans Frank: Hitlers Kronjurist und Generalgouverneur*. Frankfurt am Main: S. Fischer, 2006.

Witte, P., M. Wildt, M. Vogt, D. Pohl, P. Klein, C. Gerlach, C. Dieckmann and A. Angrick, ed. *Der Dienstkalender Heinrich Himmlers 1941/42*. Hamburg: Christians, 1999.

9

Roland Freisler

Reich Ministry of Justice

Hitler's "Political Soldier"

Silke Struck

Illustration 9.1 Unknown photographer, undated (1933), SZ, 00059078.

> While Heydrich was making his introductory remarks I thoroughly scruti-
> nized the others present. Freisler, the Minister of Justice [State Secretary in
> the Reich Ministry of Justice], sat bolt upright, pressing his backside into
> his seat and constantly turning a pencil in his outstretched hand . . . Not
> one word of disapproval was uttered. Every time he [Heydrich] paused,
> they [the participants] nodded their heads vigorously even though it was
> quite clear that the Final Solution meant nothing other than extermination.
> —Otto Adolf Eichmann, *Meine Flucht*

By Adolf Eichmann's account, Roland Freisler did not stand out at the
Wannsee Conference for anything but his eager bearing. It is a surprising picture, given that the name Freisler is usually associated with a
far from inconspicuous man. Rather, he is remembered as "Rasender
Roland" (the German equivalent of Orlando Furioso), a nickname he
acquired as a young lawyer in Kassel in the late 1920s, or as the formi-
dable "red-robed judge" (*"Richter in roter Robe"*), whose habit it was to
berate and humiliate defendants in the People's Court before alluding
to the death penalty, and finally stridently announcing the same. He
described himself as a "political soldier" in a letter to Adolf Hitler of
15 October 1942, in response to his appointment as President of the
People's Court, who was ready "to judge cases how he believes you, my
Führer, would judge them."[1] The image of Freisler as a radical who was
unconditionally loyal to the Führer originated mainly from film recordings of the trials of those involved in the 20 July Plot to assassinate

Hitler,[2] which Freisler presided over as the draconian president of the First Senate of the People's Court. Commissioned by Reich Propaganda Minister Goebbels in 1944, the recordings were later withdrawn and classified as highly confidential. After the war, Freisler's image became cemented as Germany debated the criminal nature of the Nazi judiciary and the failure of its legal system to confront the history of the People's Court judges. Reports that Freisler's widow drew a full pension, based on his earnings in the "Third Reich," contributed to the controversy. But Freisler had previously been active as a lawyer during the 1920s and 1930s; and he was a rhetorically skilled, ethnonationalistic Nazi politician, the author of various specialist articles and books on matrimonial, inheritance and criminal law, the editor and author of several legal journals and commentaries, and State Secretary of the Reich Ministry for Justice. Even his participation in the Wannsee Conference has not factored significantly into his public image. So who was this man who died on 3 February 1945 during a U.S. bombing raid on Berlin and had supposedly been so quiescent at the Wannsee Conference on 20 January 1942?

Rasender Roland—Orlando Furioso

Freisler was born on 30 October 1893 in Celle, the first-born son of the engineer Julius Freisler of Klantendorf, Moravia, and his wife Charlotte Auguste Florentine Schwerdtfeger of Celle. The family, practicing members of the Evangelical-Reformed Church, moved house several times as Julius Freisler pursued his career. Following periods in Hameln[3] and Aachen, Freisler attended school in Kassel, where he took his Abitur school-leaving diploma, gaining the best result in his class at the Wilhelmsgymnasium in Kassel-Wilhelmshöhe.[4] Kassel henceforth remained Freisler's main geographical base. Nevertheless, when it came to choosing a university, he opted for Jena in Thuringia. Like Gerhard Klopfer and Rudolf Lange after him, he enrolled at the faculty of law of the University of Jena. As a student, he continued the political activities he had begun at school and joined the right-wing students' fraternity SBV Alemania Jena, part of the Schwarzburgbund fraternity association.[5]

While a student of law, the outbreak of the First World War forced Freisler—like many other young men of his generation—to put his professional plans on ice. On 4 August 1914, he joined the 167th infantry regiment as an Officer Cadet. In late 1914 he was wounded in the battle of Langemarck in Flanders—later glorified by the Germans—and on recovery in 1915, was sent to the Eastern Front, where he was taken prisoner on 18 October 1915 by Russian forces. By this time, Freisler was already a lieutenant and holder of an Iron Cross for his services leading a reconnaissance patrol. The Russian troops treated him correspondingly, and he was given work as commissar of a prisoner-of-war camp administration after the 1918 October Revolution. By his own account, he was responsible for maintaining food supplies and not involved in any political tasks.[6] This activity as a commissar under the Bolsheviks was the cause of some controversy in later years, especially after 1933. At one point Hitler even described Freisler himself as a "Bolshevik." For his part, in his curriculum vitae of 22 January 1921, Freisler soberly recounted "returning home" from Russian imprisonment and having learned the Russian language during his long detention.[7] To mark Freisler's 40th birthday, the newspaper *Völkischer Beobachter* published a somewhat more embellished account on 4 November 1933. This described how he had escaped from imprisonment shortly after being made a commissar, and had resourcefully made the best of his circumstances:

> He was in Russia until 1920, when he managed to flee to Germany, having been made commissar for food supplies and industry by the Bolsheviks a short time previously. On his return home, Dr Roland Freisler sat for an examination in the Russian language at the Oriental Seminary, which he passed with an overall grade of "good."[8]

Freisler's imprisonment ended when the prisoner-of-war camp was dissolved in July 1920. A short time later, he was officially discharged from the old army.[9] Once this crucially formative episode in his life was over, he continued his study of law in Jena, his ambition not in the least diminished. He obtained a doctorate in law under Justus Wilhelm Hedemann (1878–1963)[10] and Otto Koellreuther (1883–1972)[11] on the subject of the "basics of company organization"[12] and was awarded the highest distinction of "summa cum laude" by his two doctoral supervisors, both later to become prominent Nazis. In spite of the top grade awarded, Koellreuther, the second assessor, viewed Freisler's work somewhat critically. He declined to attend Freisler's thesis defense, seeing in him "a pronounced dogmatic talent," an uncritical approach to everything new, and a tendency to hail the zeitgeist—an interesting assessment considering both Freisler's later development and Koellreuther's own career under Nazism.[13] One year later, Freisler's doctoral thesis was accepted and published by the Institute of Commercial Law of Jena University.[14] While still a young man, Freisler gained a reputation as a serious jurist on the legal scene of the Weimar

Republic. He completed his legal training on 2 October 1923, when he took his main state examination. Together with his brother Oswald, now also a doctor of law, he set up a law firm in Kassel in early 1924.[15] The two brothers divided their firm's commissions according to their diverging preferences. Oswald took over the civil law cases while Roland dealt with criminal law and worked as a defense attorney. In the latter capacity, he soon made an impression on the senate of the Reich Court in Leipzig, which had jurisdiction over the greater Kassel district, as a combative and eloquent lawyer in political trials.[16] He became known in Kassel for acting as defense attorney in political proceedings against anti-Semitic and right-wing defendants and, after 1925, particularly members of the SA and the Nazi Party. He became an early Party member himself on 9 July 1925, holding the membership number 9,679. The two brothers' political convictions also earned them repeated reprimands, fines and summonses before professional tribunals.

Roland Freisler was alternately accused of breaching his duty as a lawyer, injuring the dignity of the court, and defamation, as well as other, similar offences.[17] In the case against Philipp Fischer, a Nazi charged with insulting a Jewish tradesman, Freisler declared: "We followers of Hitler take the viewpoint that a Jew cannot be the object of an insult at all."[18] A professional tribunal consequently found that "his remarks cannot have been made for the purpose of upholding the rights of his client; instead, he [Roland Freisler] used the opportunity to publicly express his contempt for the Jews."[19] By openly expressing his anti-Semitism, Freisler proved he was not one of the so-called "March fallen" ("Märzgefallenen"), but a member of the old guard, a convinced nationalist — from 1933 onward he always made sure he wore the appropriate Party badge — who chose his moments for impressing the Party according to when he sensed opportunities for gaining political power.

In 1924 Freisler had become a member of Kassel city council for the right-wing Völkisch-Sozialer Block, with whom he had sympathized since 1923. But shortly after Hitler's early release from Landsberg prison, he joined the Nazi Party, and his activity as a verbally dexterous representative of the Nazi Party on Kassel city council launched his rise within the Party. Soon he was made deputy Gauleiter of Hessen-Nassau-Nord and did not conceal his interest in taking over the post of acting Gauleiter Dr Walter Schultz. The latter was only able to prevent Freisler usurping him in 1928 by rallying the support of Rudolf Heß, with whom he was in close contact, and denouncing Freisler as "moody," "hectic and ranting."[20] Freisler did not let this setback deter him but remained ambitious and manipulative. He invited many high-ranking Hessen Nazis to his marriage with eighteen-year-old Marion Russegger on 23 March 1928.[21] As the marriage remained childless for many years—their sons Harald and Roland were not born until the late 1930s[22]—Freisler continued unabated to work on his professional and political advancement. He effectively raised his public profile in 1930 by applying for motion of censure against the Kassel chief of police, Dr Adolf Hohenstein, who was responsible for enforcing a ban on uniforms issued by the Prussian state government. Under Freisler's leadership, the Kassel Nazi Party deliberately disregarded the ban, appearing in various places in town in uniform. Consequently, their political opponents did likewise. Riots in the center of Kassel erupted as a result. Freisler accused chief of police Hohenstein, in outraged tones, of not having taken firm enough action against the communists. As a Jew, moreover, and one who was seconded by a Social Democrat (the commander of the uniformed police), Freisler said he was incapable of dealing objectively with Nazis. By this time, Freisler had a national reputation as the "leader of the National Socialists in Kassel" and an "incorrigible enemy of the Jews."[23] Despite being sentenced to pay a fine of 300 Reichmarks for slander and defamation, he continued to provoke high-profile and lucrative—for himself as a lawyer—disputes with his political opponents.[24] In 1931 he and Hans Frank, Hitler's attorney and head of the legal department of the Reich leadership of the Nazi Party, defended SA leader Graf Wolf-Heinrich von Helldorff—the later chief of police in Potsdam and Berlin, whom Freisler was to sentence to death in August 1944—in the case of the anti-Jewish Kurfürstendamm riots of 12 September 1931, and managed to secure him a lenient sentence on appeal.[25] From 1932 onward, Freisler not only worked as a lawyer and member of the Kassel city council (1924–33) but was also a member of the Prussian parliament (1932–33) and, after 1933, represented the Nazi Party in the Reichstag.

From State Secretary to Bloody Judge

To mark Hitler's election as Chancellor in January 1933, Freisler arranged for Kassel town hall to be occupied by Nazis and the Kassel courthouse hung with swastika flags. After news of these actions appeared in the national press, Freisler was appointed *Ministerialdirektor* in the Prussian Ministry of Justice under Dr Hanns Kerrl. Functioning as head of the personnel department, he used his position to exert pressure on Jewish members of staff. The newspaper *Völkischer Beobachter* of 30 October 1933 stated in a review of his career: "He started working for the Prussian Minister of Justice Hanns Kerrl in late March 1933, initially as Ministerialdirektor in the Ministry of Justice, and in late May was named State Secretary in the Prussian Ministry of Justice. In this capacity he has made excellent contributions to the reforms of the Prussian judiciary."[26] In summer 1933 the newly appointed Prussian State Secretary was made a member of the Prussian state council by Hermann Göring, along with the other Wannsee Conference attendees Wilhelm Stuckart and Erich Neumann. From Freisler's point of view, however, his promotion to the Prussian ministerial administration also had disadvantages. He reluctantly applied to have his name deleted from the attorneys' register of the Kassel Regional and District Courts on 19 June 1933. At this time, Freisler earned an annual income of 24,000 Reichmarks. But as he had no additional income as a lawyer, he deemed it appropriate to ask for household assistance, given that his wife Marion would have to run the household at Hinzepeter Straße 8 in Kassel for another month. He did not take his many commissions as an expert assessor into account, for which he charged and accepted fees.

On 1 April 1934, following the merging of the Prussian and Reich ministries, Freisler became State Secretary in the Reich Ministry of Justice under Dr Franz Gürtner.[27] His place of work was now Wilhelmstraße 65 in Berlin.[28] Having received the Golden Party Badge two months previously, he wore it henceforth at all public appearances. New in Berlin, he and his wife took up residence at Herder Straße 9 in the elegant district of Zehlendorf.[29] Under Gürtner, Freisler continued to cultivate his reputation as an expert in criminal, matrimonial and inheritance law. In the fields of matrimonial and inheritance law, he was soon dealing with cases concerning so-called "Mischlinge" ("cross-breeds") and sought to shape the law according to his own convictions, one example being the blood-and-soil notions behind the land heritage law (Reichserbhofgesetz).[30] In the Academy of German Law, founded in Munich in 1933 by Hans Frank, Freisler acted as chairman of the criminal law committee, head of the department of scientific studies and editor of the Academy newspaper. In 1934 the Academy of German Law was made a public corporation of the Reich, lending the writings it published, including Freisler's, the official seal of approval. In 1935 Frank praised Freisler as a "defender of National Socialism in the field of legislation reform."[31] He was partly referring to Freisler's declaration in 1934 that the so-called Röhm putsch murders were right and proper, by which he showed his support for the radical, "preventative" enforcement of criminal law. Other members of the Academy in Freisler's professional and personal circles included his doctoral supervisor Justus Wilhelm Hedemann, his second assessor Koellreuther, the State Secretary in the Reich Ministry of Justice and later interim Minister of Justice Dr Franz Schlegelberger, the first President of the People's Court and later Minister of Justice Otto Thierack,[32] the State Secretary in the Reich Ministry of Education and later in the Ministry of the Interior Stuckart, and even the non-lawyer Friedrich Minoux. It was in his villa, which he had sold to the SS foundation Nordhav in 1940, that the participants in the Wannsee Conference, including Academy members Freisler and Stuckart, discussed the "Final Solution."

Although Freisler was once again described as a "champion of Nazi national law" in a statement to the press by the Reich Ministry of Justice, marking his forty-third birthday in October 1936,[33] his hitherto meteoric career unexpectedly faltered one year later. The reason was his brother Oswald, now also working in Berlin as a lawyer and notary. In the show trials of Berlin Catholics, which Goebbels wanted staged in the People's Court for publicity purposes, Oswald Freisler defended three co-defendants of main defendant Dr Joseph Roissant and managed to get them acquitted. Propaganda Minister Goebbels was outraged by Oswald Freisler's performance in court—appearing in plain clothes with his Golden Party Badge attached to the collar of his suit—and wrote to Minister of Justice Gürtner that "a party comrade, and a holder of a badge of honor at that, has no place acting as the attorney of the defendants' choice in a case of high treason."[34] Even if Goebbels was under the mistaken impression that Oswald had represented main defendant Joseph Roissant, who was charged with forming a united front between Catholics and communists, his reaction sparked a fierce debate about the role of the Freisler brother as defense attorney in a highly political, and after Goebbels' design, public trial. At Hitler's request, and as a result of Goebbel's intervention, Oswald Freisler was expelled from the Nazi Party by an order of Hitler's Chancellery.[35] Probably as a consequence, he committed suicide on 4 March 1939—a watershed for, and blemish on the name of, State Secretary Freisler.[36]

During and after this affair, in 1938 and 1939, Freisler published many writings and embarked on intensive lecture tours, apparently in a concerted effort to raise his profile as a leading jurist and an ethnonationalistic, anti-Semitic German politician throughout Europe. In April 1938 he published a groundbreaking article entitled "The basics of reforming criminal proceedings; the purpose of the criminal procedure and its legal framework," which he introduced with the words: "German criminal law should serve the preservation of the German people and the safeguarding of the National Socialist state," and in which he commented on the necessity of reforming German criminal law to correspond with "ethno-national law" *(Volksrecht)*.[37] In fall 1938,

Freisler followed a prestigious invitation from the Italian Ministry of Justice to attend the first major international criminal biology congress in Rome. From 3 to 8 October, Freisler led the fifty-person German delegation, consisting not only of criminal biologists but also members of the Reich administration of justice, the Reich Legal Office of the Nazi Party, members of the Academy of German Law, the Reich Ministry of the Interior, the Ministry of Foreign Affairs, representatives of the Supreme Command of the Armed Forces (OKW), and scholars. Freisler was not only the head of the delegation but also addressed the congress on 7 October, which with 500 delegates from thirty-four countries, was well attended. His talk included the following remarks on criminality, crime-fighting and personality research:

> Crime prevention in general! That is a declaration! And to have made this declaration at the first congress of this kind is a great achievement. Hygiene is even more important than cure; it dries out the cesspools that release bubbles of individual and mass infection. It deprives the pathogenic bacteria of their source of life and effectiveness, along with their breeding ground. We Germans have overcome the separation of law from ethos, we declare our belief in the fact that the commandments of the law grow in the soil of an ethno-nationalist ethos.[38]

In his report on the congress to the Reich Chancellery, Freisler also mentioned that he had had a meeting with Benito Mussolini in the Palazzo Venezia in Rome. With some pride, he pointed out that "the Duce talked to me about the race laws passed in Italy the previous day."[39] While this event further enhanced the standing of Freisler's delegation, it was not the only honor he received in Rome. On 6 January 1939, Freisler wrote to the Ministry of Justice to inform his colleagues that he had been awarded the order known as Cavaliere di Gran Croce dell'Ordine della Corona d'Italia by King Victor Emanuel III for his participation in the criminal biology congress in Rome.[40] The week in Italy, then, not only demonstrated the high regard in which Freisler was held in Italy and his own very clear position on racial topics but also bolstered his position in comparison to the older, second State Secretary in the Reich Ministry of Justice, Schlegelberger, who was much esteemed internationally but did not yet show any commitment to Nazi politics.[41]

One month after his trip to Rome, Freisler represented the Reich Ministry of Justice at the "Göring conference on the Jewish Question" in the Reich Ministry of Aviation, also attended by Stuckart, Neumann, Heydrich and Eichmann. Held on 12 November 1938, one of the points discussed at this conference was the so-called atonement tax (*"Sühnelesitung"*), levied on Jews to raise 1 billion Reichsmark to "compensate" for the damages caused in the night of pogroms on 9 November.[42] Policy on Jews, supporting the German minorities in other European countries, and National Socialist legal reforms remained important issues to Freisler. In fall 1940 he traveled to Hungary to give a talk about the "concept of law in the new Europe." Here he met the Hungarian Minister of Justice and representatives of the ethnic German minority in Hungary. He reassured them that German ethnicity had found "its house and home" in Hungary, too.[43]

But his activities were not confined to considering race issues on a European level and developing a new "ethnonational law" influenced by Nazism. On 8 July 1940, the Reich Ministry of Justice received a letter from Dr Lothar Kreyssig, senior local court judge and judge of a court of guardianship, protesting at the euthanasia murders in Brandenburg, the victims of which included his own wards. Thus Freisler gained knowledge of the Nazi project of killing people deemed unfit to live.[44] Kreyssig had learned of the mysterious deaths of mental patients in Hartheim and regarded it as his duty as a judge to take action against what he saw as illegal killings: "I can no longer doubt that the patients taken in batches from their accommodation to the aforementioned institution were killed."[45] He assumed that "mentally ill people in institutional care were made to die without the knowledge of their families, their legal guardians or the guardianship court, without the guarantee of an orderly legal process and without any legal grounding,"[46] and concluded: "Law is to benefit the people. In the name of this dreadful doctrine, which has still not been contradicted by any custodians of the law in Germany, entire areas of community life are exempted from the law, e.g. the concentration camps are completely, as the care and nursing homes are now completely exempted."[47] This letter prompted two meetings in the Reich Ministry of Justice. First, Freisler met Kreyssig alone to discuss the matter. Freisler agreed with the agitated guardianship court judge's criticism on a technical level. Surprisingly, he even advised Kreyssig to press charges against Reichsleiter Philipp Bouhler, whom Hitler had placed in charge of euthanasia, but ultimately, he argued that the National Socialist revolution had given rise to a new concept of law. Freisler also pointed out that the Ministry of Justice was planning an "orderly" procedure for euthanasia, involving expert committees and grievance councils, but did not question the rightfulness of the killings per se. Kreyssig continued to take a stand against euthanasia, actually pressing charges of murder against Bouhler and calling for mental hospitals to compulsorily supply information on the transport of patients to the institutions in question. Some months later, he was summoned to a meeting with Minister of Justice Gürtner. Gürtner told

Kreyssig he was assured of the legality of the measures, as he had received a notice of authorization from Hitler of 1 September 1939. Gürtner argued that this notice made the Führer's will evident and thus legitimized the procedure, adding: "Well, if you will not accept the will of the Führer as the source and basis of the law, then you cannot remain a judge."[48] Kreyssig reportedly agreed with Gürtner on one point only—that he could no longer be a judge—and was made to retire under paragraph 6 of the Law for the Restoration of the Professional Civil Service.[49]

In late 1941 Freisler was preoccupied with anti-Jewish measures. On 31 October 1941 he issued orders for Jews to wear the Star of David in Reich prisons,[50] and a short time later, in January 1942, he decreed that imprisoned Jews and Poles should no longer be addressed as "Herr."[51] In summer 1941 Freisler had begun cooperating closely with the governor in Wartheland, Reichstatthalter Arthur Greiser, on the regulation of penalties against Jews and Poles in the occupied Eastern territories, staying with his wife in the Poznań area. Freisler and Greiser agreed that the death penalty, or at least terms of concentration camp imprisonment, imposed by specially set-up court-martials, were the only appropriate punishment even for minor offences where Poles and Jews were concerned. In the course of these talks in the Reichsgau Wartheland, in June 1941, Freisler met another later participant in the Wannsee Conference, Klopfer, who agreed to tell the head of the Nazi Party Chancellery, Reichsleiter Martin Bormann, that he endorsed Freisler's agreement with Greiser on the matter of penal legislation for Poles and Jews.[52] Four days before the Wannsee Conference, Freisler wrote about the recently launched deportations from the Reich to the Eastern territories with reference to applying the penal regulations for Poles, which came into force in December 1941. The new legislation naturally also applied to those Jews "who come from the other parts of the Reich into the incorporated Eastern territories." Furthermore, he wrote that he expected the judges and attorneys active in Poland to "feel like soldiers in the political troop of German ethnicity, which has been assigned the task of fulfilling the German mission in the incorporated East" and to regard those persons as Jews who "are Jews [under the] general German Reich regulations."[53]

Freisler was one of eight lawyers at the Wannsee Conference on 20 January 1942. He and Stuckart were the legal experts who established the legal and administrative framework for identifying, isolating and deporting German Jews, and thus prepared the ground for the Nuremberg race laws, which were finally written by the Ministry of the Interior together with the Nazi Party Chancellery. At the conference, he embodied a lawyer who was active in the Reich Ministry of Justice and had plenty of experience of dealing with issues of matrimonial and inheritance law, as well as matters such as the definition and significance of mixed-blood marriages, and kindred blood and its importance for successive generations. Back in 1933, in an "exposé on National Socialist penal law,"[54] published by Minister of Justice Kerrl, he had argued in favor of classifying "racial treason" (*"Rasseverrat"*) as a statutory offense under the new Nazi laws. In an article in August 1937, part of a series on "legal regeneration" (*"Beiträge zur Rechtserneuerung"*) in the newspaper *Deutsche Justiz*, Freisler wrote with reference to distinguishing the concept of mixed-blood marriages from mixed-faith marriages: "But we are thinking of blood kinship . . . National Socialism has brought this into the open through the Nuremberg Laws presented at the Party Congress." Freisler, then, surely approved of taking Nuremberg as the yardstick for policy on "Mischlinge." But he probably did not think the last word had been spoken on the matter, as his ideas on racial mixing and heredity spanned several generations and therefore went far deeper than recorded in the Protocol. In fact, the topic was discussed further at subsequent conferences in spring and fall 1942. Following the Wannsee Conference, some participants felt emboldened to express their own ideas. In a secret letter of 16 March 1942 to all attendees of the Wannsee Conference with respect to the "Final Solution of the Jewish Question," Stuckart wrote: "There is complete clarity and agreement on the fact that Jewish blood, even if the carriers are half-Jews, is to be eliminated from the German, and beyond that, the European bloodstream, i.e. that first and foremost any mixing of blood with Germans or related peoples is to be prevented."[55]

On 5 April 1942 Schlegelberger—interim Minister of Justice following the death of Gürtner in January 1941—declared that it was imperative to clearly delineate the circle of people affected by the "Final Solution of the Jewish Question." Measures toward the "Final Solution" were to be taken against full Jews and "first-degree crossbreeds" (*"Mischlinge ersten Grades"*); "second-degree crossbreeds," in contrast, should be given the choice between sterilization or deportation.[56] Stuckart's proposal to enforce compulsory divorces was dismissed, but divorce procedures were to be greatly simplified. Freisler and Stuckart apparently met again later the same year to discuss other politically charged topics. On 6 August 1942, Freisler wrote to the Reich Minister of the Interior in connection with the punishment of violations of wartime regulations: "I must speak a word of warning against replacing one system of criminal justice with another, such as administrative jurisdiction. Following my conversation with Herr State Secretary Dr Stuckart, I would like to ask that, should there be any objections to my suggestions, they are discussed at the State Secretaries' meeting."[57]

In other respects, 1942 was a year of professional advancement and personal changes for Freisler. Six days after the Wannsee Conference, he traveled to The Hague in the Netherlands to give a talk on "the jurisprudence of young Europe" (*"Das Rechtsdenken des jungen Europa"*)[58] to a large audience including Reichskommissar Dr Seyß-Inquart. In late summer 1942, he was made president of the highest political court, the 1934-founded People's Court, more as a result of tactical personnel changes in the judicial system than of his own ambitions.[59] He was actually hoping to become Reich Minister of Justice. But Freisler embraced his task as a judge, assigned him by Hitler on 20 August, as an opportunity to apply his ideas of justice, and did not let it prevent him from publishing further groundbreaking legal writings, such as his commentary on "German law."

Under his aegis as President of the People's Court and chief judge of the First Senate, more death sentences were imposed than ever before and distinctly fewer "incomprehensibly lenient sentences," as Freisler saw them.[60] As a consequence, he gained a reputation as a "bloody judge" who presided over all the most important political trials. In 1943 he pronounced death sentences for most members of the White Rose resistance group and, in 1944 and 1945, for most of those involved in the 20 July Plot to assassinate Hitler. Yet Freisler was not entirely trusted by the top men in the Reich.[61] Following talks with Hitler, Goebbels saw reason to meet Freisler personally in order to make his standpoint clear on "how trials are to proceed." This echoed Thierack's comments in 1942, pointing out to his successor at the People's Court that he had no experience as a judge. For his part, Freisler acted the "political soldier," who judged defendants as Hitler expected—irrespective of the person and with no mercy—particularly in the trials of those involved in the assassination attempt on Hitler. Among the defendants on 15 August 1944 were Graf Wolf-Heinrich von Helldorff, whom Freisler had once successfully defended in court in connection with the Kurfürstendamm riots in 1931/32. This time, Freisler humiliated him, too, before eventually sentencing him to death.[62] Freisler died in a bombing attack on 3 February 1945, a day of hearings against parties involved in the plot to assassinate Hitler. In his death announcement, published on 16 February 1945, Minister of Justice Thierack praised his deceased colleague: "Holding a position of responsibility in the administration of justice from 1933 onward, Dr Freisler played a considerable part in shaping and creating legislation to enable the National Socialist interpretation of the law to become established in the German judiciary." All his life he had acted with "fanatical resolve" as a National Socialist who "gave supreme priority to the greater good."[63]

Thierack did not, however, attend Freisler's funeral. After the war, Marion Freisler re-adopted her maiden name and moved to Munich. News of her pension payments sparked public controversy; she had emerged "exonerated" from denazification proceedings and was thus accepted as her husband's universal successor. Roland Freisler had left his estate to his wife with the words: "She shall simply inherit everything," written in 1944. In 1955 the magazine *Der Spiegel* described Freisler's actions as "cleverer than almost all his accomplices'."[64] After 1974 his widow also received a loss adjustment pension, as the pension office responsible had found that her husband would have continued his career had he survived. The law was not changed in this respect until after Marion Russegger's death in 1997.

Summary

Freisler was an ambitious lawyer, convinced Nazi, anti-Semite, and radical judge. He knew about the use of murder as a potential instrument of politics long before the Wannsee Conference, and approved of it. As a politician and lawyer, he had connections throughout Europe and was in some respects more highly regarded outside Germany. Partly for this reason, he was familiar with other countries' positions on Jewish and race issues. Representing the Ministry of Justice at the Wannsee Conference, he was quite aware that this meeting of high-ranking Nazis was called to discuss the extermination of the Jewish population in Europe. His contribution to the talks on 20 January 1942 was to argue in favor of a radical policy on people of mixed blood; he takes responsibility for broadening the definition of those targeted. After the disappointingly ineffective Judge Trials in Nuremberg, and the early release of many of those convicted in the early 1950s, he along with his role within Nazism began to be considered more closely and critically. Freisler gained an image as "the devil's attorney," casting a long and dark shadow, under which the other National Socialist lawyers were able to continue their careers largely undisturbed.[65]

Silke Struck has a master degree in political science from the Free University of Berlin. She has been a freelance employee of the House of the Wannsee Conference since the foundation of the memorial in 1992. In 2005, she was a consultant to BBC London for the television documentation "Auschwitz: Inside the Nazi State." Until 2009 she worked as a contract historian for the War Crimes Section of the Department of Justice Ottawa /Canada. Since the 90s, she has been working as a private researcher at the Bundesarchiv Berlin Lichterfelde.

Notes

1 Helmut Ortner, *Der Hinrichter: Roland Freisler, Mörder im Dienste Hitlers* (Frankfurt am Main, 2014), 148.
2 See the movie: *Verräter vor dem Volksgerichtshof*, BArch 3179.
3 Roland Freisler's brother Oswald was born here on 29 December 1895.
4 The Wilhelmsgymnasium in Kassel still exists today and actively remembers Roland Freisler as a former pupil.
5 See also *Schwarzburgbund: Ein Bund christlicher Verbindungen*. Retrieved 15 October 2016 from http://www.schwarzburgbund.de. Freisler was later thrown out of the fraternity for trying to change the student movement.
6 Ortner, *Hinrichter*, 51.
7 See: Universitätsarchiv Jena, Bestand K, no. 308. In his analysis of Freisler's curriculum vitae, the author Manfred Overesch found that he "conspicuously" emphasized the fact that he had been taken a prisoner of war "through no fault of his own" and could have been released following the Treaty of Brest-Litovsk. See Manfred Overesch, *Gott, die Liebe und der Galgen: Helmuth J. und Freya von Moltke in ihren letzten Gesprächen 1944/45*, (Hildesheim, Zurich and New York, 2015), 74 et seq.
8 "Staatssekretär Freisler 40 Jahre," *Völkischer Beobachter*, 4 November 1933.
9 "Personalbogen," undated, BArch, R 3001/56247.
10 In 1933 he became a member of the Academy of German Law founded by Hans Frank.
11 A Nazi politician and jurist who campaigned against denazification after 1945.
12 Freisler's dissertation was originally titled "Die zivilrechtliche Stellung der Betriebsvertretung" ["The Status According to Civil Law of Employees' Representation"]. In order to take contemporary changes to the law into account, Freisler agreed on a slightly different topic with his doctoral supervisor, Hedemann. See Overesch, *Helmuth J. und Freya von Moltke*, 78.
13 Overesch, *Helmuth J. und Freya von Moltke*, 83.
14 A second edition of Freisler's thesis was published by the institute (Schriften des Instituts für Wirtschaftsrecht der Universität Jena) as early as 1923.
15 Oswald Freisler obtained his doctorate in 1923 with the grade "satisfactory." His career was crucially influenced by his brother Roland and his party-political leanings. Oswald joined the Nazi Party in 1927 and was a founding member of the League of Nazi German Lawyers. He became a member of the Academy of German Law in 1933. However, he was thrown out of the Nazi Party in 1937 after successfully defending Catholic members of the resistance in court. In 1939 Oswald Freisler committed

suicide under mysterious circumstances; BArch R 3001/56246 (Personalakte, Reichsjustizministerium).

16 Ortner, *Hinrichter*, 50 et seq.
17 "Zusammenstellung der ehrengerichtlichen und strafrechtlichen Verfahren, der Aufsichtsmaßnahmen gegen Rechtsanwalt Oswald Freisler und der Äußerungen über seine Persönlichkeit," BArch, R 3001/56246, 355–57.
18 "Anklageschrift des Generalstaatsanwalts Cassel vom 15. Juni 1924 gegen die Rechtsanwälte Dr Roland und Dr Oswald Freisler wegen Pflichtverletzung," BArch R 3001/56246, 172 et seq.
19 "Anklageschrift vom 15. Juni 1924," BArch R 3001/56246, 172 et seq.
20 Ortner, *Hinrichter*, 55.
21 Ortner, *Hinrichter*, 53.
22 Harald on 1 November 1937, Roland on 12 October 1939. Both children were baptized. The birth announcements are in Freisler's personal file from the Reich Ministry of Justice, BArch R 3001/56247.
23 "Aus den Gerichtssälen," *CV Zeitung* 49 (5 December 1930): 628.
24 Ortner, *Hinrichter*, 56.
25 "Urteil des Landgerichts," 9 February 1932, LAB, A Rep. 358-01, 20. See also Stefan Hördler, "Entgrenzung und Eingrenzung der Gewalt: Berliner SA, SS und Polizei (1933–1939)," in *Berlin 1933–1945*, ed. M. Wildt and C. Kreutzmüller (Munich, 2013), 299.
26 "Staatssekretär Pg. Freisler 40 Jahre," *Völkischer Beobachter*, 30 October 1933. According to his personal file, Freisler actually entered service in the Prussian Ministry of Justice on 27 March 1933, BArch, R 3001/56247. See also Roland Freisler, *Grundzüge eines Allgemeinen Deutschen Strafrechts: Denkschrift des Zentralausschusses der Akademie für Deutsches Recht* (Berlin, 1934).
27 On Dr Franz Gürtner (26 August 1881–29 January 1941), see: BArch R 3001/58396-58400 and R 3001/82231 and 82232.
28 For a while Freisler was only listed in the Berlin directory under his work address, Wilhelmstraße 65. In 1934 (vol. I, sheet 594) and 1935 (vol. III, sheet 14), he was listed as State Secretary in the Reich Ministry of Justice, in 1935 also as a member of the Reichstag. His private addresses Habelschwerter Allee 9/Hüttenweg 14 A were entered for the first time in 1943 (vol. IV, sheet 1414). Freisler left his properties to his wife, Marion Freisler, in his will of 1 October 1944. After 1945 the question of whether Roland or Marion Freisler had paid for the houses in Berlin became a topic of dispute.
29 BArch, Ortskartei der NSDAP, Film 3200/E0079, sheet 480.
30 RGB1, vol. I, 29 September 1933, sheet 686, 2. Abschnitt, Paragraph 13.
31 Cit. from Günter Neliba, *Staatssekretäre des NS-Regimes: Ausgewählte Aufsätze* (Berlin, 2005), 4.
32 On Otto Thierack, see: BArch R 3001/78253.
33 BArch, R 3001/56247, 53.
34 Joseph Goebbels to Dr Franz Gürtner, 27 April 1937, BArch R 3001/56246, 78.
35 "Vermerk RJM," 23 December 1937, BArch, R 3001/56246, 131.

36 A. Niedostadek, "Roland Freisler: Williger Vollstrecker im Namen des Führers," *Legal Tribune Online*, 3 February 2015. See also the letter from RJM of 23 March 1939 to the Devisenamt Berlin, BArch R 3001/56246, 162.

37 Roland Freisler, "Grundsätzliches zur Strafrechtserneuerung," in *Das kommende deutsche Strafverfahren: Bericht der amtlichen Strafrechtskommission*, ed. F. Gürtner (Berlin, 1938), 13.

38 R. Freisler and F. Schlegelberger, ed., *Römischer Kongreß für Kriminologie* (Berlin, 1939), 9.

39 BArch R 43/II 1418a, 30 et seq. Freisler attended several breakfasts and dinners in Rome, meeting not only the Duce but also the Italian Minister of Justice, Arrigo Solmi, the president of the court of cassation, Mario Dàmelio, and the German ambassador in Rome, Rom Mackensen.

40 BArch, R 3001/56247, 78. However, Freisler was never invited to meet Hitler, neither on the occasion of his decoration nor at any later date.

41 On Schlegelberger and the state secretaries in the Reich Ministry of Justice, see Neliba, *Staatssekretäre*, 2–36.

42 Shorthand record, 12 November 1938, International Military Tribunal [IMT], *Der Prozeß gegen die Hauptkriegsverbrecher vor dem Internationalen Militärgerichtshof (IMT): Nürnberg 14. November 1945 — 1. Oktober 1946, gemäß den Weisungen des Internationalen Militärgerichtshofes vom Sekretariat des Gerichtshofes unter der Autorität des Obersten Kontrollrats für Deutschland veröffentlicht*, 42 vols., ed. L.D. Egbert and P.A. Joosten (Nuremberg, 1947–49), vol. 28, 499–540, PS-1816.

43 BArch, R 3001, 56247, 96–100.

44 Karl Binding and Alfred Hoche, *Die Freigabe der Vernichtung lebensunwerten Lebens* (Leipzig, 1920). This book can be regarded as the intellectual foundation on which the policy of euthanasia was developed; Kreyssig referred to it in his report.

45 Estate of Lothar Kreyssig, letter (copy) from the guardianship court judge in Brandenburg, Havel, Dr Lothar Kreyssig of 8 July 1940 to the Minister of Justice, in: Evangelisches Zentralarchiv Berlin, EZA 614/161, 5.

46 Estate of Lothar Kreyssig, EZA 614/161, 5 et seq.

47 Estate of Lothar Kreyssig, EZA 614/161, 6 et seq.

48 Cit. from "Bericht des Amtsgerichtsrats i.R. Dr Lothar Kreyssig vom 16. Oktober 1969," IfZ, ZS-1956, 6.

49 For a biography of Lothar Kreyssig, see L. Gruchmann, "Ein unbequemer Amtsrichter im Dritten Reich: Aus den Personalakten des Dr Lothar Keyßig," *Vierteljahrshefte für Zeitgeschichte* 32, no. 3 (1984): 462–90.

50 Nikolaus Wachsmann, *Gefangen unter Hitler: Justizterror und Strafvollzug im NS-Staat* (Munich, 2006), 160 et seq.

51 R. Möhler, "Volksgenossen und Gemeinschaftsfremde hinter Gittern: Zum Strafvollzug im 'Dritten Reich,'" *Zeitschrift für Strafvollzug und Straffälligenhilfe* 42 (1993): 19.

52 Letter from Roland Freisler of 24 June 1941 to Arthur Greiser, R 3001/20849, 108 et seq.

53 Roland Freisler, "Das deutsche Polenstrafrecht," *Deutsche Justiz* 104 (16 January 1942): 45.

54 Hanns Kerrl, *Nationalsozialistisches Strafrecht: Denkschrift des preußischen Justizministers* (Berlin, 1933). On Freisler's stance on "racial treason" and his role in the Law for the Protection of German Blood, see: L. Gruchmann, "'Blutschutzgesetz' und Justiz: Zu Entstehung und Auswirkung des Nürnberger Gesetzes vom 15. September 1935," *Vierteljahrshefte für Zeitgeschichte* 31, no. 3 (1983): 419.

55 Kurt Pätzold and Erika Schwarz, *Tagesordnung: Judenmord: Die Wannsee-Konferenz am 20. Januar 1942: Eine Dokumentation zur Organisation der 'Endlösung'* (Berlin, 1992), 121 et seq.

56 PA AA Berlin, R 100857, 1661 et seq.

57 BArch, R 3001/25003, 11.

58 See Europeana Collections, record 2021622. Retrieved 15 October 2016 from http://europeana.eu

59 The interim Minister of Justice and former first State Secretary in the Reich Ministry of Justice, Schlegelberger, was pensioned off; the first President of the People's Court, Otto Thierack, was made Reich Minister of Justice, and Freisler was made President of the People's Court. See "Schreiben der Reichskanzlei vom 24. August 1942 an den RJM," BArch, R 3001/26248, sheet 256.

60 On 27 June 1942, when Freisler was still State Secretary, he had criticized the sentences in cases of treachery at Berlin special courts for being too lenient. On this and the statistics on People's Court sentences, see: "Anklage gegen Dr Paul Reimers," Staatsarchiv beim LG Berlin, 3 P (K) Js 6/79, 76, 203.

61 See Ingo Müller, *Furchtbare Juristen: Die unbewältigte Vergangenheit unserer Justiz* (Munich, 1987), 150 et seq.

62 Peter Longerich, *Goebbels: Biographie* (Munich, 2010), 637.

63 *Deutsche Justiz* 3, 16 February 1945, 33.

64 "Sie soll alles erben," *Der Spiegel* 30 (1955): 17.

65 See Anton Geldner, *Roland Freisler: Der Anwalt des Teufels* (Munich 1952); a series of articles in *Neue Illustrierte Köln*; Gert Buchheit, *Richter in roter Robe: Freisler, Präsident des Volksgerichtshofs* (Munich, 1968). Later, critical articles appeared on the People's Court judges Rehse and Reimers and, in *Der Spiegel*, on Freisler and the history of the judiciary under Nazism.

Bibliography

Binding, Karl and Alfred Hoche. *Die Freigabe der Vernichtung lebensunwerten Lebens*, Leipzig: Meiner, 1920.

Buchheit, Gert. *Richter in roter Robe: Freisler, Präsident des Volksgerichtshofs.* Munich: List, 1968.

Freisler, Roland. 1934. *Grundzüge eines Allgemeinen Deutschen Strafrechts: Denkschrift des Zentralausschusses der Akademie für Deutsches Recht.* Berlin: R. v. Decker.

———. "Grundsätzliches zur Strafrechtserneuerung." In *Das kommende deutsche Strafverfahren: Bericht der amtlichen Strafrechtskommission,* edited by F. Gürtner. Berlin: F. Vahlen, 1938.

Freisler, R. "Das deutsche Polenstrafrecht," *Deutsche Justiz* 104 (16 January 1942): 25–33 and 41–46

Freisler, R. and F. Schlegelberger, ed. *Römischer Kongreß für Kriminologie*. Berlin: R. v. Decker, 1939.

Geldner, Anton. *Roland Freisler: Der Anwalt des Teufels*. Munich, 1952.

Gruchmann, L. "'Blutschutzgesetz' und Justiz: Zu Entstehung und Auswirkung des Nürnberger Gesetzes vom 15. September 1935." *Vierteljahrshefte für Zeitgeschichte* 31, no. 3 (1983): 418–42.

———. "Ein unbequemer Amtsrichter im Dritten Reich: Aus den Personalakten des Dr Lothar Keyßig." *Vierteljahrshefte für Zeitgeschichte* 32, no. 3 (1984): 462–90.

Hördler, Stefan. "Entgrenzung und Eingrenzung der Gewalt: Berliner SA, SS und Polizei (1933–1939)." In *Berlin 1933–1945*, edited by M. Wildt and C.Kreutzmüller, 297–310. Munich: Siedler, 2013.

International Military Tribunal [IMT]. *Der Prozeß gegen die Hauptkriegsverbrecher vor dem Internationalen Militärgerichtshof (IMT): Nürnberg 14. November 1945 – 1. Oktober 1946, gemäß den Weisungen des Internationalen Militärgerichtshofes vom Sekretariat des Gerichtshofes unter der Autorität des Obersten Kontrollrats für Deutschland veröffentlicht*, edited by L.D. Egbert and P.A. Joosten. Nuremberg, 1947–1949.

Kerrl, Hanns. *Nationalsozialistisches Strafrecht: Denkschrift des preußischen Justizministers*. Berlin, 1933.

Longerich, Peter. *Goebbels: Biographie*. Munich: Siedler, 2010. [English: *Goebbels: A Biography*. New York: Random House, 2015.]

Möhler, R. "Volksgenossen und Gemeinschaftsfremde hinter Gittern: Zum Strafvollzug im 'Dritten Reich.'" *Zeitschrift für Strafvollzug und Straffälligenhilfe* 42 (1993): 17–21.

Müller, Ingo. *Furchtbare Juristen: Die unbewältigte Vergangenheit unserer Justiz*. Munich: Droemer Knaur, 1987. [English: *Hitler's Justice: The Courts of the Third Reich*. Cambridge, MA: Harvard University Press, 1991.]

Neliba, Günter. *Staatssekretäre des NS-Regimes: Ausgewählte Aufsätze*. Berlin: Duncker und Humblot, 2005.

Niedostadek, A. "Roland Freisler: Williger Vollstrecker im Namen des Führers." *Legal Tribune Online*, 3 February 2015. Retrieved 7 October 2016 from http://www.lto.de/recht/feuilleton/f/roland-freisler-volksgerichtshof-rechtsgeschichte-hitler-nsdap/

Ortner, Helmut. *Der Hinrichter: Roland Freisler, Mörder im Dienste Hitlers*. Frankfurt am Main: Nomen, 2014.

Overesch, Manfred. *Gott, die Liebe und der Galgen: Helmuth J. und Freya von Moltke in ihren letzten Gesprächen 1944/45*. Hildesheim, Zurich and New York: Olms, 2015.

Pätzold, Kurt and Erika Schwarz. *Tagesordnung: Judenmord: Die Wannsee-Konferenz am 20. Januar 1942: Eine Dokumentation zur Organisation der 'Endlösung.'* Berlin: Metropol, 1992.

Wachsmann, Nikolaus. *Gefangen unter Hitler: Justizterror und Strafvollzug im NS-Staat*. Munich: Siedler, 2006.

10

GERHARD KLOPFER

Nazi Party Chancellery

A Nationalist Ideologue and a
Respectable West German

Markus Heckmann

Illustration 10.1 Unknown photographer,
27.11.1942, BArch Koblenz, 119-09-44-12.

On 2 February 1987, a death notice appeared in the Ulm newspaper *Südwest-Presse* that caused some readers to double take: "In memory of Dr Gerhard Klopfer, who passed away after a fulfilled life in the service of all those in his sphere of influence." The announcement was signed by his wife, sister and four daughters with their husbands and nineteen children.[1] It would not have been remarkable had the deceased not been the former state secretary in Martin Bormann's Party Chancellery, and the longest surviving participant in the Wannsee Conference. The chairman of Berlin's Jewish Community, Hans Galinski, found the tribute to Klopfer "shocking," especially as Berlin had just commemorated forty-five years since the Wannsee Conference a few days previously.[2] The members of the German Social Democratic Party on Ulm's local council released a statement that the wording of the notice was an insult to all victims of the Nazi regime and called for the Ulm public prosecution office to launch an inquiry into this "slander of the memory of the deceased"[3]—ultimately, without success. In the ensuing days, the local press ran several articles on the Nazi past and this SS-Gruppenführer who had lived "unobtrusively" in Ulm for thirty years.[4] Gerhard Klopfer remains a shadowy figure of the Nazi past. Yet he held the high rank of State Secretary in the Nazi Party Chancellery, a pivotal department that mediated between the Party and the state. This chapter will consider not only how his career in the Nazi state but also his life after 1945 were typical of the "uncompromising generation."[5]

War Youth and Career

Gerhard Klopfer was born on 18 February 1905, the son of Otto, an agriculturist, and his wife Ida Klopfer, both Protestants, in the Silesian village of Schreibersdorf (now Pisarzowice, some 30 km south east of Gliwice). Shortly after the outbreak of the First World War, Klopfer left his local village school to attend high school in Lauban (now Luban). The collapse of the German Empire in November 1918, probably the most significant political event in Klopfer's early life, had immediate consequences for his Silesian home. The Treaty of Versailles demanded that a plebiscite be held in Upper Silesia on whether the region remain part of Germany. The vote on 20 March 1921 was preceded by bitter fighting between Polish military and German Freikorps units. In the event, 59.6 percent voted to stay in the German Reich and 40.4 percent voted to join Poland. As the result was so close, in October 1921, the allied conference of ambassadors in Paris ruled that Upper Silesia be divided. The eastern part, including the industrial town Katowice, was to be absorbed by Poland, sparking fierce protests by the German-speaking population.

In 1923, when inflation was at its peak, Klopfer completed his Abitur school-leaving exams and enrolled to study law in Breslau. A short time later he transferred to the University of Jena, where Roland Freisler was also a student. Here he became involved in the ethnonationalistic student organization Deutscher Hochschulring, where he met later companions such as Werner Best and Wilhelm Stuckart. After passing his first state examinations with "cum laude" in 1927, he wrote his doctoral thesis on "the employee's duty of allegiance in employment" in 1929. He completed his legal clerkship in Breslau. In 1931 he passed his second state examination with "cum laude" in Berlin and started working as a junior judge at Düsseldorf magistrates' court and regional court.[6]

Klopfer joined the Nazi Party on 1 April 1933. He became a member of the SA later the same month. After a short period from November to December 1933 acting as a state prosecutor and judge in Düsseldorf, Klopfer worked for the Ministry for Agriculture, Domains and Forestry under Walther Darré until Werner Best assigned him to the planning staff of the Prussian Gestapo. One year later, Klopfer left this post to join Rudolf Heß on the Staff of the Deputy Führer.

Heß needed well-qualified and ideologically reliable lawyers to ensure his department functioned efficiently. Appointed Deputy Führer by Hitler immediately after the Nazis' election victory in March 1933, Heß had two main tasks: first, to act as a leader within the Party and, second, to represent the Party's interests toward the state. Hitler entrusted him with substantial authority to this end. Heß's department was involved in law-making processes, and had a right to veto the promotion of senior officials. But the main function of the Staff of the Deputy Führer was to realize the goals of the National Socialist movement as uncompromisingly as possible. In the fight against political opponents, it consistently supported the most radical solution. Following Heß's mysterious flight to Scotland in May 1941, the Staff of the Deputy Führer was renamed Party Chancellery and Martin Bormann appointed as head.[7]

Klopfer's rapid professional advancement is an indication that he performed impeccably in the Party Chancellery. He was even promoted in disregard of "Reich principles." In May 1938, Bormann suggested promoting Klopfer to assistant head of the department. The Reich Ministry of the Interior responded by pointing out that this would "violate Reich principles on the appointment, employment and promotion of Reich and regional officials." Aged thirty-three, Klopfer did not meet the age requirements for an assistant head of a government department, nor had he served long enough as a regular official. But the Ministry of the Interior waived the rules for the Deputy Führer's sake, "as Klopfer is Chief of Staff Bormann's personal aide and both the nature and extent of his work and the efficient manner in which he has fulfilled the obligations of his office justify his preferential promotion."[8] Just one year later, Klopfer was promoted again, to head of section. The Staff of the Deputy Führer was now organized as a three-section department: Internal Affairs (Section I), Tasks of the Party Leadership (Section II) and Questions of State (Section III). As the staff of Section III assumed governmental functions, like their colleagues in the Reich ministry, they were appointed, promoted and paid according to civil service law. Their salaries were paid out of the budget of the ministry in whose remit they worked.[9]

Until 1941, Klopfer's immediate superior was Walther Sommer, an extremely "problematic man, very difficult to describe, who enjoyed provocatively living out the role of the bully."[10] Bormann and Heß doubted whether the undiplomatic Sommer would be able to successfully represent the interests of the Party Chancellery. For this reason, shortly before Heß's mysterious flight to Scotland, Bormann engineered Sommer's appointment as president of the newly founded Reich administrative court. Klopfer was subsequently put forward as Sommer's replacement. In April 1941, Klopfer was duly promoted, and as head of Section III, now controlled coordination between the Party and the state.[11] The reconstructed Party Chancellery files are too fragmentary

Illustration 10.2 Gerhard Klopfer with his first wife Hildegard. It was common for SS-members to pose together for a picture for the obligatory application to receive the allowance to get married (August 1937). Unknown photographer, 1937; BArch R 9163-III 98446.

to give a rounded impression of Klopfer and his work.[12] But simply by dint of his position as head of Section III, he can be regarded as one of the most influential administrative officers in the "Third Reich." His superior, Bormann, was one of Hitler's travel escorts and rarely present in the Party Chancellery, so Klopfer was the main contact person on the ground for colleagues from the ministerial administration. His field of responsibility included coordinating work with the ministries and finalizing legislation. To this end, he had weekly briefings with the head of the Reich Chancellery, Hans Lammers.[13] Klopfer ensured that the Führer's decrees and complex implementing orders were swiftly and efficiently enforced.[14] Cooperation between the Party Chancellery and ministerial offices improved under his direction.[15] He had a reputation as an "experienced and intelligent man of administration,"[16] with whom one could also "smooth out difficulties"[17] in an informal manner.

In parallel with his advancement in the Party Chancellery, he also climbed the ranks of the SS to eventually become Gruppenführer.[18] In his SS file, Klopfer's "personal conduct" is described as "decent and obliging" with an "adequate amount" of "strength of will and personal rigor"; his "mental agility" praised as "very brisk and lively." Overall, Klopfer was deemed a "willing and ambitious SS leader with a very good knowledge of administrative law."[19] After the war, Klopfer liked to claim that he was merely an administrative official carrying out orders. But the fact that he co-edited the ethnonationalistic journal *Reich Volksordnung Lebensraum — Zeitschrift für völkische Verfassung und Verwaltung* shows that he was also a convinced Nazi who was in favor of putting ideology into practice. This magazine was published between 1941 and 1943 and dealt with questions of race policy and the restructuring of territories conquered by Germany. It mainly addressed the elite leadership of the SS. Alongside Klopfer, the editors included Werner Best, Wilhelm Stuckart, specialist in state law Reinhard Höhn, and head of the legal department of the German Armed Forced High Command, Rudolf Lehmann.[20]

As head of Section III in the Party Chancellery, Klopfer regularly commuted between the Berlin branch of the Party Chancellery in Wilhelmstraße and the "Braunes Haus" in Munich. In 1937, he moved into a house in the "Rudolf Heß" estate in Pullach. This model development of detached houses with gardens was especially built for Nazi functionaries working in Munich. Klopfer lived at Sonnenweg 10 with his wife Hildegard, née Müller, whom he married in 1937. Here they raised their four daughters, born in 1938, 1940, 1941 and 1943.[21]

Klopfer and the *"Mischling* Question"

Gerhard Klopfer's name would probably have been forgotten like those of dozens of other high-ranking Nazi functionaries had he not been present at the Wannsee Conference. After the war, Klopfer maintained that he was driven to the conference along with head of department Friedrich Kritzinger without knowing what exactly was awaiting him.[22] The Wannsee Protocol shows that Klopfer did not speak during the talks. He did not have any reason to: where the main point under discussion was concerned—how to deal with "crossbreed Jews" *("Mischlingsjuden")*—he agreed with Heydrich. Apart from certain exceptional cases, "first-degree crossbreeds" *("Mischlinge ersten Grades")* were to be treated the same as other Jews "with regard to the Final Solution," while "second-degree crossbreeds" were to be exempted from "evacuation."[23] The Party Chancellery and the Reich Security Main Office joined forces to organize the persecution of Jews as the events preceding the Wannsee Conference show.

As far as the Party Chancellery was concerned, the Nuremberg race laws, which revoked the equal civil rights for Jews introduced in 1871, did not go far enough. They did not define who was actually Jewish.[24] During consultations over the race laws, the Party Chancellery had called for people with one Jewish grandparent to be legally classified as Jews. Again, when the first implementing regulation on the Reich Citizenship Law and the Reich Law for the Protection of German Blood in 1935 was discussed, the Party Chancellery urged the legislators to broaden the classification of Jews. But the Ministry of the Interior's draft envisaged classifying people with one Jewish grandparent as "quarter Jews" and therefore "German-Jewish crossbreeds." Only those who descended from three Jewish grandparents were to be classified as Jews. The Party Chancellery found this definition of "Mischlinge" too loose. It called for the law to differentiate between "quarter Jews" and "half Jews" and proposed introducing assessment on a case-by-case basis, paying special attention to appearance and character. The Party Chancellery wanted all those defined as Jews who were "descendants of Eastern Jews, those with a pronounced Jewish appearance, hereditary diseases, and all those . . . who have a bad reputation or criminal tendencies."[25] Ultimately, a compromise was reached. Under the regulations announced on 14 November 1935, the legal classification of "half Jews" was dependent on whether they belonged to a Jewish congregation or were married to a Jew. If either was the case, they were excluded from the "Reich civil community" *(Reichbürgerschaft)*; if not, they were to be classified as "crossbreeds" ("Mischlinge"). The Party Chancellery had more influence over the Law for the Protection of German Blood, and managed to have marriages between "half Jews" and those "of German blood" prohibited.[26]

No further developments regarding the "Mischling Question" occurred until after the outbreak of war. By this time, the driving force behind such matters was the newly formed Reich Main Security Office (Reichssicherheitshauptamt, RSHA), an office essentially conceived by Werner Best. In January, March, August and September 1941, talks were held between the RSHA, the office of the Four Year Plan and the Party

Chancellery. The participants agreed on basically classifying "cross-breeds" as Jews and in exceptional cases, affecting some 10,000 people, carrying out sterilizations. The minutes of the meetings show that it was again the Party Chancellery, represented by Herbert Reischauer, that made the most radical proposals. In a meeting on 15 January 1941, Reischauer suggested declaring Jews living in "privileged mixed-blood marriages" to be stateless and so include them in the deportations. At the meeting on August 1941 he called for the definition of Jews to be extended in the German-occupied territories to include "crossbreeds."[27] At around the same time, Klopfer was promoted to head of department and head of Section III (State Affairs) in the Party Chancellery. As such, he must have been well informed about the measures regarding the "Mischling Question" and the many other regulations against Jews. Devised by a circularized process of writing and reviewing, Klopfer was probably more deeply involved in the law-making than can today be proven from the surviving files.[28]

It is therefore hardly likely that Klopfer was surprised at the points discussed at the Wannsee Conference. Although the "Mischling Question" was not conclusively settled, Klopfer and Heydrich had every reason to be satisfied with the outcome of the talks. According to the minutes, Stuckart proposed the sterilization of "crossbreeds" and compulsory divorces for "mixed-blood marriages." Both proposals were intended to accommodate Heydrich's wishes.[29] In the event, however, these measures were not put into practice. At talks between the ministries in March and October 1942, it was decided that a mass-scale compulsory sterilization program would be unfeasible. Where compulsory divorces were concerned, the Reich Propaganda Ministry and Reich Justice Ministry feared protests from the Catholic Church. For this reason, in October 1943, Minister of Justice Otto Thierack and Heinrich Himmler agreed to refrain from deporting "Mischlinge" as long as the country was at war.[30]

The Party Chancellery continued to work on anti-Jewish legislation even after the deportations and systematic murder of the European Jews had begun. One example, in which Klopfer was undoubtedly involved, was the ruling to cancel Jews' eligibility for food ration cards. The minutes of an inter-ministry meeting on 29 June 1942 meticulously recorded the participants' decisions on which foodstuffs were no longer to be distributed among Jews, and that extra allowances were to be stopped for children, pregnant women, women who had recently given birth and nursing mothers of Jewish descent.[31] That year Klopfer reached the zenith of his career. On 22 November 1942, he was made State Secretary with forty-eight civil servants at his command.[32]

"... then you must have slept through the meeting ..."

Despite Klopfer's close involvement in the genocide of the Jews, he was able to blend into postwar German society and start working as a lawyer after just a few years. In the immediate aftermath of the war, he managed to go into hiding. He was not arrested until 1 March 1946, by American Counter Intelligence Corps (CIC) agents in Munich. At the time of his arrest he was carrying forged identification documents bearing the name Otto Kunz. Klopfer was held in several internment camps: initially interned in Dachau at the same time as Wilhelm Stuckart, he was later transferred to Ludwigsburg and lastly to Nuremberg-Langwasser. By this time, the war crimes trials had begun in Nuremberg. Klopfer acted as a witness during the Wilhelmstraße trials, and was interrogated a total of ten times by U.S. prosecutors between March 1947 and January 1948. Questioning was led by Peter Beauvais and assistant chief attorney Robert Kempner. The trials were certainly very tense. Kempner came from Germany; like Klopfer, he had studied law in Berlin and Breslau, albeit a few years earlier, and had worked in the Ministry of the Interior before fleeing to the United States. He was quite familiar, then, with Nazi ministerial bureaucracy and the system within which Klopfer had operated. The investigators had collected extensive evidence against Klopfer, including the Wannsee Protocol, and correspondence concerning the "Mischling Question" and the implementation of the Nuremberg Laws.

Klopfer responded cleverly to questioning. He did not dispute anything that the investigators clearly already knew but acted unwitting where all other matters were concerned. He shifted all political responsibility onto his superior, Martin Bormann, who was missing, presumed dead. He did not lose his nerve when confronted with the Wannsee Protocol, claiming that Heydrich had merely talked about the "emigration of the Jews." In response to the demur that the evidence suggested he was told exactly what was to happen to the Jews, Klopfer pleaded ignorance, prompting Peter Beauvais to remark, "Then you must have slept through the meeting, I think."[33] Eventually the charges against Klopfer were dropped. The U.S. prosecutors stopped their work and handed the case over to the Nuremberg denazification court.

Denazification courts were non-professional tribunals staffed by untainted members of the public. Every German over eighteen years of age was required to complete a registration form, giving information about their personal involvement in Nazism. On the basis of these forms, the denazification courts conducted proceedings against the implicated by placing them in one of five criminal categories: Major Offenders *(Hauptschuldige)*, Offenders *(Belastete)*, Lesser Offenders *(Minderbelastete)*, Followers *(Mitläufer)*, and Exonerated *(Entlastete)*. How, then, did Klopfer's denazification case proceed? The prosecution called for charging Klopfer as a Main Offender on grounds of his high position in the state apparatus and the SS. The prosecutors had put together twenty-seven documents as evidence, including the minutes of the Wannsee Conference. The strategy of the defense consisted of denying the conclusiveness of these documents, playing down Klopfer's position as State Secretary and SS-Gruppenführer, and trying to convince the court that Klopfer had used his position to moderate the more radical propositions for legislation. The supposed evidence produced by the defense consisted of two dozen statutory declarations in lieu of an oath, sworn by staff members of the Party Chancellery and their colleagues in the ministries, most of whom were in the dock themselves in other trials. Several witnesses claimed that Klopfer, together with Albert Speer, had made sure that Hitler's order to leave "scorched earth" — destroy all infrastructure — wherever the Allies were advancing was not carried out. Klopfer's personal assistant in the Party Chancellery, Dr Karl Lang, wrote that "in Dr Klopfer" he had "got to know a man whose untiring, positive activities had scotched the evil forces which were at play in the Nazi state at constant risk of his own life."[34] Stuckart claimed that "Dr Klopfer always tried to act as a counterbalance and reduce the severity of Bormann's radical demands. With regard to the Jewish Question, too, Dr Klopfer always took a moderate standpoint, informed by reason and humaneness."[35]

Having weighed up the arguments of the prosecution and the defense, the court came to the following conclusion:

> Bormann completely trusted [Klopfer] as a dutiful civil servant. He also regarded him as a good Nazi, otherwise he would not have left him in his post for so long. His work, and particularly his activity as Bormann's advisor, was a crucial support to the Nazi regime. No further proof is needed of the fact that the accused personally held Nazi views, that he agreed with the party program.[36]

With regard to Klopfer's participation in the Wannsee Conference, the verdict ran: "Even if the accused cannot be proven by this document to have committed any criminal action, he can be seen to have been informed of the procedure on the Jewish Question . . . and continued to work on the Mischling problem."[37] The court did not give any credence to the affidavits, viewing them merely as attempts at "sophistic proof of mutual non-responsibility."[38]

The denazification court did, however, acknowledge mitigating circumstances. First, it accepted the defense's argument that Klopfer did not have the authority of a State Secretary or an SS-Gruppenführer, despite the fact that he held these titles. Second, it accorded credibility to Klopfer's claim that he was able to have a moderating influence on legislation in certain cases, such as the case of Hitler's scorched earth order, and third, it took Klopfer's contemporary situation into account—he had a family of five and an elderly mother to provide for. Consequently, the Nuremberg denazification court classified the former State Secretary as a Lesser Offender. He was sentenced to a fine of 2,000 Deutschmarks and a probation period of three years, during which he was restricted to carrying out a simple occupation.

Klopfer's lenient sentence was by no means an isolated case but actually typical of the denazification of high-ranking Nazi functionaries. It was almost the norm for those initially charged with being Major Offenders to be relegated to a lower offence category—as in Klopfer's case—by a denazification court. Overall, 3.5 percent of the defendants in denazification court trials were deemed Major Offenders by the prosecution. But only 0.03 percent were sentenced as such. The historian Lutz Niethammer has therefore concluded that, "the more serious the formal charges, the further the accused had advanced into the inner circle of Nazi organization, the higher up its ladder he had climbed, the earlier he had joined and the more memberships he had accumulated, the more leniently he was treated by the denazification court."[39] This conclusion certainly tallies with Klopfer's case. On receiving his sentence from the denazification court, Klopfer was released from imprisonment after four years in various camps. During his probation period he worked as a carpenter. His former secretary, Emma Hölzle, arranged for him to work in her father-in-law's carpentry firm in Altenstadt an der Iller, 30 km south of Ulm. In 1952 Klopfer also started working as an "advisor on tax affairs" for various companies in the region as a sideline.

Return to Civilian Life

When denazification was stopped, a cross-party consensus prevailed in the new Federal Republic of Germany that the resultant professional bans and convictions should be reversed. Konrad Adenauer addressed the issue in his first government policy statement in September 1949. Without uttering a single word about the crimes committed under Nazism, he condemned the Allies' policy of denazification, which, in his view, had caused "much harm and much misfortune." He also announced his intention to ask the Allied High Commission for an amnesty for all those convicted by Allied military tribunals.[40] Three months later, the Bundestag enacted an amnesty law — its first legislative act, passed by all parliamentary groups. A second followed in 1954. Under these amnesty laws, certain offences committed after 1933 could no longer be prosecuted and sentences could be revoked.[41]

A further political measure that enabled many former Nazi Party members to resume their jobs, having been dismissed from public service due to their implication in Nazism, was the implementing laws on article 131 of the Basic Law. This obliged the legislator to clarify the legal status of those who "had been in public service on 8 May 1945 and quit for grounds other than of civil service law or collective bargaining law and who have not been employed since, or not in the capacity of their former positions."[42] The persons implied were administrative officials, police officials, professional soldiers and even members of the Gestapo who had lost their jobs due to denazification. When the implementing laws for article 131 were debated in the Bundestag, many members of parliament stressed the need to exploit the potential of experienced public servants and get them back into employment as important for society.[43]

In this context, it is no wonder that Klopfer managed to return to civilian life. Toward the end of his probation period, he tried to become established as a lawyer in Bavaria. But the Bavarian Ministry of Justice rejected his application for technical reasons: Klopfer had not taken his state examinations in Bavaria. He had better luck with the Ministry of Justice in Stuttgart, in the state of Baden-Württemberg. Having belatedly completed his advocacy trial period in a law firm in Memmingen, he was able to set up as a lawyer. On 29 February 1956, he opened a law office at Zinglerstraße 40 in Ulm. The file on Klopfer that is still held in the Stuttgart Ministry of Justice shows that he did not try to cover up his activity in the Party Chancellery in his application but gave honest information about his past. It obviously did not trouble anyone at the Baden-Württemberg Ministry of Justice.[44]

Four years after his release, Klopfer became a matter of record again. The Ulm public prosecutor started investigations against him on charges of assisting murder. The proceedings were triggered by an incident in the Bundestag. During question time on 28 September 1960, Social Democratic member of the Bundestag Franz Neumann asked the house whether it was aware if Martin Bormann's deputy, State Secretary Klopfer, was being prosecuted at any German court. Then Minister of Justice Schäffer (Christian Democratic Union) replied that the government knew nothing about criminal proceedings against Klopfer but would consider the possibility of initiating them. Neumann's attention had been drawn to Klopfer by an article in the New York journal *Aufbau* about the participants of the Wannsee Conference. In this article, Robert Kempner, Klopfer's interrogator in Nuremberg, criticized the fact that Klopfer had never been convicted by a German court.

The investigations by the Ulm public prosecutor had better prospects of ending in a conviction. By this time, the Central Office of the State Justice Administration for the Investigation of National Socialist Crimes had been set up in Ludwigsburg to support the work of local public prosecutors. And statements about the Wannsee Conference by Adolf Eichmann, who had been arrested by Mossad agents and questioned in Jerusalem, severely incriminated the Party Chancellery. The investigations into Klopfer's role in the Holocaust dragged on for over one and a half years, and centered on his participation in the Wannsee Conference. Klopfer himself made one written statement in response to the accusations against him and was questioned once by the prosecutor responsible for the case. He adhered to his earlier position; no new findings were brought to light. On 29 January 1962, the charges were dropped on the following grounds:

> The charges of aiding and abetting murder under § 211 and 49 StGB are untenable due to the fact that the accused had no possibility of influencing the fate of the Jews. Once Hitler, Himmler and Heydrich had resolved to exterminate the Jews, and even begun implementing the corresponding measures by the time of the Wannsee Conference in January 1942, there was no way the accused could have prevented or obstructed the implementation of the mass murder program.[45]

Here, too, Klopfer's case is no exception but typical of the Federal Republic of Germany's handling of Nazi criminals. Only a fraction of the cases investigated actually resulted in convictions. Many offences, such as manslaughter, became statute-barred or fell under the provisions of the amnesty laws of 1949 and 1954. In some cases, the perpetrators could not be conclusively identified, or were declared unfit for trial. The charges of "aiding and abetting murder" in Klopfer's case are also typical. The legal construct of "aiding and abetting" was based on the assumption that the main offenders—the actual murderers—were those at the very end of the chain of command: Hitler, Himmler and Heydrich. By this logic, all the other persons involved could only ever be accused of aiding and abetting murder.[46]

The case against Klopfer did not damage his reputation in Ulm. Eyewitnesses described him as a "Prussian official of the old school" whose only slightly conspicuous trait was his rather submissive bearing. "If he saw me, a known SPD party hack, on the street, he would doff his hat while still at a distance and make an unduly low bow," remembered Klaus Beer, a judge and councilor in Ulm.[47] Baden-Württemberg's Minister of Justice Eyrich saw fit to congratulate Klopfer on his seventy-fifth and eightieth birthdays. In preparation, he checked with the president of the Ulm regional court whether Klopfer was still practicing and if he was in good health. The Landgericht president replied, "as a legal counsellor and trial lawyer, he [Klopfer] is extremely punctilious, with perfect manners, a model of an upright and noble lawyer of the old school, who is highly esteemed and respected at the court."[48] The only historian to interview Klopfer was Dieter Rebentisch. He arranged a meeting with Klopfer in his home in Ulm on 11 May 1985 as part of the research for his postdoctoral thesis. Subsequently, he noted down the following impressions:

> On the one hand, his material circumstances are very frugal, but on the other, he pays conscious attention to accumulating assets and valuables. The table at which we sat would not be kept today by less wealthy families. But the cake was served on Meissen porcelain . . . His negative views on the failure of democracy, which show that he has not discarded his ultra-reactionary standpoint of the thirties and has learned nothing from the catastrophe that was Nazism, were disconcerting.[49]

Klopfer also repeatedly told Rebentisch that he hailed from a family of farmers and that he, too, now had a farm, explaining, "I grow spelt there, which is good for making brown bread." Klopfer was apparently convinced that the black soup eaten by the Spartans had also been made out of this grain. In any case, since he had been eating bread made out of spelt, he claimed to have noticed his "mental vigor" increase.[50] Klopfer's farm is in Langenburg, 130 km west of Nuremberg, and is still owned by his family today. It is not known how Klopfer, who emerged penniless from denazification, paid for the running of the farm and the leasehold on the land. Until his death, he fought for a pension taking his years of service in the Party Chancellery into account. But he did not live to see his application processed by the regional salaries and pensions office. Klopfer died in early 1987—the same year that his former employer Rudolf Heß committed suicide in Spandau—and is now buried near his farm outside Langenburg.

Markus Heckmann has studied Contemporary History, Sociology and Political Science at the Humboldt University in Berlin and at the University of Essex. His research and writing investigates the life and impact of Dr Gerhard Klopfer and the integration of Nazi perpetrators in postwar Germany.

Notes

1 *Südwest-Presse*, 2 February 1987, reprinted in: Markus Heckmann, *NS-Täter und Bürger der Bundesrepublik: Das Beispiel des D Gerhard Klopfer* (Ulm, 2010), 13.
2 *Frankurter Rundschau*, 5 February 1987; *Die Tageszeitung*, 5 February 1987.
3 *Südwest-Presse Ulm*, 11 February 1987.
4 *Neu-Ulmer Zeitung*, 7 February 1987.
5 Michael Wildt, *Die Generation des Unbedingten: Das Führungskorps des Reichssicherheitshauptamtes* (Hamburg, 2002).
6 Heckmann, *NS-Täter und Bürger der Bundesrepublik*, 18–21; Armin Nolzen, "Gerhard Klopfer, die Abteilung III in der Parteikanzlei und deren 'Judenpolitik' 1941/1942," in *Die Wannsee-Konferenz am 20. Januar 1942: Dokumente, Forschungsstand, Kontroversen*, ed. N. Kampe and P. Klein (Cologne, 2013), 306.
7 Peter Longerich, *Hitlers Stellvertreter: Führung der Partei und Kontrolle des Staatsapparates durch den Stab Heß und Bormanns Partei-Kanzlei* (Munich, 1992), 8–24; Dieter Rebentisch, *Führerstaat und Verwaltung im Zweiten Weltkrieg: Verfassungsentwicklung und Verwaltungspolitik 1939–1945* (Stuttgart, 1989), 68–91.
8 Letter from the Secretary of State in the Reich Ministry of the Interior, Hans Pfundtner, to the Reich Minister of Finance of 23 March 1938, ending with a request to agree to this deviation from "Reich principles," Akten der Parteikanzlei, 101 12337.
9 Rebentisch, *Führerstaat*, 80 et seq.
10 According to Rebentisch's description, *Führerstaat*, 83 et seq.
11 Rebentisch, *Führerstaat*, 454.
12 Most of the Party Chancellery files were destroyed in the war. However, the German Institute of Contemporary History (IfZ) reconstructed the archives in a project lasting over ten years, by searching the holdings of all party offices, authorities and ministries for correspondence with the Party Chancellery. The reconstructed archive is now available in a four-volume microfiche edition.
13 "Dienstkalender Lammers," Akten der Parteikanzlei, 101 29075-29124.
14 This is clearly shown by the Party Chancellery files on "the Führer's order of 13 January 1943" *(Führerbefehl vom 13. Januar 1943)*, introducing compulsory registration for men between sixteen and sixty-five years of age and women between seventeen and fifty years of age. This order co-formed the basis for the later "Führer's decree on the mission of total war" *(Erlass des Führers über den totalen Kriegseinsatz)*, Heckmann, *NS-Täter*, 29 et seq.
15 This is the conclusion drawn by Rebentisch. See idem, *Führerstaat*, 456.
16 This was the view of Hans Kehrl, head of the natural resources agency in the Ministry for Armament from 1943 and head of the planning office for the Four Year Plan. See Hans Kehrl, *Krisenmanager im Dritten Reich: 6 Jahre Friede, 6 Jahre Krieg: Erinnerungen* (Düsseldorf, 1973), 252.

17 As noted in a memo to Heinrich Himmler's personal assistant, SS-Standartenführer Dr Rudolf Brandt, undated, signed illegible, Akten der Parteikanzlei 107 00802.

18 Here, too, he was rapidly promoted: after joining in 1935, he was made Hauptsturmführer on 20 April 1936, Sturmbannführer on 20 January 1937, Obersturmbannführer on 20 January 1939, SS-Standartenführer on 20 April 1939, SS-Oberführer on 20 April 1941, SS-Brigadeführer on 30 January 1942 and finally SS-Gruppenführer on 9 November 1944.

19 "SS-Personalakte Klopfer," Akten der Parteikanzlei, 306 00365-00636, reprinted in Heckmann, *NS-Täter*, 35.

20 Michael Stolleis, Geschichte des Öffentlichen Rechts in Deutschland: Weimarer Republik und Nationalsozialismus (Munich, 2002), 308–9; Ulrich Herbert, *Best: Biographische Studien über Radikalismus, Weltanschauung und Vernunft 1903–1989* (Bonn, 1996), 284.

21 Susanne Meinl and Bodo Hechelhammer, *Geheimobjekt Pullach: Von der NS-Mustersiedlung zur Zentrale des BND* (Berlin, 2014), 12–87.

22 Klopfer made this claim in a written statement to the Ulm public prosecution department on 31 January 1962, Ermittlungsakten in der Ludwigsburger Zentralstelle Barch 162/AR1187/61, sheet 6.

23 According to an invitation from Heydrich to Hofmann, reproduced in Peter Klein, *Die Wannsee-Konferenz vom 20. Januar 1942: Analyse und Dokumentation* (Berlin, 1995), 489 et seq.

24 Jeremy Noakes, "Wohin gehören die 'Judenmischlinge'? Die Entstehung der ersten Durchführungsverordnung zu den Nürnberger Gesetzen," in *Das Unrechtsregime: Internationale Forschung über den Nationalsozialismus*, ed. U. Büttner (Hamburg, 1986), vol. 2, 70.

25 Noakes, "Wohin gehören die 'Judenmischlinge'?

26 Noakes, "Wohin gehören die 'Judenmischlinge'?, 70–87; Peter Longerich, *Politik der Vernichtung: Eine Gesamtdarstellung der nationalsozialist-ischen Judenverfolgung* (Munich, 1998), 102–15; John A.S. Greenville, "Die 'Endlösung' und die 'Judenmischlinge' im Dritten Reich," in *Das Unrechtsregime: Internationale Forschung über den Nationalsozialismus* (Hamburger Beiträge zur Sozial- und Zeitgeschichte, vol. 22), ed. U. Büttner (Hamburg, 1986), 91–121.

27 Longerich, *Hitlers Stellvertreter*, 220–22; Mark Roseman, *The Villa, the Lake, the Meeting: Wannsee and the Final Solution* (London, 2002), 79–83.

28 The reconstructed archive of the Party Chancellery does, however, contain fairly clear evidence of Klopfer's involvement in the implementation of the "Führer decree" of 13 January 1943 on mobilizing the population for war. Heckmann, *NS-Täter*, 29 et seq.

29 Roseman, *Wannsee and the Final Solution*, 97–99.

30 Roseman, *Wannsee and the Final Solution*, 100 et seq. C. Gerlach, "Die Wannsee-Konferenz, das Schicksal der deutschen Juden und Hitlers politische Grundsatzentscheidung, alle Juden Europas zu ermorden," *WerkstattGeschichte* 18 (1997): 136 et seq.

31 Akten der Parteikanzlei, 101 08002 — 101 08003, Heckmann, *NS-Täter*, 45.

32 Rebentisch, *Führerstaat*, 454.

33 "Protokoll des Verhörs am 12 Juni 1947," 2, Staatsarchiv Nürnberg KV-Anklage Interrogations K93, Klopfer, Gerhard; Heckmann, *NS-Täter*, 53.

34 "Eidesstattliche Erklärung von Karl Lang verfasst in Brackenheim/ Württemberg," 20 January 1949, Staatsarchiv Ludwigsburg EL 840 II Bü 867, sheet 81/7.

35 "Eidesstattliche Erklärung von Wilhelm Stuckart verfasst im Nürnberger Gerichtsgefängnis am 16. Juni 1948," Staatsarchiv Ludwigsburg EL 840 II Bü 867, sheet 92/2.

36 "Spruch vom 28 März 1949," Staatsarchiv Ludwigsburg EL 840 II Bü 867, sheet 18/6.

37 Staatsarchiv Ludwigsburg EL 840 II Bü 867, sheet 18/7.

38 Staatsarchiv Ludwigsburg EL 840 II Bü 867, sheet 18/22. Excerpts of the denazification court protocol are reproduced in: Heckmann, *NS-Täter*, 64 et seq.

39 Lutz Niethammer, *Entnazifizierung in Bayern: Säuberung und Rehabilitierung unter amerikanischer Besatzung* (Frankfurt am Main, 1972), 584.

40 This section of German Chancellor Konrad Adenauer's government statement of 20 September 1949 is cited from Norbert Frei, "Hitlers Eliten nach 1945—eine Bilanz," in *Karrieren im Zwielicht: Hitlers Eliten nach 1945*, ed. N. Frei (Frankfurt am Main and New York, 2001), 303–37, 310.

41 Norbert Frei, *Vergangenheitspolitik: Die Anfänge der Bundesrepublik und die NS-Vergangenheit* (Munich, 1996), 25–69.

42 "Grundgesetzartikel 131 (1)" [translation: CK].

43 Frei, *Vergangenheitspolitik*, 69–100.

44 Justizministerium Baden-Württemberg, Personalakte Dr Gerhard Klopfer, no. 33947, Heckmann, *NS-Täter*, 70 et seq.

45 Statement by the Ulm public prosecution office on the suspension of proceedings against Klopfer of 29 January 1962 [translation: CK], in Heckmann, *NS-Täter*, 81.

46 "Erklärung zur Einstellung des Verfahrens der Staatsanwaltschaft Ulm vom 29 Januar 1962," Bundesarchiv, B 162/AR 1187/61, sheet 16/7.

47 Klaus Beer, *Auf den Feldern von Ulm: In den wechselnden Winden von Adenauer bis Willy Brandt* (Blaubeuren, 2008), 259 [translation here: CK].

48 File note of 8 February 1980, Justizministerium Baden-Württemberg, Personalakte Dr Gerhard Klopfer 33947, sheet 69, Heckmann, *NS-Täter*, 89.

49 Memorandum by Rebentisch on his conversation with Klopfer on 11 May 1985, in Heckmann, *NS-Täter*, 91 [translation: CK].

50 Heckmann, *NS-Täter*, 91.

Bibliography

Beer, Klaus. *Auf den Feldern von Ulm: In den wechselnden Winden von Adenauer bis Willy Brandt,* Blaubeuren: Verlag Ulmer Manuskripte, 2008.

Frei, Norbert. *Vergangenheitspolitik: Die Anfänge der Bundesrepublik und die NS-Vergangenheit.* Munich: C.H. Beck, 1996.

Frei, N., ed. *Karrieren im Zwielicht: Hitlers Eliten nach 1945*. Frankfurt am Main and New York: Campus, 2001.

Gerlach, Christian. "Die Wannsee-Konferenz, das Schicksal der deutschen Juden und Hitlers politische Grundsatzentscheidung, alle Juden Europas zu ermorden." In *Krieg, Ernährung, Völkermord: Forschungen zur deutschen Vernichtungspolitik im Zweiten Weltkrieg*, edited by C. Gerlach, 79–153. Hamburg: Hamburger Edition, 1998 [first in: *WerkstattGeschichte* 18 (1997): 7–44)]. [English: "The Wannsee Conferenz: The Fate of German Jews, and Hitler's Decision in Principle to Exterminate all European Jews." *Journal of Modern History* 70, no. 4 (1998): 759–812.]

Greenville, John A.S. "Die 'Endlösung' und die 'Judenmischlinge' im Dritten Reich." In *Das Unrechtsregime: Internationale Forschung über den Nationalsozialismus*, edited by U. Büttner, vol. 2, 91–121. Hamburg: Christians, 1986.

Heckmann, Markus. *NS-Täter und Bürger der Bundesrepublik: Das Beispiel des Dr Gerhard Klopfer*. Ulm: Klemm + Oelschläger, 2010.

Herbert, Ulrich. *Best: Biographische Studien über Radikalismus, Weltanschauung und Vernunft 1903–1989*. Bonn: Dietz, 1996.

Kehrl, Hans. *Krisenmanager im Dritten Reich: 6 Jahre Friede, 6 Jahre Krieg: Erinnerungen*. Düsseldorf: Droste, 1973.

Klein, Peter. *Die Wannsee-Konferenz vom 20. Januar 1942: Analyse und Dokumentation*. Berlin: Edition Hentrich, 1995.

Longerich, Peter. *Hitlers Stellvertreter: Führung der Partei und Kontrolle des Staatsapparates durch den Stab Heß und Bormanns Partei-Kanzlei*. Munich: Saur, 1992.

———. *Politik der Vernichtung: Eine Gesamtdarstellung der nationalsozialistischen Judenverfolgung*. Munich: Piper, 1998. [English: *Holocaust: The Nazi Persecution and Murder of the Jews*. Oxford and New York: Oxford University Press, 2010.]

Meinl, Susanne and Bodo Hechelhammer. *Geheimobjekt Pullach: Von der NS-Mustersiedlung zur Zentrale des BND*. Berlin: Links, 2014.

Niethammer, Lutz. *Entnazifizierung in Bayern: Säuberung und Rehabilitierung unter amerikanischer Besatzung*. Frankfurt am Main: S. Fischer, 1972.

Noakes, Jeremy. "Wohin gehören die 'Judenmischlinge'? Die Entstehung der ersten Durchführungsverordnung zu den Nürnberger Gesetzen." In *Das Unrechtsregime: Internationale Forschung über den Nationalsozialismus*, edited by U. Büttner, vol. 2, 69–91. Hamburg: Christians, 1986.

Nolzen, Armin. "Gerhard Klopfer, die Abteilung III in der Parteikanzlei und deren 'Judenpolitik' 1941/1942." In *Die Wannsee-Konferenz am 20. Januar 1942: Dokumente, Forschungsstand, Kontroversen*, edited by N. Kampe and P. Klein, 303–22. Cologne: Böhlau, 2013.

Rebentisch, Dieter. *Führerstaat und Verwaltung im Zweiten Weltkrieg: Verfassungsentwicklung und Verwaltungspolitik 1939–1945*. Stuttgart: Steiner, 1989.

Roseman, Mark. *Die Wannsee-Konferenz: Wie die NS-Bürokratie den Holocaust organisierte*. Berlin: Propyläen, 2002. [English: *The Villa, the Lake, the Meeting: Wannsee and the Final Solution*. London: Penguin Press, 2002.]

Stolleis, Michael. *Geschichte des Öffentlichen Rechts in Deutschland: Weimarer Republik und Nationalsozialismus*. Munich: C.H. Beck, 2002. [English: *A History of Public Law in Germany: 1914–1945*. Oxford: Oxford University Press, 2004.]

Wildt, Michael. *Die Generation des Unbedingten: Das Führungskorps des Reichssicherheitshauptamtes*. Hamburg: Hamburger Edition, 2002. [English: *An Uncompromising Generation: The Nazi Leadership of the Reich Security Main Office*. Madison, WI: University of Wisconsin Press, 2009.]

11

Friedrich Wilhelm Kritzinger

Reich-Chancellery

A Prussian Civil Servant under the Nazi Regime

Stefan Paul-Jacobs and Lore Kleiber

Illustration 11.1 Unknown photographer, undated (1936/1938), BArch Berlin, R 43-I/3171, 5.

Of all the protagonists of the Wannsee Conference, Friedrich Wilhelm Kritzinger was not one who featured significantly in later appraisals of its import. This can be explained, firstly, by his premature death in spring 1947; secondly, by his function at the Reich Chancellery, which appeared to have been more that of a coordinator than of a policymaker; and, thirdly, his own preference to be viewed as a traditional Prussian civil servant rather than as an ardent representative of the Nazi Party. This is the view that the history books reflect. The last major works focused specifically on Kritzinger were written by Hans Mommsen, who authored a report on him for the Institute of Contemporary History in 1966[1] and by Dieter Rebentisch, who took an in-depth look at Kritzinger some twenty years later as part of his study of bureaucracy in the Führerstaat.[2]

What is most striking about Kritzinger is the effort made by his family, in particular his son, to cast him in a positive light and to minimize his association with the Wannsee Conference. This was made apparent in laborious legal proceedings in the 1960s that examined his widow's entitlement to benefits, and in an exchange of letters between his son and the House of the Wannsee Conference.[3] This chapter will look at Kritzinger's life and legacy, focusing not only on his role and duties as state secretary in the Reich Chancellery but also on the way subsequent generations dealt with their parents' war guilt.

Personal Biography

In his biography of Kritzinger, Rebentisch described him as the "classic conservative Prussian ministry official." After studying law, Kritzinger fought in the First World War, attaining the rank of Reserve Lieutenant, and was wounded several times. He was highly decorated and was held in France as a prisoner of war until 1920. He passed the second state law exam in 1921 and began working at the Reich Justice Ministry (RJM). In 1925/26 he became an associate judge and entered the Prussian Ministry of Trade, a route subsequently followed by Erich Neumann. In 1926 he returned to the RJM. By 1931 he had been promoted to the position of undersecretary, also serving as advisor on state law, and to the Secret Cabinet Council. He was one of the few ministry officials allowed to attend cabinet meetings. Kritzinger was the oldest participant at the Wannsee Conference. Like Neumann, he had climbed the career ladder in what the Nazis referred to as "the System"—the Weimar Republic. He grew up in a Protestant parish rectory in Grünfier/Netzekreis in Grenzmark province in Posen, West Prussia. He embraced a national-ist standpoint from an early age and voted in the Weimar Republic for the anti-democratic National People's Party (DNVP), Hitler's coali-tion partner.[4] He welcomed Hitler's seizure of power and dismissed Nazi violence and attacks as mere revolutionary excesses.[5] He initially remained in the RJM, a ministry where there tended to be few staff changes.[6] A member of the DNVP, Justice Minister Franz Gürtner only joined the Nazi Party when the ban on membership was lifted in 1937.[7] Kritzinger was held in high esteem at the RJM not as an ideological aco-lyte of the new leader but as an expert on law. Responsible for matters of state law, he was directly complicit in Nazi atrocities. Referring to the Night of the Long Knives begun on 30 June 1934, Kritzinger revealed in 1946[8] that he had helped draft a law[9] that legitimized as acts of self-defense by the state the murders of a number of SA leaders, as well as of former Reich Chancellor Kurt von Schleicher and members of the conservative elite such as Erich Klausener and Edgar Jung.[10] Kritzinger also admitted that he helped establish a legal framework for the Nazis' expropriation of trade union property.

In the Reich Chancellery

The Head of the Reich Chancellery, Hans Heinrich Lammers, cultivated close ties to the Justice Ministry. When a member of his staff died in

1938 he was keen to fill the vacated position with an expert who would give him the freedom to devote his attention to day-to-day matters. By this point, the role of the Reich Chancellery was already more or less solely to lend the Nazi state legal legitimacy. According to Kritzinger himself, he hesitated before moving to the Reich Chancellery, especially when he was informed by Lammers that membership of the Nazi Party was one of the main prerequisites of the job—and at this point, he was not a member. However, he accepted the position after seeking assurances that joining the party would not necessitate party-political activity and, even more importantly, after lobbying by Gürtner, his superior at the RJM, who preferred to see "his" people in important positions rather than ardent members of the Nazi Party. His new job began on 1 February 1938 and entailed a promotion as ministerial director. Financial considerations were unlikely to have been his main motivation. Kritzinger was married to a relative of the Reich finance minister, and a member of the Schwerin von Krosigk family. In 1939, his father-in-law gave the Kritzingers a house in Blücherstraße, in the Berlin suburb of Zehlendorf.[11] Ultimately, the question as to whether his resistance to the new position and to the party membership it called for was as great as he later maintained it was is irrelevant. It was without question a promotion and afforded him added prestige in a body close to the nerve center of Nazi power. In November 1942 he advanced another step up the career ladder when he was appointed state secretary.

With its staff of seventy-five, the Reich Chancellery was a small body, given the vast amount of work being done and in comparison with the other ministries, whose work it coordinated. By the end of the war, the ten senior permanent positions that had existed at the end of the Weimar Republic had risen to just fourteen, despite their increased significance in the "Third Reich." With such modest staff numbers, close perusal of the ministries' draft laws and petitions was not possible. In the "Third Reich" there was ten times the workload there had been in the Weimar Republic.[12] Polycratic structures and the elimination of cabinet meetings after 1938 led to an increase in the number of petitions to the Reich's central institutions. According to Kritzinger, between 200 and 300 petitions and pleas were submitted to the Reich Chancellery every day.[13] A look at the résumés of other staff members of the Reich Chancellery shows how few members of the so-called "uncompromising generation" found their way into this institution. It was run by generalists and seconded specialists covering a range of areas.[14]

The start of the war further intensified government activity's focus on Hitler. The Reichstag decision in April 1942 to appoint Hitler to the highest legal office *(Oberster Gerichtsherr)* in the country, putting him above the law, effectively turned the Reich Chancellery into a clearing house (Mommsen) coordinating laws, decrees and regulations to be signed by Hitler. This meant that Kritzinger held a key position in the Nazis' legislature as an "interface manager" ensuring the smooth operation of a polycratic control structure.[15] However, such a legislature had its limitations. The Reich Chancellery had little influence on the powers of Speer, Goebbels and Himmler, including in matters relating to occupied and annexed territories.[16] Kritzinger represented the legalistic face of the regime but was undoubtedly aware of Nazi crimes against people with disabilities, Jews and other groups. It is unclear whether he knew of the full scale of the Nazis' murderous activities, or, for example, whether he processed SS mission reports.[17]

As head of Division B of the Reich Chancellery, Kritzinger was in charge of matters relating to "Jews and Persons of Mixed Blood," such as the issuing of permits for exemption from the Nuremberg Laws.[18] It also entailed cooperating on new laws drawn up under the supervision of Wilhelm Stuckart, State Secretary at the Interior Ministry. These included the 11th decree on the Reich Citizens Act of 25 November 1941, which deprived German Jews of German citizenship and stripped them of their assets in the wake of deportation, as well as the notorious 13th decree on the Reich Citizens Act of 1 July 1943, which specified that the assets of Jews would become the property of the Reich in the event of their death and transferred responsibility for criminal proceedings against Jews from the judiciary to the police.[19] Kritzinger coordinated both decrees, which served as a legal framework for the deportation and mass murder of Jews and legalized the looting of Jewish assets. With regard to Stuckart's legislative proposal for the 11th decree, Kritzinger noted that it seemed odd that "Jews, of all people, should be named protected persons" and wondered, given that "Jews might have disappeared from Germany in the not too distant future," whether it was "worth granting them special legal status" when they were not even Reich citizens.[20] These remarks suggest that Kritzinger demonstrated no overt resistance to developments in this area. After the war, however, he maintained he had hampered them in certain cases by employing the tactic of bureaucratic delay.

The Reich Chancellery altered its position in the course of the Nazi dictatorship. The Enabling Act gave the executive—in effect, Hitler, Führer and Reich Chancellor—the power to enact laws without the involvement of the Reichstag. Even though the cabinet still existed on paper, its role shrank.[21] Numerous Führer decrees and regulations consolidated the regime's centralized focus. The law-making process became circular and was coordinated by the Reich minister and Lammers, the head of the Reich Chancellery, who, along with Hitler and the relevant Reich minister, co-signed any new laws.[22] The respective Reich ministers no longer reported directly to the Reich Chancellor and it was the head of the Reich Chancellery who informed Hitler of ongoing projects and legislative proposals. This meant that Lammers played a key role in the law-making process,[23] while Kritzinger represented an institution that was not "operationally" active but responsible for making sure this process could proceed as smoothly as possible.[24] Senior members of staff were instructed in no uncertain terms to refrain from taking a policy stance in any discussions between divisions.[25] Nevertheless, they exerted considerable influence. As was the case throughout the regime's administrative arm, they were able to speed up or hamper procedures, pass on or withhold informal memos as they saw fit.[26] In later questioning, Kritzinger stated that:

> My consultations with Hitler were of course tailored to his mentality. It goes without saying that it would have been insane to say that such and such a decision would adversely affect Jews. One had to phrase it differently, and say that it would trigger serious public unrest. Obviously we could not say anything to Hitler he did not want to hear. Especially when it came to those decisions.[27]

Examples of how staff influenced decisions[28] include the introduction of special criminal laws for Poles and Jews, and the stripping of German Jews' citizenship rights.[29] However, it must be stressed that, in the main, the Reich Chancellery's job was to ensure government business could be carried out efficiently.[30]

Kritzinger's Role at the Wannsee Conference

As a representative of the institution that coordinated the regime's legislation, Kritzinger was formally required to attend the Wannsee Conference. The many laws and regulations that advanced the deprivation of the Jewish population's rights and provided a legal framework for mass murder to be perpetrated were processed by his office. However, Kritzinger did not actively participate in the meeting and is not quoted in the minutes. He presumably only contributed to the discussion when it revolved around laws and decrees that did not accord with existing legal regulations, such as questions relating to "persons of mixed-blood" and "marriages between full Jews and persons of German blood," who had so far been exempted from the deportations. It is possible that he supported Stuckart's attempts to oppose the RSHA's bid to give "persons of mixed-blood" the same legal status as "full Jews." Stuckart argued that this would "create endless administrative work" and proposed as an alternative forced sterilization.[31] Policy regarding these two categories had long been a source of conflict and one with which Kritzinger was familiar, given the number of petitions submitted to his office by parties affected.[32]

It subsequently became apparent that the Reich Chancellery was keen to maintain a distance from the question of the "Final Solution" and to postpone its resolution until the war was over. This was how Lammers interpreted Hitler's demand not to discuss the "Final Solution" with him. When the various ministries' "Jewish experts" were invited to attend a follow-up conference focused on "*Mischling* Questions" on 6 March 1942, the Reich Chancellery sent a young official named Gottfried Boley. Kritzinger instructed him to refrain from taking any policy stance, but merely to report back from the meeting.[33] The evidence suggests that this was the approach taken by Kritzinger himself at the Wannsee Conference. According to the minutes of the follow-up conference, which were sent to all the parties who had attended, the RSHA issued an unequivocal demand that they all take a position on policy. The Reich Chancellery refused to comply.[34]

It is likely that Kritzinger was privy to Stuckart's efforts, after the Wannsee Conference and the first follow-up conference, to oppose Heydrich's proposals. The archives contain a copy of a letter dated 22 May 1942, sent by Lammers to Frick, in which the head of the Reich Chancellery refers to a memo written on 12 May 1942 by Frick or Stuckart, which has unfortunately been lost. The memo, he writes, prompted him to write a secret note to Heydrich, which he nonetheless enclosed.[35] In the secret note, Lammers urged Heydrich to take into account the issues laid out in the RMdI's letter dated 12 May 1942, "concerning the status of persons of mixed blood of the first degree" in his upcoming report to Göring on the "Final Solution." He added that he would himself be bringing them to the attention of the Führer. There is no evidence in the archives to suggest that Hitler reached any categorical decision regarding "persons of mixed blood" or issued any decree bringing the policy to a halt. Given that a third conference was convened on 27 October 1942, it seems unlikely he ever did.[36]

It also seems unlikely that Kritzinger took part in the Wannsee Conference with any degree of enthusiasm, despite the fact that he was on agreeable terms with his colleagues in the ministries. He traveled there on 20 January 1942 with Gerhard Klopfer, his much younger colleague from the Party Chancellery and a close personal friend.[37]

After the Conference, Kritzinger remained Lammers' most important member of staff. While Lammers tended to work closely with
Hitler in the field, Kritzinger dealt with day-to-day affairs in the Reich
Chancellery in Berlin. His service was rewarded when he was appointed
state secretary—on the same day as Gerhard Klopfer was. Lammers'
personal meetings with Hitler became more infrequent. Meanwhile,
Martin Bormann was made the Führer's personal secretary and was
soon demanding a say in all matters relating to the Führer and, even
more significantly, controlling access to him. This further weakened the
influence of Lammers and the Reich Chancellery, and Bormann even
began to sit in on Lammers' meetings with Hitler. By now, Kritzinger's
heavy workload was taking its toll.[38] In spring 1943 he took six weeks'
sick leave, citing high blood pressure and impaired vision. He helped
organize the "relocation" of government offices in late April 1945, an
important task that shows his professionalism was highly valued. He
remained state secretary in the so-called Flensburg Government, the
short-lived government formed following Hitler's suicide.[39]

Kritzinger—As Portrayed by his Son

Kritzinger's premature death meant he could neither reflect on his
professional trajectory against the backdrop of the altered political parameters of the postwar era nor attempt to rewrite it, as other
Nazi perpetrators did, including Albert Speer and Adolf Eichmann.
Kritzinger had only a small window of opportunity to explain himself.
He was interrogated by Robert W. Kempner, who attempted to find a
category of perpetrator that Kritzinger fitted in to. "When someone
tells us that the Reich Chancellery was a type of letter sorting center
then of course we know instantly, he was complicit, but is trying to tell
us he was merely an employee who sorted letters."[40]

The comprehensive minutes of Kempner's questioning served as the
basis for Hans Mommsen's Report as well as for the strong attempt made
by Kritzinger's son to cast his father in a positive light after he died.
He compiled two comprehensive legal documents in the opposition
proceedings against the revocation of the pension paid to Kritzinger's
widow, in 1963 and 1965. His goal was not only to defend his mother's
right to a pension but also to defend his father's honor. Kritzinger's
son later wrote a professional biography of his father, over 700 pages
long and completed in 1998, intended for his family. It is striking how
Kritzinger's son largely adopts his late father's social and professional
standpoints. As a lawyer, he worked in the same field as his father and

was at pains to legitimize his father's professional involvement with the Nazi regime as tactical, and also to reclaim control over how his career was interpreted. In order to back up his arguments, he examined in depth the court cases involving other relatives of participants at the Wannsee Conference, such as the case brought between 1960 and 1969 by the widow of Wilhelm Stuckart[41] and the case brought by the widow of Erich Neumann in 1964 against the revocation of her civil service pension claim. On 22 February 1963 the State Office of Personnel in Hessen revoked Kritzinger's widow's pension, which she had received for six years. Among the reasons it cited was that Kritzinger "participated in the issuing of a number of decrees contrary to the rule of law and attended the meeting of state secretaries on 20 January 1942."[42] It is not surprising that, in his appeal, his son attempted to exonerate Kritzinger by describing his professional role as one with limited scope of action (thereby adopting the same strategy as Kritzinger and his colleagues) that, in his opinion, often consisted of choosing between "the greater and the lesser evil." The benchmark of this evaluation was always set from the position of "a radical Jewish policy" that the Reich Chancellery supposedly resisted. Kritzinger's actions did indeed appear ambiguous: for example, with regard to the 11th decree on the Reich Citizens Act, "The only justifiable question would be why my father used arguments that sound anti-Semitic."[43] His son resorted to the same explanation as Nazi perpetrators used to defend themselves: the oddity of his father's actions was a result of a sophisticated deceptive trick employed to "convince [Hitler], i.e: they had to make the issuing of a decree seem unwelcome or inexpedient from the point of view of a radical Nazi."[44] His son saw in this approach evidence of Kritzinger's strength and finesse: "His repeated attempts to hamper the introduction of an anti-Semitic measure with a skillfully worded objection, and a decision made by Hitler himself, attest to unparalleled courage, intelligence and psychological empathy."[45]

The accusation, also made by Mommsen in his 1966 report, that Kritzinger could have given up his job was rebuffed by his son on the grounds that Kritzinger would have considered such a move to be an act of cowardice and desertion. Moreover, "an attempt to be released from his office on the ground that he could not condone the political goals ... would have landed him in a concentration camp."[46] His son argued that no petition to be released from his office or for transfer would have been approved "because no position was any less problematic ... The decisive factor for my father was that no successor would carry on doing the job as he did it."[47] At this point the son cited the Nazis' ever-tightening grip on leading government bodies, which his father and other functionaries who saw themselves as nonpartisan complained about at the time. "He [Kritzinger] requested a halt to the Party's encroachment and forced the more radical members of the leadership to adhere to positive law rather than other, dubious legislation such as Führer decrees etc. He was genuinely at pains to protest against the incipient administrative chaos."[48] In short, this version of events again confirmed a view of Kritzinger as a man ultimately walking a tightrope with extraordinary courage, whose decision to remain in his job was ethically sound because there was no option. His son rejected out of hand historian Hans Mommsen's description of Kritzinger as a "civil servant who collaborated." He also rejected the idea that "weakness made him a fellow traveller."[49] Kritzinger's silence at the Wannsee Conference, in his son's view, reflected well on him. "His silence was not an unlawful failure to act because the conference produced no result."[50]

Kritzinger's son then became increasingly emotional and altered the rhetoric of his argument, referring to the personal danger facing his father. He went so far as to compare it with the threat facing victims of political persecution, citing Clemens August Graf von Galen, the Bishop of Münster, who resisted the Nazis and became an icon of civil courage for his opposition to Nazi euthanasia. In the dramatic climax of his argument, Kritzinger's son emphasized the moral dilemma in which his father found himself:

> Should my father have protested out loud? . . . Insubordination would have served no moral purpose because he could not demonstrate his resistance to the public, like the Bishop of Münster . . . He would have been risking his life without the slightest hope that open resistance would have helped the people who were being oppressed and persecuted . . . Instead, my father pursued a far more effective course of action: he monitored the development of the Final Solution as far as he was able and did what he could to mitigate it.[51]

While he had previously seemed to suggest that Kritzinger was forced into a position of powerlessness, he now suggested his father did indeed have room for maneuver, saying that Kritzinger closely monitored the radicalization of the Nazis' policy of persecution—which he supposedly was barely aware of—and intervened when he could. All in all, his son painted a contradictory and incoherent picture of Kritzinger's professional activities. With undisguised indignation, his son referred to the pension paid to Hans Lammers, the head of the Reich Chancellery and Kritzinger's former superior. Sentenced in Nuremberg to twenty years in prison, he was released after a few years. "Although he was a convicted war criminal, he received a civil servant pension until his death. But the widow of his state secretary is to be denied any right to dependents' benefits even though my father was not among the war criminals who were convicted or are still to be charged."[52]

The House of the Wannsee Conference as a Memorial and Educational Site opened in 1992. The exhibition focused on the participants at the 1942 meeting, but the curators had no photographs of three of them at their disposal. One of the three was Kritzinger. Staff at the memorial site therefore turned to relatives of these men for assistance. An initial letter was sent to Kritzinger's son in June 1994. He gave the site's request for photographs careful consideration and asked for further details of the context in which his father would appear in the exhibition and the precise wording of the information about him. Gerhard Schoenberner, the director of the memorial site at the time, was well aware that the matter was a delicate one. Past experience had made him familiar with the reactions sparked by the sort of request the site had sent Kritzinger's son. He assured him that the information the exhibition would contain would be completely objective, pointing out that it was in the public interest and appealing for his cooperation.[53]

In July 1994 Kritzinger's son refused the request for a photograph of his father and expressed fundamental criticism of the memorial site's concept. He said he was unwilling to "support the historically spurious bias by supplying a photograph."[54] He repeated the argument he had put forward in his father's defense in the court case that the significance of the Wannsee Conference was vastly overestimated. He even took exception to the name, "The House of the Wannsee Conference," where the conference room, as the nerve center of the memorial, would feature as an original historical site, and criticized the fact that the conference participants would misleadingly appear to "impartial and uninformed visitors" as a group of perpetrators in league with each other, "a decision-making body colluding in the drawing up and execution of the so-called Final Solution."[55] His basic objection was to what he saw as "an underlying reinterpretation of the conference," and the "historical distortion" and "simplistic" depiction of the participants. His final point—which perhaps amounted to wishful thinking—was that in terms of history, his father might as well be left out of the equation, thereby erasing his association with the other perpetrators:

> We believe that his [Kritzinger's] presence was so irrelevant as to be not worthy of mention . . . The entire concept of the exhibition completely unfairly places him together with Heydrich, Eichmann and other accomplices in a gallery of perpetrators.[56]

In October 1994 Kritzinger's son wrote to the memorial site once again, offering his own suggestion for captions in the exhibition that pertained to the role played by his father, Lammers and the Reich Chancellery in general. This, he said, would satisfy his wish for an amendment to the historical documentation. Visitors to the exhibition would be informed that the Reich Chancellery obstructed the murder of nearly 100,000 so-called "Mischlinge" and partners in "privileged mixed marriages," and his father would be depicted as a silent but outraged witness to the Wannsee Conference. The memorial site did not accede to his wish. In a subsequent letter in June 2005, Kritzinger's son expressed skepticism, curiosity and even some respect for the historical exhibition at the House of the Wannsee Conference after director Norbert Kampe informed him of the intention to revise it. In 2006 an entire room devoted to the institutional context of the authorities invited to the Wannsee Conference was opened.[57]

Conclusion

"Justice being taken away, then, what are kingdoms but great robberies?" (St. Augustine). This might not be a quote from Kritzinger, but it serves as a reminder that, by working as a lawyer for a regime, which he had known from the start to be criminal, he made himself a stooge. When questioned by Robert W. Kempner, Deputy Chief U.S. Prosecutor at the U.S.-led Nuremberg Military Tribunals, about what happened between 1933 and 1945, he said that "to me, the worst atrocities were perpetrated in the occupied territories and against the Jews. I was ashamed to visit my home and my father's grave." His father's grave lay in a region that used to belong to the German Reich but which was ceded to Poland under the terms of the Treaty of Versailles.[58] However, the shame he felt regarding the regime's crimes did not extend to an admission of his own active complicity in the organization of this criminal system. In Nuremberg he picked up on a nautical metaphor used by Kempner: "When a ship is in distress at sea—and Germany was a ship in distress—then the sailors do not jump ship when they realize it's the captain's fault."[59]

The fact is that, from 1933 on, Kritzinger held positions of responsibility and colluded in disguising major breaches of law and maintaining the illusion that the Nazi dictatorship was a constitutional state. The Wannsee Conference marked a further step in the regime's use of legal norms to flank and rationalize its genocidal agenda. The facade of legality helped ensure that the Nazi regime and its crimes were accepted even by its detractors, and their participation in the system

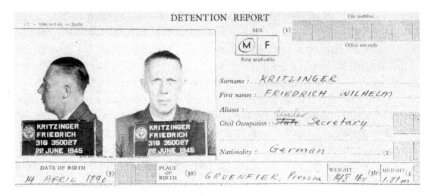

Illustration 11.2 On this report issued to document Kritzinger's imprisonment in Nuremberg, an unknown person changed the entry stating his previous occupation from "state secretary" to "undersecretary" to make it clear he had not been a minister. Unknown photographer, 22 June 1947, Yad Vashem, 84185.

thereby facilitated. The Nazi regime saw itself as a constitutional state. The Nazis appeared to reject the possibility of a revolution that did not appear to be supported by traditional legal norms.

No one chooses their family. The descendants of the Wannsee Conference participants—the descendants of perpetrators—all dealt very differently with their family's past. Almost fifteen years after the death of Friedrich Wilhelm Kritzinger, his son assumed the role of his legal and ethical defender. Perhaps he made this emotional family pact in light of the personal shame that Kritzinger expressed on several occasions during questioning, coupled with his strong identification with his father. He argued for a compassionate evaluation of his father's complicity and strongly resisted contemporary interpretations. He was especially opposed to the institutionalization of the villa that hosted the Wannsee Conference. Kritzinger's son aimed to ensure his father would go down in history as a minor figure, which would be, in his eyes, a fitting historicization.

Lore Kleiber is a Political Scientist who has studied history, German philology, media studies and political science. She was a curator for exhibitions, and has been the research assistant of the educational department of the House of the Wannsee Conference since 1992. Kleiber is a member of the "Historikerlabor" (Documentary-theater group).

Stefan Paul-Jacobs is an editor, historian, curator and dramaturg for cultural historical exhibitions, and has written numerous publications about everyday history and cultural history. He also conducted research about Friedrich Wilhelm Kritzinger for the documentary-theater "Die Wannsee-Konferenz", which was shown for the first time in the House of the Wannsee Conference in 2012.

Notes

1 Hans Mommsen, "Aufgabenkreise und Verantwortlichkeit des Staatssekretärs der Reichskanzlei Dr. Wilhelm Kritzinger," in *Gutachten des Institutes für Zeitgeschichte, vol. 2: Gutachten,* ed. Institutes für Zeitgeschichte (Munich, 1966), 369–98. An exhaustive assessment of the Report can be found in Nicolas Berg, *Der Holocaust und die westdeutschen Historiker: Erforschung und Erinnerung* (Göttingen, 2003), 557–63.

2 Dieter Rebentisch, "Friedrich Wilhelm Kritzinger (1890–1947)," in *Persönlichkeiten der Verwaltung: Biographien zur deutschen Verwaltungsgeschichte 1648–1945,* ed. K.G.A. Jeserich and H. Neuhaus (Stuttgart, 1991), 445–48.

3 See, for instance, Friedrich Wilhelm Kritzinger, "Ausarbeitung über die Tätigkeit und Haltung meines Vaters im Dritten Reich" — arguments submitted to the State Staff Office in connection with the administrative proceedings against Walti Kritzinger of 22 February 1963, BArch, N 1635/2.

4 Minutes of the interrogation of Kritzinger by Robert Kempner on 5 March 1947, IFZ. Retrieved 15 October 2016 from http://www.ifz-muenchen.de/archiv/zs/zs-0988.pdf.

5 Self-reported by Friedrich Wilhelm Kritzinger on 9 September 1946, 5, Barch, N 1635, 3–6.

6 The twelve ministerial advisors, almost half of whom had been working in-house since 1920, all remained in office in 1933. In an SD Report (probably from 1941) it is stated that "When one went into the Justice Ministry, one had to take off one's Party badge." Quoted in M. Broszat, E. Fröhlich and F. Wiesemann, ed., *Bayern in der NS-Zeit: Soziale Lage und politisches Verhalten der Bevölkerung im Spiegel vertraulicher Berichte* (Munich, 1977), 612.

7 Lothar Gruchmann, *Justiz im Dritten Reich 1933–1940: Anpassung und Unterwerfung in der Ära Gürtner,* (Munich, 2001), 243.

8 Self-reported, Kritzinger, 5.

9 Self-reported, Kritzinger, 5.

10 "Gesetz über Maßnahmen der Staatsnotwehr [Law on Measures taken by the State in Legitimate Self-defence]," 3 July 1934, RGBl. I, 529. See Hans-Detlef Heller, *Die Zivilrechtsgesetzgebung im Dritten Reich: Die deutsche bürgerlich-rechtliche Gesetzgebung unter der Herrschaft des Nationalsozialismus: Anspruch und Wirklichkeit* (Münster, 2015), 356.

11 Self-reported, Kritzinger, 18.

12 Dieter Rebentisch, *Führerstaat und Verwaltung im Zweiten Weltkrieg: Verfassungsentwicklung und Verwaltungspolitik 1939–1945* (Stuttgart, 1989), 56, footnote 105.

13 Self-reported, Kritzinger, 10.

14 Georg Franz-Willing, *Die Reichskanzlei 1933–1945: Rolle und Bedeutung unter der Regierung Hitler* (Tübingen, 1984), 106 et seq.

15 S. Reichardt and W. Seibel, ed., *Der prekäre Staat: Herrschen und Verwalten im Nationalsozialismus* (Frankfurt am Main, 2011), 19.

16 Friedrich Hartmannsgruber, who worked on files of the Reich Chancellery, refers to sectoral, territorial and temporal limits. See Conference Report of J. Retterath, "Die bürokratische Dimension der NS-Herrschaft: Die Reichsverwaltung im Zweiten Weltkrieg: Konflikt, Verflechtung, Koordination, 13 October 2015 Munich," in *H-Soz-Kult* (26 January 2016). Retrieved 15 October 2016 from http://www.hsozkult.de/conferencereport/id/tagungsberichte-6346

17 Hans Mommsen writes, in his Report on Kritzinger, that although he might not have been aware of "the full extent of the Final Solution," nevertheless there is no doubt that Kritzinger "was informed of all decisive political operations, including the persecution of Jews and the Final Solution, the issues surrounding special commando units, euthanasia, persecution of the Church, political measures in the occupied Eastern Territories, slave labor, etc. and knew of all draft legislation relating to them before it was published." Mommsen, "Aufgabenkreise und Verantwortlichkeit," 372.

18 Mommsen, "Aufgabenkreise und Verantwortlichkeit," 370.

19 "Reichsgesetzblatt 1943," 372; see Mommsen, "Aufgabenkreise und Verantwortlichkeit," 393–96.

20 Hitler, presented with Stuckart's proposal, together with the proposal for a decree on the German People's List, stated—as Lammers noted on 20 December 1940—that he was "decisively" against Jews being designated in any law or decree as "protected persons," a view that Lammers reported to the Interior Ministry shortly thereafter. Quote from Mommsen, "Aufgabenkreise und Verantwortlichkeit," 382.

21 Rebentisch, *Führerstaat*, 41.

22 While, in 1933, the Cabinet met every second day, in 1934 it met nineteen times, in 1935 twelve times, in 1936 four times, in 1937 six times, and in 1938 once, see Hans-Ulrich Wehler, *Das deutsche Kaiserreich 1871–1918* (Deutsche Geschichte, vol. 9) (Göttingen, 1994), 65. Rebentisch, *Führerstaat*, 41, described the meeting on 9 December 1937 as the last regular Cabinet meeting, while the meeting to discuss the "Fritsch-Krise" on 5 February 1938 was solely a ministerial discussion or a speech by Hitler on the political situation.

23 Lammers stated in an interrogation by Robert Kempner at Nuremberg in 1948: "Because the Reich Cabinet no longer met, as the Führer usually forbade, so to speak, meetings of Ministers, the only way to coordinate current activities between the various spheres of competence was to hold meetings between the State Secretaries as the opportunity arose, and these had then, in the last months of the war, become an almost daily consultation, because otherwise there would have been no contact at all." Quoted by Kurt Pätzold and Erika Schwarz, *Tagesordnung: Judenmord: Die Wannsee-Konferenz am 20. Januar 1942: Eine Dokumentation zur Organisation der 'Endlösung'* (Berlin, 1992), 154 et seq.

24 Rebentisch, *Führerstaat*, 48.

25 Rebentisch, *Führerstaat*, 54 et seq.

26 Rebentisch, *Führerstaat*, 55 et seq.

27 Interrogation of Friedrich Wilhelm Kritzinger by Dr Robert Kempner, 5 March 1947, IfZ ZS 988/1, 17.

28 Exhaustively documented by Uwe Dietrich Adam, *Judenpolitik im Dritten Reich* (Düsseldorf, 1972), 192–212.

29 Ultimately these efforts were in vain however: Adam concludes: "The criminal law regime for Poland entailed for all affected the end of the existing criminal law system."

30 Mommsen, "Aufgabenkreise und Verantwortlichkeit," 375.

31 Adam, *Judenpolitik*, 226.

32 Self-report, Kritzinger,10.

33 Interrogation of Hans Ficker, 20 December 1946, BArch Berlin, Film 44312.

34 Interrogation of Gottfried Boley, 10 June 1947, BArch Berlin, Film 55001.

35 BAB R 1501/5519, sheet 239 et seq.

36 See, on this point, Cornelia Essner, *Die "Nürnberger Gesetze" oder die Verwaltung des Rassenwahns 1933–1945* (Paderborn, 2002), 428; Hans-Christian Jasch, *Staatssekretär Wilhelm Stuckart und die Judenpolitik: Der Mythos von der sauberen Verwaltung* (Munich: , 2012), 342 et seq. Lammers' colleague, Reich Cabinet Advisor Dr Ficker stated that in the wake of the meeting on 6 March 1942, Lammers brought the issue to the attention of Hitler in April or May 1942. Hitler then decided that "resolving the matter should be postponed until the end of the war." See testimony of Ficker of 22 December 1947 on behalf of Hofmann in RuSHA-Trial (case 8, Hofmann doc. no. 135 c), excerpts copied as doc. no. 669 of Stuckart's defense, BArch 99 US 7, Case XI/871, sheet 95.

37 After Kritzinger's death, contact between the Kritzinger family and Gerhard Klopfer did not come to an end, as letters from Klopfer from between 1947 and 1968 show. See letter from Friedrich Wilhelm Kritzinger (son) to the author of 12 November 2011 with two copy letters.

38 See Wolfgang Heintzeler, *Der rote Faden: Fünf Jahrzehnte Staatsdienst, Wehrmacht, Chemische Industrie, Nürnberg, Marktwirtschaft, Mitbestimmung, Kirche* (Stuttgart, 1983), 51.

39 See Ian Kershaw, *The End: Hitler's Germany, 1944–45* (London, 2011), 469 et seq.

40 Interrogation of Friedrich Wilhelm Kritzinger by Dr Robert Kempner, 5 March 1947, IfZ, ZS 988, 14 et seq.

41 On 1 June 1960 the Director of the State Office of Personnel in Hessen determined, by reference to Paragraph 3(3) of the Law on Art. 131 of the Basic Law, that the deceased, Stuckart, and his dependents had no rights under Chapter I of G 131. Lotte Stuckart appealed against that decision right up to the Hessen Administrative Court, which referred the case to the Federal Constitutional Court for consultation on the constitutionality of Paragraph 3(3) of G 131 and then wholly rejected the appeal. The appeal against the refusal to refer the case to the Federal Constitutional Court

in 1969 was also unsuccessful. See: Hessisches Staatsarchiv, Wiesbaden (HessStA): Decision of the Hessen Administrative Court, 10 December 1963 (Az: AS I 3/62).

42 Copy of a letter from Friedrich Wilhelm Kritzinger to the State Office of Personnel in Hessen of 28 May 1963, 1, BArch, N 1635/2.

43 1, BArch, N 1635/2, 21.

44 1, BArch, N 1635/2, 22.

45 1, BArch, N 1635/2, 43.

46 1, BArch, N 1635/2, 29.

47 Copy of a letter from Friedrich Wilhelm Kritzinger to the State Office of Personnel in Hessen of 28 May 1963, 29, BArch, N 1635/2.

48 29, BArch, N 1635/2, 29.

49 29, BArch, N 1635/2, 42.

50 29, BArch, N 1635/2, 35.

51 29, BArch, N 1635/2, 33.

52 29, BArch, N 1635/2, 46.

53 Letter from Gerhard Schoenberner to Kritzinger, 23 June 1994, in: Archives of the House of the Wannsee Conference Memorial.

54 Letter from Kritzinger to Schoenberner of 19 June 1994, 4.

55 Letter from Kritzinger to Schoenberner of 19 July 1994, 1.

56 Letter from Kritzinger to Schoenberner of 19 July 1994, 4.

57 Letter from Friedrich Wilhelm Kritzinger to Norbert Kampe, 14 June 2005, in: Archives of the House of the Wannsee Conference Memorial.

58 Questioning of Wilhelm Kritzinger by Dr Robert Kempner, 5 March 1947, IfZ, ZS 988, 14.

59 Questioning of Wilhelm Kritzinger by Dr Robert Kempner, 5 March 1947, IfZ, ZS 988, 14.

Bibliography

Adam, Uwe Dietrich. *Judenpolitik im Dritten Reich*. Düsseldorf: Droste, 1972 [reprint Düsseldorf: Droste, 2003].

Berg, Nicolas. *Der Holocaust und die westdeutschen Historiker: Erforschung und Erinnerung*, Göttingen: Wallstein, 2003. [English: *The Holocaust and the West German Historians: Historical Interpretation and Autobiographical Memory*. Madison, WI: University of Wisconsin Press, 2015.]

Broszat, M., E. Fröhlich and F. Wiesemann, ed. *Bayern in der NS-Zeit: Soziale Lage und politisches Verhalten der Bevölkerung im Spiegel vertraulicher Berichte*. Munich: Oldenbourg, 1977.

Essner, Cornelia. *Die "Nürnberger Gesetze" oder die Verwaltung des Rassenwahns 1933–1945*. Paderborn: Schöningh, 2002.

Franz-Willing, Georg. *Die Reichskanzlei 1933–1945: Rolle und Bedeutung unter der Regierung Hitler*. Tübingen: Grabert, 1984.

Gruchmann, Lothar. *Justiz im Dritten Reich 1933–1940: Anpassung und Unterwerfung in der Ära Gürtner*. 3rd ed. Munich: Oldenbourg, 2001.

Heintzeler, Wolfgang. *Der rote Faden: Fünf Jahrzehnte Staatsdienst, Wehrmacht, Chemische Industrie, Nürnberg, Marktwirtschaft, Mitbestimmung, Kirche.* Stuttgart: Seewald, 1983.

Heller, Hans-Detlef. *Die Zivilrechtsgesetzgebung im Dritten Reich: Die deutsche bürgerlich-rechtliche Gesetzgebung unter der Herrschaft des Nationalsozialismus: Anspruch und Wirklichkeit.* Münster: Verlagshaus Monsenstein und Vannerdat, 2015. Retrieved 6 October 2016 from http://nbn-resolving.de/urn:nbn:de:0168-ssoar-450022

Jasch, Hans-Christian. *Staatssekretär Wilhelm Stuckart und die Judenpolitik: Der Mythos von der sauberen Verwaltung.* Munich: Oldenbourg, 2012.

Kershaw, Ian. *The End: Hitler's Germany, 1944–45.* London: Allen Lane, 2011.

Mommsen, Hans. "Aufgabenkreise und Verantwortlichkeit des Staatssekretärs der Reichskanzlei Dr. Wilhelm Kritzinger." In *Gutachten des Institutes für Zeitgeschichte,* edited by Institutes für Zeitgeschichte, ed. Institut für Zeitgeschichte, vol. 2, 369–98. Munich: Institutes für Zeitgeschichte, 1966.

Pätzold, Kurt and Erika Schwarz. *Tagesordnung: Judenmord: Die Wannsee-Konferenz am 20. Januar 1942: Eine Dokumentation zur Organisation der 'Endlösung.'* Berlin: Metropol, 1992.

Rebentisch, Dieter. *Führerstaat und Verwaltung im Zweiten Weltkrieg: Verfassungsentwicklung und Verwaltungspolitik 1939–1945.* Stuttgart: Steiner, 1989.

———. "Friedrich Wilhelm Kritzinger (1890–1947)." In *Persönlichkeiten der Verwaltung: Biographien zur deutschen Verwaltungsgeschichte 1648–1945,* edited by K.G.A. Jeserich and H. Neuhaus. Stuttgart: Kohlhammer, 1991.

Reichardt, S. and W. Seibel, ed. *Der prekäre Staat: Herrschen und Verwalten im Nationalsozialismus.* Frankfurt am Main: Campus, 2011.

Wehler, Hans-Ulrich. *Das deutsche Kaiserreich 1871–1918.* Göttingen: Vandenhoeck & Ruprecht, 1994 [first published 1973]. [English: *The German Empire: 1871–1918.* Warwickshire: Berg Publishers, 1985.]

12

GEORG LEIBBRANDT

Reich Ministry for the Occupied
Eastern Territories

An Academic Radical

Martin Munke

Illustration 12.1 Unknown
photographer, undated (1942), Ullstein,
00263185.

> Diversity of nationalities . . . brought with it further enrichment, whether
> in the field of business, spiritual life or religious, cultural, political and
> social consensus-building . . . It was a colloquium humanum, a humane
> and spiritual coexistence that allowed each and everyone to retain their
> individuality . . ., with the overarching principle of human community
> transcending nationality.
> —Georg Leibbrandt, "Wechselwirkungen zwischen den Völkern"

This was how Georg Leibbrandt described the coexistence of various
nationalities in Ukraine prior to the First World War. The description
conveys a vision of a harmonious coexistence of nationalities, cooperation, exchange, acceptance—a vision, which allegedly informed
Leibbrandt in his role as a high-ranking official at the NSDAP Office of
Foreign Affairs (APA) and the Reich Ministry for the Occupied Eastern
Territories (RMO). Christian Gerlach suggests that a different picture
of ethnic Germans in Russia prevailed in Nazi offices. "Former Russian
and Soviet Germans were among the most active and fanatical perpetrators, frequently serving as strategists in occupation policy and mass
murder . . ."[1] These included Leibbrandt himself, who was born near
Odessa. Among those who subscribed to this point of view was Ernst
Piper in his biographical study of Alfred Rosenberg, Leibbrandt's long-
term superior.[2] Coupled with the tendency of many former protagonists
in the Nazi regime to play down their own roles,[3] the latter assessment
seems the more plausible in the light of Leibbrandt's attendance at the

Wannsee Conference, where he and Rosenberg's deputy, Alfred Meyer, represented the RMO.

This chapter will examine the reasons for Leibbrandt's attendance at the meeting on 20 January 1942. He has featured in previous writings on the Wannsee Conference merely as a marginal figure.[4] Historians also disagree on his role in the Nazis' systematic extermination of the Jewish population in the Eastern territories. To some he was a dilettante;[5] to others, a leading force.[6] Along with Otto Hofmann and Gerhard Klopfer, Leibbrandt is just one of three participants at the conference who continued to live in what became West Germany after the war for a number of decades, seeking to build a new life. This chapter sets out to show that Leibbrandt was a significant contributor to nationalistic research on the East *(Ostforschung),*[7] based on ideas concerning the restructuring of a Europe dominated by Germany that seemed superficially more "humane" than the reality of the German occupation in the East. However, his work on policy regarding German ethnography and implementation of his ideas was clearly carried out under the aegis of National Socialism in order to further its political and ideological aims, with all their terrible consequences, whether intended or not.

Ethnographic Researcher

Born on 5 September 1899, in Hoffnungsfeld/Torosovo, Hoffnungstal/Tsebrykove near Odessa, Georg Leibbrandt was the descendant of German emigres.[8] His first language was German. He attended secondary schools in Dorpat/Tartu, Verro/Võru and Odessa, where he learned Greek and Latin, Russian, Ukrainian and, later, French and English. In 1918 he served as an interpreter for the German occupying troops in Ukraine and in 1919, he fled the Ukrainian War of Independence and settled in Germany. His experiences as a young man, including losing a number of family members in the wake of the forced resettlements and the purges ordered by Stalin, laid the foundations for Leibbrandt's deep anti-Bolshevism, which formed the core of his world view.

In the 1920s he graduated in theology, history and philosophy from the University of Leipzig, having also spent several terms in Tübingen and two months in Marburg. He went on to spend time in Paris and London, where he attended lectures on international law and international relations. He earned a living as an interpreter for foreign visitors at the Leipzig Trade Fair and as a private tutor. As a student, Leibbrandt was an active member of the "Wingolf" Christian student association and rejoined it in 1945. In 1927 he completed his doctorate on the

Swabian emigration to Russia, which his forebears had joined,[9] and was awarded a Ph.D. from the University of Leipzig. During and after a spell working at the Institute of Culture and Universal History, headed by his doctoral supervisor Walter Goetz,[10] Leibbrandt made research trips to Canada, the U.S., the Soviet Union (three times) and Switzerland. These trips were funded by the Emergency Association of German Science and the Rockefeller Foundation. He was briefly employed at the Stiftung für deutsche Volks- und Kulturbodenforschung and the Potsdam Reich Archive, where he researched *"Auslandsdeutschtum"* (ethnic Germans in border areas and foreign countries). His published work stressed the "colonization skills" of German settlers in Russia — and, later, in the Soviet Union — and the United States.[11] In a preface to a source edition, Leibbrandt wrote that the point of the book was to "help foster in Germans themselves a love for their national tradition and an interest in the history of colonialism."[12] The book was published by the German Foreign Institute (DAI) in Stuttgart as the first in a new series intended to illustrate the "cultural achievements of ethnic Germans in foreign countries"[13] and to raise their profile in Germany's foreign policy.[14]

Leibbrandt had taken an active interest in these issues since he was a student, publishing an article on Wingolf's "national duties."[15] He later joined organizations such as the Student Union of Ethnic Germans from Foreign Countries (Vereinigung auslandsdeutscher Studierender) and the Student Union of Colonialist Germans (Verein Deutscher Studierender Kolonisten).[16] After a research trip, he delivered reports on the state of German minorities in the Soviet Union to the Foreign Ministry.[17] His interest was also apparent in his editorial contributions to a "Concise Dictionary of Ethnic German Identity in Border Areas and Foreign Countries" ("Handwörterbuch des Grenz- und Auslandsdeutschtums") during his employment at the Stiftung für deutsche Volks- und Kulturbodenforschung. The dictionary, which linked *Volk* (nation) and *Raum* (space),[18] was one of the main projects completed in the field of research on ethnic Germans and the areas in which they settled in the period between the two World Wars.

Ethno-politician

Until the 1930s there is no evidence of any contact between Leibbrandt and the Nazi movement. But ahead of his stay in the United States, Leibbrandt referred to knowing Kurt Lüdecke,[19] the Washington correspondent for the *Völkischer Beobachter.* Lüdecke reported to Munich on

Leibbrandt's work on "nationalist questions," bringing Leibbrandt to the attention of the NSDAP Office of Foreign Affairs (APA), established in April 1933. Hjalmar Schacht secured him an introduction to Alfred Rosenberg at the APA.[20] As "chief ideologist"[21] Rosenberg identified broad agreement in ideas on policy regarding the east—this applied primarily to the plan to divide the Soviet Union into states defined by nationality, known as the decomposition concept,[22]—and appointed Leibbrandt head of the Eastern Division, on condition that he join the party. Leibbrandt submitted two applications for membership: to Berlin on 20 June and via the Nazis' Geneva chapter on 17 September. Because of the temporary suspension of new admissions, Rosenberg had to intervene at the Nazi Party Chancellery and Leibbrandt's application was only approved on 30 September, backdated to 1 July. He was given membership number 1,976,826[23] and assumed his new office at the APA. Leibbrandt would later maintain that he had been working for the party prior to 1933 in a bid to boost his status.[24] In fact, he joined the Nazi Party in order to advance his career and implement his own political ideas.

He rose to the new challenge with enthusiasm. After all, it was his "deepest wish ... to be of service to the German nation by means of foreign policy."[25] But Leibbrandt's approach to his work at the APA was far from systematic. For example, his contacts with various groups of emigres were often based on personal relationships.[26] He attempted to steer their respective activities so long as these activities did not impede the own foreign policy. In the early days of his appointment, he made few plans for any later structuring of Russia and treatment of ethnic Germans. In the early 1930s, Germany's eventual expansionist policy did not yet seem viable. Policy was restricted to vague plans to create a buffer zone of states on the border to the Soviet Union.[27]

However, Leibbrandt did succeed in bringing into line the various associations of Russian Germans active in the Reich and uniting them in the League of Germans from Russia (Verband der Deutschen aus Rußland, VDR).[28] The VDR was set up to help quantify the number of ethnic Germans living in the Reich and to keep tabs on them. Ultimately, they were to be primed to perform political tasks in the East. Leibbrandt also sought to banish what he saw as "a prevailing lack of clarity among Nazi officials regarding the nature, worth and significance of Russia's ethnic Germans." Hitler and Himmler in particular apparently underestimated the biological might of this ethnic group, "which, thanks to its natural reproductive values and uttermost frugality, even after severe blows of fate, has repeatedly shown itself to be a valuable element of colonization in the east."[29]

His words indicate that he had embraced the biological principles of Nazi ideology. Prior to 1933 and again after 1945, Leibbrandt extolled a definition of nation anchored in culture theory. Predicated on the superiority of "Germanness," this lent itself well to the Nazi regime's political aims. Leibbrandt's altered views were also evident in propaganda material he published, a series of pamphlets entitled "Bolshevism" as well as numerous articles for the *Völkischer Beobachter* and the *Nationalsozialistische Monatshefte* that examined the supposed connection between "Jewishness" and Bolshevism.[30] Leibbrandt's increasingly evident deep anti-Bolshevism tied in with the focus on German minorities outside the Reich. He wrote countless drafts, exposés and speeches for Rosenberg containing strong anti-Semitic messages,[31] which he also integrated into his own presentations and publications.[32]

Leibbrandt's central "ethnographic" venture was the project "Sammlung Georg Leibbrandt" (SGL).[33] With its supposed historical explanation of Germany's claims to dominion and territory as well as its categorization—conducted with supposedly modern methods[34]—of ethnic German groups, it lent weight, on the one hand, to the thinking that consolidated those claims;[35] on the other hand the results of research conducted in this field were later seen as laying the groundwork for and justifying the advance of the Wehrmacht as well as occupation and resettlement policy.

The foundations of Leibbrandt's work were laid on the research trips he undertook in the late 1920s. In 1937/38 he gave his collected documents and records relating to Russian Germans to the geographer Emil Meynen.[36] These were collated into the SGL. After 1945, the later director of the West German Research Institute for Regional Geography (Institut für Länderkunde) described it as "scientifically analytical" and "strictly scientific documentation."[37] Under the aegis of the SGL (later renamed the "Publications Office East/Publikationsstelle Ost") a series of "ethno-political projects" were compiled strictly for "official use". These projects constituted the self-perception of the SGL staff to be the the central research office for ethnic Germanness in the East.[38] Among its tasks was the compilation of local card indexes on all German communities in the Soviet Union, including information as to how their respective populations were made up; their topographic position and an "ethno-map" of the Soviet Union.[39] Further tasks included routine examination of the Ukrainian and Russian press and the compilation of an index of significant Russian-German figures, with the aim of establishing their "ethnographic standpoint." There were more indexes of literature related to Russia's ethnic Germans as well as a library. This was later extended with material looted by the Künsberg special unit (Sonderkommando Künsberg), which was under the control of the Foreign Ministry and which systematically plundered art and cultural resources primarily in the east. The SGL came into possession of over 65,000 volumes from the Ukraine. Most of them belonged to collections in Kiev. Leibbrandt was also personally involved in library and archival plunder, examining collections in the Ukraine and in France as part of the "Einsatzstab Reichsleiter Rosenberg" (Reichsleiter Rosenberg Taskforce).[40]

Occupation and Extermination Policy

These activities constituted a link to Leibbrandt's complicity in Nazi extermination policy. Between summer 1941 and spring 1943, his old acquaintance Karl Stumpp[41] headed a unit of up to eighty men. This was directly assigned to Leibbrandt's Department I (Politics) in the newly created Reich Ministry for the Occupied Eastern Territories. In August 1941 it began compiling ethnobiological statistics on rural populations in the Ukraine. In late 1942 these statistics were used to divide ethnic German communities into the categories on the German People's List (Deutsche Volksliste, DVL).[42] Stumpp's reports amount to a chronicle of the murder of the Jewish population.[43] At the RMO, Leibbrandt was directly briefed about the beginnings of the Jewish genocide. The most obvious example was his often-cited exchange of letters[44] with Hinrich Lohse, the Reich Commissar for the Ostland,[45] in autumn 1941. This exchange saw Leibbrandt requesting an explanation for Lohse's "prohibition" of "Jewish executions." The last letter sent by Leibbrandt's deputy, Otto Bräutigam,[46] contained the statement: "economic considerations . . . must not be taken into account when dealing with the Jewish problem."[47] Plans to spark off pogroms by local populations against Jews had been drawn up within the SS and the APA ahead of the invasion of the Soviet Union,[48] and Leibbrandt was informed of the implementation of these "methods" shortly after the invasion. In July 1941 Bräutigam, who initially served as the RMO's liaison officer to the Supreme High Command of the German Army (Oberkommando des Heeres, OKH), referred to such assaults in his diary.[49] Similar accounts of the shooting of "a few thousand Jews" reached Leibbrandt from the Baltic region at the same time.[50]

In this respect, Leibbrandt's attendance at the Wannsee Conference appears understandable. The fact that the RMO was the only office involved to send two representatives has repeatedly been cited as an indication of the particular intensity of his complicity.[51] But in fact the reason it did so had more to do with Alfred Meyer, Rosenberg's State Secretary for the Eastern occupied territories, therefore a more senior official and a Gauleiter. He usually had specialist support when he attended talks outside the RMO.[52] Leibbrandt's statement that he had been ordered by Meyer at short notice to accompany him to the conference therefore seems plausible.[53] Despite the fact that Leibbrandt himself did not speak,[54] he was familiar with the questions addressed at the conference. He too had been affected by Himmler's efforts to push through his demands ahead of the conference. On 4 October he and Meyer had been the guests of Reinhard Heydrich[55] and on 15 November 1941 he and Rosenberg visited the SS-Reichsführer himself.[56] He subsequently hosted a follow-up conference focused on the treatment of "Mischlinge" on 29 January 1942. There the RMO argued the case for introducing a broad-based definition of Jewishness in order to reduce red tape in the racial selection process.[57]

After the war, Leibbrandt maintained he had kept a mental distance from the Nazis' Jewish policy. In actual fact the RMO made a number of efforts to restructure occupation policy. However, these concerned mainly the more general treatment of prisoners of war and forced laborers, as well as the treatment of the local populations, who were to be recruited to the fight against Bolshevism. No criticism of the treatment of the Jewish population was voiced.[58] Leibbrandt and Bräutigam expressed disgust at the members of the civil government who were keen to participate in the murder of Jews[59] but, nevertheless, his post meant he dealt daily with matters relating to the "Jewish Question."[60]

Members of the Wehrmacht close to Quarter-Master General Eduard Wagner[61]—who was involved with the hunger plan and extermination policies, but also with the 20 July plot in 1944—were identified by Rosenberg and Leibbrandt as potential allies in the push for a restructured occupation policy. In October 1942 Leibbrandt—by now ministerial director[62]—took part in consultations with the Wehrmacht's head office.[63] At the behest of Leibbrandt and Wagner, a meeting with high-ranking representatives from both sides took place on 11 December.[64] In late January/early February 1943, Leibbrandt, the OKH and the Wehrmacht propaganda decided on a "program of reform," which Rosenberg presented without success to Hitler on 8 February.[65]

Leibbrandt may also have been led by political reservations as to occupation policy in another case he cited subsequently in his defense.[66] The issue this time was the classification of the Crimean Karaites. It had been decided that this ethnic group should be considered Turkic despite the fact that the majority were Jewish—a decision made by Leibbrandt in June 1943 after nearly two years of debate. As a result, the Crimean Karaites were largely exempted from the Nazis' extermination policy.[67] The decision was one of the last made by Leibbrandt during his period of office, which he had to give up in the autumn. This was partly due to his ongoing disagreements with Erich Koch, the Reich Commissioner for Ukraine.[68] Moreover, Himmler wanted to replace Leibbrandt—whom he saw as siding with the Ukrainians and being led by "sentimental humanitarianism"[69]— with one of his own men in the RMO, in a bid to further consolidate his leading role in developing and implementing the policies of occupation and extermination. His choice as director of Department I (Politics) was Gottlob Berger, chief of the SS main office. By the time the war ended, Leibbrandt was in the navy. This does not, however, make his account of himself as a bureaucrat who had nothing to do with the policy of extermination any more plausible. During his tenure with the Ostministerium, he was involved at a senior level with the mass murder and occupation policy carried out between mid 1941 and mid 1943.[70]

From Perpetrator to Victim

At the end of the war, Leibbrandt was interned in the Fallingbostel camp under automatic arrest. Although he was released in July 1947, he was arrested again two months later and taken to Nuremberg. He gave evidence in the Wilhelmstrasse Trial, so-named because the Foreign Ministry was located at the Wilhelmstrasse in Berlin.[71] When he was interrogated by Robert Kempner[72] the acting chief prosecutor, Leibbrandt initially maintained he could not remember the Wannsee Conference. He went on to say: "I took the first available opportunity to tell the minister that I did not share the lunacy."[73] Leibbrandt remained in Allied detention. After an investigation, the proceedings against Leibbrandt and Bräutigam on charges of being accessories to murder initiated by the Nuremberg-Fürth public prosecutor's office were terminated in 1950.[74] Leibbrandt was considered to be rehabilitated and in 1951 he was deemed "not incriminated" by a denazification committee in Kiel.[75] He subsequently served as a lobbyist for the city of Wilhelmshaven and the administrative district Friesland in Bonn.[76] At a later point he represented Salzgitter, a company with which Erich Neumann had cultivated close ties.[77] He continued to research the history of German enclaves around the world and was an active member of the Territorial Association of Russian Germans

(Landsmannschaft der Deutschen aus Russland).[78] He unsuccessfully applied to join the Foreign Ministry, citing Otto Bräutigam as a referee. Their efforts were thwarted when Bräutigam's Nazi past surfaced in public in the mid 1950s.[79] Leibbrandt also stayed in touch with other former comrades active in the field of ethnography, such as Stumpp and Meynen.

Despite his complicity—however ambivalent[80]—in the Nazis' extermination policy, Leibbrandt saw the part he played as that of an "objective scholar"[81] working towards a noble objective—the liberation of the Eastern European people from Bolshevik rule, being unable to assert himself against various objections and obstacles.[82] This was his defense against accusations of having collaborated with the Nazi leadership.[83] He painted the same picture to experts querying the role he had played, such as Alexander Dallin, the Berlin-born son of Russian emigrants[84] and author of the seminal book *German Rule in Russia* (1957). Dallin described Leibbrandt as too much of an apologist for his own role to offer objective insights.[85] For the rest of his life, Leibbrandt saw himself as a man with a clear conscience, who had suffered himself from his opponents in the Nazi hierarchy. As such, he is emblematic of the functionary élite that later cultivated the illusion of having themselves been victims.[86] However, he was never wholly able to escape his past. In March 1958, ahead of a trip to Tunis via Paris, he inquired at the Foreign Ministry if he had grounds to fear arrest in France.[87] Leibbrandt frequently had to give evidence in Nazi war criminal trials, such as those of Hinrich Lohse and Erhard Wetzel, the "race expert" in his former division. Lawsuits were also filed against the former ministerial director himself, for example in the case brought by the Association of Victims of the Nazi Regime against the participants at the Wannsee Conference.[88] The last of these lawsuits was only brought to a close when Leibbrandt died.

Martin Munke studied at universities in Leipzig, Chemnitz, and Prague. He holds a BA in European History and a MA in European Integration (with specialization in Eastern and Central Europe). After several years as a research assistant at Technische Universität Chemnitz and a term as visiting lecturer at Technische Universität Dresden, he now is the deputy head of the department Manuscripts, Rare Prints and Saxony at Saxon State and University Library Dresden. His Ph.D. thesis on Georg Leibbrandt has been submitted. Amongst others, he has published on German-Russian, German-Polish and German-Czech relations, transfers and perceptions from the Age of Enlightenment to the "Age of Extremes".

Notes

For the introductory quote, see Literary Estate of Georg Leibbrandt (NL Leibbrandt), manuscript "Wechselwirkungen zwischen den Völkern," 35. I am very grateful to Hansgeorg Leibbrandt, Berlin, for allowing me access to his father's papers. This chapter was supported by the Hanns-Seidel-Stiftung, to whom I would also like to express my heartfelt thanks.

1 Christian Gerlach, *Kalkulierte Morde: Die deutsche Wirtschafts- und Vernichtungspolitik in Weißrußland 1941 bis 1944* (Hamburg, 1998), 225.
2 See Ernst Piper, *Alfred Rosenberg: Hitlers Chefideologe* (Munich, 2005), 536.
3 See Martin Munke, "Täter, Mitläufer, Opponent? Fremd- und Selbstwahrnehmung der Rolle Georg Leibbrandts (1899–1982) im 'Dritten Reich,'" in *Fragmentierung oder glatte Linien? Biographie und biographische Selbstwahrnehmungen im 20. Jahrhundert*, ed. E. Lommatzsch (Berlin, 2017) (forthcoming).
4 The references do not go much beyond the fact of his presence, see Gedenk- und Bildungsstätte Haus der Wannsee-Konferenz, ed., *Die Wannsee-Konferenz und der Völkermord an den europäischen Juden: Katalog der ständigen Ausstellung* (Berlin, 2006); Peter Klein, *Die Wannsee-Konferenz vom 20. Januar 1942: Analyse und Dokumentation* (Berlin, 1995); Steven Lehrer, *Wannsee House and the Holocaust* (Jefferson, 2000); Kurt Pätzold and Erika Schwarz, *Tagesordnung: Judenmord: Die Wannsee-Konferenz am 20. Januar 1942: Eine Dokumentation zur Organisation der 'Endlösung'* (Berlin, 1992); Mark Roseman, *Die Wannsee-Konferenz: Wie die NS-Bürokratie den Holocaust organisierte* (Berlin, 2002); lastly N. Kampe and P. Klein, ed., *Die Wannsee-Konferenz am 20. Januar 1942: Dokumente, Forschungsstand, Kontroversen* (Cologne, Weimar and Vienna, 2013).
5 See Walter Laqueur, *Deutschland und Russland* (Berlin, 1965), 231; Roseman, *Wannsee-Konferenz*, 128.
6 See Hans-Adolf Jacobsen, *Nationalsozialistische Außenpolitik 1933–1938* (Frankfurt am Main and Berlin, 1968), 61; Piper, *Rosenberg*, 292, 535.
7 See M. Munke, "Vom Scheitern eines Experten: Georg Leibbrandt im Nationalsozialismus," *Osteuropa* 67, no. 1–2 (2017): 107–19.
8 See Eric J. Schmaltz, "Georg Leibbrandt," in *Handbuch der völkischen Wissenschaften: Personen—Institutionen—Forschungsprogramme—Stiftungen*, ed. I. Haar and M. Fahlbusch (Munich, 2008), 370–73; Ernst Klee, *Das Personenlexikon zum Dritten Reich: Wer war was vor und nach 1945*, extended ed. (Frankfurt am Main, 2005), 364; Juliana Wetzel, "Georg Leibbrandt," in *Biographisches Lexikon zum Dritten Reich*, ed. H. Weiß (Frankfurt am Main, 2002), 295 et seq.
9 Georg Leibbrandt, *Die Auswanderung aus Schwaben nach Rußland 1816–1823: Ein schwäbisches Zeit- und Charakterbild* (Stuttgart, 1928).
10 See Wolf Volker Weigand, *Walter Wilhelm Goetz 1867–1958: Eine biographische Studie über den Historiker, Politiker und Publizisten* (Boppard am Rhein, 1992); Matthias Middell, *Weltgeschichtsschreibung im Zeitalter der*

Verfachlichung und Professionalisierung: Das Leipziger Institut für Kultur- und Universalgeschichte 1890–1990, 3 vols. (Leipzig, 2005), in particular at vol. 2: "Von der Kulturgeschichte unter Walter Goetz zur historischen Soziologie Hans Freyers."

11 See Georg Leibbrandt, *Die deutschen Kolonien in Cherson und Bessarabien: Berichte der Gemeindeämter über Entstehung und Entwicklung der lutherischen Kolonien in der ersten Hälfte des 19. Jahrhunderts* (Stuttgart, 1926), quote from 5; G. Leibbrandt, "Forschungen zur Geschichte des deutschen Volkstums in Russland," *Archiv für Kulturgeschichte* 21, no. 1 (1930): 81–94; G. Leibbrandt, "The Emigration of the German Mennonites from Russia to the United States and Canada in 1873–1880, I," *The Mennonite Quarterly Review* 6, no. 4 (1932): 205–26; G. Leibbrandt, "The Emigration of the German Mennonites from Russia to the United States and Canada in 1873–1880, II," *The Mennonite Quarterly Review* 7, no. 1 (1933): 5–41.

12 Leibbrandt, *Kolonien*, 5.

13 Leibbrandt, *Kolonien*, 3 et seq. The dissertation also appeared in a DAI Series. See Ernst Ritter, *Das Deutsche Ausland-Institut in Stuttgart 1917–1945: Ein Beispiel deutscher Volkstumsarbeit zwischen den Weltkriegen* (Wiesbaden, 1976).

14 G. Leibbrandt and F. Dickmann, ed., *Auswanderungsakten des Deutschen Bundestags (1817–1866) und der Frankfurter Reichsministerien (1848/49)* (Schriften des deutschen Ausland-Instituts Stuttgart, Series C, vol. 3) (Stuttgart, 1932), 2 et seq. See also Martin Munke, "Zwischen Russland, Deutschland und Amerika: Russlanddeutsche Identitätskonstruktionen im 'kurzen' 20. Jahrhundert am Beispiel von Georg und Gottlieb Leibbrandt," in *Jenseits der "Volksgruppe": Neue Perspektiven auf die Russlanddeutschen zwischen Russland, Deutschland und Amerika*, ed. J. Panagiotidis, H-C. Petersen and J. Tauber (Berlin, 2017) (forthcoming).

15 See Georg Leibbrandt, "Völkische Pflichten für den Wingolf," in *Festschrift des Leipziger Wingolf zum 60. Stiftungsfeste, 1865–1925* (Leipzig, 1925), 19–23.

16 BArch, VBS 1027-ZC, 14364 A.02, CV of Georg Leibbrandt, undated.

17 See the political archive of the Foreign Ministry (PA AA), R 60201, "Die gegenwärtige Lage der Deutschen Kolonisten im Schwarzmeergebiet," March 1927.

18 See Michael Fahlbusch, *"Wo der Deutsche . . . ist, ist Deutschland!" Die Stiftung für Deutsche Volks- und Kulturbodenforschung in Leipzig 1920–1933* (Bochum, 1994).

19 See R.V. Layton Jr., "Kurt Ludecke and 'I Knew Hitler': An Evaluation," *Central European History* 12, no. 4 (1979): 372–86; A.L. Smith, "Kurt Lüdecke: The Man Who Knew Hitler," *German Studies Review* 26, no. 3 (2003): 597–606.

20 See NL Leibbrandt, "Meine Erinnerungen," typed manuscript, 1968, 72; IfZ, Zeitzeugenschrifttum, ZS 636, sheet 14.

21 Thus, as distinct from older research opinion, Piper, *Rosenberg*; Frank-Lothar Kroll, "Alfred Rosenberg: Der Ideologe als Politiker," in *Deutschbalten, Weimarer Republik und Drittes Reich*, ed. M. Garleff (Cologne, Weimar and Vienna, 2001), vol. 1, 147–66.

22 Trial of the major war criminals before the International Military Tribunal Nuremberg, 14 November 1945 to 1 October 1946, Nuremberg 1947, see: International Military Tribunal [IMT], *Der Prozeß gegen die Hauptkriegsverbrecher vor dem Internationalen Militärgerichtshof (IMT): Nürnberg 14. November 1945 — 1. Oktober 1946, gemäß den Weisungen des Internationalen Militärgerichtshofes vom Sekretariat des Gerichtshofes unter der Autorität des Obersten Kontrollrats für Deutschland veröffentlicht*, 42 vols., ed. L.D. Egbert and P.A. Joosten (Nuremberg, 1947–49), vol. 26, doc. 1017-PS, 547–54; 1030-PS, 576–580; doc. 1039–PS, 584–627, in particular at 616. See Andreas Zellhuber, *"Unsere Verwaltung treibt einer Katastrophe zu . . ."*: *Das Reichsministerium für die besetzten Ostgebiete und die deutsche Besatzungsherrschaft in der Sowjetunion 1941–1945* (Munich, 2006), 258–63.

23 See the Party Files in the collections of the former Berlin Document Center, BArch, R 9361-V/26888 (formerly VBS 1, N 0080).

24 See the application to award the "Ehrenzeichens für deutsche Volkspflege 1. Stufe" to Leibbrandt, Rosenberg to Hess, 26 March 1941, BArch, NS 8/185.

25 NL Leibbrandt, "Erinnerungen", 43.

26 This involved ethnic Germans, Russian and Ukrainian groups. See Frank Golczewski, *Deutsche und Ukrainer 1914–1939* (Paderborn, 2010), in particular at 667–72, 712–21, 724–28; Frank Grelka, *Die ukrainische Nationalbewegung unter deutscher Besatzungsherrschaft 1918 und 1941/42* (Wiesbaden, 2005), 132–35, 152 et seq., 162–65.

27 See Jacobsen, *Außenpolitik*, 450 et seq. (quote from 450).

28 See the files of the Verband der Deutschen aus Rußland (VRD), 4 vols., PA AA, R 60476, 60477, 60478, 60479. The literature of Ingeborg Fleischhauer, *Das Dritte Reich und die Deutschen in der Sowjetunion* (Schriftenreihe der Vierteljahrshefte für Zeitgeschichte, vol. 46) (Stuttgart, 1983), 47–60.

29 See Fleischhauer, *Das Dritte Reich*, 48 et seq.

30 Just two of numerous examples: G. Leibbrandt, "Rassisch-völkische Bedingtheit der bolschewistischen Revolution," *Nationalsozialistische Monatshefte* 7, no. 8 (1937): 1021–24; G. Leibbrandt, "Moskaus Kampf gegen die Völker der Sowjetunion," *Völkischer Beobachter*, 9 October 1937.

31 See Martin Munke, "Gemeinsam gegen den Bolschewismus: Ideen und Konzepte einer Neuen Ordnung für Europa im Nationalsozialismus," in *Bewegtes Mitteleuropa: Beiträge zur internationalen Doktorandenkonferenz des Doktoratskollegs der Fakultät für Mitteleuropäische Studien an der Andrássy Universität Budapest*, ed. A-O. Drăghiciu, F. Gouverneur and S. Sparwasser (Herne, 2014), 73–78; M. Munke, "Russlandbilder im Nationalsozialismus — Hitler, Goebbels, Rosenberg," *Ostblicke* 4 (2013): 57–63.

32 In 1937 for instance, at a training day organized by the German Labor Front (DAF) on 7 May in Erwitte; to the student body of the Technische Hochschule Danzig on 13 June; at a conference organized by the DAI in August and on 15 October at the Nazi Teacher Association in Bayreuth; see the notes in Leibbrandt's personal files to the head of the department at the APA, BArch, NS 43/9, sheet 253 (4 May 1937), 248 (4 June 1937), 238 (7 August 1937), 225 (12 October 1937).

33 See inter alia BArch, R153/1233, pamphlet "Sammelbesitz Georg Leibbrandt," undated.

34 See Willi Oberkrome, *Volksgeschichte: methodische Innovation und völkische Ideologisierung in der deutschen Geschichtswissenschaft 1918–1945* (Göttingen, 1993). For the European context, see Manfred Hettling, ed., *Volksgeschichten im Europa der Zwischenkriegszeit* (Göttingen, 2003).

35 See Jan Eckel. "Herrschaftsstabilisierende Denkmuster in der Geschichtswissenschaft während des Nationalsozialismus: Eine Skizze der Voraussetzungen, Formen und Entwicklungen," in *Wissenschaft im Einsatz*, ed. K. Mayer-Drawe and K. Platt (Paderborn and Munich, 2007), 74–91.

36 See M. Fahlbusch, "Emil Meynen," in Haar and Fahlbusch, *Handbuch der völkischen Wissenschaften*, 422–28. The two had met in the United States in the early 1930s when they were both on Rockefeller scholarships.

37 Institut für Länderkunde Leipzig (IfL), Meynen Literary Estate, 781/7, sheet 633 et seq., "Homework—Sammlung Georg Leibrandt/Publikationsstelle Ost," 10 December 1946. A distinction must be made from case to case between the source publications in a series also entitled "Sammlung Georg Leibbrandt" and the works described here. In Rosenberg's words, both were intended to serve with the SGL as a "comprehensive and exhaustive basis to identify German progress in (the European east)" (BArch, NS 43/3, sheet 118, memo, 15 February 1940).

38 Emil Meynen, "Die Sammlung Georg Leibbrandt," in *Probleme des Ostraumes*, ed. G. Leibbrandt (Berlin, 1942), 113. See Martin Munke, "Publikationsstelle Ost," in *Online-Lexikon zur Kultur und Geschichte der Deutschen im östlichen Europa*, ed. S. Doering and M. Weber (Oldenburg, 2013), available at http://ome-lexikon.uni-oldenburg.de/62681.html.

39 Julia Landau, "Publikationsstelle Ost/Sammlung Georg Leibbrandt," in Haar and Fahlbusch, *Handbuch der völkischen Wissenschaften*, 488.

40 See Ulrike Hartung, *Raubzüge in der Sowjetunion: das Sonderkommando Künsberg 1941–1943* (Bremen, 1997); A. Heuss, "Die 'Beuteorganisation' des Auswärtigen Amtes: Das Sonderkommando Künsberg und der Kulturgutraub in der Sowjetunion," *Vierteljahrshefte für Zeitgeschichte* 45, no. 4 (1997): 535–56. In the last months of the War, the Allies were already aware of Leibbrandt's involvement. See National Archives London, T209/26/1, "The 'Einsatzstab Rosenberg' Report," 2 March 1945.

41 See Karl Stumpp, *Ostwanderung: Akten über die Auswanderg der Württemberger nach Rußland 1816–1822* (Leipzig, 1941); Eric J. Schmaltz and Samuel D. Sinner, "Karl Stummp," in Haar and Fahlbusch, *Handbuch der völkischen Wissenschaften*, 678–82. Like Leibbrandt, Stumpp was born shortly before the turn of the century not far from Odessa and wrote his doctoral thesis on German colonies in the Black Sea area.

42 See Fleischhauer, *Das Dritte Reich*, 185–92.

43 Landau, "Publikationsstelle Ost," 492. See E.J. Schmaltz and S.D. Sinner, "The Nazi Ethnographic Research of Georg Leibbrandt and Karl Stumpp in Ukraine, and its North American Legacy," *Holocaust and Genocide Studies* 14, no. 1 (2000): 34–42; Samuel D. Sinner, "Sonderkommando Dr Stumpp,"

in Haar and Fahlbusch, *Handbuch der völkischen Wissenschaften*, 647–51; Fleischhauer, *Das Dritte Reich*, 97–101.

44 Through the copy in Léon Poliakov and Joseph Wulf, *Das Dritte Reich und die Juden*, (Frankfurt am Main, 1983), 190 et seq. this was already familiar to a wide section of the public.

45 See Uwe Danker, "Der schleswig-holsteinische NSDAP-Gauleiter Hinrich Lohse: Überlegungen zu seiner Biografie," in *Regionen im Nationalsozialismus*, ed. M. Ruck and K.H. Pohl (Bielefeld, 2003), 91–120.

46 See Hans Dieter Heilmann, "Aus dem Kriegstagebuch des Diplomaten Otto Bräutigam," in *Biedermann und Schreibtischtäter: Materialien zur deutschen Täter-Biographie*, ed. G. Aly et al., (Berlin, 1987), 123–87. The two had met in the 1920s, during Bräutigam's term of office as Consul General in Odessa.

47 Originally edited as Documents 3663-PS and 3666-PS in: IMT, vol. 32, 435–37, quote from 437. See, however, H. Schneppen, "Generalkonsul a.D. Dr Otto Bräutigam: Widerstand und Verstrickung: Eine quellenkritische Untersuchung," *Zeitschrift für Geschichtswissenschaft* 60, no. 4 (2012): 301–30.

48 PA AA, R 105193, "Richtlinien (Geheime Reichssache)," 29 May 1941.

49 See Heilmann, "Aus dem Kriegstagebuch des Diplomaten Otto Bräutigam," 134.

50 See Centre de documentation juive contemporaine, 54.2 Paris, CXLV-504, Kleist to Leibbrandt, 22 July 1941. As regards Peter Kleist, see H. Buchheim, "Zu Kleists 'Auch du warst dabei,'" *Vierteljahrshefte für Zeitgeschichte* 2, no. 2 (1954): 177–92.

51 Most recently, Editors' Preface in J. Matthäus and F. Bajohr (ed.). 2015. *Alfred Rosenberg: Die Tagebücher von 1934 bis 1944*, (Frankfurt am Main, 2015), 9–116, at 85.

52 See Heinz-Jürgen Priamus, *Meyer: Zwischen Kaisertreue und NS-Täterschaft. Biographische Konturen eines deutschen Bürgers* (Schriftenreihe des Instituts für Stadtgeschichte, Beiträge, vol. 14) (Essen, 2011), 355.

53 See NL Leibbrandt, "Erinnerungen", 152.

54 See the minutes, copied in: Kampe and Klein, *Wannsee-Konferenz*, 40–54.

55 See Susanne Heim and Götz Aly, ed., *Die Verfolgung und Ermordung der europäischen Juden durch das nationalsozialistische Deutschland 1933–1945* [VEJ], 16 vols. (Berlin, 2008–), vol. 7, doc. 199, 550–53.

56 See Piper, *Rosenberg*, 587 et seq.; on Leibbrandt's participation, see M. Vogt, ed., *Herbst 1941 im "Führerhauptquartier": Berichte Werner Koeppens an seinen Minister Alfred Rosenberg* (Koblenz, 2002), 124, footnote 1090.

57 See minutes of the Meeting (chaired by Bräutigam), in: W. Benz, K. Kwiet and J. Matthäus, ed., *Einsatz im "Reichskommissariat Ostland": Dokumente zum Völkermord im Baltikum und in Weißrußland, 1941–1944* (Berlin, 1998), doc. 21, 55–61.

58 See Hans Umbreit, "Die deutsche Herrschaft in den besetzten Gebieten 1942–1945," in *Das Deutsche Reich und der Zweite Weltkrieg*, vol. 5/2, ed. B. Kroener (Munich, 1999), 3–272, at 60; Bernd Wegner, "Der Krieg gegen die Sowjetunion 1942/43," in Kroener, *Das Deutsche Reich und der Zweite Weltkrieg*, vol. 6, 761–1102, 921 et seq.

59 See VEJ, vol. 8, doc. 171, 393–96, at 395 et seq.

60 A communiqué signed by Leibbrandt on behalf of Rosenberg dated 23 October 1942. See VEJ, vol. 8, doc. 202, 468.

61 The efforts took place in the context of the Caucasus experiment, involving political warfare by the 17th Army in the Caucasus, in which Bräutigam was closely involved. See Manfred Oldenburg, *Ideologie und militärisches Kalkül: die Besatzungspolitik der Wehrmacht in der Sowjetunion 1942* (Cologne, Weimar and Vienna, 2004), 259–306. On Wagner, see Roland Peter, "General der Artillerie Eduard Wagner," in *Hitlers militärische Elite: 68 Lebensläufe*, ed. G.R. Ueberschär (Darmstadt, 2015), 534–40.

62 Before moving to the RMO, Leibbrandt had served as a department head *(Reichsamtsleiter)* at the APA. He retained the position even after his move and was promoted to the position of senior division head *(Oberbereichsleiter)* with effect from 9 November 1941. He started at the RMO as a main section head *(Hauptabteilungsleiter)*. Before the Wannsee Conference had taken place, Rosenberg had recommended Leibbrandt's immediate appointment as ministerial director *(Ministerialdirektor)* as a civil servant (Rosenberg to the Reich Interior Ministry and the Reich Finance Ministry with copies to the Party Chancellery and Reich Chancellery, 13 January 1942, Akten der Partei-Kanzlei der NSDAP, 103 05244 et seq.). Given that he did not meet the formal requirements, his appointment only took effect in May after lengthy discussions (See the article "Dr Leibbrandt Ministerialdirektor," *Völkischer Beobachter*, 12 May 1942).

63 See Matthäus and Bajohr, *Alfred Rosenberg: Die Tagebücher*, 451.

64 See minutes, in: W. Schumann, ed., *Europa unterm Hakenkreuz: Die Okkupationspolitik des deutschen Faschismus (1938–1945)*, 8 vols. (Berlin, 1991), vol. 5, doc. 150, 374–78.

65 NL Leibbrandt, "Erinnerungen", 157 et seq. See Timothy Patrick Mulligan, *The Politics of Illusion and Empire: German Occupation Policy in the Soviet Union, 1942–1943* (New York, 1988), 49–51.

66 See NL Leibbrandt, "Erinnerungen", 150 et seq.

67 See Saul Friedländer, *Das Dritte Reich und die Juden: Verfolgung und Vernichtung*, 2 vols. (Munich, 2006), vol. 2, 617–19. For the beginning of the debate: VEJ, vol. 7, doc. 189, 532–34.

68 See Koch's complaints about Leibbrandt and those working in his department in a memorandum dated 16 March 1943, IMT, vol. 25, doc. 192-PS, 255–87, inter alia 260 et seq., 265 et seq., 280. See Ralf Meindl, *Ostpreußens Gauleiter: Erich Koch—eine politische Biographie* (Osnabrück, 2007), 323–97.

69 Matthäus and Bajohr, *Alfred Rosenberg: Die Tagebücher*, 470; Staatsarchiv Nürnberg, 2638/I, sheet 207.

70 See, on the role of the RMO, Zellhuber, *Das Reichsministerium für die besetzten Ostgebiete*, 217–54; Piper, *Rosenberg*, 577–97.

71 See Dirk Pöppmann, "Im Schatten Weizsäckers? Auswärtiges Amt und SS im Wilhelmstraßen-Prozess," in Priemel and Stiller, *NMT*, 320–52.

72 See Dirk Pöppmann, "The trials of Robert Kempner: From Stateless Immigrant to Prosecutor of the Foreign Office," in Priemel and Stiller, *NMT*, 23–46.

73　See Robert M. W. Kempner, *Eichmann und Komplizen* (Zurich, Stuttgart and Vienna, 1961), 155–57.

74　File Nos. 1c Js 1678/49. See Staatsarchiv Nürnberg, 2638/I–VIII.

75　See Staatsarchiv Ludwigsburg, EL 902/3, Bü 8603: Entnazifizierungs-Hauptausschuss Kiel to Zentralspruchkammer Nord-Württemberg, 28 August 1951. A lawsuit pursued in his family's hometown pleaded for his inclusion in the group of chief culprits; see Staatsarchiv Ludwigsburg, EL 902/3, Bü 8603. "Klageschrift Zentralspruchkammer Nord-Württemberg," 14 July 1951.

76　See Staatsarchiv Oldenburg, Dep. 20 FRI, Akz. 2ß12/062, no. 236.

77　See contracts NL Leibbrandt.

78　See G. Leibbrandt, H. Leibbrandt and O.G. Siegle, ed., *Hoffnungstal und seine Schwaben: Die historische Entwicklung einer schwarzmeerdeutschen Gemeinde, als Beispiel religiös bestimmter Wanderung und Siedlung und als Beitrag zur Geschichte des Russlanddeutschtums* (Bonn, 1980).

79　See press article in Landesarchiv Schleswig-Holstein, Abt. 399.65, no. 16 (Literary Estate Hinrich Lohse).

80　This was recognized while he was working abroad, on the one hand under-scoring his supposed efforts on behalf of individual ethnic groups in the Soviet Union, while on the other hand he also looked like a Soviet agent. See interviews with Soviet emigres in: Widener Library, Harvard University, Harvard Project on the Soviet Social System, for instance Schedule B, vol. 10, case 81, sheet 2 et seq.; vol. 11, case 382, sheet 11 (from where the quote is taken); vol. 11, case 429, sheet 1.

81　Staatsarchiv Nürnberg, 2638/VI, sheet 36.

82　IfZ, ZS 636, sheet 2–13.

83　A reader's letter to *Die Welt* responded to an article published on 22 October 1971, in which he was described as one of Martin Bormann's closest confidantes. See NL Leibbrandt, *Die Welt*, 12 November 1971.

84　See the Editor's introduction to: Alexander Dallin, *The Uses of History: Understanding the Soviet Union and Russia*, ed. G.W. Lapidus (Lanham, MD, 2009), 3–7.

85　Hoover Institution Archives, Alexander Dallin Collection, box 7, Interview G-12 A, 5 June 1952. Hans-Adolf Jacobsen's judgment: "Definitely important as a living source; his account is vivid and lively. Powers of memory good [!] but needs to be verified on many points." (IfZ, ZS 636, sheet 16).

86　Alf Lüdtke, "Funktionseliten—Täter, Mit-Täter, Opfer? Zu den Bedingungen des deutschen Faschismus," in *Herrschaft als soziale Praxis: historische und sozial-anthropologische Studien*, ed. A. Lüdtke (Göttingen, 1991), 590.

87　BArch, B 305/22971.

88　With the Berlin Attorney General, Berliner Generalstaatsanwaltschaft (Aktenzeichen 1 P Js 686/55); BArch, B 162/2638.

Bibliography

Benz, W., K. Kwiet and J. Matthäus, ed. *Einsatz im "Reichskommissariat Ostland"*: *Dokumente zum Völkermord im Baltikum und in Weißrußland, 1941–1944*. Berlin: Metropol, 1998.

Buchheim, H. "Zu Kleists 'Auch du warst dabei.'" *Vierteljahrshefte für Zeitgeschichte* 2, no. 2 (1954): 177–92.

Dallin, Alexander. *The Uses of History: Understanding the Soviet Union and Russia*, edited by G.W. Lapidus. Lanham, MD: Rowman & Littlefield Publishers, 2009.

Danker, Uwe. "Der schleswig-holsteinische NSDAP-Gauleiter Hinrich Lohse: Überlegungen zu seiner Biografie." In *Regionen im Nationalsozialismus*, edited by M. Ruck and K. H. Pohl, 91–120. Bielefeld: Verlag für Regionalgeschichte, 2003.

Eckel, Jan. "Herrschaftsstabilisierende Denkmuster in der Geschichtswissenschaft während des Nationalsozialismus: Eine Skizze der Voraussetzungen, Formen und Entwicklungen. " In *Wissenschaft im Einsatz*, edited by K. Mayer-Drawe and K. Platt, 74–91. Paderborn and Munich: Fink, 2007.

Fahlbusch, Michael. *"Wo der Deutsche . . . ist, ist Deutschland!" Die Stiftung für Deutsche Volks- und Kulturbodenforschung in Leipzig 1920–1933*. Bochum: Brockmeyer, 1994.

———. "Emil Meynen," in *Handbuch der völkischen Wissenschaften: Personen — Institutionen — Forschungsprogramme — Stiftungen*, edited by I. Haar and M. Fahlbusch, 422–28. Munich: Saur, 2008.

Fleischhauer, Ingeborg. *Das Dritte Reich und die Deutschen in der Sowjetunion*. Stuttgart: Deutsche Verlags-Anstalt, 1983.

Friedländer, Saul. *Das Dritte Reich und die Juden: Verfolgung und Vernichtung*. Munich: C.H. Beck, 2006. [English: *Nazi Germany and the Jews*. New York: HarperCollins, 1997.]

Gedenk- und Bildungsstätte Haus der Wannsee-Konferenz, ed. *Die Wannsee-Konferenz und der Völkermord an den europäischen Juden: Katalog der ständigen Ausstellung*. Berlin: Gedenk- und Bildungsstätte Haus der Wannsee-Konferenz, 2006.

Gerlach, Christian. *Kalkulierte Morde: Die deutsche Wirtschafts- und Vernichtungspolitik in Weißrußland 1941 bis 1944*. Hamburg: Hamburger Edition, 1998.

Golczewski, Frank. *Deutsche und Ukrainer 1914–1939*. Paderborn: Schöningh, 2010.

Grelka, Frank. *Die ukrainische Nationalbewegung unter deutscher Besatzungsherrschaft 1918 und 1941/42*. Wiesbaden: Harrassowitz, 2005.

Hartung, Ulrike. *Raubzüge in der Sowjetunion: das Sonderkommando Künsberg 1941–1943*. Bremen: Edition Temmen, 1997.

Heilmann, Hans Dieter. "Aus dem Kriegstagebuch des Diplomaten Otto Bräutigam," in *Biedermann und Schreibtischtäter: Materialien zur deutschen Täter-Biographie*, edited by G. Aly, P. Chroust, H.D. Heilmann and H. Langbein, 123–87. Berlin: Rotbuch, 1987.

Heim, S. and G. Aly, ed. *Die Verfolgung und Ermordung der europäischen Juden durch das nationalsozialistische Deutschland 1933–1945 [VEJ]*. Berlin: Oldenbourg, 2008–.

Hettling, M. ed. *Volksgeschichten im Europa der Zwischenkriegszeit*. Göttingen: Vandenhoeck & Ruprecht, 2003.

Heuss, A. "Die 'Beuteorganisation' des Auswärtigen Amtes: Das Sonderkommando Künsberg und der Kulturgutraub in der Sowjetunion." *Vierteljahrshefte für Zeitgeschichte* 45, no. 4 (1997): 535–56.

International Military Tribunal [IMT]. *Der Prozeß gegen die Hauptkriegsverbrecher vor dem Internationalen Militärgerichtshof (IMT): Nürnberg 14. November 1945 – 1. Oktober 1946, gemäß den Weisungen des Internationalen Militärgerichtshofes vom Sekretariat des Gerichtshofes unter der Autorität des Obersten Kontrollrats für Deutschland veröffentlicht*, edited by L.D. Egbert and P.A. Joosten. Nuremberg, 1947–1949.

Jacobsen, Hans-Adolf. *Nationalsozialistische Außenpolitik 1933–1938*. Frankfurt on the Main and Berlin: Metzner, 1968.

Kampe, N. and P. Klein, ed. *Die Wannsee-Konferenz am 20. Januar 1942: Dokumente, Forschungsstand, Kontroversen*. Cologne, Weimar and Vienna: Böhlau, 2013.

Kempner, Robert M. W. *Eichmann und Komplizen*. Zurich, Stuttgart and Vienna: Europaverlag, 1961.

Klee, Ernst. *Das Personenlexikon zum Dritten Reich: Wer war was vor und nach 1945*. Frankfurt on the Main: Fischer-Taschenbuch-Verlag, 2005.

Klein, Peter. *Die Wannsee-Konferenz vom 20. Januar 1942: Analyse und Dokumentation*. Berlin: Edition Hentrich, 1995.

Kroll, Frank-Lothar. "Alfred Rosenberg: Der Ideologe als Politiker." In *Deutschbalten, Weimarer Republik und Drittes Reich*, edited by M. Garleff, vol. 1, 147–66. Cologne, Weimar and Vienna: Böhlau, 2001.

Landau, Julia. "Publikationsstelle Ost/Sammlung Georg Leibbrandt." In *Handbuch der völkischen Wissenschaften: Personen—Institutionen—Forschungsprogramme—Stiftungen*, edited by I. Haar and M. Fahlbusch, 486–96. Munich: Saur, 2008.

Laqueur, Walter. *Deutschland und Russland*. Berlin: Propyläen, 1965. [English: *Russia and Germany: A Century of Conflict*. London: Transaction Publishers, 1990.]

Layton, R.V. Jr. "Kurt Ludecke and 'I Knew Hitler': An Evaluation." *Central European History* 12, no. 4 (1979): 372–86.

Lehrer, Steven. *Wannsee House and the Holocaust*. Jefferson, NC: McFarland, 2000.

Leibbrandt, Georg. "Völkische Pflichten für den Wingolf." In *Festschrift des Leipziger Wingolf zum 60. Stiftungsfeste, 1865–1925*, 19–23. Leipzig: P. Fischer, 1925.

———. *Die deutschen Kolonien in Cherson und Bessarabien: Berichte der Gemeindeämter über Entstehung und Entwicklung der lutherischen Kolonien in der ersten Hälfte des 19. Jahrhunderts*. Stuttgart: Ausland und Heimat Verlags-AG, 1926.

———. *Die Auswanderung aus Schwaben nach Rußland 1816–1823: Ein schwäbisches Zeit- und Charakterbild*. Stuttgart: Ausland und Heimat Verlags-AG, 1928.

Leibbrandt, G. "Forschungen zur Geschichte des deutschen Volkstums in Russland." *Archiv für Kulturgeschichte* 21, no. 1 (1930): 81–94.

———. "The Emigration of the German Mennonites from Russia to the United States and Canada in 1873–1880, I." *The Mennonite Quarterly Review* 6 no. 4 (1932): 205–26.

———. "The Emigration of the German Mennonites from Russia to the United States and Canada in 1873–1880, II." *The Mennonite Quarterly Review* 7, no. 1 (1933): 5–41.

———. "Moskaus Kampf gegen die Völker der Sowjetunion." *Völkischer Beobachter* (9 October 1937).

———. "Rassisch-völkische Bedingtheit der bolschewistischen Revolution." *Nationalsozialistische Monatshefte* 7, no. 8 (1937): 1021–24.

Leibbrandt, G. and F. Dickmann, ed. *Auswanderungsakten des Deutschen Bundestags (1817–1866) und der Frankfurter Reichsministerien (1848/49)*. Stuttgart: Ausland und Heimat Verlags-AG, 1932.

Leibbrandt, G., H. Leibbrandt and O.G. Siegle, ed. *Hoffnungstal und seine Schwaben: Die historische Entwicklung einer schwarzmeerdeutschen Gemeinde, als Beispiel religiös bestimmter Wanderung und Siedlung und als Beitrag zur Geschichte des Russlanddeutschtums*. Bonn: G. Leibbrandt, 1980.

Lüdtke, Alf. "Funktionseliten—Täter, Mit-Täter, Opfer? Zu den Bedingungen des deutschen Faschismus." In *Herrschaft als soziale Praxis: historische und sozial-anthropologische Studien*, edited by A. Lüdtke, 559–90. Göttingen: Vandenhoeck & Ruprecht, 1991.

Matthäus, J. and F. Bajohr, ed. *Alfred Rosenberg: Die Tagebücher von 1934 bis 1944*. Frankfurt on the Main: S. Fischer, 2015.

Meindl, Ralf. *Ostpreußens Gauleiter: Erich Koch—eine politische Biographie*. Osnabrück: Fibre, 2007.

Meynen, Emil. "Die Sammlung Georg Leibbrandt." In *Probleme des Ostraumes*, edited by G. Leibbrandt, 111–18. Berlin: Stollberg, 1942.

Middell, Matthias. *Weltgeschichtsschreibung im Zeitalter der Verfachlichung und Professionalisierung: Das Leipziger Institut für Kultur- und Universalgeschichte 1890–1990*. Leipzig: Akademische Verlagsanstalt, 2005.

Mulligan, Timothy Patrick. *The Politics of Illusion and Empire: German Occupation Policy in the Soviet Union, 1942–1943*. New York: Praeger, 1988.

Munke, M. "Russlandbilder im Nationalsozialismus—Hitler, Goebbels, Rosenberg." *Ostblicke* 4 (2013): 43–66.

———. "Publikationsstelle Ost." In *Online-Lexikon zur Kultur und Geschichte der Deutschen im östlichen Europa*, edited by S. Doering and M. Weber, available at http://ome-lexikon.uni-oldenburg.de/62681.html. Oldenburg: Carl von Ossietzky Universität and Bundesinstitut für Kultur und Geschichte der Deutschen im östlichen Europa, 2013.

———. "Vom Scheitern eines Experten: Georg Leibbrandt im Nationalsozialismus," In *Osteuropa* 67, no. 1–2 (2017): 107–19.

———. "Gemeinsam gegen den Bolschewismus: Ideen und Konzepte einer Neuen Ordnung für Europa im Nationalsozialismus." In *Bewegtes Mitteleuropa: Beiträge zur internationalen Doktorandenkonferenz des Doktoratskollegs der Fakultät für Mitteleuropäische Studien an der Andrássy Universität Budapest,* edited by A-O. Drăghiciu, F. Gouverneur and S. Sparwasser, 63–103. Herne: Schäfer, 2014.

——. "Täter, Mitläufer, Opponent? Fremd- und Selbstwahrnehmung der Rolle Georg Leibbrandts (1899–1982) im 'Dritten Reich.'" In *Fragmentierung oder glatte Linien? Biographie und biographische Selbstwahrnehmungen im 20. Jahrhundert*, edited by E. Lommatzsch. Berlin: Duncker & Humblot, forthcoming.

——. "Zwischen Russland, Deutschland und Amerika: Russlanddeutsche Identitätskonstruktionen im 'kurzen' 20. Jahrhundert am Beispiel von Georg und Gottlieb Leibbrandt." In *Jenseits der "Volksgruppe": Neue Perspektiven auf die Russlanddeutschen zwischen Russland, Deutschland und Amerika*, edited by J. Panagiotidis, H-C. Petersen and J. Tauber. Berlin: de Gruyter Oldenbourg, forthcoming.

Oberkrome, Willi. *Volksgeschichte: methodische Innovation und völkische Ideologisierung in der deutschen Geschichtswissenschaft 1918–1945*. Göttingen: Vandenhoeck & Ruprecht, 1993.

Oldenburg, Manfred. *Ideologie und militärisches Kalkül: Die Besatzungspolitik der Wehrmacht in der Sowjetunion 1942*. Cologne, Weimar and Vienna: Böhlau, 2004.

Pätzold, Kurt and Erika Schwarz. *Tagesordnung: Judenmord: Die Wannsee-Konferenz am 20. Januar 1942: Eine Dokumentation zur Organisation der 'Endlösung.'* Berlin: Metropol, 1992.

Peter, Roland. "General der Artillerie Eduard Wagner." In *Hitlers militärische Elite: 68 Lebensläufe*, edited by G.R. Ueberschär, 534–40. Darmstadt: Theiss, 2015.

Piper, Ernst. *Alfred Rosenberg: Hitlers Chefideologe*. Munich: Blessing, 2005.

Poliakov, Léon and Joseph Wulf. *Das Dritte Reich und die Juden*. 2nd ed. Frankfurt on the Main: Ullstein, 1983 [first published 1955].

Pöppmann, Dirk. "Im Schatten Weizsäckers? Auswärtiges Amt und SS im Wilhelmstraßen-Prozess." In *NMT: Die Nürnberger Militärtribunale zwischen Geschichte, Gerechtigkeit und Rechtschöpfung*, edited by K.C. Priemel and A. Stiller, 320–52. Hamburg: Hamburger Edition, 2013.

——. "The Trials of Robert Kempner: From Stateless Immigrant to Prosecutor of the Foreign Office." In *NMT: Die Nürnberger Militärtribunale zwischen Geschichte, Gerechtigkeit und Rechtschöpfung*, edited by K.C. Priemel and A. Stiller, 23–46. Hamburg: Hamburger Edition, 2013.

Priamus, Heinz-Jürgen. *Meyer: Zwischen Kaisertreue und NS-Täterschaft. Biographische Konturen eines deutschen Bürgers*. Essen: Klartext, 2011.

Ritter, Ernst. *Das Deutsche Ausland-Institut in Stuttgart 1917–1945: Ein Beispiel deutscher Volkstumsarbeit zwischen den Weltkriegen*. Wiesbaden: Steiner, 1976.

Roseman, Mark. *Die Wannsee-Konferenz: Wie die NS-Bürokratie den Holocaust organisierte*. Berlin: Propyläen, 2002. [English: *The Villa, the Lake, the Meeting: Wannsee and the Final Solution*. London: Penguin Press, 2002.]

Schmaltz, Eric J. "Georg Leibbrandt." In *Handbuch der völkischen Wissenschaften: Personen—Institutionen—Forschungsprogramme—Stiftungen*, edited by I. Haar and M. Fahlbusch, 370–73. Munich: Saur, 2008.

Schmaltz, Eric J. and Samuel D. Sinner. "Karl Stummp." In *Handbuch der völkischen Wissenschaften: Personen—Institutionen—Forschungsprogramme—Stiftungen*, edited by I. Haar and M. Fahlbusch, 678–82. Munich: Saur, 2008.

———."The Nazi Ethnographic Research of Georg Leibbrandt and Karl Stumpp in Ukraine, and its North American Legacy." *Holocaust and Genocide Studies* 14, no. 1 (2000): 28–64.

Schneppen, H. "Generalkonsul a.D. Dr. Otto Bräutigam: Widerstand und Verstrickung: Eine quellenkritische Untersuchung." *Zeitschrift für Geschichtswissenschaft* 60, no. 4 (2012): 301–30.

Schumann, W. ed. *Europa unterm Hakenkreuz: Die Okkupationspolitik des deutschen Faschismus (1938–1945)*. Berlin: Hüthig, 1991.

Sinner, Samuel D. "Sonderkommando Dr. Stumpp." In *Handbuch der völkischen Wissenschaften: Personen—Institutionen—Forschungsprogramme—Stiftungen*, edited by I. Haar and M. Fahlbusch, 647–51. Munich: Saur, 2008.

Smith, A.L. "Kurt Lüdecke: The Man Who Knew Hitler." *German Studies Review* 26, no. 3 (2003): 597–606.

Stumpp, Karl. *Ostwanderung: Akten über die Auswanderg der Württemberger nach Rußland 1816–1822*. Leipzig: Hirzel, 1941.

Umbreit, Hans. "Die deutsche Herrschaft in den besetzten Gebieten 1942–1945." In *Das Deutsche Reich und der Zweite Weltkrieg, vol. 5/2, Organisation und Mobilisierung des deutschen Machtbereichs*, edited by B. Kroener, 3–272. Munich: Deutsche Verlags-Anstalt, 1999.

Vogt, M., ed. *Herbst 1941 im "Führerhauptquartier": Berichte Werner Koeppens an seinen Minister Alfred Rosenberg*. Koblenz: Bundesarchiv, 2002.

Wegner, Bernd. "Der Krieg gegen die Sowjetunion 1942/43." In *Das Deutsche Reich und der Zweite Weltkrieg*, edited by B. Kroener, vol. 6, 761–1102. Munich: Deutsche Verlags-Anstalt, 1999.

Weigand, Wolf Volker. *Walter Wilhelm Goetz 1867–1958: Eine biographische Studie über den Historiker, Politiker und Publizisten*. Boppard am Rhein: Boldt, 1992.

Wetzel, Juliane. "Georg Leibbrandt." In *Biographisches Lexikon zum Dritten Reich*, edited by Hermann Weiß, 295–96. Frankfurt on the Main: Fischer-Taschenbuch-Verlag, 2002.

Zellhuber, Andreas. *"Unsere Verwaltung treibt einer Katastrophe zu . . .": Das Reichsministerium für die besetzten Ostgebiete und die deutsche Besatzungsherrschaft in der Sowjetunion 1941–1945*. Munich: Vögel, 2006.

13

UNDERSECRETARY MARTIN LUTHER

Defender of Foreign Office Prerogatives

Christopher R. Browning

Illustration 13.1 Unknown photographer, undated (1942), Ullstein, 00272468.

The Wannsee Conference has been referred to as the State Secretaries' Conference because Reinhard Heydrich invited representatives of the ministerial bureaucracy of equivalent rank. Beyond the high rank of many of the participants, eight of fifteen possessed the *Doktortitel*. Yet Martin Luther, who left school before obtaining even the Abitur and held the rank of *Unterstaatssekretär*, was invited to represent the Foreign Office. Who was this man? Why was he invited? What did he know about the state of Nazi Jewish policy at the time? What was his contribution to the Wannsee Conference? How did he contribute to the implementation of the "Final Solution" thereafter?

Martin Luther was an able, energetic, extremely ambitious and unscrupulous man, for whom the Nazi regime offered social mobility and access to power that would have been unimaginable for such a professionally disadvantaged man in Germany prior to 1933. He made the most of the opportunities that the Nazi regime made possible, breaking into the tradition-bound and hitherto socially exclusive ranks of higher civil service of the German Foreign Office, and climbing improbably to the rank of Unterstaatssekretär in a scant three years, before his overweening ambition got the better of him. Frustrated by the shrinking role of the Foreign Office, the incompetence of the Foreign Minister, Joachim von Ribbentrop, and the dire prospects Germany faced without a compromise peace, he attempted to organize Ribbentrop's ouster. The plot failed, and Luther's fall was even more precipitous than his rise. He spent the last two years of the war as a privileged prisoner in the concentration camp at Sachsenhausen and died of a heart attack shortly after the end of the war. Before his fall, however, much of his success owed to his ability to protect the inept Ribbentrop from the latter's party rivals and to harness the Foreign Office to serve the Nazis' most cherished projects, such as the "Final Solution," without waiting for decisions and orders from above.

Martin Luther was born on 16 December 1895. He begun Gymnasium studies but in August 1914 left school before completing his Abitur and joined the army. He served throughout the war in railway units and was promoted to the rank of Reserve Lieutenant in 1917. After the war he went into the kinds of business activities that utilized his war experience in logistics, such as hauling and furniture supply and removal. His first business went bankrupt, not an unusual phenomenon in the economic instability of the early Weimar years, but eventually he became a reasonably successful businessman. By 1933 he owned an apartment building managed by a hired caretaker, and he was sufficiently independent financially to begin devoting himself to politics.[1]

An Uncouth Upstart

Luther joined the NSDAP and SA on 1 March 1932 and became active in the district of Zehlendorf, a well-to-do section of South West Berlin, in the chapter of Dahlem. While periodically soliciting funds for Nazi charity, he made the acquaintance of Frau Ribbentrop, likewise residing in Dahlem. Luther was commissioned to redecorate the Ribbentrops' villa and enlarge their stables. Over the following years he managed to increasingly ingratiate himself with the Ribbentrops by satisfying their material needs, and in the fall of 1936 accompanied the newly appointed ambassador to London to supervise the remodeling of the interior of the German embassy.

Just months earlier Luther had joined the Ribbentrop Bureau and was commissioned to create a new *Parteiverbindungsstelle* or Party Liason Office to handle the latter's relations with other party organizations, something at which Ribbentrop—not an *alter Kämpfer* ("old fighter")—had no skill or experience. In this capacity Luther made himself useful defending the former wine merchant against various slanders and false rumors that were not uncommon in the sordid internal politics of the Nazi Party. Through incessant intriguing, he obtained relative autonomy for his liaison office within the Bureau. He was then abruptly dismissed when Ribbentrop learned that Luther's new liaison to the SS had made a very unflattering report on his bureau to the

Illustration 13.2 Luther posing at his desk in Rauchstraße, with telephone, ink-pen, documents and folders. Unknown photographer, undated (1942), Ullstein, 00272469.

SD. Luther gained reinstatement through the intercession of Gauleiter Martin Mutschmann, Reich Student Leader Dr Scheel, and the head of the Volksdeutsche Mittelstelle, Werner Lorenz.[2]

The next major challenge Luther faced was not to be left behind when Ribbentrop was appointed Foreign Minister in February 1938. Two obstacles stood in Luther's way. The new minister was not transferring many of Bureau personnel into his new ministry. Moreover Luther was facing charges of having embezzled party funds and could not be taken into state service while the threat of party expulsion hung over him. To move Ribbentrop, Luther submitted several reports on how party organizations were playing the ministry and the bureau off against one another and exploiting the lack of coordination between the two (such as applying for funding from both) and, even worse, without adequate oversight were undertaking unauthorized foreign contacts and even negotiations on their own. Luther immodestly proposed that a unified and vigilant handling of party matters could be obtained by creating a new *Referat Partei*, which he would head with the rank of *Legationsrat*.[3] Once Ribbentrop was persuaded, he intervened with Martin Bormann concerning Luther's pending trial. Bormann in turn appealed to the judge in the case, who happened to be his father-in-law, and the case was quashed.[4]

Luther was taken into the Foreign Office in November 1938 and assiduously devoted himself to protecting Ribbentrop's prerogatives. His career took a huge leap forward in the spring of 1940 when he persuaded Ribbentrop to create a new division within the Foreign Office, Abteilung Deutschland, composed of six *Referäte*, with Luther promoted to the rank of division chief. In addition to party liaison functions, foreign contacts of state and party organizations, and the management of Ribbentrop's real estate, the new division now also handled liaison to the SS and police, production and distribution of the ministry's printed materials, travel abroad by important German personalities, and Jewish policy (in Referat D *III*).[5] Over the following year, Luther inexorably expanded his domain and doubled the number of Referäte. He also became head of Sonderreferat Organisation, with the task of proposing reorganization schemes for the ministry, which was a license to interfere everywhere and led him, in a play on his name, to style himself the "Reformer" of the ministry.[6] Intruding into personnel matters, Luther was also instrumental in securing the appointment of five SA men as ambassadors to German allies and satellites in southeast Europe. This advancement was but one among many causes of friction between Luther and the SS.[7] Despised and resented even more by the "old guard" of the Foreign Office as an alien intruder and uncouth upstart,[8] Luther culminated his phenomenal rise with the appointment to the rank of Unterstaatssekretär in July 1941, just thirty-two months after his precarious entry into the Foreign Office as a mere Legationsrat. Symbolic of Luther's position as an outsider in the Foreign Office, his office was located not in the main building on the Wilhelmstrasse but rather in the confiscated Norwegian embassy at Rauchstrasse 11 next to the Tiergarten.

Luther and the Jews

As a party and SA member since 1932, a member of the Ribbentrop Bureau since 1936, and head of Referat Partei in the Foreign Office since 1938, Luther had not demonstrated any particular interest in the "Jewish Question." It was only in May 1940, when Luther's newly created Abteilung Deutschland annexed the remaining functions of the old Referat Deutschland, that he became involved in Nazi Jewish policy for the first time. However, rather than appointing one of his close associates to lead the new Judenreferat (D III), he took on a man of no prior acquaintance, Franz Rademacher, as its head. At the time of his appointment, Rademacher had just returned from Montevideo, Uruguay, where he had served as the chargé d'affaires in the German embassy. A self-made man of modest social origins, Rademacher, like Luther, was a relative outsider by traditional Foreign Office standards of recruitment. Appointed head of the Judenreferat, he zealously threw himself into becoming a self-made Jewish expert and anti-Semite. He ordered a hefty pile of anti-Semitic books from publishers all over Germany and cultivated the acquaintance of the foreign editor of *Der Stürmer*, Paul Wurm. He must have been very proud indeed when Wurm acknowledged him as "a really good authority on the Jewish Question and old fighter."[9]

For the next fifteen months Luther allowed Rademacher considerable scope to take his own initiatives and backed him when necessary, but personally did not engage in Jewish policy to any significant degree. Rademacher was eager for the Judenreferat to move beyond the routine tasks and "1,000 individual decisions" concerning potential foreign policy complications and the fate of individual Jews. As the war had "a double face: one is imperialistic—the securing of political, military, and economic space necessary for Germany as a world power, one supra-national—liberation of the world from the chains of Jewry and free masonry," Abteilung Deutschland should play a role equal to that of the Political Division in the forthcoming peace treaty negotiations with France. For this it needed to clarify the question "whereto with the Jews."

Inspired by old anti-Semitic pamphlets that he found in the files when he was trying to get up to speed as a Jewish expert, Rademacher suggested one possibility was that "all Jews" or at least "West Jews" be "removed from Europe, to Madagascar for example."[10] Luther presented Rademacher's idea that DIII be charged with preparing a solution to the "Jewish Question" within the framework of the peace treaty, to which Ribbentrop agreed.[11] At their meetings on June 17 and 18 with Mussolini and Ciano respectively, both Hitler and Ribbentrop mentioned the plan to use Madagascar as a reservation for the Jews.[12] When Reinhard Heydrich got wind of this development, he immediately asserted his own jurisdiction,[13] and Rademacher was instructed to prepare the Madagascar Plan in agreement with the SS. In reality, while Rademacher worked with others over the summer to produce a Foreign Office version of the plan that would involve widespread participation, the SS proceeded to produce its own version, which made no mention of the Foreign Office and in which Heydrich would control every aspect.[14]

Even after the Madagascar Plan became moot when expected victory over Great Britain did not materialize, this pattern, in which the SS proceeded to act unilaterally and without consultation on Jewish matters that clearly had foreign policy implications, continued. In particular, the Foreign Office learned of the roundup and expulsion of 6,504 German Jews from Baden and Pfalz into Vichy France on 22 to 23 October only following French protests that it received on 29 October 1940. Luther's request for information elicited a brief letter from Heydrich that the expulsion measure had been ordered by Hitler. It had been carried out without notifying France and had proceeded without incident. Further attempts to extract more information from the SS were unsuccessful. Ribbentrop instructed that continuing French protests were to be treated "dilatorily" and any return of the expelled Jews was totally excluded.[15] In reality, in 1940 and early 1941 the Foreign Office learned more about the implementation of Nazi Jewish policy from a persistent anonymous letter-writer than it did from official communications from the SS.[16]

Lack of communication with and even outright misinformation from the SS continued during the first months after the invasion of the Soviet Union. For example, while Luther and Rademacher learned from the German ambassador to Romania (the SA man Manfred von Killinger, whose appointment Luther had arranged) that "the Jews were exposed to unheard-of persecution on the Romanian boarder" and that 4,000 Jews had been killed in Iasi, from Heydrich they received the complaint alleging that Romanian actions in the newly occupied territories "repeatedly displayed a strong friendliness to the Jews."[17] This uncooperative relationship began to change when Eichmann telephoned Rademacher on 21 August 1941, to confidentially inform him that Hitler had just approved the marking of Jews in Germany and wanted to know if foreign Jews could be included. Rademacher and Luther responded with alacrity. They drew up a set of proposals, according to which Jews from occupied countries could be marked immediately, and the agreement of friendly European countries would be sought. Once such agreement had been secured, marking could officially be extended to all Jews, with non-European Jews exempted by secret internal instructions. Expected protests from European neutrals such as Sweden and Switzerland would be ignored. Heydrich approved these proposals *before* Luther submitted them to Ribbentrop.[18]

By the time an inter-ministerial conference was held on 29 August to finalize the marking decree, Ribbentrop had still not replied. Rademacher attended the conference, where it was agreed that no exception for foreign Jews would be made in the text, but the police would exempt through internal instruction those foreign Jews requested by the Foreign Office. Ribbentrop then belatedly responded, postponing the marking of any foreign Jews for the moment.[19] Acting as middlemen between the RSHA on the one hand and Ribbentrop on the other, Luther and Rademacher facilitated the rapid issue of the marking decree. But in their communications, they had bypassed Staatssekretär Ernst von Weizsäcker entirely. When Weizsäcker was asked several weeks later if the Foreign Office had been consulted, he asked Luther in turn if consultation had occurred without the matter ever being submitted to the Staatssekretär. When Luther confirmed that he had learned verbally from Heydrich about Hitler's decision, that a conference had been called and the decree issued very quickly, and that he had dealt directly with Ribbentrop because speedy action was required, Weizsäcker frostily told him to adhere to official channels in the future.[20]

Very soon thereafter, however, Luther cooperated even more closely and fatefully with Heydrich on expediting the implementation of Nazi Jewish policy and bypassing Weizsäcker once again. As the communist-led partisan uprising in Serbia gained momentum against the German occupation in August 1941, the German ambassador in Belgrade, Felix Benzler, urged closer cooperation with Serbian nationalists and the deportation of Serbian Jews down the Danube or to the General Government.[21] Ribbentrop sent his confidant, Edmund Veesenmeyer, to investigate, and Veesenmeyer immediately endorsed the deportation, at least of Serbia's 8,000 male Jews to Romania.[22] As Germany had just blocked Romania's attempt to expel Jews beyond Transnistria into German-occupied Ukraine, Ribbentrop in a telephone conversation with Luther rejected the proposal.[23] Benzler persisted, suggesting that if Romania was not possible, then the male Jews must be deported to the General Government or Russian territory, and Luther instructed Rademacher to explore this possibility with Eichmann. Rademacher noted Eichmann's response that "residence in Russia and GG impossible. Not even the Jews from Germany can be lodged there. Eichmann proposes shooting."[24]

Benzler appealed directly to Ribbentrop, claiming that the military commander was in agreement that the deportation of the 8,000 male Jews in Serbia was a precondition for pacification.[25] Immensely annoyed, Luther also addressed Ribbentrop:

> If the military commander is agreed with Benzler to the effect that these 8,000 Jews prevent pacification action . . ., then in my opinion the military commander must take care of the immediate elimination of these 8,000 Jews. In other areas military commanders have dealt with considerably greater numbers of Jews without even mentioning it.

This time with Weizsäcker's approval, he requested authorization to discuss the question with Heydrich. "I am convinced that in agreement with him we can come very quickly to a clear solution of this question."[26] Ribbentrop, responding to Benzler's earlier reproach, authorized Luther to contact the SS-Reichsführer as to whether he could not take over the 8,000 Jews and move them somewhere else.[27] In effect, Luther now had Ribbentrop's authorization to meet with Heydrich, but it would not be a meeting about reopening the deportation question.

Presumably Luther met with Heydrich on 4 October, when the latter was back in Berlin from his first visit to Prague as the new Reichsprotektor and meeting with other officials as well, including another subsequent invitee to the Wannsee Conference, Alfred Meyer, of the Ministry for the Eastern Occupied Territories.[28] Heydrich and Luther, both mistrustful of Benzler, agreed to send Eichmann's deputy, Friedrich Suhr, as well as the Foreign Office Jewish expert, Franz Rademacher, to examine the situation in Belgrade.[29] Rademacher later summarized the reason for his trip: "Purpose of the service trip was to check on the spot, whether the problem of the 8,000 Jewish agitators, whose deportation has been urged by the embassy, could not be settled on the spot."[30] On his subsequent travel expense form, he was more explicit concerning the purpose of the trip: "liquidation of Jews in Belgrade."[31] The travelers left Berlin on 16 October, reached Belgrade on 18 October, and met with various German officials. It turned out that, just as Luther had earlier assumed to be the expected solution, the military was already shooting the incarcerated male Jews (and *"Zigeuner"*) as the most convenient and least complicated source of victims (that is, they were already in German camps and their execution did not drive Serbs into the hands of the partisans) to meet the extraordinary reprisal ratio of 100 to one that the Wehrmacht was committed to fulfill for every German soldier killed by the partisans. The army's problem now was that it had too few male Jews, not too many, to meet its self-imposed reprisal quotas. Left to continue its reprisal procedures, the army would soon shoot all remaining male Jews in Serbia as well. But the delegation from Berlin continued to insist on deporting the remaining male Jews. Rademacher and Suhr presented a united front that deportation to Romania, the General Government or Russia was impossible, and the proposal to have the remaining male Jews shot within the framework of the military's reprisal policy carried the day. Rademacher could report: "The male Jews will be shot by the end of the week, so that the problem broached in the embassy's report is settled." The fate of the Jewish women and children in Serbia was also discussed. They would be incarcerated over the winter. "Then as soon as the technical possibility exists within the framework of the total solution of the Jewish Question, the Jews will be deported by waterway to reception camps in the east."[32]

Rademacher spent three days in Budapest on his return trip, reached Berlin on 25 October, and submitted his summary report. Luther did not send it to Weizsäcker until 7 November, but news of it had already spread quickly. On 1 November von Hassell noted what he had learned from Hans Berndt Häften, deputy head of the Information Division and later one of the 20 July conspirators, that Luther had been indignant over the "softness" of the ambassador in Belgrade concerning the "the 8,000 Jews herded together in that city" and therefore had "got in touch with Heydrich, who immediately sent a 'specialist' down to Belgrade to clean out those poor people."[33] Allegedly, the episode earned Rademacher the title of Judenschlächter or "Jew butcher" in certain circles within the Foreign Office. Weizsäcker vented his displeasure, noting that Benzler had exceeded his competency. "The same applies in my opinion then also for the Foreign Office," by which he obviously meant Luther and Rademacher. He instructed Luther to deliver a written reprimand to Benzler for going beyond the relevant foreign policy issue of deportation and involving himself in how local authorities coped with the "Jewish Question" within Serbian borders. Knowing that the Weizsacker reprimand was really aimed at himself, Luther cited Ribbentrop's instructions to discuss the entire matter with Heydrich. "I must assume, therefore, that it is in agreement with the foreign minister, when the Foreign Office involved itself in this certainly delicate matter." He therefore refused to write Benzler and considered the matter settled.[34]

The full impact of what Luther and Rademacher learned about the state of Nazi Jewish policy from the Serbian episode cannot be fully understood without noting the simultaneous reception of two other sources of information. The German military in France had arrested a large number of Jews there in retaliation for the killing of German soldiers by the emerging resistance. Included among those arrested were a number of Jews holding Spanish passports. This led the Spanish government to suggest the possibility of evacuating all Spanish Jews, some 2,000, from France to Spanish Morocco. The German ambassador in Paris, Otto Abetz, forwarded this inquiry to Berlin. On 13 October 1941, Luther prepared a memorandum, suggesting that Abetz should be instructed to explore the possibility of removing the Spanish Jews in France to Spanish Morocco (which would have been in line with the previous Nazi goal of expelling Jews from Europe). Four days later, following a telephone conversation, Luther noted that the RSHA opposed the removal of Spanish Jews from France to Spanish Morocco, because the Spanish government had neither the will nor experience effectively to guard them there. More ominously, Luther learned, "In addition these Jews would also be all too much out of the direct reach of the measures for a basic solution of the Jewish Question to be enacted after the war."[35] The following day, Himmler and Heydrich agreed upon the end of all Jewish emigration from Europe, and this decision was transmitted to various agencies of the SiPo-SD on October 23.[36] Rademacher learned of the halt to all Jewish emigration on 4 November, and relayed this information to Luther on 14 November.[37]

On 23 October 1941, Eichmann met in Berlin with his deportation experts, including those from the east, to discuss the next wave of Jewish deportation from the Reich, following the deportations to Lodz that had begun on 15 October.[38] Rademacher was in Budapest that day, on his way back from Belgrade, but he nonetheless learned something very crucial about the meeting from his old friend, Paul Wurm, who had been visiting in Berlin that day and sent Rademacher a brief note: "Dear Party Comrade Rademacher! On my return trip from Berlin I met an old party comrade, who works in the east on the settlement of the Jewish Question. In the near future, many of the Jewish vermin will be exterminated through special measures."[39]

Days later Luther learned from a Swedish intervention on their behalf that of the 600 young Dutch male Jews who had been sent to a concentration camp in Germany in the spring of 1941, over 400 had already died, most of them on specific days indicating deliberate mass killing. Luther assured Gestapo chief Heinrich Müller on 5 November 1941 that "in principle the Foreign Office held the same viewpoint as the RSHA and advocated on its part reprisal measures against Jews as causers of unrest," but urged that in the future care should be taken in the release of death notices that the impression did not arise that the deaths had all occurred on certain days.[40]

Thus, within the brief space of several weeks, Luther and Rademacher had played a pivotal role with Heydrich and the SS in assuring the mass shooting of the remaining male Jews in Serbia. Moreover, they had learned of a "total solution" or "basic solution" involving deportation of all European Jews—even the Spanish Jews in France and Jewish women and children in Belgrade—to "reception camps" in the east in place of the previous policy of expulsion, to be carried out "after the war" or "in the near future." While we do not know precisely what Rademacher may have told Luther, he now knew that this solution also involved mass extermination "through special measures."

If Luther and Rademacher were getting a clear idea of the direction Nazi Jewish policy was taking concerning the fate of European Jews, they—along with many others in the Foreign Office—were also now given detailed information about what had already transpired on Soviet territory. On 30 October 1941, on orders from Heydrich, Heinrich Müller sent the first five "Activity and Situation Reports of the Einsatzgruppen of the SiPo-SD" to Ribbentrop. They covered events from August and September. Forwarded by staff, they reached Luther on 17 November, and he passed them to Rademacher the following day.[41] It must have been clear to Luther that the reports pertained most closely to his Judenreferat. On 25 November 1941, Heydrich forwarded to Ribbentrop the sixth report, covering the month of October. On 8 December, Dr Bruns on Ribbentrop's staff requested a short summary of the six lengthy reports for the foreign minister. One of Rademacher's assistants wrote a summary of the first five, while Luther personally wrote a summary of the sixth report, which he had just received.[42]

Several aspects about the Foreign Office copies are noteworthy. First, the Foreign Office was but one of many recipients of these reports. The second report sent to the Foreign Office was one of fifty-three copies, the third one of eighty, and the fourth through sixth were one of 100 copies. Second, the information from the Foreign Office's own copy was widely circulated. The summaries were submitted to Ribbentrop through Weizsäcker and Unterstaatssekretär Ernst Woermann of the Political Division—both of whom initialed the cover letter—and circulated to a number of divisions and desks within the Foreign Office. In the end the original reports were read by at least five people and the summaries had been initialed by sixteen. Many others who did not initial them would certainly have learned of their contents as well. Finally, and most importantly, the reports and summaries left no doubt as to the extent and systematic nature of the mass killing of Jews on Soviet territory. In addition to listing many mass executions, the fourth report noted that two Sonderkommando had liquidated 85,000 and 75,000 Jews respectively by the end of September. The sixth report noted that 33,771 Jews had been killed in Kiev on 29 to 30 September. While the early reports still gave nominal justifications for the massacres, increasingly the goal of making these territories *judenfrei* was openly proclaimed. No one reading them could doubt the meaning of the term "Final Solution" as it applied to Soviet territories. And in the early months of 1942, the seventh, eight, tenth and eleventh reports (only the ninth was missing) were also sent to and circulated within the Foreign Office as well.[43]

Luther at the Conference

On 29 November 1941, after already possessing the first five reports, Luther received the first invitation to what was to become the Wannsee Conference. Luther as representative of the Foreign Office was the only invitee with the rank of Unterstaatssekretär. As the meeting approached, Luther asked Rademacher to inform Heydrich that he was ill, but was very grateful for the invitation and would attend if possible. He asked Rademacher to prepare a memorandum for the meeting of "our wishes and ideas" and to inform the Staatssekretär. On 8 December, Rademacher informed Luther that the meeting had been postponed to an as yet undetermined date and Weizäcker had been informed.[44]

By the time of the invitation, Luther's contentious relationship with the SS had been mitigated by cooperation in implementing Nazi Jewish policy on two important occasions. Negotiating directly with Heydrich, he had made it possible for the marking decree to be issued quickly, with decisions exempting some foreign Jews to be determined later and transmitted through internal instructions. Faced with the repeated insistence of the German ambassador in Belgrade to deport the male Jews of Serbia, Luther had supported Eichmann's option of shooting them instead. Again negotiating with Heydrich, he had sent Rademacher as part of a joint delegation to block deportation and force the shooting option. In both cases Luther had acted quickly and quasi-independently, getting the foreign minister's vague authorization, ignoring Weizsäcker, and working out the details himself rather than waiting for specific instructions from above. It is a fair assumption that Luther's cooperation with Heydrich in the fall of 1941 overcame earlier rancor and distrust between the two and earned Luther the invitation to the Wannsee Conference so unusual for his rank.

One can also say with certainty that by the time he received the invitation, Luther knew two things: first, that a solution of systematic mass murder was already being implemented against Jews on Soviet territory, and second, that a plan for a basic or total solution for all remaining European Jews within the German sphere—to be undertaken after the war—consisted of deporting them to "reception camps" in the east, where the likelihood of their being killed was very great. Rademacher initialed the covering letter for the compilation of "desires and ideas" requested by Luther, but the memorandum itself was unsigned, and there is also no stamp or initial to prove that Luther in fact ever read it. At the center of the memorandum was the Foreign Office desire for deportation of all German, Croatian, Slovak, and Romanian Jews in the "Third Reich," all former-German, now stateless Jews on German occupied territory, Serbian Jews, and Jews turned over to Germany by Hungary, as well as the declaration of German willingness to deport all Jews living in Romania, Slovakia, Croatia, Bulgaria and Hungary. The second major desire was to influence other European countries to introduce Jewish legislation, preferably on the Nürnberg model. All of this was to be achieved "as hitherto on friendly terms with the Gestapo."[45] Clearly the notion that the meeting originally scheduled for 9 December was to be devoted exclusively to settling issues related solely to German Jews, as argued by Christian Gerlach,[46] was not an understanding of the meeting's purpose that was shared by the compiler of the "wishes and ideas" of the German Foreign Office.

On 8 January 1942, Luther received his second invitation from Heydrich to attend the rescheduled conference on 20 January 1942. At the end of his long opening monologue, Heydrich said that Europe would be combed of its Jews from west to east. Having invited Luther as Foreign Office representative to the conference, Heydrich gave the necessary reassurance: "Concerning the treatment of the Final Solution in the European territories occupied and influenced by us, it is proposed that the relevant experts of the Foreign Office confer with the competent specialists of the Security Police and SD." He anticipated no difficulties with Slovakia, Croatia, Romania or France, but some preliminary work was still to be done in Hungary and Italy. At this point Luther appears to have been the first invitee to interrupt Heydrich, when he broke in and pointed out that:

> ... in a basic treatment of this problem in some countries, such as the northern countries, difficulties would emerge, and it is thus recommended to postpone those countries for the time being. In view of the small number of Jews in question here, this postponement constitutes no significant restriction anyhow. On the other hand, the Foreign Office sees no great difficulty for southeast and west Europe.[47]

The discussion then shifted to other topics, and the Protocol of the conference did not record any further intervention on the part of Luther. With Heydrich's announcement of a European-wide deportation program and his assurance of consultation with the Foreign Office, Luther had obtained both the chief "desire" of the Foreign Office and protection of its prerogatives. And Luther's warning concerning the Scandinavian countries would prove prescient.

In the ensuing months Luther and Rademacher insured smooth implementation of the "Final Solution" in several ways. First, the

Foreign Office did not raise any objections based on foreign policy considerations when Heydrich through Eichmann requested clearance to carry out deportation actions in various countries. Second, it often exerted pressure or supplied expertise for deportation through its own diplomats and the SS Jewish advisors housed in its various embassies. Third, the Foreign Office sought either to swell the number of victims by obtaining the permission or at least an expression of disinterest on the part of Germany's allies and European neutrals to the inclusion of their Jewish nationals in deportations from Germany and German-occupied territories, or alternatively to contribute to making these territories *judenrein* by compelling these countries to repatriate the Jews in question. And finally, the Foreign Office sought to insure that no disputed claims over Jewish property would interfere with the "Final Solution."

Luther certainly informed Rademacher of the results of the Conference but seems not to have shared this information with anyone else. When Rademacher informed the Colonial Desk of the Political Division within the Foreign Office that the Madagascar Plan was now defunct because "the Führer had decided that the Jews shall be deported not to Madagascar but to the east," Woermann immediately asked about the source of this significant decision. Luther subsequently assured Rademacher that he had answered Woermann's inquiry.[48] There is no indication that Luther shared any further information with Weizsäcker beyond the fact that he had been invited. More surprising, there is no indication that Luther consulted with Ribbentrop over his close cooperation with Heydrich until the following summer, when a growing estrangement between the two placed Luther's position in peril.

In the summer of 1942, Luther's growing sense of exasperation over Ribbentrop's endless demands for personal favors finally led to a break between the two and mutual accusations of corruption. At the same time, Luther seems to have concluded that some kind of compromise peace had to be negotiated to save Germany from defeat, and he was both susceptible to the blandishments of his disillusioned youthful recruits in Abteilung Deutschland in this regard and aware that only Ribbentrop's ouster would open the door for the Foreign Office to undertake the necessary negotiations.[49]

In August 1942 Ribbentrop became aware that the SS advisor in Bucharest had negotiated a deportation agreement directly with the Romanian government behind the back of the German ambassador von Killinger and suspected that Luther had condoned this upstaging of Foreign Office prerogatives. Ribbentrop turned on Luther and demanded an explanation not only of the events in Romania but of

Luther's conduct in the whole field of Jewish affairs.[50] Instead of exculpating himself by accusing the SS of a breach of faith in this one case, Luther chose to defend his actions and those of the SS together as a preliminary step in laying the groundwork for a possible alliance with the SS against Ribbentrop.

With the help of Rademacher and his deputy, Luther composed a lengthy and detailed *Rechtfertigungsbericht* or "justification report" in a brief two days. Accompanied by supporting documents, it was a comprehensive denial that Luther had ever behaved improperly or independently in Jewish affairs.[51] Omitting any mention of Serbia, Luther tried to explain away the fact that he had never informed the foreign minister of the Wannsee Conference, the Protocol of which he attached as a supporting document to his report. He claimed that he had not informed the foreign minister at the time because Heydrich had planned a follow-up conference, which had never taken place because of Heydrich's preoccupation with the Protectorate and then his assassination. Luther emphatically asserted:

> In the meeting on January 20, 1942, I requested that all questions concerning foreign territory must be coordinated with the Foreign Office beforehand, which Gruppenführer Heydrich promised and has also loyally complied with, as indeed the agencies of the Reich Security Main Office competent for Jewish affairs have carried out all measures from the beginning in frictionless cooperation with the Foreign Office.

As for the events in Romania, Luther tried to conjure up a veneer of Foreign Office sanction and oversight for the unilateral actions of the SS. Ribbentrop, obviously not persuaded by his Unterstaatssekretär, had Emil von Rintelen on his staff relay his displeasure. "The foreign minister requests you in the future, before taking up negotiations with any foreign government that falls within the work area of your division, to report or submit the relevant matter to him and await his approval."[52] Ribbentrop obstructed Luther for nearly a month, until Romania's deputy prime minister, Mihai Antonescu, visited Hitler's headquarters on 23 September. After Hitler's and Ribbentrop's meetings with Mihai Antonescu, Hitler must have vented his anger over the Foreign Office's failure to finalize the previously promised deportations from that country. Ribbentrop literally rushed to the telephone to retract his earlier instructions and unleash his Unterstaatssekretär. A triumphant Luther immediately communicated to Weizsäcker and other division heads: "The Reich Foreign Minister has given me instructions today over the telephone to hurry as much as possible the evacuation of Jews from the various countries of Europe."[53]

Luther's victory over Ribbentrop was short-lived. While he had been freed aggressively to pursue new deportations, he was also being investigated for corruption by a Ribbentrop-appointed commission.[54] And he was being subjected to the eternal pestering of his young co-workers and their incessant pressure to act.[55] In conjunction with Walter Schellenberg, Himmler's stalking horse for exploring contacts with the allies, Luther plotted how to oust the foreign minister. There are conflicting accounts as to how and why the plot failed. In his self-serving memoirs, Schellenberg claimed that while he was trying to bring Himmler around to the idea of ousting Ribbentrop, a tactless Luther alienated Himmler by his boorish behavior and prematurely set the plot in motion by circulating a report declaring the foreign minister mentally unfit.[56] According to Walter Büttner, one of Luther's young men, it was Himmler who gave Luther to understand that he was ready to withdraw protection from Ribbentrop, and it was Schellenberg who then urgently solicited the Luther report on the foreign minister's unfitness, though Büttner had not finished lining up other support.[57] After Himmler wavered and then turned the report over to Ribbentrop, Luther and his co-conspirators in Abteilung Deutschland were arrested on 10 February 1943.[58] Luther spent the rest of the war as a privileged prisoner at Sachsenhausen. His *Judenreferent*, Franz Rademacher, was not directly implicated in the plot and was released from the Foreign Office to serve in the navy for the remainder of the war.

Summary

As a participant at the Wannsee Conference, Martin Luther exemplified the socially disadvantaged but able and ambitious man for whom the "Third Reich" offered unprecedented opportunity for a rise to power and prestige. He repaid the regime with devotion and energy that benefited his patron, Joachim von Ribbentrop, and himself. He was particularly useful to Ribbentrop as the expert in defending the latter's prerogatives and jurisdictions in the often sordid internal politics of National Socialism, while simultaneously engaged in a relentless program of bureaucratic encroachment and expansion at the expense of his rivals in the Foreign Office. Not particularly interested in Jewish policy until the last months of 1941, he then perceived its increased importance and moved with alacrity to transcend a long history of contestation with the SS and to personally cooperate with Heydrich. In so doing, he insured that the role of the Foreign Office in this regard was not ignored or eclipsed, and it thereby became deeply implicated in the "Final Solution." But Luther also proceeded with little or no authorization or guidance from Ribbentrop, attending the Wannsee Conference without even informing the Foreign Minister either before or after. This was not a man who needed specific instructions to act or welcomed micromanagement from above. Heydrich made no mistake when he judged that Luther would be his most valuable ally in the Foreign Office and thus invited him, despite his lesser rank and previous conflicts, to the Wannsee Conference.

Christopher R. Browning is the Frank Porter Graham Professor of History Emeritus at the University of North Carolina in Chapel Hill. He is the author of numerous books, including *The Final Solution and the German Foreign Office* (1978), *Ordinary Men: Reserve Police Battalion 101 and the Final Solution in Poland* (1992), *The Origins of the Final Solution* (2004), and *Remembering Survival: Inside a Nazi Slave Labor Camp* (2010). He has served as an expert witness in several trials of accused Holocaust perpetrators as well as the "Holocaust denial" trials of Ernst Zündel vs. Crown Counsel of Ontario (1988) and David Irving vs. Deborah Lipstadt and Penguin Books (2000). He is a fellow of the American Academy of Arts and Sciences.

Notes

1   For Luther's early career, see: Berlin Document Center, Luther Party and SA files; Hans-Adolf Jacobsen, *Nationalsozialistische Außenpolitik 1933–1938* (Frankfurt am Main and Berlin, 1968), 303–9; Paul Seabury, *The Wilhelmstrasse: A Study of German Diplomats under the Nazi Regime* (Berkeley, CA, 1954), 73–74, 107–8. For Luther's business success: Politisches Archiv des Auswärtigen Amtes (hereafter PA), Luther Handakten, vol. 4, Luther to Schroeder, 24 February 1940; Landgericht Nürnberg-Fürth (hereafter LGNF) 2 Ks 3/53, Hauptakten, XI, 1812, Rademacher testimony, 1968.
2   PA, Dienststelle Ribbentrop 12/2 (old signature): Mutschmann to Ribbentrop, 16 November 1937, and Büttner note, 13 December 1937; R 27644, Luther to Lorenz, 29 September 1942.
3   PA, R 27648, Luther to Ribbentrop, 13 July 1938; draft order creating Referat Partei, 25 September 1938; and Luther to Ribbentrop, 2 November 1938.
4   Donald McKale, *Curt Prüfer: German Diplomat from the Kaiser to Hitler* (Kent, OH and London, 1987), 137.
5   PA, R 27624, Luther memorandum, 16 April 1940; and R 100305, "Geschäftsplan," 7 May 1940.
6   For the details of Luther's relentless bureaucratic imperialism, see: C.R. Browning, "Unterstaatssekretär Martin Luther and the Ribbentrop Foreign Office," *Journal of Contemporary History* 12, no. 2 (1977): 313–44, especially

320–26. Hans-Jürgen Döscher, *Das Auswärtige Amt im Dritten Reich: Diplomaten im Schatten der "Endlösung"* (Berlin, 1987), 204–12.

7   Döscher, *Das Auswärtige Amt im Dritten Reich*, 38; E. Conze et al., ed., *Das Amt und die Vergangenheit: Deutsche Diplomaten im Dritten Reich und in der Bundesrepublik* (Munich, 2010), 165–66.

8   Ulrich von Hassell deemed him "uncouth, presumptuous, false, and probably corrupt." Von Weizsäcker called him a "reptile." Ulrich von Hassell, *The Von Hassell Diaries, 1938–1944: The Story of the Forces against Hitler inside Germany* (Garden City, NY, 1947), 290; Ernst von Weizsäcker, *Memoirs of Ernst Weiszäcker* (Chicago, IL, 1951), 272.

9   PA, R 99388, Wurm to Rademacher, 5 June 1940. For the biographical information on Rademacher, see: Christopher R. Browning, *The Final Solution and the German Foreign Office: A Study of Referat D III of Abteilung Deutschland 1940–1943* (New York, 1978), 29–30.

10 PA, R 100305, Rademacher memorandum, "Gedanken über die Arbeiten und Aufgaben des Ref. D III," 3 June 1940. Nürnberg Staatsarchiv, Zz 431, no. 1, Rademacher affidavit, 20 July 1948. For detailed studies of the Madagascar Plan, see: Magnus Brechtken, *"Madagaskar für die Juden": Antisemitische Idee und politische Praxis 1885–1945* (Munich, 1997), and Hans Jansen, *Der Madagaskar-Plan: Die beabsichtigte Deportation der europäischen Juden nach Madagaskar* (Munich, 1997).

11 *Akten zur deutschen Aussenpolitik*, Series D, X, 92–94 (Rademacher memorandum "Die Judenfrage im Friedensvertrage," 3 July 1940); PA, R 100857, Rademacher memorandum, 30 August 1940.

12 Paul Schmidt, *Hitler's Interpreter* (New York, 1951), 178; Galeazzo Ciano, *The Ciano Diaries, 1939–43*, New York, 1946), 265–66.

13 PA, R 100857, Heydrich to Ribbentrop, 24 June 1940.

14 For the SS plan: PA, R 100857: RSHA Madagaskar Projekt. For Rademacher's various preparations and contacts with others, Browning, *Final Solution*, 39–42.

15 PA, R 100869, Heydrich to Luther, 29 October 1940, and Sonnleithner to Luther, 22 November 1940; *Akten zur deutschen Aussenpolitik*, D, XI, 376 (Todenhöfer to Luther, 31 October 1940).

16 PA: R 98465, Schumburg to Müller, 23 February 1940; R 100869, anonymous letter forwarded from Gaus to Luther, 3 November 1940; R 99368, anonymous letter, 15 February 1941.

17 PA, R 100883: Heydrich to Luther, 23 August 1941, and from Killinger to Luther, 1 September 1941.

18 PA, R 100851: Rademacher to Luther, 21 August 1941; Luther note, 22 August 1941; Luther to Ribbentrop, 22 August 1941.

19 PA, R 1000851: Rademacher report, 8 September 1941, and Büro RAM to Luther, 31 August 1941.

20 PA, R 100851: Weizsäcker to Luther, 15 September 1941; Luther to Weizsäcker, 19 and 22 September 1941; Weizsäcker marginal note, 24 September 1941.

21 PA, R 99424, Benzler to Foreign Office, 14 August 1941.

22 *Akten zur deutschen Aussenpolitik*, D, XIII, 378 and 386.

23 Nürnberg Document NG-3354 (Rademacher statement, 30 August 1948).

24 PA, R 100874: Benzler to Foreign Office and Luther marginal note, 12 September 1941, and Rademacher marginal note, 13 September 1941.

25 PA, R 100874, Benzler to Ribbentrop, 28 September 1941.

26 PA, R 1000874, Luther to Ribbentrop, 2 October 1941.

27 PA, R 100874, Büro RAM to Luther, 3 October 1941.

28 Philippe Burrin, *Hitler and the Jews: The Genesis of the Holocaust* (London, 1994), 123.

29 PA, R 100874: Luther to Belgrade, 4, 8 and 15 October 1941. LGNF 2 Ks 3/53, Hauptakten, VIII, 1262 (Rademacher interrogation, October 1966).

30 *Akten zur deutschen Aussenpolitik*, D, XIII, part 2, 570–72 (Rademacher summary report, 25 October 1941).

31 Landgericht Bamburg, Urteil in dem Strafverfahren gegen Franz Rademacher, 2 Ks 3/53, 44. This document was not made available to me during my research at the PA in 1972–73 but was accessible through the court records.

32 2 Ks 3/53, 53–58, and Rademacher's summary report, cited in n. 32.

33 Hassell, *The von Hassell Diaries*, 224.

34 PA, R R 100874: Rademacher memorandum, 15 November 1941, and Weizsäker handwritten note, 19 November 41; Weizsäcker to Abteilung Deutschland, 22 November 1941; and Luther to Weizsäcker, 12 December 1941.

35 PA, R 103195, Luther memoranda, 13 and 17 October 1941.

36 P. Witte et al., ed., *Der Dienstkalender Heinrich Himmlers 1941/42* (Hamburg, 1999), 238 (entry of 18 October 1941). Hans Günther Adler, *Der verwaltete Mensch: Studien zur Deportation der Juden aus Deutschland* (Tübingen, 1974), 29–30.

37 PA, R 99370 I: Huene to D III, 12 November 1941, and Rademacher note, 14 November 1941.

38 Yad Vashem Archives, O-53/76/110-111 (Abromeit Vermerk, 24 October 1941).

39 PA, R 99398, Wurm to Rademacher, 23 October 1941.

40 PA, R 100876, Luther to Müller, 5 November 1941.

41 PA, R 101122: Müller to Ribbentrop, 30 October 1941, and Picot covering letter, 15.11.1941, with Luther and Rademacher initials; and Activity and Situation Reports No. 1–5.

42 PA, R 101122: Heydrich to Ribbentrop, 25 November 1941; Bruns to D II, 8 December 1941; Luther to Ribbentrop, 10 December 1941; von Hahn report, 10 December 1941; and Activity and Situation Report No. 6.

43 PA, R 101122: Activity and Situation Reports No. 7–8, 10–11, and covering correspondence, January–April 1942. For further details, see: Browning, *Final Solution*, 72–76.

44 PA, R 100857, Heydrich to Luther, 29 November 1941, with Luther and Rademacher marginalia.

45 PA, R 100857, unsigned and undated memorandum "Wünschen und Ideen."

46 C. Gerlach, "The Wannsee Conferenz: The fate of German Jews, and Hitler's Decision in Principle to Exterminate all European Jews," *Journal of Modern History* 70, no. 4 (1998): 759–812.

47 PA, R 100857, Protocol of the Wannsee Conference, 20 January 1942.

48 *Akten zur deutschen Aussenpolitik*, E, I, 403; PA, R 100857: Woermann to Rademacher, 14 February 1942, Rademacher to Luther, 24 February 1942, and Luther handwritten notation, 26 February 1942.

49 Browning, "Unterstaatssekretär Martin Luther," 332–37.

50 PA, R 100881: Rintelen to Luther, 19 August 1942, with copy of report of SiPo-SD to Reichsführer-SS, 26 July 1942; Luther to Rintelen, 19 August 1942. LGNF 2 Ks 3/53, Hauptakten, II, 285 (Rintelen affidavit, 1949).

51 PA, R 100857, Luther to Ribbentrop, 21 August 1942. LGNF 2 Ks 3/53, Hauptakten, XI, 1836 (Rademacher testimony, 1968).

52 PA, R 100857, Rintelen to Luther 29 August 1942.

53 PA, R 100890, Luther memorandum, 24 September 1942. Hearsay evidence that Hitler violently criticized Ribbentrop on 23 September 1942 for lack of success in solving the Jewish question comes from Cecil von Renthe-Fink, the German ambassador to Copenhagen, who claimed he had heard the story from a member of Ribbentrop's staff. Leni Yahil, *The Rescue of Danish Jewry: Test of a Democracy* (Philadelphia, PA, 1969), 73.

54 D. McKale, ed., *Rewriting History: The Original and Revised World War II Diaries of Curt Prüfer* (Kent, OH, 1988), 22, 24, 37, and 39.

55 Nürnberg Staatsarchiv, Zz 431, no. 10 (Rademacher affidavit, July 1948).

56 Walter Schellenberg, *The Labyrinth* (New York, 1956), 320–25.

57 Büttner letter to Höhne, February 1967, quoted in: Heinz Höhne, *The Order of the Death's Head: The Story of Hitler's SS* (New York, 1971), 590.

58 For another account of the "Luther Revolt," see also: Döscher, *Das Auswärtige Amt im Dritten Reich*, 256–64.

Bibliography

Adler, Hans Günther. *Der verwaltete Mensch: Studien zur Deportation der Juden aus Deutschland*. Tübingen: Mohr, 1974.

Brechtken, Magnus. *"Madagaskar für die Juden": Antisemitische Idee und politische Praxis 1885–1945*. Munich: Oldenbourg, 1997.

Browning, Christopher R. *Die "Endlösung" und das Auswärtige Amt: Das Referat D III der Abteilung Deutschland 1940–1943*. Darmstadt: WBG. 2010. [English: *The Final Solution and the German Foreign Office: A Study of Referat D III of Abteilung Deutschland 1940–1943*. New York: Holmes & Meier, 1978.]

Browning, C.R. "Unterstaatssekretär Martin Luther and the Ribbentrop Foreign Office." *Journal of Contemporary History* 12, no. 2 (1977): 313–44.

Burrin, Philippe. *Hitler and the Jews: The Genesis of the Holocaust*. London: Arnold, 1994.

Ciano, Galeazzo. *The Ciano Diaries, 1939–43*. New York: Doubleday, 1946 [reprint New York: Simon Publications, 2000].

Conze, E., N. Frei, P. Hayes and M. Zimmermann, ed. *Das Amt und die Vergangenheit. Deutsche Diplomaten im Dritten Reich und in der Bundesrepublik.* Munich: Blessing, 2010.

Döscher, Hans-Jürgen. *Das Auswärtige Amt im Dritten Reich: Diplomaten im Schatten der "Endlösung."* Berlin: Siedler, 1987.

Gerlach, Christian. "Die Wannsee-Konferenz, das Schicksal der deutschen Juden und Hitlers politische Grundsatzentscheidung, alle Juden Europas zu ermorden." In *Krieg, Ernährung, Völkermord: Forschungen zur deutschen Vernichtungspolitik im Zweiten Weltkrieg,* edited by C. Gerlach, 79–153. Hamburg: Hamburger Edition, 1998 [first in: *WerkstattGeschichte* 18 (1997): 7–44]. [English: "The Wannsee Conferenz: The Fate of German Jews, and Hitler's Decision in Principle to Exterminate all European Jews." *Journal of Modern History* 70, no. 4 (1998): 759–812.]

Hassell, Ulrich von. *The Von Hassell Diaries, 1938–1944: The Story of the Forces against Hitler inside Germany.* Garden City, NY: Doubleday, 1947.

Höhne, Heinz. *The Order of the Death's Head: The Story of Hitler's SS.* New York: Ballantine, 1971.

Jacobsen, Hans-Adolf. *Nationalsozialistische Außenpolitik 1933–1938.* Frankfurt am Main and Berlin: Metzner, 1968.

Jansen, Hans. *Der Madagaskar-Plan: Die beabsichtigte Deportation der europäischen Juden nach Madagaskar.* Munich: Herbig, 1997.

McKale, Donald. *Curt Prüfer: German Diplomat from the Kaiser to Hitler.* Kent, OH and London: The Kent State University Press, 1987.

McKale, D., ed. *Rewriting History: The Original and Revised World War II Diaries of Curt Prüfer.* Kent, OH: Kent State University Press, 1988.

Schellenberg, Walter. *The Labyrinth.* New York: Harper & Brothers, 1956.

Schmidt, Paul. *Hitler's Interpreter.* New York: Heinemann, 1951.

Seabury, Paul. *The Wilhelmstrasse: A Study of German Diplomats under the Nazi Regime.* Berkeley, CA: Cambridge University Press, 1954.

Weizsäcker, Ernst von. *Memoirs of Ernst Weiszäcker.* Chicago, IL: H. Regnery, 1951.

Witte, P., M. Wildt, M. Vogt, D. Pohl, P. Klein, C. Gerlach, C. Dieckmann and A. Angrick, ed. *Der Dienstkalender Heinrich Himmlers 1941/42.* Hamburg: Christians, 1999.

Yahil, Leni. *The Rescue of Danish Jewry: Test of a Democracy.* Philadelphia, PA: Jewish Publication Society of America, 1969.

14

Alfred Meyer

Reich Ministry for the Occupied
Eastern Territories

From German Monarchist to Nazi
Desk Perpetrator

Heinz-Jürgen Priamus

Illustration 14.1 Unknown photographer,
1941, Ullstein 00193487.

"We courageously defended Rinteln and the Weser . . . In the last free
corner of my Gau I am taking my leave from the Führer . . ., from
Germany. It will become free and remain Nazi. I am taking my leave
from my beloved, my loved ones. May they fare well." These lines
belong to a suicide note found on 15 May 1945 next to a corpse, decom-
posed beyond recognition, on the Hohenstein in the Weser mountains —
the place of worship of the goddess Ostara, according to Germanic
legend. Four weeks earlier, it was here, in the border region between
the former Prussian provinces of Westphalia and Hanover, that the
Second World War had come to an end. A pistol was also found next to
the corpse. Identifying the deceased proved difficult, but it was eventually decided that it was almost certainly Alfred Meyer, the former Nazi
Gauleiter of northern Westphalia, *Reichsstatthalter* (Reich Governor)
of Lippe and Schaumburg-Lippe, Senior President of the province of
Westphalia and Permanent Representative of the Reich Minister for the
Occupied Eastern Territories.[1]

A Middle-Class Upbringing

Alfred Meyer was born in Göttingen on 5 October 1891 to Carl Ludwig
Meyer, a protestant Royal Prussian government master builder, and
his wife Elisabeth. His father's work meant that the family moved
frequently, but in 1901 the Meyers settled in the Hanseatic town of

Soest in Westphalia. Wealthy and middle-class, they fitted easily into its protestant community. Alfred Meyer's grandfather was a business-man from Essen, so his father had a considerable fortune when he married. As the director of the Prussian building department in Soest and the local building inspector, Carl Ludwig Meyer was soon highly regarded by the town's dignitaries.[2] Alfred Meyer enjoyed a privileged upbringing in late Wilhelminian imperial Germany, graduating along with six others from the Archigymnasium grammar school in autumn 1911.

Meyer's political leanings first became apparent while he was taking his school leaving exams. His ambition was to become a military officer so that he could train "brave soldiers to serve the German Reich" and educate "the lower classes" so they would become morally upstanding soldiers loyal to the Kaiser." Given his family's nationalist, conservative and middle-class roots, such ambition was hardly surprising.[3] In fact, it was not easy for a middle-class young man to become a military officer on account of noble privileges, which were no longer enshrined in law but nonetheless continued to exist.[4] Meyer was not able to pursue his ambition straight away and it apparently seemed extremely doubtful that he ever would.

As soon as he had finished school, Meyer therefore enrolled at university to study law, a subject that opened professional doors, with lawyers commanding the same respect in Wilhelminian society as military officers. Moreover, thanks to the financial support his parents were able to give him, Meyer did not enroll at merely any university but went to Lausanne in Switzerland, a university that to this day is considered one of the best for law. However, he dropped out after just one term, when he was unexpectedly awarded a place as an officer cadet in the 6th Rhenish Infantry Regiment No. 68. It was a professional dream come true, and on 16 June 1913 Meyer accepted his commission. Just one year later he exchanged his handsome officer's uniform for a grey field uniform. Alfred Meyer fought in the First World War and returned to Germany from a French POW camp with multiple battle wounds in March 1920.[5]

A Professional Failure

The year 1920 marked the nadir of Meyer's professional life. His career as an officer was over before it had even begun. Having only recently returned home, he was excluded from the German army, which was now limited to 100,000 men under the terms of the Treaty of Versailles. Aged twenty-nine, he returned to his law degree, this time at the University of Bonn, only to break it off once again. He needed financial means to complete a legal clerkship and qualify as a lawyer. But he received no state support and could no longer rely on parental help, now that inflation was steadily eroding the family fortune. Meyer switched from law to political science, a new subject at German universities, and also moved to the University of Würzburg. He completed his studies and went on to gain a Ph.D. in 1923.[6]

Nothing is known of Meyer's political activities during this period. But his thesis and a related pamphlet published by Christian Meurer, his Ph.D. supervisor, attest to fervently nationalistic political convictions.[7] His thesis topic was "The Belgian People's War" and was more of an exculpation than an academic study. His core argument was that the breach of Belgium's neutrality in the wake of the German invasion in the early days of the First World War was not a breach of international law at all and the Belgians should have allowed German troops to march through their country to France. They were therefore themselves responsible for what later happened, including the atrocities perpetrated by Germans. Meurer, a member since July 1922 of the inquiry committee of the Commission of the German Constituent Assembly and of the German Reichstag, which had been established to examine war guilt, used it as the basis of his report for the committee. He drew the same conclusions as Meyer and gave it the same title as Meyer's thesis.[8]

The following four to five years of Meyer's life revolved around work and family. After completing his studies, Meyer took a job as a business clerk with the Graf Bismarck mining company in Gelsenkirchen, a job for which he was overqualified. He would later maintain he had been a legal administrator. It was another low point in his career. In 1925 he married 29-year-old Dorothee Capell, a bookseller's daughter from Soest. Their first daughter was born a year later, and four more daughters arrived over the subsequent thirteen years.[9] At this point Meyer was not politically active but continued to demonstrate an affinity to nationalists. He was friends with Otto Schumacher, the protestant pastor who had christened his daughters and who led the anti-democratic Evangelical Association in the Gelsenkirchen city council. He was also involved with the Fürst Otto von Bismarck veterans' association, eventually becoming its chairman. It set itself apart from other military veterans' associations in the Weimar Republic by only accepting former officers and belonged to the Kyffhäuser League. It was fervently nationalist, anti-democratic and in opposition to the Weimar Republic.[10]

Illustration 14.2 Alfred Meyer carrying his two elder daughters in the bright sunshine behind his 'miner's home' in Gelsenkirchen-Bismarck. Unknown photographer, undated (1930), Landesarchiv Nordrhein-Westfalen, Abteilung Ostwestfalen-Lippe, Signatur D 72 Meyer Nr. 4.

A Middle-Class Nazi

Alfred Meyer's career as a Nazi began on 1 April 1928. Neither a political epiphany nor a specific political event spurred him to join the Nazi Party. He took the step after he and a number of his colleagues at the Graf Bismarck mine succumbed to peer pressure.[11] Meyer experienced a meteoric career rise in the party, a development facilitated by its rapid growth in membership. This called for a constant restructuring of the organization, such as the introduction of new functions within its hierarchy. Meyer also benefited from a series of coincidences. In 1929 Fritz Florian, one of the earliest members of the party and the head of the Emscher-Lippe chapter of the NSDAP, took up a new position. He was replaced by Meyer, who had so far headed the smaller Groß-Gelsenkirchen chapter. By January 1931 he made the leap to a position as Gauleiter, the most important Nazi Party paramilitary rank. The position of Gauleiter of Northern Westphalia had only just been introduced, after the rapid increase in party members had prompted the Nazi Party's organizational management to divide the existing Westphalia Gau into Southern Westphalia and Northern Westphalia. The appointment of Alfred Meyer rather than a long-standing party member sparked backroom rumors. The reason for his selection has never been fully clarified.[12]

It was not only party politics that led fortuitously to Meyer's career rise. In November 1929 he once again succeeded Fritz Florian—this time on the Gelsenkirchen city council. He soon began touting an outspoken agenda, which earned him notoriety beyond the city and brought him to the attention of the party leadership. This was no doubt how Meyer, who had been a member of the party for a mere two years, ended up on the Nazi Party's list of candidates for Northern Westphalia in the Reichstag elections on 14 September 1930. Once again fortune smiled upon him. Meyer was only number two on the list, which under normal circumstances would not have been enough to secure him a seat. Perhaps this was why there was no inner-party resistance from long-standing Nazi functionaries to the newcomer. But when the Nazis won a wholly unexpected 107 seats, Meyer found himself a member of the Reichstag.[13]

It was here that he met and befriended Alfred Rosenberg. Rosenberg was not only the chairman of the Militant League for German Culture, a body which helped Meyer raise funds for regional chapters of the party, but at this point he was also a leading foreign policy ideologue and firebrand. Thanks to his acquaintance with Rosenberg, Meyer began making trips abroad; for example, campaigning in Spain for Franco before the Spanish Civil War. Meyer possibly expected Alfred Rosenberg to be appointed foreign minister should the Nazis come to power and hoped their association would help further his career. Even though Rosenberg was never made foreign minister, he did indeed help Meyer advance professionally, albeit ten years later, when the Reich Ministry for the Occupied Eastern Territories was established.[14]

Meyer spent two years as a member of the Reichstag. In April 1932 he became a member of the Prussian House of Representatives, which was, in his eyes, a demotion. Yet again, a twist of fate turned his fortunes around. Support for the Nazi Party dropped dramatically in the Reichstag elections in November 1932. With local elections in Thuringia appearing to confirm the downward trend, the party leadership was determined to seize back the advantage in the next upcoming state elections, which happened to be in the tiny free state of Lippe. The party launched a unique, highly modern campaign with no personnel, expertise, organizational or financial investment spared.[15] Handpicked by Hitler himself, Alfred Meyer served as campaign manager, since Lippe was located within his Gau. It was a controversial appointment. Nazi Party propaganda director Joseph Goebbels, in particular, expressed reservations with regard to Meyer.[16]

The Nazis won the election on 15 January 1933, but their victory was by no means the landslide the leadership had hoped for. The Nazi Party failed to secure anywhere near enough votes to form an absolute majority, but nevertheless the new president of the state government in Lippe was now a Nazi. Alfred Meyer was seen as having played a major role in bringing this about.

Against this backdrop, Hitler appointed Meyer Reichsstatthalter (Reich governor) of Lippe and Schaumburg-Lippe on 17 May 1933.[17] The position of Reichsstatthalter was introduced on 7 April 1933 by the Law Coordinating the States with the Reich, designed to subordinate the states, which had previously been autonomous, to the Reich.[18] Compared to his role as a minister in Lippe, this was a prominent position and Meyer now felt he had arrived where he belonged—among the bourgeoisie. Once he had assumed office, he was inundated with new duties. This was fairly typical. Meyer could only cope by using proxies. For every institution and organization he headed, he selected a person he trusted and who had the necessary expertise to effectively do his job for him. This person was not allowed to become any kind of rival and had to report to Meyer on a regular basis. His wide range of duties and reliance on proxies meant that Meyer belonged everywhere and nowhere.

His appointment as senior president of the province of Westphalia marked the next step on his career ladder, although this did not happen as soon as Meyer would have liked. He did not immediately succeed Johannes Gronowski, the centrist politician whom the Nazis removed from power in late February 1933. His successor was the nationalist conservative Baron Ferdinand von Lüninck, a member of the party whose first allegiance was nonetheless to the province's catholic population. Lüninck was on excellent terms with the former Reich Chancellor Franz von Papen and the equally anti-democratic and conservative Clemens August von Galen, who would later be made a bishop. The Nazis' grip on power was not yet so firm that they could afford to ignore widespread public indignation. Göring, prime minister since the 1932 Prussian coup and in charge of appointing the senior president, had little time for Meyer, but at this point, his dislike would not have mattered much. However, it was one reason why Meyer had to wait until 1938 to become senior president.

Apart from Goebbels, Meyer was the only Gauleiter appointed to this office, and the promotion only came about because it was originally assumed that he would give up his role as Reichsstatthalter, as Lippe and Schaumburg-Lippe were to be annexed by Prussia.[19] However, he never did relinquish that role.[20] It is unclear whether Meyer undertook the tasks of both those offices. It should be pointed out that the tasks of each could only be carried out in accordance with instructions; this was included in the job description of the new position of Reichsstatthalter, while the traditional role of the senior president was adjusted in the wake of enforced conformity. There was little scope for initiative or creative thinking.

Combined with the soldierly obedience to his superiors that Meyer demonstrated throughout his life, it is worth focusing on a few specific aspects of Meyer's biography; namely, his tasks as Chief of Civil Administration, his involvement in the "Aktion T4" program of involuntary euthanasia, his introduction of comprehensive schools, as well as tasks he was instructed to carry out by his superiors and various projects he carried out on his own initiative in the cultural-political field.

When Meyer became senior president he also became the Chief of Civil Administration (CdZ),[21] a post introduced against the backdrop of German rearmament and the formation of the Wehrmacht in 1935. Henceforth, the CdZ was in charge of territories invaded and occupied by the Wehrmacht. Since it was an essential part of Germany's war preparations, the activities of this office were top secret. Meyer was assigned to the General Command of the Sixth Army Corps, then the Supreme Command of the Fifth Army. Only senior presidents whose base was also a *Wehrkreiskommando* (military district command) assumed the CdZ office. This was the case in Münster, the seat of the district's senior president. The CdZ was required to staff his office with officials not only from his own regional government but also from neighboring regional governments. This effectively meant that one senior president had jurisdiction over another senior president. A structural conflict was inevitable between Meyer and Josef Terboven in particular, who was senior president of the Rhine province. Like Meyer, he also served as a Gauleiter and was in addition a confidante and favorite of Hermann Göring. Göring did not like Rosenberg, nor his protégé Meyer.

Other senior presidents who found themselves in the same position as Terboven also expressed their displeasure. Given the scope for conflict, it is not surprising that the CdZ position was abolished on 1 June 1940 and replaced by the *Reichsverteidigungskommissar* (Reich Defense Commissioner). At this point, the tables turned. The job went to Josef Terboven, who now had authority to issue directives to Meyer, who had been stripped of his office and therefore suffered a double humiliation.[22] His track record as senior president was further undermined by his dealings with the bishop of Münster, Clemens August von Galen. Anti-democratic, nationalist and conservative, von Galen was still considered acceptable by the Nazis in 1933—"a lucky find," in fact—but his luck soon ran out. Church dignitaries changed their mind about him mainly on account of his hostility to the Nazis' schools policy, which targeted denominational schools, as well as his opposition to the anti-Christian, neopagan philosophy of Alfred Rosenberg, who had frequently spoken at mass events in Münster at the behest of Meyer, and also to the "Aktion T4" program of involuntary euthanasia. The latter was devised in Münster, the district overseen by senior president and Gauleiter Alfred Meyer. His heavy-handed response to von Galen culminated in a call to arrest the bishop and to deport anyone spreading his message to concentration camps. Given von Galen's international profile, Meyer's approach was utterly foolish and served only to undermine his own credibility.[23]

The Deputy

It is therefore all the more extraordinary that Meyer was nonetheless given an opportunity to advance yet another rung up the Nazi career ladder. The Reich Ministry for the Occupied Eastern Territories (RMO) was established in July 1941, although it was only unveiled to the public several months later in November. Alfred Rosenberg was appointed minister and Alfred Meyer made his deputy. His official title was Permanent Representative of the Reich Minister for the Occupied Eastern Territories. He was therefore more of a minister than a state secretary, as he usually appears in the history books. His unique function in the Nazi ministerial bureaucracy came about partly because he refused to give up any of his other roles, clinging especially tenaciously to his position as Gauleiter, which had the most political clout of his various positions. It was unheard of to be a state secretary who took orders from his minister and a Gauleiter at the same time. Two witness testimonies confirm that Meyer saw himself more or less as a minister. One of his closest associates at the RMO, Otto Bräutigam, appeared as a witness in the trial of Alfred Rosenberg in Nuremberg and at one point stated that Alfred Meyer saw himself as "a Gauleiter with the rank of a minister" and "superior to a state secretary." Another witness in Rosenberg's trial, Gerhard Klopfer said: "Meyer often told me that he was not a state secretary. As Gauleiter and Reichsstatthalter he had a higher rank and greater influence." [24] This explains why Meyer was the first on the list of participants at the Wannsee Conference.

But even in his new role, Meyer did not distinguish himself. This did not escape the attention of Rosenberg, who later—shortly before he was executed—said that Meyer "could not always . . . rise to the challenges of senior Reich office."[25] However, Meyer liked to show off his rank and, for some reason, Rosenberg often put him in charge of the RMO's publicity work. One year after it was set up, for example, the ministry publicly presented its first progress report, with Meyer hailing "a year of constructive work" in a radio address. He of course claimed some of the credit.[26] He also ensured the Nazi press reported extensively on his trips to the occupied Eastern territories.[27]

The Perpetrator

No sooner had the RMO been established than Meyer was confronted in August 1941 with the question of the ministry's official line regarding the "Jewish Question" in the occupied territories. In early August, Hinrich Lohse, who served as *Reichskommissar Ostland* (Reich Commissioner for the Baltic and Belorussian areas) submitted a request to the RMO for instructions as to how to handle the Jewish population in the areas within his jurisdiction. Lohse wrote in his request that it was unthinkable in the long term that Jews remain in the "Ostland." But he also ruled out highly visible deportations of the whole Jewish population, pushing instead for an "extension of police measures" to be taken against Jews in the occupied territories.[28] This boiled down to a call for the intervention of regular police and killing units. It is highly unlikely that Lohse's letter to Rosenberg was not seen by Meyer first.

Lohse's request obviously brought it to the attention of the RMO's top brass that organizational structures to deal with the "Jewish Question" had yet to be put in place in their ministry. Meyer took the opportunity to seek out Reinhard Heydrich, who had been entrusted since July with developing a "Final Solution" to the "Jewish Question," with the aim of creating new positions in the RMO for experts and clerks dedicated to Jewish matters. The RMO was disappointed by the meeting held on 4 October 1941, where it was decided that the "Jewish Question" would remain within the remit of the *Sicherheitspolizei* (Security Police) and the *Sicherheitsdienst* (Security Service). This meant that the RMO was not permitted to appoint its own Jewish experts. In forfeiting a dedicated department, the RMO would not have been in a position to take any autonomous political stance on Jewish matters.[29] It had to get creative, as repellent as that sounds. Erhard Wetzel had begun work as head of the RMO's racial policy section just two days before the meeting between Meyer and Heydrich. In this capacity, his remit included Jewish matters. A lawyer and a judge, Wetzel came to the RMO from the Party Chancellery, where he had worked in the racial policy office since 1935 and was known as one of its most radical anti-Semites. It is believed that Meyer's door was always open to Wetzel, which indicates that he would have been aware of every measure taken by Wetzel regarding Jews and possibly also ordered some of them. It was possibly as a result of Wetzel's efforts that the RMO drafted its own initiatives and proposals for the "Final Solution," as the deputy minister most certainly would have been aware.[30]

In late October 1941 Wetzel sent a letter pertaining to the "Jewish Question" to Hinrich Lohse. The letter had been drawn up in collaboration with Georg Leibbrandt, the head of the RMO's political department. Since it served as the basis for a consultation with the minister, it can be assumed that Meyer was aware of its content. In what has gone down in history as the "gas chamber letter," Wetzel blatantly recommended the use of shelters and gas apparatus. The letter documents nothing less than the perverse aim of murdering all the Jews within the RMO's jurisdiction quickly and en masse. In addition, further killing operations were carried out with gas vans that had been used to kill the sick in the occupied territories. During his trial in Jerusalem, Adolf Eichmann maintained that the initiative to "industrialize mass murder" had come from the RMO rather than the Reich Main Security Office (RSHA).[31]

The Co-organizer of Mass Murder

Against this backdrop, Alfred Meyer attended the meeting on Lake Wannsee on 20 January 1942 as the deputy to the Reich Minister for the Occupied Eastern Territories. He was accompanied by Georg Leibbrandt, director of the RMO's political department, whom he had summoned to provide him with "specialist" support. Rosenberg, who was one of Hitler's inner circle of advisors on the "Jewish Question" but who also had a close personal relationship with Meyer, must have believed that Meyer would be a credit to him and his ministry.[32]

As the only Gauleiter among the participants, Meyer had information the others did not have, straight from the horse's mouth, as it were. On 12 December 1941 he had attended a meeting of Reichleiter and Gauleiter in Hitler's private apartment. In his journal, Goebbels wrote that Hitler took the opportunity to call for nothing less than the "destruction of Jewry." Moreover, Meyer was one of the few participants at the conference who was specifically quoted in the minutes. In the context of the "different types of possible solutions" discussed towards the end of the meeting, Meyer and Josef Bühler, who was representing the General Government in occupied Poland, took the position that "certain preparatory activities for the Final Solution should be carried out immediately in the territories in question, during which process any alarming of the populace must be avoided."[33] Meyer and Bühler both represented occupied territories in the east that had previously been proposed as deportation destinations for European Jews. Neither of them wanted to be left in charge of areas that had been turned into vast slums for Jewish people. Faced with this prospect, they argued for the most radical "Final Solution" — mass murder.

Meyer and the RMO played a leading role in resolving a number of questions that were left unanswered at the Wannsee Conference. Nine days afterwards, Meyer convened a meeting in the RMO offices of subordinate representatives of the various ministries, the Party Chancellery and the Supreme Command of the Wehrmacht. Only eight of the meeting's sixteen participants came from the RMO. Otto Bräutigam took the chair.[34] The representatives of the RMO spelt out their interest in a draconian resolution to the "Jewish Question." There is no doubt that this standpoint had been dictated by the ministry's directorate. The term "Jew" had to be made as broad as possible and regulations pertaining to previous definitions tightened, especially regarding "persons of mixed blood" and "persons of mixed blood of the first degree." As Heydrich had proposed at the Wannsee Conference, the latter were now to be considered "full Jews." The participants also agreed on a "standardization plan" for the occupied Eastern territories. This foresaw the definition of Jewishness being expanded to include all people of the Jewish faith, non-Jewish wives of Jews as well as legitimate and illegitimate children born to couples of whom one person was Jewish.[35]

The meeting gave rise to a flurry of communications between the various authorities involved in the murder of Jews. One key letter written by Meyer on 16 July 1942 proposed requesting that a decision be made by the Führer as to whether "Mischlinge" should be included in the destruction plans.[36] The fact that bureaucracy allowed the murder of the Jewish population to be carried out was not only the result of the efforts of the RSHA but also due to Rosenberg's zealous deputy. In the light of these facts and events, Meyer can most certainly be described as a desk perpetrator and a war criminal, even if he was not in the vanguard of the Nazis' campaign.

The Vanquished

Geared to resolving the "Jewish Question" and recruiting slave laborers in the occupied Eastern territories, Meyer's political activity was soon overshadowed by the RMO's existential problems.[37] By the time the Nazis lost the battle of Stalingrad in February 1943, it was apparent that the RMO was becoming increasingly obsolete. Not only was there nothing to build upon, there was ever less to administer now that the Nazis were retreating from the occupied territories. The military was in charge of managing the retreat. The ministry's dwindling significance was underscored when its premises were bombed in November 1943. Scattered across fifty-five different offices in Berlin and with its headquarters in a train carriage in Michendorf outside the city, the RMO was left more or less paralyzed. It was closed down in autumn 1944, although it continued to exist on paper until the end of the Nazi regime.[38]

The demise of the RMO was only one aspect of Meyer's unraveling fortunes. The unfolding events were a heavy blow to him and no doubt he had started to realize there was no escape. This had become manifestly obvious by the time the Allies took military control of his Gau. Even in September 1944, Meyer had naively believed that the advancing British and American troops could be stopped. Slavishly devoted to the Führer, who had ordered the expansion of Germany's Western Front on 24 August 1944, he had planned to establish the Westfalen-Wall line of defense, but the project failed, not least as a result of disputes over competences. The Allied offensive could no longer be stopped. Within three days, they had overrun the defense line. The leadership of the northern Westphalia Gau fled the bombing and retreated from Münster to Haltern in September 1944. Little is known of Meyer's whereabouts at this point. It was said that Meyer was in the Ruhr region in early April 1945 to implement Hitler's Nero Decree. But given that Allied forces had encircled the Ruhr Pocket by then, it seems unlikely that Meyer would have voluntarily taken the risk of entering "the pocket," even if he had been able to do so. Rumors as to his whereabouts abounded. In early April 1945 his family were reportedly seen in Heiligenkirchen near Detmold, where the family was registered. According to former colleagues, he took part in a meeting of Gauleiter in Obernkirchen near Bückeburg shortly before the Allied invasion. After that, the trail runs cold[39] until the discovery of his corpse in May 1945.

Heinz-Jürgen Priamus, Dr phil (Ph.D.) is a historian, the former director of the Institut für Stadtgeschichte, Gelsenkirchen and a former lecturer at the Department of History and the Department of Social Sciences at the Ruhr-Universität Bochum. He has published numerous publications on National Socialism and Urban History.

Notes

1 Quote from Pollack, Sworn declaration concerning the death of Alfred Meyer, in Staatsarchiv Münster, Amt 43 E, no. 14.

2 CV in: Alfred Meyer, "Der belgische Volkskrieg" (Ph.D. dissertation, University of Würzburg, 1922). W. Däbritz, "Carl Julius Schulz, der Begründer des Blechwalzwerks Schulz, Knaudt & Co," *Essener Beiträge* 46 (1928): 279–93; Horst A. Wessel, *Kontinuität im Wandel: 100 Jahre Mannesmann 1890–1990* (Gütersloh, 1990), 142–477; interview with Dorothee Z., Alfred Meyer's daughter, in: Soest City Archives, collected documents on Alfred Meyer.

3 Alfred Meyer's application to sit the university entrance exam in: Soest Ciy Archives, Archigymnasium files.

4 Hans-Ulrich Wehler, Das deutsche Kaiserreich 1871–1918 (Deutsche Geschichte, vol. 9) (Göttingen, 1994), 161.

5 State Archives Detmold, M1 I P no. 646, sheets 157–60; Graßmann/ Maywald (Revised), Stammliste der Offiziere, 122; Bundesarchiv Berlin, Berlin Document Center, PA Alfred Meyer; Transcript of a judgment of the Spruchkammer Berlin of 17 September 1958, in: Zentrale Stelle der Landesjustizverwaltungen Ludwigsburg (now: BArch Außenstelle Ludwigsburg), File Alfred Meyer.

6 Archive of the Rheinische Friedrich-Wilhelms-Universität Bonn, Immatrikulationsmanual no 590 and de-registration document together with list of courses taken by Alfred Meyer; Alfred Meyer's CV, in: Meyer, "Volkskrieg".

7 For Meurer: D. Blumenwitz, Der Würzburger Rechtsgelehrte Christian Meurer, S. 11-13.

8 See *Das Werk des Untersuchungsausschusses der Verfassungsgebenden Deutschen Nationalversammlung und des Deutschen Reichstages 1919–1928, Dritte Reihe: Völkerrecht im Weltkrieg* (Berlin, 1927), vols. 1 and 3.

9 Soest City Archives: Collection of documents on Alfred Meyer; private collection of Dorothee Z: Diary-type notes of Alfred Meyer; Landesarchiv NRW, Abteilung Ostwestfalen-Lippe, Einleitung des Findbuchs zu Bestand D 72, Meyer estate.

10 *National-Zeitung*, 22 June 1936; for Schumacher: Heinz-Jürgen Priamus, *Meyer: Zwischen Kaisertreue und NS-Täterschaft: Biographische Konturen eines deutschen Bürgers* (Schriftenreihe des Instituts für Stadtgeschichte, Beiträge, vol. 14) (Essen, 2011), 124 et seq.

11 Bundesarchiv Berlin, Berlin Document Center, PA Alfred Meyer and PA Böhmer and Mietz; Münster State Archive, Gauschatzamt, 176 and 178.

12 On Meyer's early career: Heinz-Jürgen Priamus, "Die Reihen noch nicht fest geschlossen: Entstehung und Aufstieg der NSDAP in Gelsenkirchen," in *Deutschlandwahn und Wirtschaftskrise: Gelsenkirchen auf dem Weg in den Nationalsozialismus, vol. 1: Die antidemokratische Allianz formiert sich*, ed. H-J. Priamus (Essen, 1991), 75–130.

13 Priamus, *Meyer*, 163–69.

14 On Rosenberg and his non-political ideas and activities, in particular in the Foreign Policy Office of the NSDAP: Ernst Piper, *Alfred Rosenberg: Hitlers Chefideologe* (Munich, 2005), 285–322.

15 On the Lippe election campaign: Jutta Ciolek-Kümper, *Wahlkampf in Lippe: Die Wahlkampfpropaganda der NSDAP zur Landtagswahl am 15. Januar 1933* (Munich, 1976).

16 Ciolek-Kümper, *Wahlkampf in Lippe*, 130 and 140 et seq.; E. Fröhlich, ed., *Die Tagebücher von Joseph Goebbels: Aufzeichnungen 1923–1941*, 14 vols. (Munich, 1998–2006), 82 and 85 (entries for 14 and 19 December 1932).

17 *National-Zeitung*, 17 May 1933; see, for the preceding controversy: Hans-Jürgen Sengotta, *Der Reichsstatthalter in Lippe 1933 bis 1939: Reichsrechtliche Bestimmungen und politische Praxis* (Detmold, 1976), 62 et seq.

18 On the role of Statthalter, see: Peter Hüttenberger, *Die Gauleiter: Studie zum Wandel des Machtgefüges in der NSDAP* (Schriftenreihe der Vierteljahrshefte für Zeitgeschichte, vol. 19) (Stuttgart, 1969), 76 et seq.

19 Hüttenberger, *Gauleiter*, 78; Sengotta, *Reichsstatthalter in Lippe*, 398 et seq.

20 On Kolbow: Karl Teppe, *Provinz, Partei, Staat: Zur provinziellen Selbstverwaltung im Dritten Reich, untersucht am Beispiel Westfalens* (Münster, 1977), 30–36; see also M. Dröge, ed., *Die Tagebücher Karl-Friedrich Kolbows (1889–1945): Nationalsozialist der ersten Stunde und Landeshauptmann der Provinz Westfalen* (Forschungen zur Regionalgeschichte, vol. 63) (Paderborn, 2009), particularly at 13 and 380; on Stangier: Priamus, *Meyer*, 132 et seq.

21 See Landesarchiv NRW (North Rhein Westphalia), section for Westphalia, Oberpräsidium 5221, 5223, 5235, 5236, 5237; on the development of the role under Meyer see also Priamus, *Meyer*, 312–24; on the question of the controversy over the role of the CdZ see generally Priamus, *Meyer*, 474, footnote 157.

22 Landesarchiv NRW, Westphalia section, Oberpräsidium 5221 and 5230; see Priamus, *Meyer*, 324–32.

23 Priamus, *Meyer*, 201–8.

24 *Völkischer Beobachter* and *National-Zeitung*, 18 November 1941; Dieter Rebentisch, *Führerstaat und Verwaltung im Zweiten Weltkrieg: Verfassungsentwicklung und Verwaltungspolitik 1939–1945* (Stuttgart, 1989), 309–31; International Military Tribunal [IMT], *Der Prozeß gegen die Hauptkriegsverbrecher vor dem Internationalen Militärgerichtshof (IMT): Nürnberg 14. November 1945—1. Oktober 1946, gemäß den Weisungen des Internationalen Militärgerichtshofes vom Sekretariat des Gerichtshofes unter der Autorität des Obersten Kontrollrats für Deutschland veröffentlicht*, 42 vols., ed. L.D. Egbert and P.A. Joosten (Nuremberg, 1947–49), vol. XXIX, doc. 1997-PS, 235 et seq.; ibid., doc. 1019-PS, "Anhang zur Denkschrift Nr. 2," 18 et seq.; ibid., vol. XXVI, 559 et seq.; Staatsarchiv Nürnberg, Staatsanwaltschaft Nürnberg-Fürth, Prov. 2638/VI, sheet 142 et seq.: interrogation of Dr Bräutigam, 14 January 1948; ibid. Prov. 2638/VIII, vol. 6: Transcript of the interrogation of Dr Gerhard Klopfer of 18 March 1949.

25 Alfred Rosenberg, *Letzte Aufzeichnungen* (Göttingen, 1955), 149.

26 Transcript of radio speech in: *National-Zeitung*, 18 September 1942.

27 See, for example: National-Zeitung, 27 August 1943

28 Christopher R. Browning, *The Final Solution and the German Foreign Office: A Study of Referat D III of Abteilung Deutschland 1940–1943* (New York, 1978), 70.

29 Staatsarchiv Nürnberg, Staatsanwaltschaft Nürnberg-Fürth, Prov. 2638/I, Indictments against Leibbrandt and Bräutigam, 20, and Leibbrandt and Bräutigam's statements in defence, 53.

30 Staatsarchiv Nürnberg, Staatsanwaltschaft Nürnberg-Fürth, Prov. 2638/I, Application by Leibbrandt's defense counsel, Dr Alfred Seidl, of 30 March 1950 to have the proceedings against Leibbrandt dismissed; ibid., Prov. 2638/II, Hanover Prosecutor's investigation report of 9 December 1961 in the criminal proceedings against Wetzel (Az. 2 Js 499/61), 2, 4 and 11; ibid., Prov. 2638/VI, Evidence of Otto Bräutigam, 15 January 1948, sheet 156; ibid, Prov. 2638/VIII, Prosecution's summary of the proceedings up to that point against Leibbrandt of 9 July 1949, sheet 148 et seq.; Roger Uhle, "Neues Volk und reine Rasse: Walter Gross und das Rassenpolitische Amt der NSDAP 1934–1945" (Ph.D. dissertation, Rheinisch-Westfälische Technische Hochschule Aachen, 1999).

31 Staatsarchiv Nürnberg, Staatsanwaltschaft Nürnberg-Fürth, Prov. 2638/I, Criminal Proceedings Js 1678/49 and Indictment of Leibbrandt and Bräutigam, 14; ibid., Prov. 2638/II, Staatsanwaltschaft Hannover, Criminal Proceedings 2 Js 499/61; ibid., Prov. 2638/III, Letter from Wetzel of 25 October 1941, sheets 1–4; Uhle, "Neues Volk," 217; see Gerald Reitlinger, *Ein Haus auf Sand gebaut: Hitlers Gewaltpolitik in Russland 1941–1944* (Hamburg, 1962), 299 et seq.

32 Facsimile of the Wannsee Protocols, in: Mark Roseman, *Die Wannsee-Konferenz: Wie die NS-Bürokratie den Holocaust organisierte* (Berlin, 2002), 170–84; see. Kurt Pätzold and Erika Schwarz, *Tagesordnung: Judenmord: Die Wannsee-Konferenz am 20. Januar 1942: Eine Dokumentation zur Organisation der 'Endlösung'* (Berlin, 1992), passim.

33 Wannsee minutes, 15, in: Roseman, *Wannsee-Konferenz*, 170–84.

34 Robert M.W. Kempner, *Eichmann und Komplizen* (Zurich, Stuttgart and Vienna, 1961), 165 et seq.

35 Bundesarchiv, R 6/74; see Kempner, *Eichmann und Komplizen*, 167.

36 Kempner, *Eichmann und Komplizen*, 167. See the comments on the meetings of 26 March and 27 October 1942, in: Staatsarchiv Nürnberg, Staatsanwaltschaft Nürnberg-Fürth, Prov. Nr. 2638/VIII, sheet 156 et seq.: prosecution's summary of the proceedings up to that point against Leibbrandt of 9 July 1949; ibid., Prov. Nr. 2638/II: prosecution's Investigation Report to the Landgericht Hannover in Criminal proceedings 2 Js 499/61 of 9 December 1961, sheet 45.

37 Priamus, *Meyer*, 389–417.

38 On the decline and winding down of the RMO: Priamus, *Meyer*, 419–25.

39 Priamus, *Meyer*, 425–27.

Bibliography

Browning, Christopher R. *Die "Endlösung" und das Auswärtige Amt: Das Referat D III der Abteilung Deutschland 1940–1943*. Darmstadt: WBG, 2010. [English: *The Final Solution and the German Foreign Office: A Study of Referat D III of Abteilung Deutschland 1940–1943*. New York: Holmes & Meier, 1978.]

Ciolek-Kümper, Jutta. *Wahlkampf in Lippe: Die Wahlkampfpropaganda der NSDAP zur Landtagswahl am 15. Januar 1933*. Munich: Verlag Dokumentation, 1976.

Däbritz, W. "Carl Julius Schulz, der Begründer des Blechwalzwerks Schulz, Knaudt & Co." *Essener Beiträge* 46 (1928): 279–93.

Dröge, M. ed. *Die Tagebücher Karl-Friedrich Kolbows (1889–1945): Nationalsozialist der ersten Stunde und Landeshauptmann der Provinz Westfalen*. Paderborn: Schöningh, 2009.

Fröhlich, E. ed. *Die Tagebücher von Joseph Goebbels: Aufzeichnungen 1923–1941*. Munich: Saur, 1998–2006.

Hüttenberger, Peter. *Die Gauleiter: Studie zum Wandel des Machtgefüges in der NSDAP*. Stuttgart: Deutsche Verlags-Anstalt, 1969.

International Military Tribunal [IMT]. *Der Prozeß gegen die Hauptkriegsverbrecher vor dem Internationalen Militärgerichtshof (IMT): Nürnberg 14. November 1945 – 1. Oktober 1946, gemäß den Weisungen des Internationalen Militärgerichtshofes vom Sekretariat des Gerichtshofes unter der Autorität des Obersten Kontrollrats für Deutschland veröffentlicht*, edited by L.D. Egbert and P.A. Joosten. Nuremberg, 1947–1949.

Kempner, Robert M.W. *Eichmann und Komplizen*. Zurich, Stuttgart and Vienna: Europaverlag, 1961.

Meyer, Alfred. "Der belgische Volkskrieg." Ph.D. dissertation, University of Würzburg, 1922.

Pätzold, Kurt and Erika Schwarz. *Tagesordnung: Judenmord: Die Wannsee-Konferenz am 20. Januar 1942: Eine Dokumentation zur Organisation der 'Endlösung.'* Berlin: Metropol, 1992.

Piper, Ernst. *Alfred Rosenberg: Hitlers Chefideologe*. Munich: Blessing, 2005.

Priamus, Heinz-Jürgen. "Die Reihen noch nicht fest geschlossen: Entstehung und Aufstieg der NSDAP in Gelsenkirchen." In *Deutschlandwahn und Wirtschaftskrise: Gelsenkirchen auf dem Weg in den Nationalsozialismus, Teil 1: Die antidemokratische Allianz formiert sich*, edited by H.J. Priamus, 75–130. Essen: Klartext, 1991.

———. *Meyer: Zwischen Kaisertreue und NS-Täterschaft: Biographische Konturen eines deutschen Bürgers*. Essen: Klartext, 2011.

Rebentisch, Dieter. *Führerstaat und Verwaltung im Zweiten Weltkrieg: Verfassungsentwicklung und Verwaltungspolitik 1939–1945*. Stuttgart: Steiner, 1989.

Reitlinger, Gerald. *Ein Haus auf Sand gebaut: Hitlers Gewaltpolitik in Russland 1941–1944*. Hamburg: Rütten & Loening, 1962. [English: *The House Built on Sand: The Conflicts of German Policy in Russia 1939–1945*. New York: Viking Press, 1960.]

Roseman, Marl. *Die Wannsee-Konferenz: Wie die NS-Bürokratie den Holocaust organisierte*. Berlin: Propyläen, 2002. [English: *The Villa, the Lake, the Meeting: Wannsee and the Final Solution*. London: Penguin Press, 2002.]

Rosenberg, Alfred. *Letzte Aufzeichnungen*. Göttingen: Plesse, 1955.

Sengotta, Hans-Jürgen. *Der Reichsstatthalter in Lippe 1933 bis 1939: Reichsrechtliche Bestimmungen und politische Praxis*. Detmold: Naturwissenschaftlicher und Historischer Verein für das Land Lippe, 1976.

Teppe, Karl. *Provinz, Partei, Staat: Zur provinziellen Selbstverwaltung im Dritten Reich, untersucht am Beispiel Westfalens*. Münster: Aschendorff, 1977.

Uhle, Roger. "Neues Volk und reine Rasse: Walter Gross und das Rassenpolitische Amt der NSDAP 1934–1945." Ph.D. dissertation, Rheinisch-Westfälische Technische Hochschule Aachen, 1999.

Wehler, Hans-Ulrich. *Das deutsche Kaiserreich 1871–1918*. Göttingen: Vandenhoeck & Ruprecht, 1994 [first published 1973]. [English: *The German Empire: 1871–1918*. Warwickshire: Berg Publishers, 1985.]

Wessel, Horst A. *Kontinuität im Wandel: 100 Jahre Mannesmann 1890–1990*. Gütersloh: Mannesmann-AG, 1990.

15

Erich Neumann

Plenipotentiary for the Four
Year Plan

A Colorless, Compliant Prussian

Christoph Kreutzmüller

Illustration 15.1 Unknown photographer,
undated (1932/33), Ullstein, 00213663.

"Then the whole business started. On 10.5.1945 I was arrested," complained Erich Neumann during an interrogation in Nuremberg on 10 January 1947.[1] But the "whole business" had of course started much earlier: Though later largely overlooked by historical research, the man who became undersecretary to the plenipotentiary for the Four Year Plan was the longest-serving government official, alongside Wilhelm Kritzinger, to attend the Wannsee Conference.[2] In the following, the stages of his almost unbroken career as a government official will be traced, from the German Empire to National Socialism. As well as Neumann's role in the genocide of the Jews, the question of why he was released from government service at his own request before 1945—the only participant of the Wannsee Conference to do so—will be given special consideration.

In the Service of Prussia

Adolf Walter Erich Neumann was born in the textile-manufacturing town of Forst in the Prussian province Brandenburg to a factory owner, Friedrich Wilhelm Neumann, and his wife, Auguste Lydia, and baptized a Protestant. Having attended the local elementary school and a high school for boarders, in 1911 he enrolled to study law and economy in Freiburg, where he joined a student fraternity. He later continued his studies in Leipzig and Halle. Like nine other participants in the Wannsee Conference, then, Neumann was a trained lawyer.

Immediately after completing his first state examination in August 1914, he was drafted for military service. He fought at the Eastern Front and was promoted to the rank of Lieutenant, as was standard procedure for high-school graduates, but was released from active service in 1917 due to a severe hand injury. Aged twenty-five by this time, he now began his traineeship in the judicial service of the Prussian administration. Having completed his second state examination in October 1920, he joined the Prussian Ministry of the Interior, and was transferred to the Essen District Office a short time later. Neumann's time as a young official in Essen coincided with the Ruhr region's occupation by French and Belgian troops, and it is likely that the experience left an enduring impression on him, as it did on Wilhelm Stuckart. In any case, he "stood the test" in Essen and was appointed senior executive officer *(Regierungsrat)* in the Prussian Ministry for Commerce in late 1923. With the currency reform accomplished and inflation stopped, he was put in charge of savings banks and other public banks. In early 1929 he became ministerial junior assistant secretary *(Ministerialrat)* and head of the—politically charged—department of reparations, subsidies and credits.[3] Although unable to speak any foreign languages, Neumann represented Germany in 1931/32 at the international debt conference in Paris.[4] He obviously performed this tricky task with some skill. A few weeks after the Chancellor Franz von Papen's coup d'etat against the incumbent Social Democratic government of Prussia, Neumann was appointed Permanent Secretary *(Ministerialdirektor)* in the Prussian Ministry of State—head of the Minister-Presidential office—in September 1932.[5] In view of the circumstances, it seems likely that he was promoted for political reasons.[6] When questioned after the war, Neumann admitted his connection with the nationalist party Deutsche Volkspartei (DVP), which had formed an alliance with the Deutsch Nationale Volkspartei, the Nazi Party's later coalition partner, for the parliamentary elections in November 1932. Although he did not deny harboring strong anti-communist feelings, he generally styled himself a non-political official whose "goal . . . it was to serve the people and the state equally by performing practical tasks, regardless of which party was currently at the helm."[7] As he himself admitted, this attitude enabled him to "occupy offices under quite different governments."[8]

At the Service of the Plenipotentiary for the Four Year Plan

Despite his purported non-political attitude, Neumann joined the Nazi Party in May 1933—one month after Hermann Göring was officially

appointed Minister-President of Prussia. Although his party membership certainly helped his career along, he joined too late to reach a
particularly high standing within the party hierarchy. Neumann was
(and remained) a latecomer, a "mayfly," in the eyes of the old guard.[9]
The situation in the SS, which Permanent Secretary Neumann joined
in August 1934, shortly after the murder of Ernst Röhm and other SA
leaders, was slightly different. By 1939 Neumann had risen to become
SS-Brigadeführer, equivalent to a higher rank than colonel in the army.[10]
Neumann was evidently also keen to climb rank in the army, having
assigned himself to several weeks' military exercises in summer 1935,
1936 and 1937, despite his injured hand, and gaining promotion to the
rank of Reserve Cavalry Master.[11]

In civilian life, too, Permanent Secretary Neumann was getting
ahead. In May 1933 he became a member of the German Society for
Public Works' supervisory board and a member of the Reich Debt
Committee. In September 1933 he was promoted to the Prussian
State Council, a prestigious advisory body under Hermann Göring,
along with his fellow Prussian officials Roland Freisler and Wilhelm
Stuckart.[12] A short time later he joined the supervisory board of the
state-owned trusteeship administration Deutsche Revisions- und
Treuhand AG, which participated as an auditing firm in some cases
of the so-called Aryanization; that is, the forced takeover of Jewish-
owned businesses by non-Jews.[13] At the same time, Neumann was
dealing with changes to the constitution of the city of Berlin. At Julius
Lippert's inauguration into office as state commissioner of the Reich
capital, on 30 April 1934, he stood on the steps of the Rotes Rathaus
city hall, forming a guard of honor with Göring's undersecretary Paul
Körner.[14] Neumann was also involved in the debt relief proceedings
that attended Graf Wolf-Heinrich von Helldorf's installation as chief
of police in Berlin.[15] In addition to all this, Neumann was responsible
for preparing administrative reforms. But it is doubtful whether he
pursued the latter task with any zeal, as the reforms aimed to merge
the Prussian ministries with the Reich ministries and thus ultimately
render the Prussian administration superfluous. In the event, the project foundered, partly due to Hitler, who "absolutely did not want a
Reich reform in writing."[16]

Neumann's career received another boost when Göring was promoted to Plenipotentiary for the Four Year Plan, as officially announced
at the Nuremberg Rally in September 1936. In this capacity, the latter
unceremoniously made the Prussian State Ministry, which he controlled, into the central office for the Four Year Plan. Within this new
authority, housed in the former Prussian House of Lords on Leipziger

Straße (where the Bundesrat, the upper house of the German parliament, now has its premises), Neumann was responsible for coordinating the various departments as well as directing the foreign currency business group.[17] With the collapse of the global economy, and Germany's declaration of a payment moratorium in 1931, the Reichsmark had stopped being a feely convertible, international currency. In view of the country's enormous foreign debts, the only way it could import vital goods was by generating foreign currency funds through exports. But intense rearmament was devouring not only imported resources, such as oil and metals, but also those which Germany could otherwise have exported, triggering a supply crisis in summer 1935. The regime responded by publicizing the slogan "butter or guns" and — with Neumann's help — by dispersing the country's last reserves.[18] This scenario explains not only the rise of the office of the Four Year Plan to become one of the "most important centres of power in the Nazi state,"[19] but also the high importance of the allocation of foreign currencies — and hence Neumann's department — for the economy.[20] Within the office of the Four Year Plan, Neumann, like Stuckart, was a member of the general council, which acted as the central control and management body.[21]

Despite postwar statements to the contrary, the Plenipotentiary for the Four Year Plan obviously valued Neumann's "sober and somewhat stuffy manner."[22] Göring preferred the company of officers, and Neumann had also served as an officer. In June 1937, Neumann accompanied Göring on a visit to Fascist Italy,[23] after which Göring had him appointed undersecretary by Hitler on 23 July 1938, "to process commissions in certain fields of the Four Year Plan."[24] From this point at the latest, Neumann had direct, personal access to the second-in-command in the Nazi state. Indeed, Neumann can be seen in the background on many press photographs of Göring's public appearances as Prussian Minister-President or Plenipotentiary for the Four Year Plan. But as well as standing in the background, he was "present at all the crucial talks."[25] On 14 October 1938, for instance, Neumann took part in the conference at which Göring called for the "Jewish Question [to be] solved as quickly as possible."[26]

Less than a month later, on 12 November 1938, Neumann, like Eichmann, Freisler, Heydrich and Stuckart, was present at the high-level conference in the Ministry of Aviation, when Göring announced that the "Jewish Question should now, once and for all, be summed up and resolved one way or another." During a phone call a few days previously, Hitler had charged him with "outlining the crucial steps."[27] Although Neumann did not contribute verbally to this conference — at

Illustration 15.2 Neumann forming part of the guard of honor on the steps of Berlin Cathedral at Hermann Göring's marriage in April 1935. Georg Pahl, 15 April 1935, BArch Koblenz, 102-16796.

least not according to the surviving minutes—the pogrom had serious implications for his field of work. This was because hundreds of thousands of Jews could only be driven out of Germany and occupied Austria, or made to "emigrate," if they were given some foreign assets to do so. But since the Reich was suffering an acute lack of foreign currencies, and its sparse reserves were almost exclusively earmarked for purchasing resources necessary for rearmament, the Jews' situation in the Reich grew increasingly desperate. Negotiations over the allocation of foreign currencies for emigration, which Wilhelm Stuckart participated in, were conducted by the Reich Ministry of Economics, so Neumann did remain in the background here.[28] Yet, following the resignation of Reichsbank president Hjalmar Schacht, Göring did not send his undersecretary Neumann but head of section Helmuth Wohlthat to attend negotiations concerning the emigration of Jews from Germany with the director of the Evian Conference, George Rublee.[29] Ostensibly signaling the importance he attributed the negotiations, Göring gave Heydrich free rein to set up a central agency for Jewish emigration in Berlin, following the Viennese example, and thus increase the pressure on Jews at the same time.[30]

Following Prague's occupation by the German army, Neumann was also involved in negotiations concerning the takeover of the Petschek business group. Eventually, the Reich authorities expropriated the Jewish brothers Julius and Ignatz Petschek by fabricating a tax debt and transferring large parts of their major coal company to the state-run industrial conglomerate Reichswerke Hermann Göring. A short time later, the Main Trustee Office for the East (*Haupttreuhandstelle Ost*) was set up within the Office of the Four Year Plan, which became a key institution involved in destroying the economic existence of Polish Jews.[31] There is no evidence to show how closely Neumann was involved in this process. But he certainly received the "guidelines for procedure toward Jews," issued in September 1939, in which Heydrich gave orders for Jews to be rounded up in ghettos "in anticipation of the final goal."[32] Neumann profited personally, moreover, from the destruction of Jewish economic existence. In early 1940 he rented a villa for himself, his wife Hildegard and their three children near the Botanical Gardens in Berlin, which the previous owner, a Jewish woman named Margarete Grünfeld, had been forced to sell to the state in order to emigrate to Great Britain.[33]

Neumann, like Kritzinger and Stuckart, took part in the first meeting of the ministerial council for the defense of the Reich (*Ministerrat für Reichsverteidigung*), at which many new regulations were passed, on 1 September 1939.[34] As Germany proceeded with military expansion, Neumann, as undersecretary to the Plenipotentiary for the Four Year Plan, cooperated on plans for infiltrating and harnessing the economies of the occupied countries. In 1940, for instance, he intervened in a disagreement between Dresdner Bank and Deutsche Bank over which of the two would take over which banks in Belgium and the Netherlands.[35] Four months later he also participated in negotiations concerning the removal of foreign currency exchange barriers between the German Reich and the occupied Netherlands.[36] In January 1941, Neumann published an article on the "goals of our economic policy" in the German-language newspaper for the Netherlands, *Deutsche Zeitung in den Niederlanden*. While stressing the absolute supremacy of the Reich following the "victory of German arms," he also warned that "not even Europe as a whole [can], as one obviously thought in the exuberance of feelings, become self-sufficient through the exchange of goods within Europe."[37] One month later, he published another article, stressing that a return to free market economy would not be likely even after the war.[38] Another month later, in March 1941, Neumann gave a talk at the Berlin academy of administration, defending the concept of an integrated, greater Germanic economy (*Großraumwirtschaft*) spanning occupied Europe. According to him, the global economy's division of responsibilities was "politically highly dangerous. This is because it stretches a country's economic reach beyond the borders of its state territory to encompass areas that are not under the military control of the country. National economies with widely diverse state and economic territories are therefore, for better or worse, linked to the continued existence of the old order."[39]

At the same time, Neumann consulted closely with Heydrich on plans to gain greater control over the British-Dutch Unilever/ Leverbrother group.[40] The acting enemy asset custodian, Karl Blessing, was dismissed, but Neumann had him transferred to the board of the oil company he had been instrumental in founding, Kontinental Öl AG.[41] Neumann was particularly concerned about setting up this company to exploit the oil reserves in Romania and the occupied territories of the Soviet Union as a public-private partnership, as we would say today, with the participation of the major German banks.[42] During the Nuremberg trials, Neumann still justified its founding as a response to German losses caused by the Treaty of Versailles.[43] As the German army marched into the Soviet Union, Neumann became a member of the executive staff for the economy in the East *(Wirtschaftsführungsstab Ost)*, through which Göring intended to organize the economic exploitation of the occupied territories.[44] As such, he inevitably played a part in the Nazis' murderous, racist plans for re-ordering the continent, known as the Generalplan Ost.

The Genocide of the Jews and the Wannsee Conference

The question of how significant a role Neumann played in planning the mass murder of Jews cannot be answered with any certainty from the information still available. But it is known that he was precisely informed of the measures. When Heydrich issued guidelines for the Security Police on the "Jewish Question in the occupied territory" on 21 September 1939, Neumann, along with Stuckart, was among the small circle to receive a circular letter also informing them.[45] Interestingly, the notice of 31 July 1941 on the "Final Solution to the Jewish Question" was not written on Göring's letter paper but by Heydrich on a plain sheet without a letterhead. Yet, Heydrich certainly did not have to call on Neumann to get Göring's signature, as he had a direct line to the *Reichsmarschall* himself. But when it came to issuing invitations to the conference, Heydrich could not overlook Neumann. For one, it would have been a slight to Göring, whom he had his position as organizer of the "total solution of the Jewish Question" to thank. And second, it was clear that the systematic murder of the Jews would have repercussions for the economy, and so increase the importance of the "Super Ministry of Economics," soon to become the Office of the Four Year Plan. Heydrich certainly also regarded Neumann's experience of dealing with economies in the Eastern territories as useful. Considered Göring's informer and mouthpiece, Neumann was not expected to harbor any fundamental misgivings.[46] In any case, he was certainly not summoned in his capacity as a representative of the Reich railways, as has been suggested by some historians. The railways *(Reichsbahn)* and the Ministry of Transport were already deeply implicated in the murder program by this point and had firmly established contacts to liaise with the Reich Main Security Office.[47]

Neumann's role at the conference is difficult to define. Eichmann mentioned him only in the margins when interrogated in Jerusalem—but he was not questioned explicitly about the undersecretary in the Four Year Plan Office. Yet on 20 January 1942, Neumann, along with Kritzinger, represented the old, Prussian administrative elite and so contributed to the "success" of the conference by his mere presence. There are two paragraphs in the minutes that point to his attendance: first, in a "brief review," filling two pages of the minutes, Heydrich talked relatively in depth about the correlation between emigration and foreign assets— familiar ground to Neumann. Emigration had hitherto cost foreign exchange, which had to be deducted from the Four Year Plan's funds for importing resources. But Heydrich had set up the Central Office for Jewish Emigration, which he now presented to the conference attendees. Having already taken 9.5 million dollars, Heydrich maintained, it contributed to saving the foreign exchange balance. However, since emigration had been stopped on Himmler's orders, it was no longer a significant economic factor.[48] Second, Neumann himself spoke, as noted at the end of the Protocol: "With regard to the effect of the evacuation of Jews on economic life, undersecretary Neumann explained that the Jews currently deployed as labor in war-relevant industries cannot be evacuated before replacements have become available."[49] Neumann did not, then, argue for not deporting Jewish slave laborers for the duration of the war (which he certainly could have done) but only for deporting them after all the others. Heydrich assured him this would be the case as, he pointed out, it followed the common practice for deportations from the Reich.[50] The deportations from Germany certainly followed this logic—a prime example is the so-called factory campaign (Fabrikaktion). The Office of the Four Year Plan was also invited to each of the follow-up conferences, where it was represented by Neumann's then deputy, Eberhard Liegner.[51]

In parallel with Albert Speer's meteoric rise, however, the significance of the Four Year Plan was diminishing, and Neumann eventually became "superfluous."[52] On 1 August 1942, he was released from government service at his own request. Without losing his entitlement to an official's pension, he became general manager of the German Potassium Syndicate, which he had first encountered during the negotiations concerning the takeover of the Petschek group.[53] For his new job, he moved from Berlin, which was increasingly the target of Allied bombs, to the far more peaceful town of Uelzen, 100 km north-east of Hanover.[54] Assistant secretary Friedrich Gramsch took over his post as director of the foreign exchange business group. In 1944, "Herr Staatssekretär Neumann" underwent treatment in Switzerland "following a severe bout of angina pectoris with myocardial infarction."[55] Showing some foresight, he had by this point already unloaded his government bonds in anticipation of Germany's military defeat. Henceforth he invested his not inconsiderable private assets in shares in industry only.[56]

Witness for the Prosecution?

As outlined above, Neumann was briefly interned in Ludwigsburg and later, from June 1946 onward, in Nuremberg. Questioned several times about the economic coherences, the role of individual officials in the economy, and rearmament in the Nazi state, he regularly drove the investigators to distraction. Claiming gaps in his memory and pointing out that he was bound by oath, he refused to make any clear statements. "Do you ever say yes?" Paul Katscher barked at him on 23 January 1947 in the middle of an interrogation that he had begun by noting that the "minutes of our last talk [contained] nothing at all."[57] Another investigator, Siegmund Kauffmann, was driven to sardonic comments: "What do you know . . . apart from an embarrassed smile?"[58] The deputy of the U.S. chief prosecutor, Robert Kempner, followed a different, not necessarily more expedient strategy. Shortly after the discovery of the Wannsee Protocol, he asked Neumann directly whether he had ever been at a conference at Wannsee. When the former undersecretary denied it, Kempner immediately exposed his lie: "Unfortunately, you were there. We have it in black and white. It was on 20 January 1942. If you want to tell the truth, you can write to me."[59] Later, Kempner, who had been dismissed from the Prussian Ministry of the Interior in

1933 because he was Jewish, tried to slip Neumann up by attacking his honor as a "Prussian undersecretary."[60] None of the approaches he tried were successful. "Neumann is a very peculiar person," Kempner noted with a hint of resignation to Paul Körner.[61] Neumann's long-time superior agreed. In his view, Neumann was, "how should one describe it, a difficult character."[62]

In late December 1947, Neumann asked to be transferred from prison to what was known as the witness house, where he hoped to receive better medical treatment for his heart problem. He supported his request with the argument that Göring's personal assistant, Erich Gritzbach, from the town of Forst like himself, "was also in the witness house. If I were to compare myself to him, I would not say that he is a no less important man. In my current situation, it would be a relief for me to get out of here."[63] Eventually, his complaints about the poor state of his health had the desired result. In summer 1948, shortly before the verdict in the IG Farben trial was announced, Göring's former undersecretary was released due to ill health. Neumann returned to his family in Grainau and acted as advisor to the Potassium Syndicate plants located in the West. He died on Good Friday, 23 March 1951, of acute circulatory collapse in Garmisch hospital.[64] A few days later, his widow published a large death notice in memory of a man she described as "undersecretary ret(d), general manager ret(d)," a "loyal father and dearly beloved husband."[65]

The association newspaper of the Freiburg student corps that Neumann had been a member of published an obituary written by his fraternity mentor A.W. Fischer, who praised his "dear corps brother's" achievements: "Every corps is rightly proud of those of its members who earn a special reputation and high esteem by their life's work. Such men are an example to the younger ones."[66] Referring to article 131 of the *Grundgesetz* (the West German constitution), his widow applied for a surviving dependant's pension a short time later. She was supported in her application by Friedrich Gramsch, among others, who introduced her to Robert Hallwachs, the former head of department who ran what amounted to the office for winding up the Prussian state ministry, and helped her to reconstruct her husband's periods of service and portray them in the best possible light.[67] At around the same time, in 1952, the Federation of Persecutees of the Nazi Regime published a first edition of the Wannsee Protocol and filed charges against the participants. Consequently, the Berlin judiciary opened "proceedings against those persons involved in the Wannsee Protocol." But finding that Neumann had "passed away several years ago," in 1956 the public prosecutors turned to investigating Liegner, who had represented

Neumann at the follow-up conferences.[68] Just like his former superior, Liegner, who by this time held a leading position at Frankfurt am Main magistrates' court, claimed that he had only played a subordinate role but successfully. In 1957, the proceedings against him were "closed due to insufficient evidence."[69]

Summary

Who was Erich Neumann? Göring's former press aide described Neumann in Nuremberg as "the official type . . . who devoted all his energy to work and punctiliously fulfilled his official duties."[70] Kurt Pätzold and Erika Schwarz characterized Neumann as "colorless."[71] Götz Aly and Susanne Heim have termed Neumann the "second éminence grise behind Göring."[72] At the Wannsee Conference, Neumann, like Kritzinger, embodied the lines of continuity within officialdom, from the old Wilhelmine empire to the "Third Reich." Loyal, reliable and exceedingly ambitious, he knew how to make the most of the opportunities the Nazi regime offered him. Hence by the mid 1930s he had become one of the "big linkers" who knew almost all the important people, forged contacts and could even translate Göring's off the cuff decisions into bureaucratic nomenclature.

Though Neumann was certainly not a brash "Sieg Heil" shouter, he had enough views in common with Nazi ideology to find his place in the regime—from his pronounced anti-communism to his equally marked opposition to the stipulations of the Treaty of Versailles. His adaptability was evident in the fact that, while he named his third child, born in 1938, Hans Adolf, he sold all his government bonds in 1944 because he knew they would become worthless in the case of Germany's defeat. Whether this professional Prussian bureaucrat was anti-Semitic cannot be ascertained from the few surviving sources. But he certainly played a crucial role in supporting the Nazis' anti-Semitic practices. And unlike Kritzinger, he did not utter a word of regret. The only person Neumann felt sorry for at Nuremberg was himself.

Neumann was the only one of the participants in the Wannsee Conference to voluntarily leave active government service before 1945. Yet he did not do so because he opposed the Nazi regime and its murderous policies but because the Plenipotentiary for the Four Year Plan had lost importance and a job in the economy was simply more lucrative. However, Neumann's decision shows that even high-level ministry officials had ways of withdrawing from the murderous regime. Very few decided to use them.

Christoph Kreutzmüller has been connected to the House of the Wannsee Conference since 1992. He studied in Berlin and the UK and wrote his Ph.D. thesis on German banks in the Netherlands between 1919 and 1945. Having coordinated two extensive research projects on the fate of Jewish owned businesses in Berlin 1930–1945 and on Jews in Berlin 1918–1938 for the Humboldt-University (Berlin), he joined the Jewish Museum in Berlin as a curator for the new permanent exhibition in 2016. Kreutzmüeller's acclaimed study *Final Sale in Berlin: The Destruction of Jewish Commercial Activity 1930–1945* was published in 2015 by Berghahn. Other publications include *Berlin 1933–1945*, Munich (Siedler) 2013 (with Michael Wildt) and *National Economies: Volks-Wirtschaft, Racism and Economy in Europe between the Wars*, Newcastle (Cambridge Scholars Publishing) 2015 (with Michael Wildt and Moshe Zimmermann).

Notes

1 Cited from the minutes of an interrogation of Erich Neumann, 10 January 1947, IfZ, ZS 1259.
2 See Kurt Pätzold and Erika Schwarz, *Tagesordnung: Judenmord: Die Wannsee-Konferenz am 20. Januar 1942: Eine Dokumentation zur Organisation der 'Endlösung'* (Berlin, 1992), 202–3.
3 CV Erich Neumann, 15 September 1947, IfZ, ZS 1259.
4 Ralf Banken, *Edelmetallmangel und Großraubwirtschaft: Die Entwicklung des deutschen Edelmetallsektors im "Dritten Reich" 1933–1945* (Jahrbuch für Wirtschaftsgeschichte. Beihefte, vol. 13) (Berlin, 2009), 727.
5 He thus "skipped" the post of "Ministerialdirigent." Letter from Robert Hallwachs to Friedrich Heinrich Neumann, 20 August 1951, in: Geheimes Preußisches Staatsarchiv (GPStA), HA I 90 A, Jüngere Registratur, 2469.
6 See Christopher Clark, *Iron Kingdom: The Rise and Fall of Prussia, 1600–1947* (London, 2006), 649–53.
7 CV Erich Neumann, 15 September 1947, IfZ, ZS 1259. Cf. Alfred Kube, *Pour le mérite und Hakenkreuz: Hermann Göring im Dritten Reich* (Munich, 1987), 59; see also Werner Maser, *Hermann Göring: Hitlers janusköpfiger Paladin: Die politische Biografie* (Berlin, 2000), 217.
8 CV Erich Neumann, 15 September 1947, IfZ, ZS 1259.
9 On these Nazi Party latecomers, known as "Maikäfer" in German, see Björn Weigel, "'Märzgefallene' und Aufnahmestopp im Frühjahr 1933: Eine Studie über den Opportunismus," in *Wie wurde man Parteigenosse? Die NSDAP und ihre Mitglieder*, ed. W. Benz (Frankfurt am Main, 2009), 91–109.
10 Information from: Deutsche Dienststelle für die Benachrichtigung der nächsten Angehörigen von Gefallenen der ehemaligen deutschen Wehrmacht (WAST), 8 October 2015.

11 "Eintrag SS-Führerkartei"; "Fragebogen zur Ergänzung der SS-Führerkartei," 22 October 1936, BArch B, BDC, SS-O, Neumann, Erich. See SS-Dienstaltersliste der Schutzstaffel der NSDAP, Stand 9 November 1944, Berlin, 1945, 26.

12 File card on Erich Neumann, undated (1933), GPStA, HA I 90 A, Jüngere Registratur, 2469; see also *Preußisches Staatshandbuch für das Jahr 1935* 139 (1935): 35 et seq.

13 "Protokoll einer Vernehmung von Erich Neumann," 26 November 1947, IfZ, ZS 1259. On the Deutsche Revisions- und Treuhand AG, see Frank Pega, "Die Tätigkeit der Deutschen Revisions- und Treuhand AG von 1925 bis 1945" (Ph.D. dissertation, Ludwig-Maximilians-University, Munich, 2009), 236–60.

14 Photograph by an unknown photographer, 30 April 1934, Landesarchiv Berlin (LAB), Bild 110680. See Christoph Kreutzmüller, "Die Verfassung und Verwaltung der Hauptstadt," in *Berlin 1933–1945*, ed. C. Kreutzmüller and M. Wildt (Munich, 2013), 51–67.

15 Letter from Erich Neumann to Graf Wolf-Heinrich von Helldorf, 20 August 1935, BArch, SA/A/001.

16 "Protokoll einer Vernehmung von Friedrich Gramsch," 15 July 1947, IfZ, ZS 717.

17 "Göring's Mitarbeiter für die Durchführung des Vierjahresplans," *Deutsche Allgemeine Zeitung*, 24 October 1936; "Erster Erlass des Ministerpräsidenten Göring über die Durchführung des Vierjahresplans, 22 Oktober 1936," *Der Vierjahresplan. Zeitschrift für nationalsozialistische Wirtschaftspolitik* 1(1) (January 1937). See also Adam Tooze, *The Wages of Destruction: The Making and Breaking of the Nazi Economy* (London, 2006), 214–30.

18 "Protokoll einer Vernehmung von Erich Neumann," 21 March 1947, IfZ, ZS 1259. See also Ludolf Herbst, *Das nationalsozialistische Deutschland 1933–1945: Die Entfesselung der Gewalt: Rassismus und Krieg* (Frankfurt am Main, 1996), 119–29.

19 Götz Aly and Susanne Heim, *Vordenker der Vernichtung: Auschwitz und die deutschen Pläne für eine neue europäische Ordnung* (Hamburg, 1991), 49.

20 "Devisenwirtschaft im Angelpunkt der Wirtschaftspolitik," *Der Vierjahresplan: Zeitschrift für nationalsozialistische Wirtschaftspolitik* 2, no.1 (January 1938).

21 Aly and Heim, *Vordenker der Vernichtung*, 51.

22 "Eidesstattliche Versicherung Erich Gritzbach," 12 August 1948, IfZ, 1554/54. See also Tooze, *Wages of Destruction*, 225.

23 Index card on Erich Neumann, undated (1936), GPStA, HA I 90 A, Jüngere Registratur, 2469.

24 "Ministerialdirektor Neumann zum Staatssekretär ernannt," *Völkischer Beobachter*, 24 July 1938; also "Staatsekretär Neumann," *Berliner Tageblatt*, 24 Juli 1938. The position was carved out of the Reich budget. See *Preußisches Staatshandbuch für das Jahr 1939* 141 (1939): 4.

25 "Aussage von Friedrich Gramsch," 15 July 1947, IfZ, ZS 717.

26 "Frage von Paul Katscher in einem Verhör mit Paul Körner," 4 March 1947, IfZ, ZS 960 I.

27 "Stenographische Niederschrift der Besprechung über der Judenfrage bei Göring," 12 November 1938, IMT, vol. 28, 499–540, doc. 1816 PS. See also "Protokoll einer Vernehmung von Erich Neumann," 18 November 1947, IfZ, ZS 1259.

28 See especially the minutes of top-level meetings 1938–39, in: SWA, A-13125. See also the minutes of the board meeting on 30 November 1938 concerning the Göring loan: "Das R.W.M. hatte zu einer Besprechung eingeladen, um über die Möglichkeit der Beschaffung einer Anleihe von RM. 300.000.000,- aus jüdischem Vermögen zu beraten. Es war an eine 10jährige Anleihe gedacht, die in Höhe von 15% in Devisen zurückgezahlt werden sollte, wobei die Verzinsung des Devisenbetrages mit 2% p.a. in Aussicht genommen wurde. Die Angelegenheit konnte zu keinem Abschluss gebracht werden," in ibid. See also "Devisen-Verordnung, Notizen," SWA, A-16253.

29 CV Helmuth Wohlthat, 30 April 1948: also statutory declaration in lieu of an oath by Günther Bergemann, 10 April 1948, both in: Hauptstaatsarchiv Düsseldorf, NW 1002-1, 49193. See also Fritz Kieffer, *Judenverfolgung in Deutschland eine innere Angelegenheit? Internationale Reaktionen auf die Flüchtlingsproblematik 1933–1939* (Stuttgart, 2003), 414 et seq.

30 Dorothea Hauser and Christoph Kreutzmüller, "Reichszentrale für jüdische Auswanderung," in *Handbuch des Antisemitismus: Judenfeindschaft in Geschichte und Gegenwart*, ed. W. Benz (Berlin and Boston, MA, 2012), vol. 5, 534–36.

31 Bernhard Rosenkötter, *Treuhandpolitik: Die "Haupttreuhandstelle Ost" und der Raub polnischer Vermögen 1939–1945* (Essen, 2003).

32. Schnellbrief des Chefs der Sicherheitspolizei und die Einsatzgruppenchefs," 21 September 1939, VEJ, vol. 4, Munich 2011, doc. 12, 88–92; also Michael Wildt, *Die Generation des Unbedingten: Das Führungskorps des Reichssicherheitshauptamtes* (Hamburg, 2002), 459 et seq.

33 "Beschluss des Wiedergutmachungsamts," 29 August 1950, LAB, B Rep. 025-01, 712/50. The house was returned to its rightful owner in 1950. See ibid.

34 Maser, *Göring*, 174 et seq.

35 Harold James, "Die Deutsche Bank und die Diktatur," in *Die Deutsche Bank 1870–1995*, ed. L. Gall et al. (Munich, 1995), 377.

36 Christoph Kreutzmüller, *Händler und Handlungsgehilfen: Der Finanzplatz Amsterdam und die deutschen Großbanken (1918–1945)* (Stuttgart, 2005), 123 et seq.

37 "Ziele unserer Wirtschaftspolitik," *Deutsche Zeitung in den Niederlanden*, 18 January 1941.

38 "Wirtschaftslenkung und Unternehmerinitiative," *Deutsche Zeitung in den Niederlanden*, 12 February 1941.

39 "Vortrag Neumann vor der Verwaltungsakademie Berlin," 29 April 1941, BArch B, R 26/I, 6. See also Richard James Overy, *War and Economy in the Third Reich* (Oxford, 2002), 248.

40 "Vermerk Reinhard Heydrichs," 26 March 1941, VEJ, vol. 7, doc. 1, 113–17, here: 115.

41 Christoph Kopper, *Bankiers unterm Hakenkreuz* (Munich and Vienna, 2005), 183–205.

42 "Protokoll einer Vernehmung von Erich Neumann," 26 November 1947, IfZ, ZS 1259.

43 "Aussage Erich Neumann, in einem Verhör Paul Körner," 21 August 1945, IfZ, ZS 1948/56. See also Dietrich Eichholtz, *Krieg um Öl: Ein Erdölimperium als deutsches Kriegsziel 1938–1943* (Leipzig, 2006).

44 Aly and Heim, *Vordenker der Vernichtung*, 64–68.

45 Aly and Heim, *Vordenker der Vernichtung*, ibid.

46 R.ichard James Overy, *Goering* (London, 2000), 128 et seq.

47 Alfred Gottwaldt, "Warum war die Reichsbahn nicht auf der Wannsee-Konferenz vertreten?" in *Die Wannsee-Konferenz am 20. Januar 1942: Dokumente, Forschungsstand, Kontroversen*, ed. N. Kampe and P. Klein (Cologne, 2013), 343.

48 In exceptional cases and on payment of large amounts in foreign currencies emigration was, however, still permitted even after October 1941. See Christoph Kreutzmüller, "An Inconceivable Emigration: Richard Frank's Flight from Germany to Switzerland in 1942," in *Microhistories of the Holocaust* (War and Genocide, vol. 24), ed. T. Bruttman and C. Zalc (New York and Oxford, 2016), 7–17.

49 "Protokoll der Besprechung über die Endlösung der Judenfrage," PArch AA, R. 100857, sheet 180.

50 Aly and Heim, *Vordenker der Vernichtung*, 511. Pätzold and Schwarz, *Tagesordnung: Judenmord*, 55.

51 See note above.

52 Pätzold and Schwarz, *Tagesordnung: Judenmord*, 238.

53 See Norbert Frei et al., *Flick: Der Konzern, die Familie, die Macht* (Munich, 2009), 229–34.

54 Transcript of a letter from the public prosecutor to the director of public prosecutions at the Supreme Court (Kammergericht), 23 January 1957, LAB, B Rep. 058, 4481.

55 Photocopy of the doctor's certificate, Dr Haemmerli-Schindler, Zurich, 27 January 1944, BArch B, R 10-V, 507.

56 Statement of securities deposited at Hardy & Co bank, 3 January 1944 and 2 January 1945, both BArch B, R 10-V, 507.

57 "Protokoll der Vernehmung von Erich Neumann," 23 Januar 1947, IfZ, ZS 1259.

58 "Protokoll der Vernehmung von Erich Neumann," 10 November 1947, IfZ, ZS 1259.

59 "Protokoll der Vernehmung von Erich Neumann," 23 April 1947, IfZ, ZS 1259.

60 See Robert M.W. Kempner, *Ankläger einer Epoche: Lebenserinnerungen* (Frankfurt am Main, Berlin and Vienna, 1983), 314.

61 "Robert Kempner in einem Verhör mit Paul Körner," 6 May 1947, IfZ, ZS 960/2.

62 "Robert Kempner in einem Verhör mit Paul Körner," 6 May 1947, IfZ, ZS 960/2.

63. "Anhang zum Protokoll der Vernehmung von Erich Neumann," 15 December 1947, IfZ, ZS, 1259.
64 See: Sterbebuch des Standesamtes Garmisch Partenkirchen, Eintrag 64, 24 March 1951.
65 "Todesanzeige," *Münchener Merkur*, 27 March 1951. I am grateful to Sebastian Lang, Munich, for pointing this out.
66 "Erich Neumann," *Verbandszeitung der Freiburger Burschenschaft*, Freiburg 1951.
67 Letter from Robert Hallwachs to Rechtsanwalt Otto Recken, GPStA, HA I 90 A, Jüngere Registratur, 2471.
68 "Abschrift eines Briefes des Staatsanwalts an den Generalstaatsanwalt beim Kammergericht," 23 January 1957, LAB, B Rep. 058, 4481.
69 "Verfügung des Staatsanwaltes," 13 September 1957, LAB, B Rep. 058, 4481.
70 "Eidesstattlche Versicherung Erich Gritzbach," 12 August 1948, IfZ, 1554/54.
71 Pätzold and Schwarz, *Tagesordnung: Judenmord*, 202.
72 Aly and Heim, *Vordenker der Vernichtung*, 63.

Bibliography

Aly, Götz and Susanne Heim. *Vordenker der Vernichtung: Auschwitz und die deutschen Pläne für eine neue europäische Ordnung*. Hamburg: Fischer-Taschenbuch-Verlag, 2004 [first published 1991]. [English: *Architects of Annihilation: Auschwitz and the Logic of Destruction*. Princeton, NJ: Princeton University Press, 2002.]

Banken, Ralf. *Edelmetallmangel und Großraubwirtschaft: Die Entwicklung des deutschen Edelmetallsektors im "Dritten Reich" 1933–1945*. Berlin: De Gruyter, 2009.

Clark, Christopher. *Iron Kingdom: The Rise and Fall of Prussia, 1600–1947*. London: Penguin, 2006.

Eichholtz, Dietrich. *Krieg um Öl: Ein Erdölimperium als deutsches Kriegsziel 1938–1943*. Leipzig: Leipziger Universitätsverlag, 2006. [English: *War for Oil: The Nazi Quest for an Oil Empire*. Washington, DC: Potomac Books, 2012.]

Frei, Norbert, Ralf Ahrens, Jörg Osterloh and Tim Schanetzky. *Flick: Der Konzern, die Familie, die Macht*. Munich: Pantheon, 2009.

Gottwaldt, Alfred. "Warum war die Reichsbahn nicht auf der Wannsee-Konferenz vertreten?" In *Die Wannsee-Konferenz am 20. Januar 1942: Dokumente, Forschungsstand, Kontroversen*, edited by N. Kampe and P. Klein, 341–54. Cologne: Böhlau, 2013.

Hauser, Dorothea and Christoph Kreutzmüller. "Reichszentrale für jüdische Auswanderung." In *Handbuch des Antisemitismus: Judenfeindschaft in Geschichte und Gegenwart*, edited by W. Benz, vol. 5, 534–36. Berlin and Boston, MA: De Gruyter Saur, 2012.

Heim, S. and G. Aly, ed. *Die Verfolgung und Ermordung der europäischen Juden durch das nationalsozialistische Deutschland 1933–1945 [VEJ]*. Berlin: Oldenbourg, 2008–.

Herbst, Ludolf. *Das nationalsozialistische Deutschland 1933–1945: Die Entfesselung der Gewalt. Rassismus und Krieg*. Frankfurt on the Main: Suhrkamp, 1996.

International Military Tribunal [IMT]. *Der Prozeß gegen die Hauptkriegsverbrecher vor dem Internationalen Militärgerichtshof (IMT): Nürnberg 14. November 1945 – 1. Oktober 1946, gemäß den Weisungen des Internationalen Militärgerichtshofes vom Sekretariat des Gerichtshofes unter der Autorität des Obersten Kontrollrats für Deutschland veröffentlicht*, edited by L.D. Egbert and P.A. Joosten.Nuremberg, 1947–1949.

James, Harold. "Die Deutsche Bank und die Diktatur." In *Die Deutsche Bank 1870–1995*, edited by L. Gall, G.D. Feldman, H. James, C-L. Holtfrerich and H.E. Büschgen, 315–408. Munich: C.H. Beck, 1995.

Kempner, Robert M.W. *Ankläger einer Epoche: Lebenserinnerungen*. Frankfurt am Main, Berlin and Vienna: Ullstein, 1983.

Kieffer, Fritz. *Judenverfolgung in Deutschland eine innere Angelegenheit? Internationale Reaktionen auf die Flüchtlingsproblematik 1933–1939*. Stuttgart: Steiner, 2003.

Kopper, Christoph. *Bankiers unterm Hakenkreuz*. Munich and Vienna: Hanser, 2005.

Kreutzmüller, Christoph. *Händler und Handlungsgehilfen: Der Finanzplatz Amsterdam und die deutschen Großbanken (1918–1945)*. Stuttgart: Steiner, 2005.

——. "Die Verfassung und Verwaltung der Hauptstadt." In *Berlin 1933–1945*, edited by C. Kreutzmüller and M. Wildt, 51–67. Munich: Siedler, 2013.

——. "An Inconceivable Emigration: Richard Frank's Flight from Germany to Switzerland in 1942." In *Microhistories of the Holocaust*, edited by T. Bruttman and C. Zalc, 7–17. New York and Oxford: Berghahn, 2016.

Kube, Alfred. *Pour le mérite und Hakenkreuz: Hermann Göring im Dritten Reich*. Munich: Oldenbourg, 1987.

Maser, Werner. *Hermann Göring: Hitlers janusköpfiger Paladin: Die politische Biografie*. Berlin: Edition q, 2000.

Overy, Richard James. *Goering*. London: Phoenix Press, 2000.

——. *War and Economy in the Third Reich*. Oxford: Oxford University Press, 2002.

Pätzold, Kurt and Erika Schwarz. *Tagesordnung: Judenmord: Die Wannsee-Konferenz am 20. Januar 1942: Eine Dokumentation zur Organisation der 'Endlösung.'* Berlin: Metropol, 1992.

Pega, Frank. "Die Tätigkeit der Deutschen Revisions- und Treuhand AG von 1925 bis 1945." Ph.D. dissertation, Ludwig-Maximilians-University Munich, 2009.

Rosenkötter, Bernhard. *Treuhandpolitik: Die "Haupttreuhandstelle Ost" und der Raub polnischer Vermögen 1939–1945*. Essen: Klartext, 2003.

Tooze, Adam. *The Wages of Destruction: The Making and Breaking of the Nazi Economy*. London: Allen Lane, 2006.

Weigel, Björn. "'Märzgefallene' und Aufnahmestopp im Frühjahr 1933: Eine Studie über den Opportunismus." In *Wie wurde man Parteigenosse? Die NSDAP und ihre Mitglieder*, edited by W. Benz, 91–109. Frankfurt am Main: Fischer-Taschenbuch-Verlag, 2009.

Wildt, Michael. *Die Generation des Unbedingten: Das Führungskorps des Reichssicherheitshauptamtes*. Hamburg: Hamburger Edition, 2002. [English: *An Uncompromising Generation: The Nazi Leadership of the Reich Security Main Office*. Madison, WI: University of Wisconsin Press, 2009.]

16

WILHELM STUCKART (1902–1953)

Reich Interior Ministry

"A Legal Pedant"

Hans-Christian Jasch

Illustration 16.1 Unknown photographer, 1939, ullstein bild, 00193567.

"What I know is that the gentlemen sat and ate together and then in very blunt terms they talked about the matter without any circumlocution," said Adolf Eichmann in Jerusalem on 24 July 1961 of the Wannsee Conference. "I certainly could not have remembered that if I had not recalled saying to myself at the time: just look at Stuckart, who was always regarded as a legal pedant, punctilious and fussy, and now what a different tone! The language being used here was very unlegalistic . . . (asked which matters were discussed). The talk was of killing, elimination and annihilation."[1] Who was this "legal pedant" who made such an impression on Eichmann?

Stuckart was born in Wiesbaden on 16 November 1902 and christened a Protestant. Like roughly half the participants at the Wannsee Conference, he belonged to the so-called "war youth generation." He was still at secondary school when he joined the youth wing of the radical German National People's Party.[2] He came from humble beginnings: his father was a porter, his mother a charlady. He had to earn a living while a law student in Munich and Frankfurt, working first at MAN and the Nassauische Landesbank, and later for the Jewish law firm Liebmann und Hallgarten in Wiesbaden. He graduated with rare honors, going on to complete a legal clerkship in Wiesbaden and a doctorate in commercial law. Stuckart then became a trial judge and soon applied for leave in order to concentrate on his work for the Nazi Party.[3] He had joined the Party on 1 December 1930, shortly after passing the examination for admission to the bar in November 1930.[4]

The freshly-minted lawyer moved to Stettin (present-day Szczecin). Like Roland Freisler in Kassel and Berlin, he served as a lawyer and legal advisor to the Nazi Party and in 1933 briefly held office as provisional mayor, state commissioner for Pomerania and member of the Pomeranian county council.[5] On 25 August 1932 he wedded 26-year-old Lotte Gertrud Köhl, the daughter of a merchant from Saarbrücken, whom he had met in Wiesbaden. Their marriage marked the start of his upward social mobility.

When the Nazis conquered Pomerania Stuckart served as head of the Gau, Pomerania's legal office, and filled key strategic administrative posts in close cooperation with Kurt Daluege, commissioner at the Prussian Interior Ministry.[6] He also made contact with other acolytes of Hermann Göring, including his state secretary Ludwig Grauert, Prussian finance minister Johannes Popitz and Erich Neumann.[7] Aged thirty-one, he was subsequently made ministerial director of the Prussian Ministry of Education and the Arts in May 1933. Shortly thereafter Göring appointed him state secretary. Like Roland Freisler and Erich Neumann, he was named a member of the Prussian Council of State. Stuckart became state secretary at the newly established Reich Ministry of Science, Education and Culture (REM) in summer 1934. He played a role in the "cleansing" of schools and universities carried out in accordance with the Law on the Restoration of the Career Civil Servant Profession.[8] However, tensions with Bernhard Rust, Minister of Science, Education and National Culture, brought his meteoric career rise to an abrupt end in autumn 1934.[9]

Temporarily stripped of his political influence, Stuckart managed to present Hitler with a radical paper on the state and the Protestant Church in January 1935, along with three draft laws relating to church affairs.[10] After a brief stint as President of the Higher Regional Court in Darmstadt, he was reappointed as general director (ministerial director) titular state secretary to the head of the office for constitutional affairs (I A) at the Reich Interior Ministry (RMdI) on 11 March 1935.[11] He worked in the former Prussian Interior Ministry at Unter den Linden 72. Over the next few years, he dealt with matters ranging from Reich reform and administrative reform[12] to the structuring of Nazi Germany's expansionist policy in accordance with the constitution and international law. This included drafting the law on the reunification of Austria with the German Reich.[13] His reward was reappointment as a fully fledged state secretary at the RMdI on 19 March 1938.[14] In Prague, a year later, he drafted the legal basis for the de facto annexation of so-called "rump Czechoslovakia."[15] Stuckart also established the framework for the invasion of Poland in autumn 1939 with a number

Illustration 16.2 Official photograph by Hitler's personal photographer Heinrich Hoffmann: Stuckart (center, standing) with Chief of the Reich Chancellery Hans-Heinrich Lammers to his left, Reich Minister of the Interior Wilhelm Frick, Martin Bormann and Hitler at Prague Castle, prior to Hitler signing the proclamation to establish the Reich Protectorate of Bohemia and Moravia on 16 March 1939. Photo by Heinrich Hoffmann, 16 March 1939, BpK, no. 30025452.

of directives formalizing Hitler's annexation of western Poland and set up the so-called General Government.[16] He was present on 17 October 1939 when Hitler outlined to a select group his heinous plans for newly subjugated Poland.[17] On 23 October 1939, in strict confidence, Stuckart told other high-ranking Nazi officials at a meeting of state secretaries how Hitler planned to deal with the Polish population.[18]

The ambitious state secretary, who bought the villa Am Sandwerder 28 in Wannsee in 1938 for 65,000 RM, began to draw up administrative plans for the occupied states.[19] He played a leading role in filling administrative posts in the occupied territories.[20] He was also involved in the Nazis' resettlement schemes: in "The Border Between Germany and France," one of his many memoranda, dated 14 June 1940, Stuckart laid out a case for an annexation of French territory, outlining the racist principles that would play a role.[21] Stuckart and his colleagues also developed the most important legal tool of Germanization policy—the decree mandating the German People's List.[22]

Together with the lawyers Reinhard Höhn, Werner Best, Rudolf Lehmann and his counterpart at the Party Chancellery, Gerhard Klopfer, who also participated in the Wannsee Conference, Stuckart published the first edition of the quarterly journal *Reich, Volksordnung, Lebensraum* (RVL) (Reich, Population Order, and Living Space) in autumn 1941. In total six volumes were published over the next two years through the Höhn Institute for State Research on Kleiner Wannsee.[23] The journal served as a platform for debate on the Nazis' racist plans for a New Order and as a bridge between ethnology and imperialistic practice. In May 1942 Stuckart set up the International Academy for State and Administrative Sciences, which took over publication of the journal. The RVL became the institute's organ.[24] Stuckart's tasks and responsibilities at the time when the Wannsee Conference took place are laid out in an organizational chart for his RMdI division. Along with constitutional, legislative and organizational duties, these included "Nationality and Race," the New Order in the West, East and South-East, the Protectorate of Bohemia and Moravia as well as civil defense of the Reich and occupied territories. This lends credibility to his "race expert" Bernhard Lösener's remark that Stuckart's appointment at the RMdI marked the start of a "gradual but marked shift in the balance of power at the ministry." Reich Minister Wilhelm Frick, he said, was a weak character with no interest in his job. Stuckart's nominal superior was Hans Pfundtner, the managing state secretary and a "former conservative" who lacked the support of the Party. In comparison, Stuckart was "talented, effective and ambitious" and soon succeeded in "seizing the reins in the ministry," rapidly becoming "the real minister" who coordinated everything.[25] Stuckart did indeed embody the link between the state and the party. As a member of the Nazi Party and the SS (since 1936) he willingly placed the administration at the service of Nazi ideology. His aim was primarily to defend and maintain its functional capability and therefore his own power against the positions and interests of the party leadership.

Stuckart and the Solution to the "Jewish Question"

The Nazis saw Jewish policy as a key, and therefore prestigious, field. Within this field, Stuckart played a leading role in developing legal tools for the implementation of the policy—legal tools shared between the RMdI and the office of the Deputy Führer, in keeping with the Reich Citizenship Law.[26] In 1935, he and his colleagues collaborated with Party deputies to draw up the Nuremberg Laws and the accompanying executive regulations that represented the core of the Nazis' race legislation. They defined Jewishness and advanced the political disfranchisement of Jews and their systematic marginalization from mainstream society by means of legal bans restricting their contact with non-Jews, including one on extramarital relations.[27] In March 1936 Stuckart became chairman of the Reich Committee for the Protection of German Blood, which issued permits for marriages between so-called "Mischlinge" (persons of mixed-blood) and "full-blooded Germans."[28] On 29 September 1936 Stuckart convened a high-level planning policy meeting to lay out the "basic direction of Jewish policy," the "expulsion of Jews from economic life" and their forced emigration.[29] Along with Neumann and Freisler, the state secretary of the Interior Ministry also took part in Göring's inter-ministerial meeting at the Reich Aviation Ministry on 12 November 1938. Stuckart published articles on the process of political, economic and social disenfranchisement of Jews,[30] writing the preface to his colleague Hans Globke's legal commentary on the Reich Citizenship Law, published by the prestigious C.H. Beck-Verlag in 1936.[31] In the fourth edition of the textbook he co-authored with Rolf Schiedermair *Considerations of Race and Heredity in the Legislation of the Reich*, published in 1943, he wrote:

> The aim of the legislation on race may be regarded as already achieved and consequently such legislation is essentially a closed chapter. It led to the temporary solution of the Jewish problem and at the same time prepared the Final Solution. Many regulations will lose their practical importance as Germany approaches the achievement of the final goal in respect of the Jewish problem.[32]

Bernhard Lösener's memo on a personal conversation with his superior on 19 December 1941 sheds light on Stuckart's position regarding the "Jewish Question."[33] Lösener had complained about the lack of promotions within his office and its steady loss of influence in relation to the Reich Main Security Office (RSHA). He then said he had heard that Jews deported from Berlin had been executed shortly after their arrival near Riga, and requested a transfer from the RMdI. Stuckart's response was that "procedures for evacuated Jews had been decided at a high level" and that Lösener would have to accept it:

> The Final Solution of the Jewish Question has to be viewed from a higher standpoint. In the last few weeks alone, 50,000 German soldiers have fallen on the eastern front; millions more will fall, because, Mr. Lösener, the war will last a very long time. Remember that the Jews are responsible for every German death, for is the fault of the Jews that we have to fight this war. Jewry has forced it upon us. If we strike back with toughness, we have to see the world historical necessity for this toughness and

should not fearfully inquire if this or that Jew who is meeting his fate is personally guilty.[34]

If we are to believe Lösener's memo, this conversation shows that Stuckart was aware that Jews were being murdered before the Wannsee Conference took place, even if he was not aware how systematic the executions were—and that he was not afraid to justify the executions in a professional conversation with a close colleague in theoretical terms. A few weeks earlier, on 25 November 1941, a decree passed on Stuckart's authority became effective, stripping Jews who had fled or been deported of their German citizenship and assets[35] and thereby giving legal cover to their persecution. A day earlier saw Stuckart lunching with Himmler and discussing jurisdiction over Jewish policy. Himmler noted in his diary that day: "Jewish Questions are my area."[36] On 1 December 1941 Stuckart conferred with Reinhard Heydrich and Karl Hermann Frank, who served as HSSPF in Prague and elsewhere in the Protectorate of Bohemia and Moravia. Given that Heydrich conducted a telephone call with Himmler to discuss "the executions in Riga," it seems highly likely that the "Final Solution to the Jewish Question" was also discussed.[37]

Stuckart at the Wannsee Conference

In a statement on the Wannsee Conference made in his defense in Nuremberg in 1947 Stuckart brazenly referred to the "Jewish Question":

> According to the Nuremberg ruling, Hitler tasked Heydrich or rather Himmler with solving the Jewish Question on 31 July 1941. I had no knowledge of this and became aware of it only after the Nuremberg ruling. Like my fellow countrymen, I only became aware of the Jewish transports after the event . . . The police carried out these procedures at all times without my or my office's instruction or knowledge. In 1942 Heydrich unexpectedly invited me to a meeting on 20 January in a building on Lake Wannsee. As far as I recall, he convened the meeting with two aims in mind:
>
> The Governor-General and the Reich Minister for the Occupied Eastern Territories must have raised objections to the scale of the Jewish transports and their resettlement in their territories with the Reich Main Security Office. As I remember, Heydrich told the office that the transports to the East were taking place on specific orders.
>
> The second goal Heydrich hoped to pursue with the conference was a series of changes to the law relating to the questions of half-Jews. During the meeting, he revealed that Hitler had ordered him to resolve this issue. Heydrich explained that he believed the solution was their deportation

and, if need be, their sterilization. As I recall, he proposed that the legal definition of Jewishness be widened to include half-Jews. He further demanded that the law should facilitate divorce between Jews, half-Jews and full-blooded Germans. He apparently convened the meeting to inform the Reich Chancellery, the Party Chancellery and the Reich Interior Ministry of his proposed changes to the law (a new definition of Jewishness and facilitated divorce).[38]

As it happened, there was disagreement at the conference regarding the question of how to deal with people with one or two Jewish grandparents who had not been fully stripped of their German citizenship in the wake of the anti-Jewish laws.[39] Heydrich wanted these people included in the deportations, thus raising an issue of respective powers: the Interior Ministry—and the Party Chancellery (at least as far as German citizens were concerned)—posed the question of jurisdiction, challenging the legal monopoly on defining who fell into this category,[40] estimated at the time to encompass approximately 70,000 to 100,000 people in the Greater German Reich[41] (and many more in the rest of occupied Europe). Lösener's pre-conference preparation for Stuckart dated 4 December 1941 shows that differences of opinion on this issue had existed since spring of that year between representatives of the Reich Main Security Office and Party representatives.[42] Heydrich's demand, in light of the "Final Solution to the Jewish Question," that people with two Jewish grandparents—with a few exceptions—should also be classified Jews, and that the fate of Jewish partners in so-called "mixed marriages" should be decided on a case by case basis, challenged the RMdI's monopoly on the definition of Jewishness. Stuckart's objection, quoted in the Protocol of the meeting, that the practical implementation of these solutions "for purifying mixed marriages and regarding 'Mischling' Questions would entail endless paperwork" therefore seems plausible. From the point of view of Stuckart, who was responsible as chief of staff of the Plenipotentiary General for Administration (GBV) for rationalizing measures and keeping paperwork to a minimum,[43] a broader definition of enemies of the state was problematic not only in terms of the war economy. He feared too that such a blurring of definitions would spread uncertainty in the population. He therefore proposed solving the problem of mixed marriages and half-Jews with forced sterilizations, stressing that "new options must be found for the problem of mixed marriages, so that the law might in effect say: these marriages have been dissolved."[44]

In a secret memo on the "Final Solution to the Jewish Problem" addressed to the participants at the Wannsee Conference and dated 16 March 1942, Stuckart reiterated his view:[45] "The question of the status to be given a Jewish 'Mischling second degree', as discussed in the meeting on 20 January 1942," he wrote, had prompted him "to reevaluate potential solutions to the problem." He went on to stress that there was "utmost clarity and unanimity" regarding the idea that "Jewish blood, even half-Jewish blood, should be eliminated from the European bloodstream." Citing reasons of racial biology, Stuckart argued that "first and foremost," this entailed "preventing any dilution of German or related blood." He pointed out that the RMdI had always considered it "extraordinarily dangerous to send German blood to the opposing side. Our adversaries will put the desirable characteristics of this blood to good use. Once the half-Jews are outside Germany, their high intelligence and education level, combined with their German heredity, will render these individuals born leaders and terrible enemies." His reservations were such, he said, that he "considered classifying half-Jews as full-Jews and therefore deporting them an unacceptable solution," instead proposing the "natural extinction" of half-Jews within the Reich territories by means of sterilization. It remains unclear whether Stuckart was truly ignorant of the facts of the "Final Solution," that is to say the murder of deported Jews, or merely pretended he was, so that his complicity was not on record. "Evacuation to the East" implied in this view the continued existence of Jews in ghettos, where half-Jews might indeed produce "leader types." In fact, the majority of half-Jews and Jewish partners in "mixed marriages" — the subject of the follow-up conference convened by Eichmann — were usually not deported from Nazi Germany. Stuckart's proposal for a law on the forced dissolution of mixed marriages was debated into 1943, but was never passed, apparently at the behest of Hitler himself.[46]

Stuckart in Nuremberg

When the Reich surrendered unconditionally and its government was arrested, Stuckart was also arrested on 26 May 1945 as the last minister of the interior and education ministries. He was called as an expert witness in the Nuremberg Trial of the Major War Criminals against his former minister Wilhelm Frick. In 1947 he himself was tried in the Ministries Trial, along with others including Ernst von Weizsäcker and Hans Heinrich Lammers. He was accused of overseeing, in the wake of the aggressive expansion of the German Reich, the provision of legal tools "that were part of an agenda involving the deportation to concentration camps of tens of thousands of foreign citizens of Jewish heritage, where they were tortured and many even murdered."[47]

Stuckart and Lammers were accused of being "principally connected with the formulation of the genocidal policy."[48] Given that the minutes of the Wannsee Conference had recently come to light, the prosecution focused heavily on Stuckart's participation:

A program for the extermination of all surviving European Jews was set up by the defendants in the winter of 1941–42 ... During interdepartmental conferences on the "Final Solution of the Jewish Question" which took place in Berlin on 20 January 1942, 6 March 1942, and 27 October 1942, the policy and techniques for the "Final Solution of the Jewish Question" were established. The policy-making session of 20 January included the state secretaries or representatives of the ministries and agencies concerned; ... In the two other conferences the details were arranged. ... The previous program for driving out the Jews as pauper émigrés was now supplanted by a program for the evacuation of eleven million European Jews to camps in Eastern Europe for ultimate extermination. They were to be transported to those areas in huge labor convoys, and there the weak were to be killed immediately, the able-bodied worked to death. Closest cooperation between the departments of which the defendants were leading officials was provided, with the RSHA in charge of the actual operations.[49]

Stuckart resorted to the same ingenious defense argued by Gerhard Klopfer, admitting only to charges that could not be disputed. In addition he orchestrated the statements provided by his former colleagues who were also incriminated to ensure that his department appeared to have been acting defensively against the Party and SS organizations, using the little room for maneuver available to them to "prevent even worse scenarios."[50] When Stuckart was questioned by his defense on 6 October 1948 as to the extent of his awareness of the murders of Jews,[51] he insisted that Lösener had never told him anything and that he had always assumed the term "Final Solution" referred to the emigration of Jews and their "territorial collection in a settlement in the East." Their "extermination" had never entered his mind, he maintained, and he had never seen the minutes of the Wannsee Conference. He claimed that those minutes distorted what had happened at the meeting and that Heydrich had never mentioned the extermination of Jews in labor camps;[52] he argued that his own proposals for sterilization and "forced dissolution of mixed marriages" had served to hamper Heydrich's demand for half-Jews and partners in "mixed marriages" to be classified as Jews. This strategy, he maintained, had been successful, with Hitler postponing the half-Jew problem until the war was over. Hans Globke, meanwhile, confirmed he had known of the mass murders of Jews but exonerated his former superior with the statement that he had often been astonished by how "uninformed" Dr Stuckart had been.[53]

Illustration 16.3 Stuckart in the dock during the Wilhelmstraße trial, in front of an organigram of the Reich Ministry of the Interior, 1 October 1948. Yad Vashem photos archive, 75238.

The judges only partially accepted Stuckart's defense and found him guilty on several counts, including crimes against humanity, the persecution of Jews, Catholics and other minorities:

> In our opinion Stuckart knew exactly what fate awaited Jews deported to the East. Without a doubt, the laws and decrees drafted or approved by Stuckart himself were a cornerstone of the plan to almost completely exterminate Jews, a plan that succeeded. If the death camp commanders who followed orders to murder their pitiable prisoners, and the people who followed orders to deport Jews to the East have gone on trial and been found guilty and sentenced—and there is no doubt they have— then the men who participated from the peace and quiet of their ministry offices, where they drew up the requisite decrees, regulations and instructions for the campaign, are just as criminal. Stuckart employed his education, his knowledge and his legal expertise in the service of the architects of this extermination policy.[54]

The judges ruled it was a proven fact that "Stuckart was a bitter enemy of Jews and had used his office before and during the war to turn his ideas into deeds."[55] They rejected Stuckart's testimony that he was merely "a more efficient civil servant":

> There were too many instances when Frick chose him to take on tasks requiring education, competence, experience and strength of character ... His advice was sought and given. Many of the original drafts for decrees and most of the regulations on the implementation of anti-Jewish measures were drawn up by him or by his division, under his supervision. When Hitler decided to introduce the Nuremberg Laws, which marked the first step towards the persecution of Jews, Stuckart was chosen to draw up those laws.[56]

However, Stuckart's stance on the "half-Jewish Question" was considered to have been at least ambiguous. In 1942 he repeatedly urged the participants of the Wannsee Conference and Himmler to exempt "half-Jews" from the deportations.[57] The court also inferred from Stuckart's proposal that "half-Jews" should be sterilized that he had aimed to delay their fate.[58] The judges concluded that Stuckart's stance was political rather than humanitarian, because he had "precisely predicted the inevitable psychological effect on Germany were "mixed marriages" to be dissolved and so-called half-Aryans condemned to the same fate as Jews."[59] But the court also concluded "that no one would have proposed sterilization as the lesser evil had they not been fully convinced that deportations would have been a greater evil and meant death." And, as the court pointed out, the planned extermination of Jews had not been kept secret at the Reich Interior Ministry. In light of Stuckart's deteriorating health, the U.S. judges sentenced the defendant to just three years, ten months and twenty days. This sentence took into account Stuckart's detention and they ruled that it had been served by the time judgment was pronounced.[60]

Stuckart was therefore released in 1949. After a denazification trial in Hannover, he was classified as a *Mitläufer* (fellow traveler). By this point he had begun working for the regional committee of the right-wing party League of expellees and those deprived of rights (Bund der Heimatvertriebenen und Entrechteten, BHE).[61] In November 1951, the *Süddeutsche Zeitung* referred to Stuckart in the light of his high-profile Nazi past as "the BHE's Nazi head."[62] With the help of his former colleagues, he also took up a new position as managing director of the Institut zur Förderung der niedersächsischen Wirtschaft (Institute for the Promotion of the Lower Saxon Economy). Fresh proceedings against Stuckart were launched in Berlin in September 1951. Stuckart's role in the "Third Reich" was judged more harshly than it had been in

Hanover on account of his participation in the Wannsee Conference. Evidence was provided by the Document Center in Berlin:

> The full stringency of the law must be applied to the irresponsible and inhuman actions of the accused. As a scholar entrusted with the senior office of state secretary, he must have had an above-average awareness of the implications of his actions; as a lawyer he must have been aware of the scale and horror of the injustice he condoned. He inflicted further suffering and despair on countless people who had already suffered unspeakable suffering in the wake of the Nuremberg Laws. Regarding reconciliation measures, the court of arbitration therefore orders the maximum penalty permitted by law and denies (the accused) the right to public benefits for three years.[63]

However, proceedings were never finalized. On the eve of his 51st birthday, Stuckart died in a car accident. His former colleagues at the Reich Interior Ministry published an obituary in the *Frankfurter Zeitung*:

> Dr Wilhelm Stuckart, former state secretary in the Reich Interior Ministry died in a tragic accident shortly before turning 51. The deceased was an upstanding and selfless man of exceptional talent who worked tirelessly. His warm-hearted and collegial manner, his willingness to help— demonstrated time and time again—his sincere disposition, remarkable achievements and towering personality, will be remembered with gratitude and affection by his colleagues. Death tore him away from his next mission. He is deeply mourned by his friends and colleagues. He will live on in their hearts. The former staff of the former Reich Interior Ministry.[64]

As his defense counsel stressed in his closing statement[65] at the Ministry Trials, Stuckart's approach to the "Jewish Question" had been, in his own opinion, "rational."[66] He succeeded in passing off his stance on the "half-Jewish" question as opposition. The little information that can be gleaned from the fragments of Stuckart's correspondence with his wife that survived suggest that he never showed any remorse after the war and possibly lacked any sense of wrongdoing with respect to his involvement in the disenfranchisement and murder of Jews. Despite the extent of his complicity and influence, he maintained throughout the criminal proceedings and process of denazification that he had merely been following orders and was just a cog in the wheel of a bureaucracy masterminded by Hitler and the Party. In reality, it was with enthusiasm that the ambitious Stuckart lent his considerable legal skills to the criminal Nazi regime, actively creating a framework for atrocities by means of legislative measures that rationalized and legitimized them. It was this framework that enabled the regime's atrocities to take place as efficiently as they did.

Dr **Hans-Christian Jasch** has been the executive director of the Memorial and Educational Site House of the Wannsee Conference since May 2014. He has authored an acclaimed biographical study on the State Secretary in the Reich Interior Ministry Wilhelm Stuckart and the role of the civil service in Jewish policy, which was published in 2012. His other research focuses on the history of state, law and administration in Nazi Germany and the early years of the Federal Republic. He has contributed to the book *The Law in Nazi Germany* (edited by Alan E. Steinweis and Robert D. Rachlin) published by Berghahn in 2013. A lawyer by training, Jasch has also gained practical experience working as a civil servant in the German Federal Ministry of the Interior since 2001. From 2005 to 2011 he was first seconded to work in Rome as a liaison officer and then to the European Commission in Brussels to work on policy development in the field of countering radicalization and terrorism.

Notes

1 Quote from P. Longerich, ed., *Die Ermordung der europäischen Juden: Eine umfassende Dokumentation des Holocaust 1941–1945* (Munich, 1989), 92.

2 CV of Stuckart, BAL, SSO Stuckart, Wilhelm, 16 November 1902. On Stuckart, see: Hans-Christian Jasch, *Staatssekretär Wilhelm Stuckart und die Judenpolitik: Der Mythos von der sauberen Verwaltung* (Munich, 2012), and idem, "Zur Rolle der Innenverwaltung im Dritten Reich bei der Vorbereitung und Organisation des Genozids an den europäischen Juden: Der Fall des Dr. Wilhelm Stuckart (1902–1953)," *Die Verwaltung* 43, no. 2 (2010): 217–71.

3 See Stuckart's personal file in Sonderarchiv Moskau, Fonds 720-5-9898.

4 In March 1932 Stuckart again—this time under his own name—joined the Nazi Party and the SA. In spring 1934 he tried to swap his high membership number (1,033,214) with his mother's—that is to say, to indicate that he first joined the Party in 1930 (378,144). He succeeded in doing so with the help of the former head of the Wiesbaden chapter, Theo Habicht. He did not maintain his original claim that he had first joined the Party in 1922 and lost his membership card in a sabotage operation against the French Occupation Authority. See letter from Stuckart to the NSDAP leadership of 17 February 1934, BAL PK 1120, M 0089, and sworn statement of Harald von Tunkl-Hohenstadt dated 19 April 1952, LAB, Rep. 031-02-01, 12647, Folder II.

5 Letter from Stuckart to the Nazi leadership, 17 February 1934, BAL PK 1120, M 0089.

6 Letter from Stuckart to Daluege, 7 March 1933, BAL PK 1120, M 0089.

7 Witness questions put to Grauert, 17 July 1953, LAB, B Rep. 031-02-01, 12647.

8   See: H-C. Jasch, "Das preußische Kultusministerium und die 'Ausschaltung' von 'nichtarischen' und politisch missliebigen Professoren an der Berliner Universität in den Jahren 1933 bis 1934 aufgrund des Gesetzes zur Wiederherstellung des Berufsbeamtentums vom 7. April 1933," *Forum Historiae Iuris*, 25 August 2005.

9   See the procedure submitted by the Reich Chancellory, BAL R 43 II/1154, sheet 20 et seq.

10 Letter from Stuckart to Lammers, 12 January 1935, BAL 43 II/163, sheet 134 et seq. See: Gerhard Besier, *Die Kirchen und das Dritte Reich, vol. 3: Spaltungen und Abwehrkämpfe 1934–1937* (Berlin, 2001), 58 et seq.

11 Letter from Frick, 18 March 1935, BAL R 2/11685.

12 See: H-C. Jasch, "Das Ringen um die Verwaltungsgerichtsbarkeit," *Die Verwaltung* 38 (2005): 546–76.

13 Law on the Reuniting of Austria with the German Reich, 13 March 1938, RGBl. I 1938, 237–38.

14 Letter from Pfundtner, 18 March 1938, BAL R 2/11687; R 43 II/1126b.

15 Decree of the Führer on the Establishment of the Protectorate of Bohemia and Moravia, 16.3.1939, RGBl. I, 485 et seq; Stuckart, "Das Protektorat Böhmen und Mähren im Großdeutschen Reich," in *Tag des Deutschen Rechts*, ed. Nationalsozialistischer Rechtswahrerbund (NRSB) (Berlin, 1939),143–62.

16 "Decree on the Organization and Administration of the East Regions" of 8 October 1939 and "Decree on the Administration of the Occupied Polish Areas" of 12 October 1939, RGBl. 1939 I, 2042 et seq; 2077. See: Stuckart's Mitarbeiter, G. Hubrich, "Gliederung und Verwaltung der Ostgebiete," *Deutsche Verwaltung* 16 (1939): 605 et seq.; Dieter Rebentisch, *Führerstaat und Verwaltung im Zweiten Weltkrieg: Verfassungsentwicklung und Verwaltungspolitik 1939–1945* (Stuttgart, 1989), 172 et seq.

17 Rebentisch, *Führerstaat*, 172.

18 Comment by Georg Hubrich, 23 October 1939, BAL R 1501/5401.

19 By a letter from Frick, 9 August 1940, BAL R 43 II/1136b, Stuckart was, for instance, appointed as from 9 August 1940 Head of the Central Office for Alsace, Lorraine and Luxembourg.

20 See S. Lehnstaedt, "'Ostnieten' oder Verwaltungsexperten? Die Auswahl deutscher Staatsdiener für den Einsatz im Generalgouvernement Polen 1939–1944," *Zeitschrift für Geschichtswissenschaft* 55, no. 9 (2007): 701–21.

21 P. Schöttler, "Eine Art 'Generalplan West': Die Stuckart-Denkschrift vom 14. Juni 1940 und die Planungen für eine neue deutsch-französische Grenze im Zweiten Weltkrieg," *Sozial. Geschichte. Zeitschrift für historische Analyse des 20. und 21. Jahrhunderts* 18, no. 3 (2003): 83–131. See also: "Globke: Vielleicht war ich nicht da," *Der Spiegel*, no. 24 (1961): 17 et seq.

22 "VO über die Deutsche Volksliste," 4 March 1941, RGBl. I., 118. On this, see: W. Stuckart, "Staatsangehörigkeit und Reichsgestaltung," *Reich—Volksordnung—Lebensraum* 5(1943): 81 et seq.

23 On the Institute for State Research at Königsstraße 71 (Kleiner Wannsee): Gideon Botsch, "Der SD in Berlin-Wannsee 1937–1945," in *Villenkolonie in Wannsee 1870–1945*, ed. N. Kampe (Berlin, 2000), 70–95.

24 H-C. Jasch, "Die Gründung der Internationalen Akademie für Verwaltungs-wissenschaften: Verwaltungswissenschaften als Herrschaftsinstrument und 'Mittel der geistigen Kriegsführung' im nationalsozialistischen Staat," *Die Öffentliche Verwaltung* 58 (2005): 709–22.

25 Sworn declaration by Lösener, 17 October 1947, Staatsrchiv Nürnberg, Interrogations; doc. NG 1944 A. See W. Strauß, "Vorbemerkung des Herausgebers zu: Dokumentation: Das Reichsministerium des Innern und die Judengesetzgebung," *Vierteljahrshefte für Zeitgeschichte* 9, no. 3 (1961): 266 et seq. and 272.

26 On this development, see: Cornelia Essner, *Die "Nürnberger Gesetze" oder die Verwaltung des Rassenwahns 1933–1945* (Paderborn, 2002), 76 et seq. Michael Mayer, *Staaten als Täter: Ministerialbürokratie und "Judenpolitik" in NS-Deutschland und Vichy-Frankreich: Ein Vergleich* (Studien zur Zeitgeschichte, vol. 80) (Munich, 2010), 110–372.

27 In the First Regulation on the Reich Citizenship Law, 14 November 1935 (RGBl. I p. 1333) the term "Jew" was defined.

28 See Circular MBliV 1936, 11; BAL R 1501/5514, sheet. 153. Committee minutes are contained in: BAL R 1501/ 125483. See also: Essner, *Nürnberger Gesetze,* 174 et seq.

29 Minutes of the discussions, BAL R 1501/5514, sheets 199–211.

30 W. Stuckart, "Die völkische Grundordnung des deutschen Volkes," *Deutsches Recht* 5 (1935): 557–64.

31 Wilhelm Stuckart and Hans Globke, *Reichsbürgergesetz vom 15. September 1935. Gesetz zum Schutze des deutschen Blutes und der deutschen Ehre vom 15. September 1935; Gesetz zum Schutze der Erbgesundheit des deutschen Volkes (Ehegesundheitsgesetz) vom 18. Oktober 1935. Nebst allen Ausführungsvorschriften und den einschlägigen Gesetzen und Verordnungen* (Munich 1936).

32 Wilhelm Stuckart and Rolf Schiedermair, *Rassen- und Erbpflege in der Gesetzgebung des Reiches* (Leipzig, 1938), 14.

33 Note by Dr Bernhard Lösener, BAL R 1501/3746a, reproduced in: W. Lenz, "Die Handakten von Bernhard Lösener, 'Rassereferent' im Reichsministerium des Innern," *Archiv und Geschichte, Schriften des Bundesarchivs* 57 (2000): 695 et seq. See also Minutes of Lösener's evidence given on 13 October 1947 to Robert Kempner, 3 et seq., Staatsarchiv Nürnberg, Interrogations.

34 See note above.

35 Eleventh Regulation on the Reich Citizenship Law, 26 November 1941, RGBl. 1941, 722.

36 Entry of 25 November 1941, in: P. Witte et al., ed., *Der Dienstkalender Heinrich Himmlers 1941/42* (Hamburg, 1999), 281.

37 See Peter Klein, "Die Wannsee-Konferenz als Echo auf die gefallene Entscheidung zur Ermordung der europäischen Juden," in *Die Wannsee-Konferenz am 20. Januar 1942: Dokumente, Forschungsstand, Kontroversen,* ed., N. Kampe and P. Klein (Cologne, 2013), 198, footnote 72 referring to the fragmentary handover of Heydrich's appointment sheets on 1 December 1941, AMV Prag, 114-9-77, sheet 31 and Witte et al., *Dienstkalender,* 280.

38 Quoted from the copy of a letter from the lawyer, K. Kauffmann, to Stuckart's former colleague, Otto Ehrensberger, 4 July 1947, BA Koblenz N 1292/125.

39 See Lösener's state secretary proposal dated 4 December 1941 for a planned conference in Wannsee on 9 December, together with annexes, BAL R 1501/5519, sheets 238–247, particularly at 477–495.

40 On the fate of "Mischlinge," see: J. Noakes, "The Development of Nazi Policy towards the German-Jewish 'Mischlinge', 1933–1945," *Leo Baeck Institute Yearbook* 34(1989): 291–354; J.M. Steiner and J.F.V. Cornberg, "Willkür in der Willkür: Befreiungen von den antisemitischen Nürnberger Gesetzen," *Vierteljahrshefte für Zeitgeschichte* 46, no. 2 (1998): 143–87; Wolf Gruner, *Widerstand in der Rosenstraße: Die Fabrik-Aktion und die Verfolgung der "Mischehen" 1943* (Frankfurt am Main, 2005), 85 et seq., 178 et seq.

41 Letter from the RMdI on the "Erfassung der Juden und jüdischen Mischlinge bei der Volkszählung 1939," 15 January 1940, BAL R 1501/5519, sheets 203–8.

42 Lösener's state secretary proposal, 4 December 1941 as in footnote 47.

43 With the adoption of the "Zweiten Reichsverteidigungsgesetzes" on 4 September 1938 and the appointment of Frick to the Plenipotentiary General for Administration (GBV) on 27 September 1938 Stuckart was made chief of staff. See on this point the undated note concerning "Die Vertretung des Generalbevollmächtigten für die Reichsverteidigung," BAL R 43 II/1293 a. The "official" appointment of Stuckart as GBV chief of staff by Göring took place, however, only after the invasion of Poland on 5 September 1939 (BAL R 43 II/ 1293 a, sheet 10 et seq.).

44 Page 14 of the minutes of the Wannsee Conference, 20 January 1942, PAAA, R 100857.

45 Letter from Stuckart to Heydrich, 16 March 1942, PAAA, R 100857. Ibid. and following quotations.

46 See the drafts of a "Law on the divorce of German-Jewish mixed marriages," on which the RMdI voted with the RJM in spring 1943, BAL R 1501/5519, sheet 513 et seq. (256 et seq.); Gruner, *Widerstand*, 178 et seq.

47 Paragraph 44 of the indictment in Case No. 11, United States of America v. Ernst von Weizsäcker et al., Nuremberg 1947, 42, NL Stuckart, BA Koblenz N 1292/95.

48 Trials of War Criminals before the Nuremberg Military Tribunals, vol. XII, Washington, undated, 47 et seq.

49 Indictment in Case No 11, United States of America v Ernst von Weizsäcker et al., Nürnberg 1947, 47 et seq., BAK N 1292/95.

50 See Jasch, *Staatssekretär Wilhelm Stuckart*, 388–429.

51 Minutes of Questioning, 6 October 1948, in: Kurt Pätzold and Erika Schwarz, *Tagesordnung: Judenmord: Die Wannsee-Konferenz am 20. Januar 1942: Eine Dokumentation zur Organisation der 'Endlösung'* (Berlin, 1992), 156 et seq. ibid. and following quotation.

52 Pätzold and Schwarz, *Tagesordnung: Judenmord*, 156 et seq. The minutes "only" refer to "evacuation" and "labor" "separated according to sex, " which would mean "a large portion will be eliminated by natural causes"

while the "final remnant" will "have to be treated accordingly." The words "extermination" and "annihilation" were avoided. In fact the minutes do not make it explicitly clear that Heydrich ever explained the true meaning of the term "Final Solution" on 20 January 1942. Possibly it was not necessary for him to do so, since the discussion was focused mainly on drumming up support for the modalities of the deportations and defining who would be deported. See Essner, *Nürnberger Gesetze*, 414 et seq.

53 Quotaton from Robert M.W. Kempner, "Begegnungen mit Hans Globke," in *Der Staatssekretär Adenauers: Persönlichkeit und politisches Wirken Hans Globkes*, ed. K. Gotto (Stuttgart, 1980), 223.

54 R.M.W. Kempner and C. Haensel, ed., *Das Urteil im Wilhelmstrassen-Prozess: Der amtliche Wortlaut der Entscheidung im Fall Nr. 11 des Nürnberger Militärtribunals gegen von Weizsäcker und andere, mit abweichender Urteilsbegründung, Berichtigungsbeschlüssen, den grundlegenden Gesetzesbestimmungen, einem Verzeichnis der Gerichtspersonen und Zeugen, und Einführungen von Dr. Robert M.W. Kempner und Dr. Carl Haensel* (Schwäbisch Gmünd, 1950), 169.

55 Kempner and Haensel, *Das Urteil im Wilhelmstrassen-Prozess*, 165.

56 Kempner and Haensel, *Das Urteil im Wilhelmstrassen-Prozess*, 165.

57 Kempner and Haensel, *Das Urteil im Wilhelmstrassen-Prozess*, 167 et seq. Ibid and following quotation.

58 The Health Division under the RMdI had already obtained extensive experience of mass human sterilization since 1934. From 1934–44, between 360,000 and 1.5 million people were sterilized on the basis of the Law for the Prevention of Genetically Diseased Offspring or "Sterilization Law." In a memo dated 22 November 1955 the Interior Ministry in Nordrhein-Westfalen referred to 1.5 million victims of the law, as quoted in: Friedemann Pfäfflin, "Zwangssterilisation im Dritten Reich," in *50 Jahre Gesetz über die Vereinheitlichung des Gesundheitswesens*, ed. Akademie für öffentliches Gesundheitswesen in Düsseldorf (Düsseldorf, 1985), 32. The SS explored methods of mass x-ray castration in German concentration camps. See the memo classed a Secret Reich Matter from Hitler's Chancellery to Himmler, dated 29 April 1944, Nürnberger Dokument NG-208, IfZ Nürnberger Dokumente.

59 Kempner and Haensel, *Das Urteil*, 169 et seq. Ibid and following quotation.

60 Kempner and Haensel, *Das Urteil*, 169 et seq.

61 See "Politisches Unkraut überwuchert Niedersachsen: Die SRP marschiert/Ein alarmierender Bericht aus einem Lande der Bundesrepublik Anno 1951," *Süddeutsche Zeitung*, 9 November 1951, 3, which survived, BAK NL Stuckart, N 1292/ 94.

62 "Politisches Unkraut überwuchert Niedersachsen".

63 See the decision in the reconciliation proceedings against W. Stuckart, 4 August 1952, LAB B Rep. 031-02-01, 12647, File V.

64 Obituary, *Frankfurter Zeitung*, 27 November 1953.

65 Closing statement, BAK N 1292/125, 28.

66 On the topos of respectability in Nazi perpetrator apologies see Ulrich Herbert, "NS-Eliten in der Bundesrepublik," in *Verwandlungspolitik:*

NS-Eliten in der westdeutschen Nachkriegsgesellschaft, ed. W. Loth and B-A. Rusinek (Frankfurt am Main and New York, 1998), 110 et seq. In his notorious Posen speeches, in 1943, which Stuckart most probably attended, Himmler also stressed respectability in order to underline the "ethics" of his men regarding the genocide. See Nbg.-Dok. 1919-PS, Nazi Conspiracy and Aggression, vol. IV, USGPO, 616–34.

Bibliography

Besier, Gerhard. *Die Kirchen und das Dritte Reich, vol. 3. Spaltungen und Abwehrkämpfe 1934–1937.* Berlin: Propyläen, 2001.

Botsch, Gideon. "Der SD in Berlin-Wannsee 1937–1945." In *Villenkolonie in Wannsee 1870–1945*, edited by N. Kampe, 70–95. Berlin: Edition Hentrich, 2000.

Essner, Cornelia. *Die "Nürnberger Gesetze" oder die Verwaltung des Rassenwahns 1933–1945.* Paderborn: Schöningh, 2002.

Gruner, Wolf. *Widerstand in der Rosenstraße: Die Fabrik-Aktion und die Verfolgung der "Mischehen" 1943.* Frankfurt on the Main: Fischer-Taschenbuch-Verlag, 2005.

Herbert, Ulrich. "NS-Eliten in der Bundesrepublik." In *Verwandlungspolitik: NS-Eliten in der westdeutschen Nachkriegsgesellschaft*, edited by W. Loth and B-A. Rusinek, 93–115. Frankfurt on the Main and New York: Campus, 1998.

Hubrich, G. "Gliederung und Verwaltung der Ostgebiete." *Deutsche Verwaltung* 16(1939): 605–9.

Jasch, H-C. "Das preußische Kultusministerium und die 'Ausschaltung' von 'nichtarischen' und politisch missliebigen Professoren an der Berliner Universität in den Jahren 1933 bis 1934 aufgrund des Gesetzes zur Wiederherstellung des Berufsbeamtentums vom 7. April 1933." *Forum Historiae Iuris*, 25 August 2005. Retrieved 7 October 2016 from http://www.forhistiur.de/zitat/0508jasch.htm

———. "Das Ringen um die Verwaltungsgerichtsbarkeit." *Die Verwaltung* 38 (2005): 546–76.

———. "Die Gründung der Internationalen Akademie für Verwaltungswissenschaften: Verwaltungswissenschaften als Herrschaftsinstrument und 'Mittel der geistigen Kriegsführung' im nationalsozialistischen Staat." *Die Öffentliche Verwaltung* 58(2005): 709–22.

———. "Zur Rolle der Innenverwaltung im Dritten Reich bei der Vorbereitung und Organisation des Genozids an den europäischen Juden: Der Fall des Dr Wilhelm Stuckart (1902–1953)." *Die Verwaltung* 43, no. 2 (2010): 217–71.

Jasch, Hans-Christian. *Staatssekretär Wilhelm Stuckart und die Judenpolitik: Der Mythos von der sauberen Verwaltung.* Munich: Oldenbourg, 2012.

Kempner, Robert M.W. "Begegnungen mit Hans Globke." In *Der Staatssekretär Adenauers: Persönlichkeit und politisches Wirken Hans Globkes*, edited by K. Gotto, 213–29. Stuttgart: Klett-Cotta, 1980.

Kempner, R.M.W. and C. Haensel, ed. *Das Urteil im Wilhelmstrassen-Prozess: Der amtliche Wortlaut der Entscheidung im Fall Nr. 11 des Nürnberger Militärtribunals gegen von Weizsäcker und andere, mit abweichender Urteilsbegründung, Berichtigungsbeschlüssen, den grundlegenden Gesetzesbestimmungen, einem Verzeichnis der Gerichtspersonen und Zeugen, und Einführungen von Dr Robert M.W. Kempner und Dr Carl Haensel.* Schwäbisch Gmünd: Alfons Bürger, 1950.

Klein, Peter. "Die Wannsee-Konferenz als Echo auf die gefallene Entscheidung zur Ermordung der europäischen Juden." In *Die Wannsee-Konferenz am 20. Januar 1942: Dokumente, Forschungsstand, Kontroversen,* edited by N. Kampe and P. Klein, 182–201. Cologne: Böhlau, 2013.

Lehnstaedt, Stephan. "'Ostnieten' oder Verwaltungsexperten? Die Auswahl deutscher Staatsdiener für den Einsatz im Generalgouvernement Polen 1939–1944," *Zeitschrift für Geschichtswissenschaft* 55, no. 9 (2007): 701–21.

Lenz, W. "Die Handakten von Bernhard Lösener, 'Rassereferent' im Reichsministerium des Innern." *Archiv und Geschichte, Schriften des Bundesarchivs* 57 (2000): 684–99.

Liebmann, Max. 1929. "Justizpersonalakte im Sonderarchiv Moskau, Fonds 720-5-9898." 4 November.

Longerich, P., ed. *Die Ermordung der europäischen Juden: Eine umfassende Dokumentation des Holocaust 1941–1945.* Munich: Piper, 1989.

Mayer, Michael. *Staaten als Täter: Ministerialbürokratie und "Judenpolitik" in NS-Deutschland und Vichy-Frankreich: Ein Vergleich.* Munich: Oldenbourg, 2010.

Noakes, J. "The Development of Nazi Policy towards the German-Jewish 'Mischlinge', 1933–1945." *Leo Baeck Institute Yearbook* 34 (1989): 291–354.

Pätzold, Kurt and Erika Schwarz. *Tagesordnung: Judenmord: Die Wannsee-Konferenz am 20. Januar 1942: Eine Dokumentation zur Organisation der 'Endlösung.'* Berlin: Metropol, 1992.

Pfäfflin, Friedemann. "Zwangssterilisation im Dritten Reich." In *50 Jahre Gesetz über die Vereinheitlichung des Gesundheitswesens,* edited by Akademie für öffentliches Gesundheitswesen in Düsseldorf, 31–42. Düsseldorf: Akademie für öffentliches Gesundheitswesen, 1985.

Rebentisch, Dieter. *Führerstaat und Verwaltung im Zweiten Weltkrieg: Verfassungsentwicklung und Verwaltungspolitik 1939–1945.* Stuttgart: Steiner, 1989.

Schöttler, P. "Eine Art 'Generalplan West': Die Stuckart-Denkschrift vom 14. Juni 1940 und die Planungen für eine neue deutsch-französische Grenze im Zweiten Weltkrieg." *Sozial. Geschichte. Zeitschrift für historische Analyse des 20. und 21. Jahrhunderts* 18, no. 3 (2003): 83–131.

Steiner, J. M. and J. F. V. Cornberg. "Willkür in der Willkür: Befreiungen von den antisemitischen Nürnberger Gesetzen." *Vierteljahrshefte für Zeitgeschichte* 46, no. 2 (1998): 143–87.

Strauß, W. "Vorbemerkung des Herausgebers zu: Dokumentation: Das Reichsministerium des Innern und die Judengesetzgebung." *Vierteljahrshefte für Zeitgeschichte* 9, no. 3 (1961): 262–313. Retrieved 6 October 2016 from http://www.ifz-muenchen.de/heftarchiv/1961_3_4_strauß.pdf

Stuckart, W. "Die völkische Grundordnung des deutschen Volkes." *Deutsches Recht* 5 (1935): 557–64.

——. "Staatsangehörigkeit und Reichsgestaltung." *Reich—Volksordnung—Lebensraum* 5(1943): 57–91.

Stuckart, Wilhelm. "Das Protektorat Böhmen und Mähren im Großdeutschen Reich." In *Tag des Deutschen Rechts,* edited by Nationalsozialistischer Rechtswahrerbund (NRSB), 143–62. Berlin, 1939.

Stuckart, Wilhelm and Hans Globke. *Reichsbürgergesetz vom 15. September 1935. Gesetz zum Schutze des deutschen Blutes und der deutschen Ehre vom 15. September 1935; Gesetz zum Schutze der Erbgesundheit des deutschen Volkes (Ehegesundheitsgesetz) vom 18. Oktober 1935. Nebst allen Ausführungsvorschriften und den einschlägigen Gesetzen und Verordnungen.* Munich, 1936.

Stuckart, Wilhelm and Rolf Schiedermair. *Rassen- und Erbpflege in der Gesetzgebung des Reiches.* Leipzig: Kohlhammer, 1938.

Witte, P., M. Wildt, M. Vogt, D. Pohl, P. Klein, C. Gerlach, C. Dieckmann and A. Angrick, ed. *Der Dienstkalender Heinrich Himmlers 1941/42.* Hamburg: Christians, 1999.

Index

CPSIA information can be obtained
at www.ICGtesting.com
Printed in the USA
JSHW021441311220
10687JS00006B/310

9 781785 336713